THE ABC OF COMMUNISM

The
ABC
of
Communism

A Popular Explanation of the Program
of the
Communist Party of Russia

———

N. Bukharin and E. Preobrazhensky

———

New Introduction by Sidney Heitman

Ann Arbor Paperbacks for the Study of
Communism and Marxism
The University of Michigan Press

Third printing 1977
First edition as an Ann Arbor Paperback 1966
All rights reserved
ISBN 0-472-06112-7
Translated from the Russian by Eden and Cedar Paul
Originally published in England in 1922
Published in the United States of America by
The University of Michigan Press and simultaneously
in Rexdale, Canada, by John Wiley & Sons Canada, Limited
Manufactured in the United States of America

Dedication

To the adamantine incarnation of all the greatness and vigour of the proletariat ; to that which incorporates its heroism, the definiteness of its class-consciousness, its deadly hatred for capitalism, and its splendid impulse towards the creation of a new society—to the great Communist Party—we dedicate this book.

> We dedicate it to the Party which commands an army of a million men, dwells in the trenches, administers a vast realm, carts wood on Communist Saturdays, makes ready for the resurrection day of mankind.
>
> We dedicate it alike to the veterans of the Party, steeled in battles and victories, and to the young recruits of the Party, destined to carry our work to its end.

To the warriors and martyrs of the Party, to those who have perished on the numberless fronts, who have been done to death in prison, who have perished under torture, who when doing the Party's work have been hanged or shot by our enemies, we dedicate this book.

NEW INTRODUCTION

By Sidney Heitman

Leon Trotsky once observed that "revolutions are always verbose." In the mountainous literature produced by the Russian Revolution during the past half century, only a few works have endured the passage of time and change. One such classic is *The ABC of Communism*. Originally written in 1919 with the simple purpose of explaining the newly adopted Program of the Russian Communist Party to recent recruits in its ranks, the book achieved a stature and international renown that made it one of the most widely read and best-known political documents of the twentieth century. So great was the demand for it in its heyday that the initial Russian edition was followed by no fewer than seventeen subsequent editions and numerous printings, while translations into a score of other languages spread its message to every part of the civilized world. For dedicated Communists in Russia and abroad during the 1920's and 1930's the book became Holy Writ, whose mastery constituted an unofficial initiation rite into the fold of the faithful; and millions of others throughout the world first acquired and for long derived their main knowledge of the international Communist movement from its pages. As the *Communist Manifesto* became the symbolic statement of nineteenth-century revolutionary Marxism, *The ABC of Communism* in its day came to be widely regarded as the "manifesto" of latter-day Marxism embodied in the Bolshevik Party, the Soviet state, and the Communist International.

Despite its one-time renown and ubiquitous circulation, however, today this book has become exceedingly rare. Only a few copies have survived in the West, and in the Communist world it has not been accessible at all since its official proscription in the late 1930's, when its authors were purged and executed by Stalin.[1] The re-issue of this volume in English translation nearly thirty years after its virtual disappearance from general circulation provides again, therefore, an opportunity to study at first hand one of the most significant and instructive documents bearing on the early, formative history of Soviet communism, which it not only illuminates with unique clarity, but which it also helped to shape.

An appreciation of the historical importance of this book and of its value for the student of modern communism must take account of the circumstances under which it was written and the purpose it was intended to fulfill. When *The ABC of Communism* was conceived by its authors in 1919, Russia stood at a critical juncture in its turbulent history. Less than two years before, the Bolshevik Party had seized political power

---

[1] In March 1965 the United Press International reported that a new edition of *The ABC of Communism* was to be published in the Soviet Union. By year's end, however, this report remained unconfirmed, and the book has not yet appeared.

in the old tsarist empire from the defunct Provisional Government, proclaiming the onset of the international proletarian revolution that was to liberate mankind from the shackles of capitalism and usher in the communist millenium forecast by Karl Marx and Friedrich Engels. The first acts of the new regime had been to establish a soviet republic, nationalize and distribute land, declare productive enterprises to be the property of the people, and promulgate far-reaching democratic social reforms. At the same time, the disastrous war against Germany was brought to a close by concluding a harsh peace that deprived Russia of much of its territory but providing the Communists with a "breathing space" in which to consolidate their gains.

But the changes had come too late, and within a few months the dream of utopia had turned into a nightmare of chaos. Wracked by years of war and political upheaval, Russia lay in ruins, its economy paralyzed, its people exhausted, and its territories splintered. To the threat of political collapse from within, a new danger was added in the summer of 1918 in the form of armed counter-revolution aided by outside powers bent on crushing the new Soviet state. Moreover, anticipated revolutions in western Europe, which were to have followed in Russia's wake and to have rescued the Bolsheviks from military encirclement and economic backwardness, failed to materialize on schedule.

Confronted by these crises, the Party, led by Lenin, resorted to extreme measures designed to maintain itself in power until aid from the West could arrive. The pre-revolutionary utopian objectives were temporarily deferred to a more favorable time; the liberal reforms enacted in 1917 were rescinded or ignored. The democratic system of soviets was replaced by dictatorial Party rule. The regulation of industrial production was taken from the workers' committees and supplanted by centralized state control. In the countryside, food produced by the peasants on their newly acquired land was forcibly confiscated by the state and allocated to select groups on whom the regime depended, and thus millions of other persons were condemned to destitution. In the new proletarian Red Army, recent democratic reforms were scrapped and harsh military discipline was restored. At the same time, former supporters of the tsarist regime or the Provisional Government who had been disfranchised and dispossessed in 1917 but whose skills were now needed by the Soviet regime were restored to positions of authority and rewarded with preferential treatment for serving the Communist state.

Lenin and his supporters consoled themselves that these extraordinary measures, which admittedly contradicted the ideals of the revolution, were unavoidable under the emergency conditions of the time and that as soon as circumstances permitted Russia would resume the offensive on communism interrupted by the outbreak of the civil war and hampered by the delay in the European proletarian revolution. Meanwhile, it was imperative to retain power at all costs and by whatever means necessary.

Not all members of the Party supported Lenin's views, however. A small but determined group of radical idealists, flushed with the Bolshevik

NEW INTRODUCTION

victory of 1917 and intent upon pushing on toward communism regardless of all obstacles, accused Lenin of betraying the workers by repudiating the democratic reforms and making an accommodation with their class enemies. Others in the Party, who held an internationalist outlook, urged that all efforts be directed toward bringing about the European proletarian revolution, even at the expense, if need be, of sacrificing the gains made in Russia. Still others, who had joined the Party after 1917 mainly in order to advance their own self interests, cared nothing for either socialism or world revolution but only for their own personal fortunes.

It was in this atmosphere of crisis and dissension that the issue of the revision of the Party Program came to a head early in 1919. The Program with which the Bolsheviks had come to power had been adopted in 1903, before the Russian Social Democratic Workers Party had divided into irreconcilable Bolshevik and Menshevik factions and when it still looked only toward a "bourgeois democratic" revolution in Russia, which was to replace the feudal monarchy with a democratic republic and pave the way for capitalism. Soon after the revolution, Lenin had called for the adoption of a new program that would reflect the changed conditions in Russia and in the Party and which would chart the way for the immediate future. After months of bitter debate, in which the divergent views regarding the nature and the course of the Russian Revolution were reflected in disagreements over the text of the Program, a draft was adopted in March 1919 by the Eighth Party Congress.[2]

The revised Program was a compromise among the contending positions. A brief introductory section summarized the Marxist-Leninist theory of capitalist development and imperialism, hailed the Russian Revolution as the first breach in the network of world capitalism, and proclaimed the onset of the international proletarian revolution. It then enumerated the achievements of the Bolshevik revolution, outlined the distance still to be traveled toward socialism, and detailed the measures necessary to achieve it. Finally, the Program ended with an exhortation to all Party members to work with energy and dedication for the attainment of its aims. Although it made concessions to both the radical and internationalist factions in the Party, it was essentially a moderate, limited, and short-term program of action reflecting Lenin's measured and practical approach to the problems of the day.

Resolving the Party debates and enlisting active support for the Program among the rank and file of the Party were two quite different problems, however. If the Program were to become anything more than a paper proclamation, it would have to be implemented on all levels of society by every Party worker throughout the country. However, not only did unreconciled differences of opinion continue to divide the Party, but the chaotic conditions of the time, the poor communications, and the low level of political consciousness and discipline among the newer members of the Party all posed serious obstacles to united and common efforts.

[2] The 1919 Program, which was appended to all editions of *The ABC of Communism*, will be found at the end of this volume.

THE ABC OF COMMUNISM

Since it was not practical either to purge the Party of dissident elements or to conduct a systematic program of ideological education and indoctrination, a special effort to win voluntary support for the Program was needed. In response to this need, two young Party leaders—Nikolai I. Bukharin and Evgeny A. Preobrazhensky—undertook to furnish "a popular explanation of the Program of the Russian Communist Party of Bolsheviks" and the theoretical principles underlying it intended to bridge the ideological gap between the Party leaders and the rank and file.

The two authors were well suited to collaborate on a joint statement of Communist principles and doctrine, for in 1919 they shared common characteristics and outlooks. Both belonged to the younger generation of Lenin's followers who had joined the Bolshevik movement during the decade preceding the First World War. Bukharin, who was barely out of his twenties, and Preobrazhensky, two years his senior,[3] had both worked up through the ranks as Party organizers and propagandists before 1917 to responsible posts in the Party during the revolution and civil war. Both men were trained intellectuals and respected theoreticians, and they were regarded as the Party's two ablest economists. In 1919 they also shared somewhat radical and doctrinaire views on the tasks of the revolution in Russia. A shared internationalist viewpoint had led them the year before to form within the Party a "Left-Communist" faction opposed to certain of Lenin's foreign and internal policies, but when civil war broke out in the summer of 1918, they rejoined the Party majority.

Eventually Bukharin resolved his remaining differences with Lenin and in time rose to the pinnacle of power and authority as the leading theoretician and spokesman of the Party, while Preobrazhensky's continued radical views drove him into opposition to the Party center—led by Bukharin after Lenin's death in 1924—and into alliance with Trotsky. Stalin's rise to power in the 1930's again brought them together in a new coalition—Bukharin because of his opposition to the Five Year Plan offensive, Preobrazhensky because of his continued support of the disgraced Trotsky. Both men shared a common fate during the Stalinist purges, Preobrazhensky meeting an unknown death in 1937, Bukharin being executed the next year after a spectacular public trial. In 1919 the shape of the future could not be seen, however, and despite their differences with Lenin and even with part of the Program itself, they placed the interests of the revolution and the Party above their own personal views and turned to the task of marshaling support for the Program.

The product that emerged from their pens toward the end of the year was a remarkable and unprecedented document. Although written in great haste and amidst innumerable distractions resulting from the heavy demands upon their time and energies, the book far exceeded the original intent to provide simply an exegesis of the 1919 Program and became

[3] Preobrazhensky was born in 1886, Bukharin in 1888.

NEW INTRODUCTION

instead a major effort to fill a serious and neglected gap in the literature of revolutionary Marxism. Though Marx and his followers had produced a voluminous outpouring of theoretical works during the preceding half century, there still did not exist a single comprehensive statement of the basic tenets of Marxism expressed in systematic and thorough fashion. Moreover, while a great body of commentaries on the evils of capitalism and the causes for its demise had been built up over the years, conspicuous gaps in Marxian revolutionary theory remained—most notably the virtual lack of any detailed treatment of the revolutionary process itself and the nature of the future Communist society which it was to bring about. Even the Bolsheviks had come to power with only the barest of notions regarding what they would do afterward, and at that the rapid course of events after November 1917 rendered their pre-revolutionary forecasts obsolete. The adoption of a program of action for the transition period as late as 1919 was itself a reflection of the fact that until then the Party lacked a set of concrete aims to guide it through the period of proletarian dictatorship, and the controversies that attended its adoption were attributable in large measure to the uncertainty and disagreements arising from the shortcomings in Marxian doctrine.

In undertaking to elaborate and explain the Party Program to relatively uninitiated readers, therefore, Bukharin and Preobrazhensky were compelled to start with the most basic tenets of Marxism and to develop systematically a comprehensive statement of the doctrine, as well as to attempt to fill in the gaps and resolve the ambiguities in Marxism along the way. Consequently, *The ABC of Communism* became not merely a commentary on the Program, but rather the most complete and systematic compendium of Marxist-Leninist theory produced until that time, encompassing the entire spectrum of Communist theory and practice as it had evolved since the appearance of the *Communist Manifesto* and incorporating into a consistent synthesis the classical theories of the founders of scientific socialism, world developments since their death, the distinctive Bolshevik revisions of the original Marxian doctrine, and the experience of the Russian Revolution to that time. Moreover, in contrast to the esoteric and turgid writings often produced by professional Marxists for the benefit mainly of other professional Marxists, *The ABC of Communism* was written for mass consumption in simple and lively language, making it comprehensible to even the most unsophisticated reader.

The immediate success of the book surprised even its authors. Successive Russian editions and translations barely kept pace with demand among both supporters and opponents of the Communists in all countries, all of whom thirsted for dependable information about the Russian Revolution. Among the former, it became a veritable Bible of communism, enjoying greater currency and authority than any of the works of such well-known figures as Lenin or Trotsky, while among the latter, it furnished the confirmation they needed for their worst apprehensions, stimulated determined efforts to crush the Communist movement, and generated an avalanche of literature of rebuttal.

THE A B C OF COMMUNISM

Whatever the reaction, the book became a major world force in the decade of the Twenties by shaping the thought and actions of millions of persons within and beyond the Soviet Union, for no one who read it could remain unmoved or indifferent to it. Even when events in Russia and elsewhere in the world after 1919 rendered parts of the book obsolete, its popularity among Communists did not dim, and it continued to circulate widely well into the 1930's, until its fate was sealed by the purge and execution of its authors. Its persistent appeal beyond the borders of Russia continued even then, however, and in 1937, the year of Preobrazhensky's death, a Spanish language edition was published in Barcelona during the Spanish civil war, while in 1952 a Japanese edition was issued in Tokyo, followed two years later by a new Spanish edition in Bolivia, and as late as 1963 it was re-issued in Paris in French. Moreover, clear evidence that interest in Bukharin and in the book he co-authored was never fully repressed in the Communist bloc of states and since 1953 has been on the rise provides further testimony to the unique place this volume occupies in the literature and the history of modern communism.

The re-issue of this significant and rare document at this time, therefore, provides an opportunity for a new generation of readers to become acquainted with one of the major contributions to the literature of revolutionary Marxism with the benefit of a broad historical perspective. The edition reprinted here, translated by Eden and Cedar Paul, retains the organization of the Russian original: the book is divided into two major parts, with chapters and sub-sections within each. Part One consists of a theoretical exposition of historical materialism, an analysis of the causes of proletarian revolution, and a description of the future Communist society that in Marxian doctrine is to replace capitalism at the end of the revolutionary process. In only a few other places in the entire body of Communist literature produced since 1917 will a more succinct and readable account of the basic tenets of Marxism-Leninism be found, and however brief the section on the Communist society of the future may be, considering its importance in Communist theory, it was in its day and still remains one of the most comprehensive and detailed descriptions by any Marxist of the goals toward which communism claims to be striving. It might also be noted that this section of the book retains its currency even today, for few of its principles have been modified or repudiated over the years since its writing.

Part Two is devoted to the practical aspects of the revolutionary process itself, both in general terms applicable to all Communist revolutions and specifically with respect to the distinctive conditions in Russia in 1919. Although this section of the book became increasingly outmoded as Russia emerged from the civil war and passed through the successive periods of the New Economic Policy and the Five Year Plans, its historic value today is undiminished. Finally, the Program of the Russian Communist Party adopted in 1919 is appended at the end of the volume with marginal references to corresponding sections of the book where the separate provisions of the Program are discussed in detail.

NEW INTRODUCTION

Although the haste with which the book was written and the adverse conditions under which the authors worked is evident in many places, *The ABC of Communism* merits careful study and thoughtful reflection for the insight it provides into a crucial period of Soviet history. It stands today as a classic monument to an earlier period in the evolution of modern communism, when the humanistic and idealistic values it expressed were vital forces in the international Communist movement, however diluted they may have been by the methods advocated to achieve its ends. At the same time, the book illuminates the complex process by which the higher ideals of the Russian Revolution were gradually eroded away, for in it may also be discerned the seeds of the dialectical destruction of these very ideals as its authors wrestled with the dilemma of conflicting ends and means inherent in Marxian doctrine, resolving the conflict on the basis of considerations that ultimately led to the sacrifice of the one to the other. Finally, the book is no less instructive for the light it sheds on contemporary developments in the Communist world. Though it is too early to form sound judgments, there is evidence to support the belief that the present Soviet leadership is seriously attempting to moderate the legacy of Stalinism and revive some of the humanitarian goals of the revolution, as evidenced, in part, by the adoption of the 1961 Program of the Communist Party of the Soviet Union. A careful reading today of *The ABC of Communism,* written nearly fifty years ago to explain the intent of the Party's preceding Program, helps to clarify not only the meaning of recent events by providing historical perspective, but also their possible future significance.

CONTENTS

CONTENTS

PAGE

FOREWORD

The ABC of Communism should, in our opinion, be an elementary textbook of communist knowledge. Daily experience of propagandists and agitators has convinced us of the urgent need for such a textbook. There is an unceasing influx of new adherents. The dearth of teachers is great, and we have not even a sufficiency of textbooks for such institutions as the party schools. Obviously, the older Marxist literature, such as *The Erfurt Program*, is largely inapplicable to present needs. Answers to new problems are extremely difficult to find. All that the student requires is scattered in various newspapers, books, and pamphlets.

We have determined to fill this gap. We regard our *ABC* as an elementary course which is to be followed in the party schools ; but we have also endeavoured to write it in such a manner that it can be used for independent study by every worker or peasant who desires to acquaint himself with the party program.

Every comrade who takes up this book should read it all through, so that he may acquire an idea of the aims and tasks of communism. The book has been written in such a way that the exposition forms a running commentary upon the text of the party program. At the end of the volume, for the convenience of our readers, we have appended this text, which is divided into numbered paragraphs ; to each paragraph of the program there correspond certain explanatory paragraphs of the book, the numeration in the text being identical with that in the program.

Fundamentals are printed in ordinary type, whilst smaller type is used for more detailed explanations, examples, numerical statements, etc. The paragraphs in small type are chiefly intended for those comrades who are studying the work without assistance, and who have neither time nor opportunity for access to information concerning matters of fact.

For those who wish to carry their studies further, a brief bibliography is appended to each chapter.

The authors are well aware that their book is defective in many ways ; it was written fragmentarily, and in scant intervals of leisure. Communists have to pursue their literary labours under conditions that can hardly be described as normal. The present work affords an interesting example of this, for the manuscript (to say nothing of both its authors) narrowly escaped destruction in the explosion at the Moscow Committee Rooms. . . . Nevertheless, with all its defects, we have decided to publish the book at once. We merely ask that comrades should furnish us with any relevant information which practice discloses to them.

The theoretical section, comprising Part One, the beginning of Part Two, together with the chapters on The Soviet Power, The Organisation of Industry, Labour Protection and Social Welfare, and Public Hygiene, were written by Buharin ; the rest of the work was penned by Preobrazhensky. Obviously, however, both the authors accept full responsibility for the work.

The title of our book, *A B C*, is an expression of the task we set ourselves. Should the work prove helpful to beginners and to propagandists, we shall feel sure that our labour has not been in vain.

October 15, 1919.

PART ONE

THEORETICAL

GROWTH AND DECAY OF CAPITALISM

OUR PROGRAM

§ 1. What is a Program ?   § 2. What was our previous Program ?   § 3. Why was it necessary to draw up a new Program ?   § 4. The Meaning of our Program.   § 5. The scientific Character of our Program.

§ 1.

What is a Program? Every party pursues definite aims, whether it be a party of landowners or capitalists, on the one hand, or a party of workers or peasants, on the other. Every party must have definite aims, for otherwise it is not a party. If it be a party representing the interests of landowners, it will pursue the aims of landowners ; it will endeavour to tighten the grasp of the owners upon the soil ; to hold the peasants in bondage ; to secure a high price for the produce of the landowners' estates ; to hire labour cheaply ; to rackrent the farms. If it be a party of capitalists and factory owners, it will likewise have its own aims : to procure cheap labour, to keep the workers well in hand, to find customers to whom the wares can be sold at the highest possible price, to obtain ever larger profits, for this purpose to compel the workers to toil harder—but, above all, so to arrange matters that the workers will have no tendency to allow their thoughts to turn towards ideas of a new social order ; let the workers think that there always have been masters and always will be masters. Such are the aims of the factory owners. It is self-evident that the workers and peasants will have utterly different aims from these, seeing that their interests are utterly different from those of the capitalists and landowners. People used to say : " What is wholesome for a Russian is death to a German." It would, in fact, be more accurate to say : " What is wholesome for a worker is death to a landowner or capitalist." That is to say, the worker has certain things to do, the capitalist other things, and the landowner yet others. Not every landowner, however, thinks out logically what is the best way of getting the last farthing out of the peasants; many landowners are drunk most of the time, and do not even trouble to consider their bailiff's reports. The same thing happens in the case of the peasants and of the workers. There are some who say: " Oh, well, we shall get along somehow; why bother? We shall go on living as our fathers have always lived." Such persons never achieve anything, and do not even understand their own interests. On the other hand, those who realise how they can best defend their own interests, organise themselves into a party. Of course the class as a whole does not enter the party, which is composed of the best and most energetic members of the class; thus those who enter the party lead the rest. To the Workers' Party (the Party of Communist Bolsheviks) adhere the best of the workers and poorer peasants; to the Party of Landowners and Capitalists (Cadets, the Party of Popular Freedom) adhere the most energetic among the landowners, the capitalists, and their hangers-on—lawyers, professors, military officers, etc. Consequently, every party is composed of the most intelligent elements in the class to which it corresponds. For this reason a landowner or capitalist who is a member of an organised party will combat the peasants and workers far more successfully than if he were not in such an organisation. In like manner an organised worker will be better able than an unorganised worker to strive against the capitalists and landowners; for the organised worker has well pondered the aims and interests of the working class, knows how these interests are to be pursued, and has learned the shortest road.

ALL THE AIMS WHICH A PARTY REPRESENTING THE INTERESTS OF ITS CLASS VIGOROUSLY PURSUES, CONSTITUTE THE PARTY PROGRAM. Thus in the program is specified that for which any particular class has to strive. In the program of the Communist Party is specified that for which the workers and the poorer peasants have to strive. The program is for every party a matter of supreme importance. From the program we can always learn what interests the party represents.

§ 2.

What was our previous Program ? Our present program
was adopted by the eighth Party Congress at the end
of March, 1919. Prior to this we had not a precise
program, written on paper. We had nothing but the
old program elaborated at the second Party Congress
in the year 1903. When this old program was compiled,
the bolsheviks and the mensheviks constituted a single
party, and they had a common program. At that date
the organisation of the working class was only just beginning.
There were very few factories and workshops. Disputes
were actually still going on as to whether a working class
would ever come into existence in Russia. The " narodniks " (the fathers of the present social revolutionaries)
considered that the working class was not destined to develop
in Russia, that in our country there would be no extensive
growth of factories and workshops. The Marxists—the
social democrats, subsequently to divide into bolsheviks
and mensheviks—supposed, on the other hand, that in
Russia, as elsewhere, the working class would continue to
grow and would constitute the main strength of the revolution. Time proved that the views of the narodniks were
wrong and that those of the social democrats were right.
But at the date when the program of the social democrats
was elaborated by the second Party Congress (both Lenin
and Plehanoff participating in the work), the strength of
the Russian working class was extremely small. That is
why no one then imagined that it would be possible to undertake the direct overthrow of the bourgeoisie. At that time
the best policy seemed : to break the neck of tsardom ;
to win freedom of association for the workers and peasants
in conjunction with all others ; to establish the eight-hour
day ; and to reduce the power of the landowners. No
one then dreamed that it would be possible to realise the
rule of the workers once and for all, or immediately to dis-
possess the bourgeoisie of its factories and workshops.
Such was our old program of the year 1903.

§ 3.

Why was it necessary to draw up a new Program ?
A considerable period intervened between 1903 and the

revolution of 1917, and during this time circumstances altered profoundly. In Russia, large-scale industry advanced with giant strides, and concomitantly there occurred a great increase in the numbers of the working class. As early as the revolution of 1905, the workers showed their strength. By the time of the second revolution (1917) it had become plain that the victory of the revolution could only be achieved through the victory of the working class. But in 1917 the working class could not be satisfied with that which might have contented it in 1905. The workers had now so fully matured that it was inevitable they should demand the seizure of the factories and workshops, the overthrow of the capitalists, and the establishment of working-class rule. That is to say, since the formulation of the first program there had occurred in Russia a fundamental change in internal conditions. Yet more important is it that in like manner there had taken place a change in external conditions. In the year 1905, " peace and quiet " prevailed throughout Europe. In the year 1917, no intelligent person could fail to see that the world war was leading up to the world revolution. In 1905, the Russian revolution was followed by nothing more than a slight movement among the Austrian workers, and by revolutions in the more backward countries of the east—Persia, Turkey, and China. The Russian revolution of 1917 is being followed by revolutions in the west as well as in the east, by revolutions in which the working class raises its banner on behalf of the overthrow of capitalism. Both at home and abroad, therefore, conditions are very different from those of the year 1903. It would be absurd for the party of the working class to have one and the same program in 1903 and in 1917–19, seeing that now the circumstances are utterly different. When the mensheviks find fault with us on the ground that we have " repudiated " our old program, and that in so doing we have repudiated the teaching of Marx, we reply that the essence of Marx's teaching is to construct programs, not out of the inner consciousness, but out of life itself. If life has undergone great changes, the program cannot be left as it was. In winter we have to wear thick overcoats. In the heat of summer only a madman wears a thick overcoat. It is just the same in politics. Marx himself taught us that we should always study the existing conditions of life and act accordingly. This does not mean that we should change our convictions as a fine lady changes her gloves. The primary aim of the working class is the realisation of the communist order. This aim is a permanent aim. It is, however, self-evident that, according as the working class stands far from or close to its goal, it will put forward different demands. Under tsarist rule working-class organisations were driven underground and the workers' party was persecuted as if its members had been criminals. Now, the working class is in power, and its party is the ruling party. Obviously no intelligent person could advocate exactly the same program for the year 1903 and for the present time.

Thus, the changes in the internal conditions of Russian life and the changes in international circumstances have necessitated changes in our program.

§ 4.

The Meaning of our Program. Our new (Moscow) program is the first program drawn up by the party of the working class since it attained to power some time ago. It is therefore necessary for our party to turn to account all the experience which the working class has gained in administering and upbuilding the new life. This is important, not only for ourselves, not only for the Russian workers and poorer peasants, but also for our foreign comrades. For from our successes and failures, from our mistakes and oversights, experience will be gained, not by ourselves alone, but by the whole international proletariat. This is why our program contains, not merely what our party wishes to accomplish, but also that which it has to some extent accomplished. Every member of our party must be familiar with the program in all its details. It constitutes the most important guide to the activities of every group and of every individual member of the party. For no one can be a member of the party unless he has accepted the program, unless he regards the program as sound. And no one can regard it as sound without knowing it. There are of course many persons who have never glanced at the program, but who thrust themselves into the communist ranks and swear by communism, simply in the hope of snatching up some unconsidered trifle or of feathering their nest. We have no use for such members, who can do us nothing but harm. Without knowledge of the program no one can be a genuine communist bolshevik. Every intelligent Russian worker and poor peasant ought to become acquainted with the program of our party. Every non-Russian proletarian ought to study it, that he may profit by the experience of the Russian revolution.

§ 5.

The scientific Character of our Program. We have already said that it is wrong to manufacture a program out of our own heads, and that our program should be taken from life. Before the time of Marx, those who represented working-class interests were apt to draw fancy pictures of a future paradise, without troubling to ask themselves whether this paradise could ever be reached, and without seeing the right road for the workers and peasants to follow. Marx taught us another way. He examined the evil, unjust, barbaric social order which still prevails throughout the world, and studied its structure. Precisely after the manner in which we might study a machine, or, let us say, a clock, did Marx study the structure of capitalist society, in which factory owners and landowners rule, while workers and peasants are oppressed. Let us suppose we have noticed that two of the wheels of our clock are badly fitted, and that at each revolution they interfere more and more with one another's movements. Then we can foresee that the clock will break down and stop. What Marx studied was not a clock, but capitalist society; he examined it thoroughly, examined life under the dominion of capital. As the outcome of his researches, Marx recognised very clearly that capitalism is digging its own grave, that the machine will break down, and that the cause of the break-down will be the inevitable uprising of the workers, who will refashion the whole world to suit themselves.

Marx's chief instruction to all his followers was that they should study life as it actually is. Thus only can a practical program be drawn up. It is self-evident, therefore, why our program begins with a description of the capitalist regime.

The capitalist regime has now been overthrown in Russia. What Marx prophesied is being fulfilled under our very eyes. The old order is collapsing. The crowns are falling from the heads of kings and emperors. Everywhere the workers are advancing towards revolution, and towards the establishment of soviet rule. In order fully to understand how all this has come about, it is necessary to be thoroughly well acquainted with the nature of the capitalist system. Then we shall realise that its breakdown was inevitable. Once we grasp that there will be no return of the old system and that the victory of the workers is assured, we shall have full strength and confidence as we carry on the struggle on behalf of the new social order of the workers.

Literature. 1. Reports of the April Conference, 1917. 2. Materials for the Revision of the Party Program. 3. BUHARIN, and SMIRNOFF, articles in " Spartakus " Nos. 4–9. 4. LENIN, article in " Prosveshchenie " Nos. 1 and 2, 1917. 5. Reports of the eighth Congress.

Concerning the scientific character of the Marxist program, consult the literature of scientific socialism : GOLUBKOFF, Utopian and Scientific Socialism ; ENGELS, Development of Socialism from Utopia to Science ; MARX and ENGELS, Communist Manifesto.

For the study of the general aspects of the program consult BUHARIN, The Program of the Communist Bolsheviks.

Of the above-mentioned literature, only Buharin's pamphlet and part of Golubkoff's pamphlet are written in a popular style. The other works are for comparatively advanced students.

CHAPTER ONE

THE CAPITALISTIC SOCIAL ORDER

§ 6.

Commodity Economy. If we study how economic life is carried on under the capitalist regime, we see that its primary characteristic is the production of *commodities*. " Well, what is there remarkable about that ? " the reader may ask. The remarkable point is that a commodity is not simply a product, but something produced for the *market*.

A product made for the producer himself, made for his own use, is not a commodity. When a peasant sows rye, gathers in the harvest, threshes it, mills the grain, and bakes bread for himself, this bread is certainly not a commodity ; it is simply bread. It only becomes a commodity when it is bought and sold ; when, that is to say, it is produced for a buyer, for the market. Whoever buys it, owns it.

Under the capitalist system, all products are produced for the market, they all become commodities. Every factory or workshop produces in ordinary circumstances one particular product only, and it is easy to understand that the producer is not producing for his own use. When an undertaker, in his workshop, has coffins made, it is perfectly clear that he does not produce these coffins for himself and his family, but for the market. Again, in the case of a castor oil manufacturer, it is equally clear that even if the man continually suffers from digestive disorder it will be impossible for him to use for his own purposes more than an infinitesimal proportion of all the castor oil which his factory turns out. The same considerations apply, under capitalism, to any products you like to consider.

In a button factory, buttons are made; but these millions of buttons are not produced in order that they may be sewn on to the manufacturer's waistcoat; they are for sale. Everything produced under the capitalist system is produced for the market. To this market come gloves and sausages; books and blacking; machines and whisky; bread, boots, and small-arms—in a word, everything that is made.

A commodity economy necessarily implies *private owner-ship*. The independent artisan who produces commodities owns his workshop and his tools; the factory owner or workshop owner owns the factory or the workshop, with all the buildings, machinery, etc. Now, wherever private ownership and commodity production exist, there is a struggle for buyers, or competition among sellers. Even in the days before there were factory owners, workshop owners, and great capitalists, when there were only inde-pendent artisans, these artisans struggled one with another for buyers. The strongest and most acquisitive among them, the one who had the best tools and was the cleverest, especially the one who put by money, was always the one who came to the top, attracted custom, and ruined his rivals. Thus the system of petty ownership and the com-modity economy that was based upon it, contained the germs of large-scale ownership and implied the ruin of many.

WE SEE, THEREFORE, THAT THE PRIMARY CHARACTERISTIC OF THE CAPITALIST SYSTEM IS A COMMODITY ECONOMY; THAT IS, AN ECONOMY WHICH PRODUCES FOR THE MARKET.

§ 7.

Monopolisation of the Means of Production by the capitalist Class. The mere existence of a commodity economy does not alone suffice to constitute capitalism. A commodity economy can exist although there are no capitalists; for instance, the economy in which the only producers are independent artisans. They produce for the market, they sell their products; thus these products are undoubtedly commodities, and the whole production is commodity pro-duction. Nevertheless, this is not capitalist production;

it is nothing more than *simple commodity production*. In order that a simple commodity economy can be transformed into capitalist production, it is necessary, on the one hand, that the means of production (tools, machinery, buildings, land, etc.) should become the private property of a comparatively limited class of wealthy capitalists; and, on the other, that there should ensue the ruin of most of the independent artisans and peasants and their conversion into wage workers.

We have already seen that a simple commodity economy contains within itself the germs that will lead to the impoverishment of some and the enrichment of others. This is what has actually occurred. In all countries alike, most of the independent artisans and small masters have been ruined. The poorest were forced in the end to sell their tools; from " masters " they became " men " whose sole possession was a pair of hands. Those on the other hand who were richer, grew more wealthy still; they rebuilt their workshops on a more extensive scale, installed new machinery, began to employ more workpeople, became factory owners.

Little by little there passed into the hands of these wealthy persons all that was necessary for production : factory buildings, machinery, raw materials, warehouses and shops, dwelling houses, workshops, mines, railways, steamships, the land—in a word, all the means of production. All these means of production became the exclusive property of the capitalist class ; they became, as the phrase runs, a " monopoly " of the capitalist class.

THE SMALL GROUP OF THE WEALTHY OWNS EVERYTHING ; THE HUGE MASSES OF THE POOR OWN NOTHING BUT THE HANDS WITH WHICH THEY WORK. THIS MONOPOLY OF THE MEANS OF PRODUCTION BY THE CAPITALIST CLASS IS THE SECOND LEADING CHARACTERISTIC OF THE CAPITALIST SYSTEM.

§ 8.

Wage Labour. The vast numbers who were left without any property were transformed into the wage labourers of capital. What indeed was left for the impoverished peasant or artisan to do ? Either take service as agricultural labourer under the capitalist landowner, or else go to the town and there seek employment in factory or workshop. There was no other way out. Such was the origin of wage labour, the third characteristic of the capitalist system.

What is wage labour ? In earlier days, when there were serfs or slaves, every serf or slave could be bought and sold. Persons with skin, hair, arms, and legs, were the private property of their lord. The lord would flog one of his serfs to death in the stable as lightly as, in a drunken fit, he would break a stool or a chair. The serf or slave was merely a chattel. Among the ancient Romans, a master's property, all that was necessary for production, was classified as " *dumb* tools " (things), " *half-speaking* tools " (beasts of burden, sheep, cows, oxen, etc.—in a word, inarticulate animals), and " *speaking* tools " (slaves, human beings). A spade, an ox, a slave, were for the master all alike *tools* or *utensils*, which he could buy, sell, misuse, or destroy, at pleasure.

The wage labourer can be neither bought nor sold. What can be bought and sold is his *labour power* ; not the man or woman, but the capacity for labour. The wage labourer is personally free ; the factory owner cannot flog him in the stable, or sell him to a neighbour, or exchange him for a wolf-hound puppy, though all these things could be done when serfdom prevailed. The wage worker can merely be hired. To all appearance the capitalist and the wage worker are equals. " Don't work if you don't want to ; there is no compulsion," says the factory owner. The employer actually declares that he feeds the worker, gives work to the employee.

As a matter of fact, however, the conditions are far from being the same for wage earner and capitalist. The workers are enchained by hunger. Hunger compels them to hire themselves out, that is, to sell their labour power. There is no other solution for the worker ; he has no choice. With his hands alone he cannot produce " his " product. Just try without tools and machinery to found steel, to weave, to build railway carriages. Under capitalism, the very land is all in private hands ; there remains no spot unowned where an enterprise can be carried on. The freedom of the worker to sell his labour power, the freedom of the capitalist to buy it, the " equality " of the capitalist and the wage earner—all these are but hunger's chain which compels the labourer to work for the capitalist.

In this manner, the essence of wage labour consists in the sale of labour power, or in the transformation of labour power into a commodity. In the simple commodity economy which was described in § 6, there were to be found in the market : milk, bread, cloth, boots, etc. ; but not labour power. Labour power was not for sale. Its possessor, the independent artisan, had in addition his own little dwelling and his tools. He worked for himself, conducted his own enterprise, applied his own labour power to the carrying of it on.

Very different is it under capitalism. The worker no longer owns the means of production ; he cannot make use of his labour power for the conduct of his own enterprise ; if he would save himself from starvation, he must sell his labour power to the capitalist. Side by side with the markets where cotton, cheese, and machines are sold, there also comes into existence the *labour market* where proletarians, that is to say wage workers, sell their labour power.

WE SEE, THEN, THAT THE DIFFERENCE BETWEEN THE CAPITALIST ECONOMY AND THE SIMPLE COMMODITY ECONOMY CONSISTS IN THIS, THAT IN THE CAPITALIST ECONOMY LABOUR POWER ITSELF BECOMES A COMMODITY. THUS, THE THIRD CHARACTERISTIC OF THE CAPITALIST SYSTEM IS THE EXISTENCE OF WAGE LABOUR.

§ 9.

Conditions of Production under Capitalism. There are, therefore, three characteristics of the capitalist system, namely : production for the market (commodity production) ; the monopolisation of the means of production by the capitalist class ; wage labour, that is, labour founded upon the sale of labour power.

All these characteristics are associated with the question, What are the mutual relationships between the individuals engaged in production and distribution ? When we say " commodity production " or " production for the market," what does the phrase mean ? It means that individuals work for one another, but that each produces for the market in his own enterprise, not knowing beforehand who will buy his wares. Let us suppose that there are an artisan named John and a peasant named George. John the artisan, a bootmaker, takes boots to the market and sells them to George, and with the money which George pays for them he buys bread from George. When John went to the market he did not know that he would meet George there, nor did George know that he would meet John ; both men simply went to the market. When John bought the bread and George bought the boots, the result was that George had been working for John and John had been working for George, although the fact was not immediately obvious. The turmoil of the market place conceals from people that in actual fact they work for one another and cannot live without one another. In a commodity economy, people work for one another, but they do so in an unorganised manner and independently of each other, not knowing how necessary they are to one another. Consequently, in commodity production, individuals stand in definite relationships one to another, and what we are here concerned with is these mutual relationships.

In like manner, when we speak of " the monopolisation of the means of production " or of " wage labour," we are really talking about the relationships between individuals. What, in fact, does " monopolisation " signify ? It signifies that persons work under such conditions that those who labour do so with means of production belonging to others ; it signifies that the workers are subordinated to the owners of these means of production, namely to the capitalists. In a word, here also we are concerned with the question, What are the mutual relationships between individuals when they produce goods ? The mutual relationships between individuals during the process of production are termed *the relationships of production.*

It is easy to see that the relationships of production have not always been the same. Very long ago, when people lived in small communities, they worked together in comradely fashion (hunting, fishing, gathering fruit and roots), and they divided everything among themselves. Here we have one kind of relationships of production. In the days of slavery, the relationships of production were of another kind. Under capitalism there is a third kind of relationships. There are, therefore, various kinds of relationships of production. We speak of these kinds of relationships of production as the *economic systems* (types) of society or as the *methods of production*.

" Capitalist relationships of production," or in other words " a capitalist type of society," or " the capitalist method of production "—these terms express the relationships between individuals in a commodity economy characterised by the monopoly ownership of the means of production on the part of a small group of capitalists, and characterised by wage labour on the part of the working class.

§ 10.

The Exploitation of Labour Power. The question now arises, For what reason does the capitalist class hire workers ? Everyone knows that the reason is by no means because the factory owners wish to feed the hungry workers, but because they wish *to extract profit from them.* For the sake of profit, the factory owner builds his factory ; for the sake of profit, he engages workers ; for the sake of profit, he is always nosing out where higher prices are paid. Profit is the motive of all his calculations. Herein, moreover, we discern a very interesting characteristic of capitalist society. For society does not itself produce the things which are necessary and useful to it ; instead of this, the capitalist class compels the workers to produce those things for which more will be paid, those things from which the capitalists derive the largest profit. Whisky, for example, is a very harmful substance, and alcoholic liquors in general ought to be produced only for technical purposes and for their use in medicine. But throughout the world the capitalists produce alcohol with all their might. Why ? Because to ply the people with drink is extremely profitable.

We must now make it perfectly clear, how profit is made. For this purpose we must examine the question in detail. The capitalist receives profit in the form of money when he sells commodities that have been produced in his factory. How much money does he get for his wares ? That depends upon the price. The next question is, How is the price determined, or why does one commodity fetch a high price and another a low price ? It is easy to understand that if, in any branch of production, new machinery is introduced and labour is advantageously applied (or, as the phrase goes, is very productive), then the price of the commodity falls. If, on the other hand, production is difficult, if the quantity of goods produced is small, if labour is unsuccessfully applied or is comparatively unproductive, then the price of the commodity rises.[1]

If society must expend on the average much labour in order to produce any article, the price of that article is high ; if on the average little labour is required, the price of the article is low. Assuming average efficiency of manufacture (that is to say, when the machinery and tools employed are neither the very best nor the very worst), *the amount of social labour requisite for the production of a commodity is termed the value of that commodity.* We see that price depends upon value. In actual fact, price is sometimes higher than value and sometimes lower, but for simplicity we may here assume that they are one and the same.

We must now recall what we said concerning the hiring of wage workers. The hiring of a worker is the sale of a peculiar commodity, the name of which is " labour power." As soon as labour power has become a commodity, what applies to other commodities applies to labour power. When the capitalist hires the worker, the former pays the latter the price of his labour power (or, to speak simply, the value of his labour power). By what is this value determined ? We have seen that the value of all commodities is determined by the quantity of labour expended in producing them. The same thing applies to labour power.

What, however, do we mean by the production of labour power ? Labour power is not indeed produced in a factory, like cloth, blacking, or machinery. How then are we to

---

[1] We are now speaking of a change of price without reference to money, without reference to the question whether there be much money or little, or whether the currency be gold or paper. Changes in price due to changes in the standard of value may be very large, but such changes affect all commodities simultaneously, and this does not explain the differences in price as between one commodity and another. For example, the great extension of paper currency has enormously inflated prices in all countries. But this universal dearness does not explain why one commodity should be dearer than another.

explain it ? We have merely to look at contemporary life under capitalism in order to understand with what we are concerned. Let us suppose that the workers have just finished their day's work. They are tired out, all their vital energy has been used up, they cannot work any more. Their labour power is practically exhausted. What is needed to restore it ? Food, rest, sleep, recuperation, and therewith strength will be restored. Then will reappear the capacity for work ; then, once more, they will have labour power. This means that food, clothing, and shelter —in a word, the necessaries that the worker consumes— effect the production of his labour power. Additional elements have to be considered, such as expenditure upon training when skilled workers are needed, and so on.

Everything that the working class consumes in order to restore its labour power, has value. For this reason, the value of articles of consumption and also of expenditure upon training constitute the value of labour power. Different commodities possess different values. In like manner, each kind of labour power has its peculiar value. The labour power of the compositor has one value, the labour power of the unskilled labourer has another.

Let us now return to the factory. The capitalist buys raw materials, fuel, machinery, lubricants, and other necessaries ; then he buys labour power, " engages hands." He pays cash for everything. The work of production begins. The workers work, the wheels turn, the fuel is burned, the lubricant is used, the factory buildings suffer wear and tear, the labour power is expended. As a result, there issues from the factory a new commodity. The commodity, like all commodities, has value. What is this value ? First of all, the commodity has absorbed into itself the value of the means of production that have been used up ; that which has passed into it—raw materials, fuel consumed, the worn parts of the machinery, and so on. All this has now been transformed into the value of the commodity. In the second place, there has passed into the commodity the labour of the workers. If the workers were 30 in number, and if in the production of the commodity each worked for 30 hours, then there will have been expended in all 900 working hours. The full value of the product will therefore consist of the value of the utilised materials (let us assume that the value of these is equivalent to 600 hours), together with the new value which the workers have added by their labour, namely 900 hours. The total is therefore 600 + 900 = 1,500 working hours.

But how much did the commodity cost the capitalist ? For the raw materials he paid in full ; that is to say, he paid a sum of money corresponding to the value of 600 working hours. But what did he pay for labour power ? Did he pay for the whole 900 hours ? Here lies the key to the riddle. By our hypothesis, he has paid the full value of the labour power for the working days. If 30 workers have worked 30 hours, three days for 10 hours a day, the factory owner will have paid them whatever sum was necessary for the recuperation of their labour power during these days. How much will this sum have been ? The answer is plain ; it will have been considerably less than 900. Why ? Because the quantity of labour which is necessary to recuperate my labour power is one thing, whereas the quantity of labour which I am able to expend is another thing. I can work 10 hours a day. To provide a sufficiency of food, clothing, etc., my daily needs are a quantity of articles the total value of which is equal to 5 hours. That is to say, I can do more work than the work which is requisite to recuperate my labour power. In our example, the workers consume, let us say, in the form of food, clothing, etc., during the three days, articles to the value of 450 working hours ; but they supply 900 hours of labour. There remain for the capitalist 450 hours ; these form the source of his profit. In fact, the commodity has cost the capitalist, as we have seen, 600 + 450 = 1050 hours ; but he sells it for the value of 600 + 900 = 1500 hours ; 450 hours are *surplus value* created by labour power. It results that for half their working time (namely for 5 hours in a ten-hour working day) the workers are working to redintegrate what they have used up for themselves ; but during the other half of the day they are working entirely for the capitalist.

Let us now consider society as a whole. What the individual factory owner or the individual worker does is of very little interest to us. What interests us is the structure

of the huge machine which goes by the name of capitalist
society. The capitalist class hires the working class, the
latter being numerically of enormous size. In millions of
factories, in mines and quarries, in forest and field, hundreds
of millions of workers labour like ants. Capital pays them
their wages, the value of their labour power, with which
they unceasingly renew this labour power for the service
of capital. By its labour, the working class does not
merely pay its own wages, but it creates in addition the
income of the upper classes, creates surplus value. Through
a thousand runnels, this surplus value flows into the pockets
of the master class. Part goes to the capitalist himself,
in the form of entrepreneur's profit ; part goes to the landowner ; in the form of taxes, part enters the coffers of the
capitalist State ; other portions accrue to merchants, traders,
and shopkeepers, are spent upon churches and in brothels,
support actors, artists, bourgeois scribblers, and so on.
Upon surplus value live all the parasites who are bred by the
capitalist system.

Part of the surplus value is, however, used over again
by the capitalists. They add it to their capital, and the
capital grows. They extend their enterprises. They engage
more workers. They instal better machinery. The increased
number of workers produces for them a still greater quantity
of surplus value. The capitalist enterprises grow ever
larger. Thus at each revolution of time, capital moves
forward, heaping up surplus value. Squeezing surplus value
out of the working class, *exploiting* the workers, capital
continually increases in size.

§ 11.

Capital. We now see clearly what capital is. Before
all else, it is a definite value : it may be in the form of money ;
it may be in the form of machinery, raw materials, or factory
buildings ; it may be in the form of finished commodities.
But it is value of such a kind as serves for the production
of new value, for the production of surplus value. CAPITAL
IS VALUE WHICH PRODUCES SURPLUS VALUE. CAPITALIST
PRODUCTION IS THE PRODUCTION OF SURPLUS VALUE.

In capitalist society, machinery and factory buildings
take the form of capital. But do machinery and buildings

always take the form of capital ? Certainly not. If the whole of society were a cooperative commonwealth producing everything for itself, then neither machinery nor raw materials would be capital, seeing that they would not be means for the creation of profit for a small group of rich persons. That is to say, machinery, for example, only becomes capital when it is the private property of the capitalist class, when it serves the purpose of exploiting wage labour, when it serves to produce surplus value. The *form* of the value is here unimportant. The value may be in the form of gold coins or paper money, with which the capitalist buys the means of production and labour power. It may be in the form of the machines with which the workers work ; or of the raw materials out of which they make commodities ; or of the finished articles which will subsequently be sold. If, however, this value serves for the production of surplus value, it is capital.

As a rule capital is continually assuming new aspects. Let us study how these transformations take place.

I. The capitalist has not yet bought labour power or the means of production. He is, however, eager to engage workers, to procure machinery, to obtain raw materials of the best quality, to get a sufficient supply of coal, and so on. As yet, he has nothing except money. Here we have capital in its *monetary form.*

II. With this supply of money the capitalist makes his way to the market—not of course in his own person, since he has the telephone, the telegraph, and a hundred servants. Here takes place the purchase of the means of production and of labour power. The capitalist returns to the factory without money, but with workers, machinery, raw materials, and fuel. These things are now no longer commodities. They have ceased to be commodities ; they are not for sale. The money has been transformed into means of production and into labour power. The monetary wrapping has been cast aside ; the capital has assumed *the form of industrial capital.*

Now the work begins. The machinery is set in motion, the wheels turn, the levers move to and fro, the workers drip with sweat, the machinery undergoes wear and tear, the raw materials are used up, the labour power is tired out.

III. Thereupon, all the raw material, the wear and tear of the machines, the labour power, undergo a gradual transformation into masses of commodities. Thus the capital assumes a new guise ; its factory embodiment vanishes, and it takes the form of quantities of commodities. We have capital in its *commodity form.* But now, when production is completed, the capital has not merely changed its wrapping. It has increased in value, for in the course of production there has been added to it surplus value.

IV. In production, the aim of the capitalist is not to provide goods for his own use, but to produce commodities for the market, for sale. That which was stored up in his warehouse, must be sold. At first the capitalist went to market as a buyer. Now he has to go there as a seller. At first he had money in his hands, and he wanted to buy commodities (the means of production). Now he has commodities in his hands, and he wants to get money. When these commodities are sold, capital jumps back from its commodity form into its monetary form. But the quantity of money which the capitalist receives differs from the quantity which he originally paid out, *inasmuch as it is greater by the whole amount of the surplus value.*

This, however, does not end the movement of capital. The enlarged capital is set in motion once again, and acquires a still larger quantity of surplus value. This surplus value is in part added to capital, and begins a new cycle. Capital rolls on like a snowball, and at each revolution there adheres to it a larger quantity of surplus value. The result of this is that capitalist production continually expands.

Thus capital sucks surplus value out of the working class and everywhere extends its dominion. Its peculiarities account for its rapid growth. The exploitation of one class by another took place in earlier days. Let us consider, for example, a landowner when serfdom prevailed, or a slave-owner in classical antiquity. They lived on the backs of their serfs and slaves. But all which the workers produced, the landowners and slaveowners ate, drank, and wore— either themselves, or else their servants and their numerous hangers-on. At that time there was very little commodity production. There was no market. If the landowner or slaveowner had compelled his serfs or slaves to produce vast quantities of bread, meat, fish, etc., all this would simply have rotted. Production was restricted to the gratification of the animal needs of the landowner and his household. It is very different under capitalism. Here production takes place, not for the gratification of immediate needs, but for profit. Under capitalism, the commodity is produced for sale, for the sake of gain, in order that profits may be heaped up. The larger the profit, the better. Hence the mad hunt for profit on the part of the capitalist class. This greed knows no limits. It is the pivot, the prime motive, of capitalist production.

§ 12.

The capitalist State. As we have seen, capitalist society is based upon the exploitation of labour. A small minority owns everything; the working masses own nothing. The capitalists command. The workers obey. The capitalists exploit. The workers are exploited. The very essence of capitalist society is found in this merciless and ever-increasing exploitation.

Capitalist production is a practical instrument for the extraction of surplus value.

Why has this instrument been able to continue in operation so long? For what reason do the workers tolerate such a state of affairs?

This question is by no means easy to answer at first sight. Speaking generally there are two reasons for it: in the first place, because the capitalist class is well organised and powerful; secondly, because the bourgeoisie frequently controls the brains of the working class.

The most trustworthy means at the disposal of the bourgeoisie for this purpose is its organisation as the State. In all capitalist countries the State is merely a union of the master class. Let us consider any country you like: Britain, the United States, France, or Japan. Everywhere we find that the ministers, high officials, members of parliament, are either capitalists, landowners, factory owners, and financial magnates, or else the faithful and well-paid servants of these—lawyers, bank managers, professors, army officers, archbishops, and bishops, who serve the capitalists, not from fear but from conviction.

The union of all these individuals belonging to the bourgeoisie, a union which embraces the entire country and holds everything in its grasp, is known as the State. This organisation of the bourgeoisie has two leading aims. The first and most important of these is to suppress disorders and insurrections on the part of the workers, to ensure the undisturbed extraction of surplus value from the working class, to increase the strength of the capitalist means of production. The second aim is to strive against other organisations of the same kind (that is to say, against other bourgeois States), to compete with them for a larger share in surplus value. Thus the capitalist State is a union of the master class, formed to safeguard exploitation. The interests of capital and nothing but the interests of capital—here we have the guiding star towards which are directed all the activities of this robber band.

Against such a view of the bourgeois State, the following considerations might be adduced.

You say that the State is exclusively run in the interests of capital. Consider this point, however. In all capitalist countries there is factory legislation forbidding or restricting child labour, limiting the working day, and so on. In Germany, for example, in the days of William II, there prevailed a fairly good system of State insurance for the workers. In England, the typically bourgeois minister Lloyd George introduced the Insurance Act and the Old-Age Pensions Act. In all bourgeois lands, there are hospitals, dispensaries, and sanatoriums for the workers ; railways are constructed, and by these all can travel, rich and poor alike ; waterworks are instituted for the supply of the towns, and so on. Such things are for the public service. This implies, many will say, that even in those countries where capital rules, the State is not run solely in the interests of capital, but is concerned likewise with the interests of the workers. The State actually punishes factory owners who infringe factory legislation.

These arguments are fallacious, for the following reasons. It is perfectly true that the bourgeois authority occasionally passes laws and regulations useful to the working class. They are, however, passed in the interest of the bourgeoisie. Let us take as an example the railways. The workers travel by them, and for this reason they are useful to the workers. But they are not built for the sake of the workers. Merchants and factory owners need railways for the carriage of their wares, for the transport of troops, for the conveyance of workers, etc. Capital needs railways, and builds them in its own interest. They are useful to the workers too, but that is not why the capitalist State constructs them. Again, let us take the cleaning of the towns, or urban sanitation as it is called, and let us consider the hospitals. In these cases the bourgeoisie is concerned about the working-class districts as well as about the others. It is true that, in comparison with the bourgeois quarters in the centre of the town, we find, in the working-class suburbs, dirt, the abomination of desolation, disease, etc. Nevertheless, the bourgeoisie does do something. Why ? Because illness and epidemics sometimes spread all through the town, and if such a thing should happen the bourgeoisie, too, would suffer. In this matter, therefore, the bourgeois State and its urban instruments are simply pursuing bourgeois interests.

Here is another example. During the nineteenth century, the French workers learned from the bourgeoisie the practice of birth control. By artificial means they arranged either to have no children at all or no more than two children. The poverty of the workers was so great that to rear a larger family was difficult or almost impossible. As a result of this practice, the population of France remained nearly stationary. The French bourgeoisie began to be short of soldiers. A clamour was raised : " The nation is perishing ! The Germans are increasing more rapidly than we are ! They will have more soldiers ! " It may be remarked in passing that year by year those who were called up for military service proved less and less fit ; they were shorter, had a smaller chest measurement, were more weakly. And now, behold, the bourgeoisie grew " free-handed " ; it began to insist upon improved conditions for the working class, in order that the workers might rear more children. Undoubtedly, if you kill the hen, you will not get any more eggs.

In all these cases, the bourgeoisie has certainly taken steps useful to the workers ; but it has done so solely in its own interests In many instances, however, measures useful to the workers have been inaugurated by the bourgeois State owing to the pressure of the working class. Nearly all the factory laws were secured in such a manner, in consequence of threats on the part of the workers. In England, the first legal limitation of the working day (to 10 hours) was brought about by working-class pressure. In Russia, the tsarist government passed the first factory laws owing to its alarm on account of disorders and strikes among the workers. In these matters the State, which consists of the enemies of the working class, the State, which is an *economic organisation*, reckons up its own interests, saying : " It is better to yield a certain amount to-day than to yield twice as much to-morrow ; and it is better to yield than to risk one's skin." The factory owner who yields to the demands of his workers on strike and concedes them an extra halfpenny, does not cease to be a factory owner ; nor does the bourgeois State in any way lose its bourgeois characteristics when it makes some small concession owing to working-class pressure.

The capitalist State is not only the largest and most powerful among bourgeois organisations ; it is at the same time the most complex of these organisations, for it has a very large number of subdivisions, and tentacles issue from these in every direction. The primary aim of all this is to protect, to consolidate, and to expand the exploitation of the working class. Against the working class, the State can employ measures of two different kinds, brute force and spiritual subjugation. These constitute the most important instruments of the capitalist State.

Among the organs of *brute force*, must first be enumerated the army and the police, the prisons and the law-courts. Next must be mentioned accessory organs, such as spies, provocative agents, organised strikebreakers, hired assassins, etc.

The *army* of the capitalist State is organised in a peculiar fashion. At the head is the officers' corps, the group of " epaulet wearers." They are drawn from the ranks of the landed gentry, from those of the wealthier bourgeoisie, and in part from those of the intelligentsia (professional classes). These are the bitterest enemies of the proletariat. From childhood they have been brought up in special schools (in Russia, in cadet corps and in junker schools) where they have been taught how to knock the men about, and how " to maintain the honour of the uniform," this meaning to keep the rankers in absolute subjection and to make mere pawns of them. The most distinguished members of the nobility and the wealthier bourgeoisie, if they enter the military or naval profession, become generals or admirals, persons of high rank, wearing orders and ribbons.

Nor are the officers ever drawn from among the poor. They have the mass of common soldiers entirely in their hands. These latter are so completely under the influence of their environment that they never ask what they are fighting for, but simply keep their ears cocked for orders. Such an army is primarily intended to hold the workers in check.

In *Russia*, the tsarist army was repeatedly used to keep down the workers and peasants. During the reign of Alexander II, before the liberation of the serfs, there were numerous risings of the peasantry, and these were all suppressed by the army. In the year 1905, the army shot down the workers during the Moscow rising ; it carried out punitive expeditions in the Baltic provinces, in the Caucasus, and in Siberia ; in the years 1906–1908, it suppressed peasant risings and protected the property of the landowners. During the war, the army shot down the workers at Ivanovo-Voznesensk, at Kostroma, and elsewhere. The officers were especially ruthless. Foreign armies behave in just the same way. In *Germany*, the army of the capitalist State has likewise been used to keep the workers down. The first naval rising was suppressed by the army. Risings of the workers in Berlin, Hamburg, Munich, all over Germany, were crushed by the army. In *France*, the army has frequently shot down strikers ; quite recently it has shot the workers, and also a number of Russian revolutionary soldiers. In the *British Empire*, in quite recent days, the army has frequently crushed risings of the Irish workers, risings of the Egyptian fellahin, risings in India ; in England itself, the soldiers have attacked great meetings of the workers. In *Switzerland*, during every strike, the machine-gun corps is mobilised and the so-called militia (the Swiss army) is summoned to the colours ; so far, however, the militia has not fired on the proletarians. In the *United States*, the army has frequently burned working-class settlements and has razed houses to the ground (for instance, during the strike in Colorado). The armies of the capitalist States are to-day combining to strangle the workers' revolutions in Russia, Hungary, the Balkans, and Germany ; they are crushing revolts all over the world.

The *police* and the *gendarmerie*. In addition to the regular army, the capitalist State has an army of picked ruffians, and of specially trained troops, peculiarly adapted for the struggle with the workers. These institutions (the police, for instance) have, indeed, the function of combating theft and of " protecting the persons and property of citizens " ; but at the same time the police are maintained for the arrest, prosecution, and punishment, of discontented workers. In Russia, the police have been the most trustworthy protectors of the landlords and the tsar. Especially brutal, in all capitalist countries, have been the members of the secret police and of the corps of gendarmes—in Russia the secret police force or " political police " was known as the *ohrana* (protection). Large numbers of detectives, provocative agents, spies, strikebreakers, etc., work in cooperation with the official police.

Interesting, in this connexion, are the methods of the American secret police. They are in league with a vast number of private and semi-official " detective bureaux." The notorious adventures of Nat Pinkerton were really a campaign against the workers. The detectives palmed off bombs on the workers' leaders, incited them to kill the capitalists, and so forth. Such " detectives " likewise

recruit vast numbers of strikebreakers (known in the United States
as " scabs "), and troops of armed ruffians who murder strikers
when opportunity arises. There is no villainy too black for these
assassins, who are employed by the " democratic " State of the
American capitalists !

The *administration of justice* in the bourgeois State is a
means of self-defence for the bourgeois class. Above all,
it is employed to settle with those who infringe the rights
of capitalist property or interfere with the capitalist system.
Bourgeois justice sent Liebknecht to prison, but acquitted
Liebknecht's murderer. The *State prison service* settles
accounts quite as effectively as does the executioner of the
bourgeois State. Its shafts are directed, not against the
rich, but against the poor.

Such are the institutions of the capitalist State, institutions which effect the direct and brutal oppression of the
working class.

Among the means of *spiritual subjugation* at the disposal
of the capitalist State, three deserve especial mention : the
State school ; the State church ; and the State, or State-
supported, press.

The bourgeoisie is well aware that it cannot control
the working masses by the use of force alone. It is necessary
that the workers' brains should be completely enmeshed as
if in a spider's web. The bourgeois State looks upon the
workers as working cattle ; these beasts must labour, but
they must not bite. Consequently, they must not merely
be whipped or shot when they attempt to bite, but they
must be trained and tamed, just as wild beasts in a menagerie
are trained by beast-tamers. Similarly, the capitalist State
maintains specialists to stupefy and subdue the proletariat ;
it maintains bourgeois teachers and professors, the clergy,
bourgeois authors and journalists. In the State schools
these specialists teach children from their earliest years
to obey capital and to despise and hate " rebels." The
children's heads are stuffed with fables about the revolution and the revolutionary movement. Emperors, kings,
and industrial magnates are glorified. In the churches, the
priests, who are salaried by the State, preach that all
authority comes from God. Day after day, the bourgeois
newspapers trumpet these lies, whilst working-class papers

are in most cases suppressed by the capitalist State.   Under such conditions, is it easy for the workers to extract themselves from the quagmire ?   A German imperialist bandit wrote : " We do not only need the soldiers' legs, but also their brains and their hearts."   The bourgeois State, in like manner, aims at educating the workers so that they may resemble domestic animals, who will work like horses, and eat humble pie.

In this manner the capitalist system ensures its own development.   The machine of exploitation does its work. Surplus value is continually extracted from the working class.   The capitalist State stands on guard, and takes good care that there shall be no uprising of the wage slaves.

§ 13.

Fundamental Contradictions of the capitalist System. We must now examine whether capitalist or bourgeois society is well or ill constructed.   Anything is sound and good when the mutual adaptation of its parts is entirely satisfactory.   Let us consider the mechanism of a clock.   It works accurately and freely if all the cog-wheels are properly adjusted one to another.

Let us now look at capitalist society.   We can perceive without difficulty that capitalist society is far less soundly constructed than it appears to be at the first glance.   On the contrary, it exhibits grave contradictions and disastrous flaws.   In the first place, under capitalism the production and distribution of goods is quite unorganised ; " anarchy of production " prevails.   What does this mean ?   It means that all the capitalist entrepreneurs (or capitalist companies) produce commodities independently of one another. Instead of society undertaking to reckon up what it needs and how much of each article, the factory owners simply produce upon the calculation of what will bring them most profit and will best enable them to defeat their rivals in the market.   The consequence often is that commodities are produced in excessive quantities—we are talking, of course, of pre-war days.   There is then no sale for them. The workers cannot buy them, for they have not enough money.   Thereupon a crisis ensues.   The factories are shut down, and the workers are turned out into the street.

Furthermore, the anarchy of production entails a struggle for the market; each producer wants to entice away the others' customers, to corner the market. This struggle assumes various forms: it begins with the competition between two factory owners; it ends in the world war, wherein the capitalist States wrestle with one another for the world market. This signifies, not merely that the parts of capitalist society interfere with one another's working, but that there is a direct conflict between the constituent parts.

THE FIRST REASON, THEREFORE, FOR THE DISHARMONY OF CAPITALIST SOCIETY IS THE ANARCHY OF PRODUCTION, WHICH LEADS TO CRISES, INTERNECINE COMPETITION, AND WARS.

THE SECOND REASON FOR THE DISHARMONY OF CAPITALIST SOCIETY IS TO BE FOUND IN THE CLASS STRUCTURE OF THAT SOCIETY. Considered in its essence, capitalist society is not one society but two societies; it consists of capitalists, on the one hand, and of workers and poor peasants, on the other. Between these two classes there is continuous and irreconcilable enmity; this is what we speak of as the *class war*. Here, also, we see that the various parts of capitalist society are not merely ill-adapted to one another, but are actually in unceasing conflict.

Is capitalism going to collapse, or is it not? The answer to the question depends upon the following considerations. If we study the evolution of capitalism, if we examine the changes it has undergone in the course of time, and if we perceive that its disharmonies are diminishing, then we can confidently wish it a long life. If, on the other hand, we discover that in the course of time the various parts of the capitalist machine have come to clash with one another more and more violently, if we discern that the flaws in the structure are becoming positive chasms, then it is time to say, " Rest in peace."

We have now, therefore, to study the evolution of capitalism.

Literature. BOGDANOFF, A short Course of Economic Science. KAUTSKY, The Economic Doctrines of Karl Marx. KAUTSKY, The Erfurt Program. LENIN, The State and Revolution. ENGELS, The Origin of the Family, of Private Property, and of the State. ENGELS, Development of Socialism from Utopia to Science.

CHAPTER TWO

THE DEVELOPMENT OF THE CAPITALISTIC SOCIAL ORDER

§ 14.

The Struggle between small-scale and large-scale Production (between working Ownership and capitalistic non-working Ownership).

(a) *The struggle between small-scale and large-scale capital in manufacturing industry.* Huge factories, sometimes employing more than ten thousand workers, and having enormous machines, did not always exist. They appeared by degrees, growing up upon the remnants of artisan production and small-scale industry when these were undergoing ruin. In order to understand why this came about, we must first of all take into account the circumstance that, under private property and commodity production, a struggle for buyers, *competition*, is inevitable. Who is the winner in this struggle ? He is the winner who knows how to attract buyers to himself and to wrest them from his competitors. Now the chief means for the attraction of buyers is to offer commodities for sale at a lower price.[1] Who can sell at a very low price ? This is the first question we have to answer. It is obvious that the large-scale producer can sell more cheaply than the small-scale producer or the independent artisan, for the large-scale

[1] We are talking in the text of pre-war days. Thanks to the destructive effects of the war, at present buyers are running after sellers instead of sellers after buyers.

47

producer can buy more cheaply. Large-scale production
has in this respect many advantages. Above all, large-
scale production has this advantage, that the entrepreneur
who commands much capital can instal better machinery,
and can procure better tools and apparatus generally.
The independent artisan or the small master finds it very
difficult to get along ; he cannot usually command a power
plant ; he dares not think of installing better and larger
machines ; he has not the wherewithal to buy them. Nor
is the small capitalist able to procure the newest machines.
Consequently, THE LARGER THE UNDERTAKING, THE MORE
PERFECT IS THE TECHNIQUE, THE MORE ECONOMICAL IS
THE LABOUR, AND THE LOWER IS THE COST OF PRODUCTION.

In the large factories of the United States and Germany there
are actually scientific laboratories where new and improved methods
are continually being discovered. Thus science is wedded to industry.
The discoveries made in such a laboratory remain secrets of the enterprise to which it is attached, and bring profit to that enterprise alone.
In small-scale production and hand production, one and the same
worker conducts nearly all the stages of production. In machine
production, on the other hand, where numerous workers are employed, one worker is responsible for one stage only, a second worker
for a second stage, a third for a third, and so on. In this way, under
the system known as the *division of labour*, the work goes much quicker.
How great is the advantage of this system was made manifest by
some American researches instituted in the year 1898. Here
are the results. *The manufacture of* 10 *ploughs.* By hand labour :
2 workers, performing 11 distinct operations, worked in all 1180
hours, and received $54. By machine labour : 52 workers, per-
forming 97 operations (the more numerous the workers, the more
varied the operations), worked in all 37 hours and 28 minutes, and
received $7.90. (We see that the time was enormously less and that
the cost of labour was very much lower.) *The manufacture of* 100
sets of clock wheels. By hand labour : 14 workers, 453 operations,
341·866 hours, $80.82. By machine labour : 10 workers, 1088 opera-
tions, 8·343 hours, $1.80. *The manufacture of* 500 *yards of cloth.*
Hand labour : 3 workers, 19 operations, 7534 hours, $135.6. Machine
labour : 252 workers, 43 operations, 84 hours, $6.81. Many similar
examples might be given. Furthermore, small manufacturers and
hand workers are quite unable to undertake those branches of production for which a highly developed mechanical technique is essential
For instance, the manufacture of locomotive engines and ironclads ;
coal mining ; and so on.

Large-scale production effects economies in every direction : in buildings, machinery, raw materials, lighting and

heating, cost of labour, utilisation of waste products, etc. In fact, let us suppose that there are one thousand small workshops, and that there is one large factory which produces the same quantity of commodities as all the little workshops put together. It is much easier to build one large factory than a thousand small workshops; the raw materials for the workshops will be used far more wastefully; lighting and heating will be much easier in the case of the large factory; the factory will have the advantage in the matter of general supervision, cleaning up, repairs, etc. In a word, there will unquestionably be in all respects an economy, a saving, in running the large factory.

In the purchase of raw materials and of all that is necessary for production, large-scale capital is likewise at an advantage. The wholesale buyer buys more cheaply, and the goods are of better quality; furthermore, the great factory owner is better acquainted with the market, knows better where to buy cheaply. In like manner, the small enterprise is always at a disadvantage when entering the market as seller. Not only does the large-scale producer know better where to buy cheaply (for this purpose, he has travellers; he conducts his business in the exchange, where news concerning various commodities is always coming in; he has commercial ties extending almost all over the world): in addition, he can afford to *wait*. If, for instance, the price of his product is too low, he can retain it in his warehouses, pending a rise in prices. The small producer cannot do this. He lives from hand to mouth. As soon as he has sold his product, he begins to use for immediate expenses the money he has received; he has no margin. For this reason he is forced to sell willy-nilly, for otherwise he will starve to death. It is obvious that this is a great disadvantage to him.

It need hardly be said that large-scale production enjoys an additional advantage, in the matter of *credit*. If a great entrepreneur has urgent need of money, he can get it. Banks will always lend money to a " solid " firm at a comparatively low rate of interest. But hardly anyone will give credit to the small producer. If he can borrow at all, exorbitant interest will be demanded. Thus the small producer readily falls into the hands of the usurer.

All these advantages attaching to large-scale enterprise explain why small-scale production must invariably succumb in capitalist society. Large-scale capital crushes the small producer, takes away his customers, and ruins him, so that he drops into the ranks of the proletariat or becomes a tramp. In many cases, of course, the small master continues to cling to life. He fights desperately, puts his own hand to the work, forces his workers and his family to labour with all their strength; but in the end he is compelled to give up his place to the great capitalist. In many instances, one who seems to be an independent master is in truth entirely dependent on large-scale capital, works for it, and cannot take a single step without its permission. The small producer is frequently in the toils of the money-lender. Ostensibly independent, he really works for this spider. Or he is a dependent of the purchaser of his commodities. In other cases he is a dependent of the shop for which he works. In the last instance, though apparently independent, he has really become a wage worker in the service of the capitalist who owns the large shop. It may happen that the capitalist provides him with raw materials, and sometimes with tools as well; in Russia many of those engaged in home industry are in this position. In such cases it is perfectly clear that the home worker has become a satellite of capital. Another form of subordination to capital is that in which small repairing workshops are grouped around a large undertaking, so that they are, as it were, mere screws in the wall of the big building. Their independence is only apparent. We sometimes see that small masters, independent artisans, home workers, traders, or petty capitalists, when they have been driven out of one branch of manufacture or commerce, enter some other branch in which large-scale capital is less powerful. In many cases, persons who have been ruined in this way become small traders, pedlars, and the like. Thus large-scale capital tends, step by step, to replace small production everywhere. Huge enterprises come into existence, each employing thousands or tens of thousands of workers. Large-scale capital is becoming the ruler of the world. The working owner is disappearing. His place is being taken by large-scale capital.

As examples of the decline of small-scale production in *Russia*, let us consider the home workers. Some of these, such as furriers and basket-weavers, worked with their own raw materials and sold to anyone who would buy. In course of time the home worker began to work for one particular capitalist ; this is what happened in the case of the Moscow hatmakers, toymakers, brushmakers, etc. In the next stage, home workers procure the raw materials from their own employer, and thus pass into bondage to him (e.g. the locksmiths of Pavlovsk and of Burmakino). Finally, the home worker is paid by his employer at piece-work rates (the nailmakers of Tver, the bootmakers of Kimry, the matmakers of Makarieff, the knifeforgers of Pavlovo). The hand-loom weavers have been similarly enslaved. In *England*, the expiring system of small-scale production was nick-named the " sweating system," owing to the abominable conditions that prevailed. In *Germany*, during the period 1882 to 1895, the number of small enterprises diminished by 8·6 per cent. ; the number of middle-sized enterprises (those employing from 6 to 50 workers) increased by 64·1 per cent. ; and the number of great enterprises increased by 90 per cent. Since 1895 a notable number of middle-sized enterprises have also been crushed out. In *Russia*, the victory of the factory system over home industry has been fairly rapid. The textile industry (weaving) is one of the most important branches of manufacture in Russia. If we consider the changes that have taken place in the cotton industry, if we compare the number of factory workers with the number of home workers, we are able to judge how rapidly the factory system is displacing home industry. Here are the figures :

Year.	No. of Factory Workers.	No. of Home Workers.
1866	94,566	66,178
1879	162,691	50,152
1894–5	242,051	20,475

In the year 1866, for every hundred workers engaged as weavers in cotton factories, there were 70 weavers working at home ; in the years 1894–5, for every hundred factory workers there were only 8 home workers. In Russia the growth of large-scale production was extraordinarily rapid because foreign capital undertook its direct organisation. By the year 1902, large enterprises were already employing nearly half (40 per cent.) of all the Russian industrial workers.

In 1903, in European Russia, the factories employing more than 100 workers numbered 17 per cent. of all factories and workshops ; and of the total number of workers engaged in factories and work-shops 76·6 per cent. worked in these large factories.

The victory of large-scale production all over the world entails much suffering upon small producers. Sometimes whole occupations perish and entire districts are depopulated (e.g. the Silesian weavers in Germany, the Indian weavers, etc.).

(b) *The struggle between small-scale and large-scale capital in agriculture.* The same struggle between small-scale and large-scale production which is carried on in industry, occurs also under capitalism in agriculture. The landlord, who administers his estate just as the capitalist administers his factory; the rich peasant, grasping and usurious; the middle peasant; the poor peasant, who often accepts a job from the landlord or the rich peasant; and the agricultural labourer—we may compare this agricultural series with the industrial series of great capitalist, small capitalist, independent artisan, home worker, wage worker. In the country, as in the town, extensive possessions give an advantage when compared with small.

On a large farm, it is comparatively easy to introduce up-to-date methods. Agricultural machinery (electric or steam ploughs, harvesters, cutters and binders, drillers, threshers, steam threshers, etc.) is almost beyond the reach of the small farmer. The independent artisan cannot think of installing expensive machinery in his little workshop; he has no money to pay for it, nor could he turn such machinery to good account even if he could buy it. In like manner, the peasant cannot buy a steam plough, for, if he had the money, a steam plough would be of no use to him. A great machine like this, for its profitable utilisation, needs a large area of land; it is valueless on a patch where there is hardly room for a fowl-run.

The efficient utilisation of machinery and tools depends on the area of land under cultivation. For the full utilisation of a horse plough we need 30 hectares of land; for that of a set comprising driller, harvester, and thresher, about 70 hectares; for a steam thresher, about 250 hectares; for a steam plough, about 1000 hectares. Recently, machines driven by electric power have been used in agriculture; for these, also, large-scale farming is indispensable.

As a rule, only for farming on the large scale is it practicable to undertake irrigation, to drain swamps, to provide field drainage (the laying of earthenware pipes in the fields to carry off superfluous water), to build light railways, and so on. In agriculture, just as in manufacturing industry, where work is done on a large scale we save upon tools and machinery, materials, labour power, fuel, lighting, etc.

In large-scale farming, there will be per desyatina less waste space between the fields, fewer hedges, ditches, and fences ; less seed will be lost in these waste areas.

Furthermore, the owner of a large farm finds it worth while to engage expert agriculturists, and he can work his land by thoroughly scientific methods.

In matters of trade and credit, what applies to industry, applies also to agriculture. The large-scale farmer is better acquainted with the market, he can await favourable opportunities, he can buy all he needs more cheaply, can sell at a better price. Only one thing remains for the small competitor ; he struggles with all his might. Small-scale agriculture is able to continue in existence only through strenuous labour, in conjunction with the restriction of needs, with semi-starvation. Thus alone can it maintain itself under the capitalist regime. It suffers still more severely owing to heavy taxation. The capitalist State lays crushing burdens upon the smallholder. It suffices to remember what tsarist taxation signified to the peasant —" Sell all you have, so long as you pay your taxes."

In general it may be said that small-scale production is far more tenacious of life in agriculture than in manufacturing industry. In the towns, the independent artisans and other small-scale producers are for the most part rapidly undergoing ruin, but in the rural districts of all countries peasant farming still leads a tolerably sturdy existence. Nevertheless, in the country, too, the impoverishment of the majority proceeds apace, only here the results are less obvious than in the towns. Sometimes it seems, as far as the amount of land is concerned, that an agricultural enterprise is very small, when in reality it is quite an extensive affair, because much capital has been put into it, and because it employs a considerable number of workers ; this applies, for instance, to market gardens in the neighbourhood of large towns. Sometimes, on the other hand, those who seem to be independent

smallholders are really for the most part wage workers;
sometimes they are employed on neighbouring farms,
sometimes they engage in seasonal occupations elsewhere,
and sometimes they work in the towns. What is happening to the independent artisans and to the home workers,
is in like manner happening to the peasants of all lands.
A few of them become " kulaks " (liquor sellers, usurers,
rich peasants who by degrees round off their possessions).
Some of them manage to struggle on as they are. The
remainder are ultimately ruined, they sell their cow and
their nag, becoming " horseless men "; finally, the plot
of land goes the way of the rest, the man will either settle
in the town or make his living as an agricultural labourer.
The " horseless man " becomes a wage worker, whereas
the kulak, the rich peasant who hires workers, becomes a
landlord or a capitalist.

Thus in agriculture a vast quantity of land, tools,
machines, cattle, horses, etc., passes into the hands of a
small group of capitalist landlords, for whom millions of
workers labour, and upon whom millions of peasants are
dependent.

In the *United States*, where the capitalist system has developed
more fully than elsewhere, there are great estates which are worked
like factories. And just as, in factories, only one product is turned
out, so it happens on these farms. There may be huge fields where
nothing but strawberries are grown, or gigantic orchards; enormous
poultry farms; colossal wheat fields, worked by machinery. Many
branches of agricultural production are concentrated in a few hands.
In this way, for example, there comes to exist a " chicken king "
(a capitalist into whose hands is concentrated, more or less completely,
the rearing of chickens), an " egg king," and so on.

§ 15.

**The dependent Position of the Proletariat; the reserve
Army of Labour; Women's Labour and Child Labour.**
Under capitalism, the masses of the population are to an
increasing extent transformed into wage workers. Ruined
artisans, home workers, peasants, traders, minor capitalists—in a word, all who have been thrown overboard,
who have been driven down by large-scale capital, fall
into the ranks of the proletariat. The more that wealth

undergoes concentration and passes into the hands of a small group of capitalists, the more do the masses of the people become the wage slaves of these capitalists.

Owing to the continuous decay of the middle strata and classes, the number of the workers always exceeds the requirements of capital. For this reason, the workers are bound hand and foot by capitalism. The worker must work for the capitalist. If he refuses, the employer can find a hundred others to take his place.

But this dependence upon capital has another cause besides the ruin of new and ever-new strata of the population. The dominion of capital over the workers is further strengthened by the way in which the capitalist is continually turning superfluous workers into the street and making of them a reserve of labour power. How does this come about ? As follows. We have already seen that every factory owner endeavours to reduce the cost of production. This is why he is continually installing new machinery. But the machine commonly replaces labour, renders part of the workers superfluous. The introduction of new machinery signifies that some of the workers will be discharged. Among those hitherto employed in the factory, a certain number will be thrown out of work. Since, however, new machinery is perpetually being introduced in one branch of production or another, it is clear that *unemployment must always exist under capitalism.* For the capitalist is not concerned to provide work for all, or to supply goods to everyone ; his aim is to secure increasing profit. Obviously, therefore, he will discharge any workers who are unable to produce for him as much profit as before.

In actual fact, we see in all capitalist countries a huge number of unemployed workers in every large city. Among the ranks of these unemployed we find Chinese and Japanese workers, ruined peasants who have come from the ends of the earth in search of work ; we find lads fresh from the country, ex-shopkeepers, and ex-artisans. We find also metal workers, printers, textile workers, and the like, men who have worked in factories for years, and have then been thrown out of employment owing to the introduction of new machinery. They all combine to form a reserve supply of labour power for capital, to form what Marx termed the *reserve army of labour*. Owing to the existence of this reserve army of labour, owing to perennial unemployment, the dependence and subjection of the working class continually increase. With the aid of new machinery, capital is able to extract more gold from some of the workers, while the others, the superfluous workers, are thrown into the street. But those who have been thrown into the street constitute a scourge in the hands of the capitalist, a whip which he uses to keep in order those who remain in employment.

The industrial reserve army gives examples of complete brutalisation, destitution, starvation, death, and even crime. Those who are out of work for years, gradually take to drink, become loafers, tramps, beggars, etc. In great cities—London, New York, Hamburg, Berlin, Paris—there are whole quarters inhabited by these out-of-works. As far as Moscow is concerned, Hitrof Market furnishes a similar example. Here, we no longer find the proletariat, but a new stratum, consisting of those who have forgotten how to work. This product of capitalist society is known as the *lumpenproletariat* (loafer-proletariat).

The introduction of machinery also led to the employment of *women's labour* and *child labour*, which are cheaper, and are therefore more profitable to the capitalist. In earlier days, before the introduction of machinery, special skill was requisite for the work of production, and sometimes a long term of apprenticeship was indispensable. Some machines can be managed by children ; all that is necessary is to move the arm or the leg until fatigue becomes overpowering. This is why, after the invention of machinery, the labour of women and children came to be more widely used. Women and children offer less resistance than male workers to capitalist oppression. They are more submissive, more easily intimidated ; they are more ready to believe the priest and to accept everything they are told by persons in authority. Hence the factory owner often replaces male workers by females, and compels little children to transmute their blood for him into the golden coins of profit.

In the year 1913, the number of women workers of all kinds (i.e. not manual workers alone) was as follows : France, 6,800,000 ; Germany, 9,400,000 ; Austria-Hungary, 8,200,000 ; Italy, 5,700,000 ; Belgium, 930,000; U.S.A., 8,000,000; England and Wales, 6,000,000. In Russia, the number of women workers continually increased. In 1900, the women workers numbered 25 per cent. of all factory workers ; in 1908, they numbered 31 per cent. ; in 1912, 45 per cent. In some branches of production, the women outnumbered the men. For example, in the textile industry, out of 870,000 workers in the year 1912, 453,000 were women—more than half, over 52 per cent. During the war, the number of women workers increased enormously.

As regards child labour, this flourishes in many places, despite prohibitions. In countries of advanced capitalist development, as for instance in the U.S.A., child labour is met with at every turn.

This leads to the break-up of the working-class family. If the mothers, and very often the children as well, go to the factory, what becomes of family life ?

When a woman enters the factory, when she becomes a wage worker, she is from time to time exposed, just like a man, to all the hardships of unemployment. She, like-wise, is shown the door by the capitalist ; she, likewise, joins the ranks of the industrial reserve army ; she, just like a man, is liable to undergo moral degradation. Associated with this we have *prostitution*, when a woman sells herself to the first comer in the street. Nothing to eat, no work, hunted from everywhere ; and even if she has work, the wages are so low that she may be compelled to supplement her earnings by the sale of her body. After a time, the new trade becomes habitual. Thus arises the caste of professional prostitutes.

In big towns, prostitutes are found in very large numbers. In such cities as Hamburg and London, these unfortunates are reckoned by tens of thousands. Capital uses them as a source of profit and enrichment, organising vast brothels on capitalistic lines. There is an extensive international commerce in white slaves. The towns of Argentina used to be the centres of this traffic. Especially repul-sive is child prostitution, which flourishes in all European and American towns.

In capitalist society, as better and better machinery is invented, as larger and larger factories are built, and as the quantity of commodities increases, there is a con-comitant increase in capitalist oppression, the industrial reserve army becomes more degraded and impoverished, and the working class grows more dependent upon its exploiters.

If private ownership did not exist, if everything were cooperatively owned, a very different state of affairs would prevail. Then people would shorten the working day, would husband their strength, economise toil, enjoy ample leisure. When the capitalist introduces machinery, his concern is for profit ; he does not think of reducing the working day, for he would only lose by this. The capitalist does not use machinery to emancipate people, but to enslave them. As capitalism develops, an ever-increasing proportion of capital is devoted to machinery, enormous buildings, huge furnaces, and so on. On the other hand, the proportion of capital expended upon the wages of labour grows continually smaller. In earlier days, when hand labour still prevailed, the expenditure upon looms and other gear was trifling ; nearly all the expenditure of capital was upon the wages of labour. Now, conversely, much the larger portion is devoted to buildings and machinery. The result is that the demand for working hands does not keep pace with the increase in the number of proletarians, does not suffice to absorb the influx of those who are ruined by capitalism. The more vigorous the advance of technique under capitalism, the more cruelly does capital oppress the working class ; for it grows ever harder to find work, more and more difficult to live.

§ 16.

The Anarchy of Production ; Competition ; Crises. The miseries of the working class continually increase concomitantly with the progress of manufacturing technique. Under capitalism this progress, instead of bringing advantages to all, brings increased profit to capital, but unemployment and ruin to many workers. There are, however, additional causes for the increasing misery.

We have already learned that capitalist society is very badly constructed. Private ownership holds sway, and there is no definite plan whatever. Every factory owner conducts his business independently of the others. He struggles with his rivals for buyers, " competes " with them.

The question now arises whether this struggle becomes enfeebled or intensified as capitalism develops.

At first sight it might seem that the struggle is enfeebled. In actual fact, the number of capitalists grows continually smaller; the great fish eat up the small fry. Whereas in earlier days ten thousand entrepreneurs were fighting one with another and competition was embittered, since now there are fewer competitors it might be imagined that the rivalry would be less acute. But this is not so in reality. The very opposite is the case. It is true that there are fewer competitors. But each one of these has become enormously stronger than were the rivals of an earlier stage. The struggle between them is greater, not less; more violent, not more gentle. If in the whole world there should rule only a few capitalists, then these capitalist governments would fight with one another. This is what it has come to at long last. At the present time the struggle goes on between immense combinations of capitalists, between their respective States. Moreover, they fight with one another, not solely by means of competitive prices, but also by means of armed force. Thus it is only in respect of the number of competitors that competition can be said to diminish as capitalism develops; in other respects it grows continually fiercer and more destructive.[1]

One more phenomenon must now be considered, the occurrence of what are termed *crises*. What are these crises? What is their real nature? The matter may be stated as follows. One fine day it appears that various commodities have been produced in excessive quantities. Prices fall, but the stock of goods cannot be cleared. The warehouses are filled with all kinds of products, for which there is no sale; buyers are lacking. Needless to say, there are plenty of hungry workers, but they receive no more than a pittance, and cannot buy anything in excess of their usual purchases. Then calamity ensues. In some particular branch of industry the small and middle-sized undertakings collapse first, and are closed down; next comes the failure of the larger enterprises. But the branch of production thus affected bought commodities from

[1] For further details see the chapter on the imperialist war.

another branch of production; this latter bought from a third. For instance, tailors buy cloth from the cloth makers; these buy wool from the yarn spinners; and so on. The tailors come to grief, and in consequence there are no customers for the cloth makers. Now the cloth makers fail, and their failure reacts upon the firms that supply them with woollen yarn. Factories and workshops everywhere close their doors, tens of thousands of workers are thrown on the streets, unemployment grows to unprecedented proportions, the workers' life becomes even worse. Yet there are plenty of commodities. The warehouses are bursting with them. This was continually happening before the war. Industry flourishes; the manufacturers' businesses work at high pressure. Suddenly there is a crash, followed by misery and unemployment, and business is at a standstill. After a time, recovery sets in; there comes a renewed period of excessive activity, to be followed in turn by a new collapse. The cycle is repeated over and over again.

How can we explain this absurd state of affairs, wherein people become paupers in the midst of wealth?

The question is not easy to answer. But we must answer it.

We have already learned that in capitalist society there prevails a disorder, or so to say an anarchy, of production. Every factory owner, every entrepreneur, produces for himself, on his own responsibility, and at his own risk. The natural result in these circumstances is that sooner or later too many commodities are produced— there is overproduction. When there was production of goods but not of commodities, when, that is to say, production was not effected for the market, then there was no danger of overproduction. It is quite otherwise in the case of commodity production. Every manufacturer, in order that he may buy what he requires for further production, must first of all sell his own products. If in any particular place there is a stoppage of machinery on account of the anarchy of production, the trouble quickly spreads from one branch of production to another, so that a universal crisis ensues.

These crises have a devastating influence. Large

quantities of goods perish.   The remnants of small-scale production are swept away as if by an iron broom. Even the big firms often fail.

Most of the burden of these crises is of course borne by the working class.

Some factories close down altogether ;   others reduce production, working only half-time ;   others are temporarily closed.   The number of unemployed increases.   The industrial reserve army grows larger.   Simultaneously there is an increase in the poverty and oppression of the working class.   During these crises, the condition of the working class, bad at the best of times, grows even worse.

Let us consider, for example, the data of the crisis of 1907–1910, affecting both Europe and America, in fact the whole capitalist world. In the *United States*, the number of unemployed trade unionists increased as follows : June, 1907, 8·1 per cent. ;   October, 18·5 per cent. ; November, 22 per cent. ;   December, 32·7 per cent. (in the building trades, 42 per cent.; in the dressmaking trade, 43·6 per cent. ; among tobacco workers, 55 per cent.).   It goes without saying that the total number of unemployed, taking into account the unorganised workers as well, was still larger.   In *England*, the percentage of unemployed in the summer of 1907 was 3·4 to 4 per cent. ;   in November, it rose to 5 per cent. ;   in December, to 6·1 per cent. ;   in June, 1908, it reached 8·2 per cent.   In *Germany*, during January, 1908, the percentage of unemployed was twice as great as during the same month of the previous year.   Like conditions were observable in other countries.

As regards the falling-off in production, it may be mentioned that in the United States the production of cast-iron, which had been 26,000,000 tons in 1907, was only 16,000,000 tons in 1908.

In times of crisis, the price of commodities falls.   The capitalist magnates, eager to continue profit making, do not hesitate to impair the quality of production.   The coffee-growers of Brazil dumped innumerable sacks of coffee into the sea in order to keep up prices. At the present time the whole world is suffering from hunger and from the non-production of goods, the result of the capitalist war. For these things are the offspring of capitalism, which decreed the disastrous war.   In times of peace, capitalism was overwhelmed by a glut of products, which, however, did not advantage the workers. Their pockets were empty.   The glut brought nothing to the workers except unemployment, with all its attendant evils.

§ 17.

The Development of Capitalism and of Class.   The Intensification of the Class Struggle.   We have seen that capitalist society is affected by two fundamental contra-

dictions, two fundamental ills. In the first place, it is
" anarchistic " ; it lacks organisation. In the second place,
it is in fact composed of two mutually hostile societies
(classes). We have also seen that, as capitalism develops,
the anarchy of production, finding expression in competition, leads to ever-increasing strife, disorder, and ruin.
The disintegration of society, far from diminishing, is
actually increasing. Now all this arises from the splitting-
up of society into two portions, into classes. As capitalism
develops, this severance, this cleavage between classes,
likewise continues to increase. On one side, that of the
capitalists, all the riches of the world are heaped up ; on
the other side, that of the oppressed classes, is an accumulation of misery, bitterness, and tears. The industrial
reserve army gives birth to a stratum of debased and
brutalised individuals, crushed to the earth by extreme
poverty. But even those who remain at work are sharply
distinguished from the capitalists by their manner of life.
The differentiation of the proletariat from the bourgeoisie
continually increases. Formerly there was quite a number
of lesser capitalists, many of whom had close relationships
with the workers and lived little better than these. Things
are very different to-day. The lords of capital live in a
manner of which no one dreamed in earlier days. It is
true that the workers' standard of life has improved in
the course of capitalist development. Down to the beginning
of the twentieth century, there occurred a general rise in
wages. But during this same period, capitalist profits
increased still more rapidly. To-day there is a great gulf
fixed between the toiling masses and the capitalist class.
The capitalist now leads an entirely different sort of life ;
he himself produces nothing. The more capitalism develops,
the more exalted becomes the position of the small group
of extremely wealthy capitalists, and the wider grows the
chasm between these uncrowned kings and the millions
upon millions of enslaved proletarians.

We have said that the wages of the workers have risen
on the whole, but that profit has increased still more
rapidly, and that for this reason the chasm between the
two classes has widened. Since the beginning of the
twentieth century, however, wages have not risen but

fallen ; whereas during the same period profits have increased as never before. Hence there has during recent years been an exceptionally rapid increase in social inequality.

It is perfectly clear that this social inequality, in its continued growth, must sooner or later lead to a clash between the workers and the capitalists. If the contrast between the two classes were diminishing, if the life conditions of the workers were becoming approximated to those of the capitalists, then, of course, we might look for a regime of " peace on earth and goodwill towards men." What actually occurs, however, is that in capitalist society the worker is day by day farther removed from the capitalist instead of drawing nearer to him. The inevitable result of this is a continuous accentuation of the class war between the proletariat and the bourgeoisie.

Bourgeois theorists put forward many objections to such a view. They would like to show that in capitalist society the condition of the working class undergoes continuous improvement. The socialists of the right wing sing the same tune. Writers of both these schools contend that the workers grow gradually richer, and can look forward to becoming petty capitalists themselves. Such expectations have been falsified. In actual fact the condition of the workers as compared with that of the capitalists has persistently grown worse. Here is an example drawn from the United States, the land of most advanced capitalist development. If we consider the purchasing power of labour (that is to say, the quantity of necessaries which the workers can buy), taking the years from 1890–1899 as a standard at 100, the purchasing power in various years was as follows : 1890, 98·6 ; 1895, 100·6 ; 1900, 103·0 ; 1905, 101·4 ; 1907, 101·5. This means that the workers' standard of life has undergone practically no improvement. The quantities of food, clothing, etc., bought by the average worker in 1890 was increased by no more than 3 per cent. in subsequent years ; this was the utmost rise in the purchasing power of his wages. But during the same period the American millionaires, the industrial magnates, were making enormous profits, and the quantity of surplus value they were receiving was increasing to an immeasurable extent. As far as the capitalist standard of life, capitalist luxuries, and capitalist incomes, are concerned, it is obvious that these were increased many times over.

The class war arises out of the conflict of interests between the bourgeoisie and the proletariat. These interests are as essentially irreconcilable as are the respective interests of wolves and sheep.

It is plain that the capitalist will find it advantageous to make the workers work as long as possible and to pay them as little as possible ; on the other hand, the workers will find it advantageous to work for the minimum hours and for the maximum wages. Obviously, therefore, since the time when the working class first began to exist, there must have been a struggle for higher wages and shorter hours.

This struggle has never been interrupted, and has never been stilled. It has not, however, been restricted to a struggle for a trifling advance in wages. Wherever the capitalist system has developed, the toiling masses have become convinced that they must make an end of capitalism itself. The workers began to consider how this detested system could be replaced by a just and comradely system based upon work. Such was the origin of the communist movement of the working class.

In their struggle, the workers have experienced numerous defeats. But the capitalist system bears within its womb the final victory of the proletariat. Why ? For this reason, because the development of capitalism entails the proletarianisation of the broad masses of the people. The victory of large-scale capital effects the ruin of independent artisans, small traders, and peasants ; it swells the ranks of the wage workers. At each step in capitalist development, the proletariat grows more numerous. It is like the Hydra, the many-headed monster of fable ; if you cut off one of its heads, ten new ones grow. When the bourgeoisie suppressed a working-class rising, it thereby strengthened the capitalist system. But the development of this capitalist system ruined petty proprietors and peasants by the million, throwing them under the feet of the capitalists. By this very process it increased the number of proletarians, the enemies of the capitalist class. But the increase in strength of the working class was not numerical merely. In addition, the working class became more strongly integrated. Why did this happen ? Because, as capitalism developed, there was an increase in the number of great factories. Each great factory assembles within its walls a thousand workers, sometimes as many as ten thousand. These workers labour shoulder to shoulder.

They recognise how their capitalist employer is exploiting them. They perceive that to each worker his fellow-workers are friends and comrades. In the course of their work the proletarians, united in the factory, learn how to unite forces. They more readily come to an agreement one with another. That is why, as capitalism develops, there is not merely an increase in the number of the workers, but an increase in *working-class solidarity*.

The more rapidly huge factories extend, the more rapidly does capitalism develop, and the more speedy is the ruin of independent artisans, home workers, and peasants. The faster, likewise is the growth of gigantic cities with millions of inhabitants. Finally, in large towns, there is gathered together upon a comparatively restricted area an immense mass of persons, and the great majority of them belong to the factory proletariat. These masses are housed in foul and smoky quarters of the town, whilst the small group of the master class, the owners of all things, lives in luxurious mansions. The numbers of those constituting this small group are continually diminishing. The workers incessantly increase in numbers and their solidarity grows ever greater.

Under such conditions, the inevitable increase in the intensity of the struggle cannot fail in the long run to lead to the victory of the working class. Sooner or later, notwithstanding all the wiles of the bourgeoisie, the workers will come into violent collision with the master class, will dethrone it, will destroy its robber government, and will create for themselves a new order, a communist order based on labour. In this manner, capitalism, by its own development, inevitably leads to the communist revolution of the proletariat.

The class struggle of the proletariat against the bourgeoisie has assumed various forms. Three leading types of working-class organisation have arisen in the course of this struggle. First of all we have the *trade unions*, grouping the workers according to occupation. Next come the *cooperatives*, which are mainly concerned with distribution, for it is their aim to free the workers from the grip of middlemen and traders. Last of all we have the *political parties* of the working class (socialist, social-democrat, and communist) whose program it is to guide the working class in its struggle for political power. The fiercer the struggle between the two classes became,

the more essential was it that all sections of the working-class movement should concentrate upon a single aim—the overthrow of the
bourgeois State. Those leaders of the working-class movement who
have most perfectly realised the situation have always insisted upon
the necessity for a close collaboration between all working-class
organisations. They pointed out, for example, the essential need
for unity of action between the trade unions and the political parties
of the proletariat ; and they declared that the trade unions could
not remain " neutral " (that is to say, indifferent in political matters).
The unions, they said, must march shoulder to shoulder with the
political parties of the working class.

Quite recently, the workers' movement has assumed yet newer
forms. The most important of these is the constitution of *councils
of workers' delegates* (soviets). We shall have to speak of these again
and again in the course of the book.

Thus from our study of the development of the
capitalist system we can confidently deduce the following
conclusions : THE NUMBER OF THE CAPITALISTS GROWS
SMALLER, BUT THESE FEW CAPITALISTS GROW RICHER AND
STRONGER ; THE NUMBER OF THE WORKERS CONTINUALLY
INCREASES, AND WORKING-CLASS SOLIDARITY LIKEWISE
INCREASES, THOUGH NOT TO THE SAME EXTENT ; THE
CONTRAST BETWEEN THE WORKERS AND THE CAPITALISTS
GROWS EVER GREATER. INEVITABLY, THEREFORE, THE
DEVELOPMENT OF CAPITALISM LEADS TO A CLASH BETWEEN
THE TWO CLASSES, THAT IS, IT LEADS TO THE COMMUNIST
REVOLUTION.

§ 18.

**The Concentration and Centralisation of Capital as Causal
Factors of Communism.** Capitalism, as we have seen, digs
its own grave. For it creates its own grave-diggers, the
proletarians. The more it develops, the more does it
multiply those who are its mortal enemies, and the more
does it unite them against itself. But it does not merely
breed its enemies. It likewise prepares the ground for
a new organisation of social production, for a new
economic order which will be comradely and communistic.
How does it do this ? We shall speedily give the answer.

We have previously seen (glance at or reread § 11.
" Capital ") that capital is continually increasing in amount.
The capitalist adds to his capital, part of the surplus value
which he extracts from the working class. By such means,

capital grows larger. But if capital increases in amount, this implies that production must extend. The increase in capital, the growth of the amount held by one pair of hands, is termed the *accumulation* or *concentration of capital*.

We have likewise seen (refer to § 14. " The Struggle between large-scale and small-scale Production ") that the development of capitalism involves the decay of small-scale and medium-scale production ; that the small and medium producers and traders are ruined, not to speak of the independent artisans ; we have seen that the great capitalist gobbles them all up. The capital which was previously owned by the small and medium capitalists slips from their grasp, and by various routes finds its way into the maw of the big sharks. The capital owned by the great capitalists is consequently increased by the amount which they have wrested from the lesser capitalists. There is now an accumulation of capital in the hands of one individual, an accumulation of what had previously been distributed among various hands. Now, after the ruin of the lesser capitalists, their capital has become the spoil of the victors. This accumulation of capital which had previously been dispersed is spoken of as the *centralisation of capital*.

The concentration and centralisation of *capital*, the accumulation of capital in a few hands, does not as yet imply the concentration and centralisation of *production*. Let us suppose that a capitalist has used the accumulation of surplus value to buy a small factory from a neighbour, and that he keeps this factory running on the old lines. Here accumulation has taken place, but there is no change in production. Usually, however, things take a different course. In actual fact it much more frequently happens that the capitalist (because it is profitable to him) remodels and extends production, that he enlarges his factories. This results, not merely in the expansion of capital, but in the expansion of production itself. Production is conducted on an enormous scale, utilising vast quantities of machinery, and assembling many thousands of workers. It may happen that a dozen or so of huge factories will supply the demand of a whole country for a particular commodity. Essentially what happens is that the workers are producing for the whole of society, that labour, as the phrase goes, has been *socialised*. But control and profit are still in the hands of the capitalist.

Such a centralisation and concentration of production actually paves the way for cooperative production after the proletarian revolution.

Had this concentration of production not taken place, if the proletariat were to seize power at a time when the work of production was carried on in a hundred thousand tiny workshops each employing no more than two or three workers, it would be impossible to organise these workshops satisfactorily, to inaugurate social production. The further capitalism has developed and the more highly centralised production has become, the easier will it be for the proletariat to manage production after the victory.

THUS CAPITALISM DOES NOT MERELY CREATE ITS OWN ENEMIES AND DOES NOT ONLY LEAD TO THE COMMUNIST REVOLUTION, BUT IT BRINGS INTO BEING THE ECONOMIC BASIS FOR THE REALISATION OF THE COMMUNIST SOCIAL ORDER.

Literature. The books mentioned at the end of Chapter One. In addition read the following : BOGDANOFF and STEPANOFF, Course of Political Economy, vol. ii, part 2 " The Era of Industrial Capital." MARX and ENGELS, The Communist Manifesto. LONDON, Under the Yoke of Imperialism.—Concerning the agrarian problem, consult the following works : KAUTSKY, The Agrarian Problem. LENIN, The Agrarian Problem and the Critics of Marx. KAUTSKY, Socialism and Agriculture (an answer to David). LENIN, New Data concerning the Development of Capitalism in Agriculture in the U.S. LENIN, The Development of Capitalism in Russia. KRZHIVITSKY, The Agrarian Question. PARVUS, The World Market and the Agrarian Crisis.

CHAPTER THREE

COMMUNISM AND THE DICTATORSHIP OF THE PROLETARIAT

§ 19.

Characteristics of the communist System. Production under Communism. We have seen why the destruction of the capitalist system was inevitable. It is now perishing under our very eyes. It is perishing because it is affected by two fundamental contradictions : on the one hand, anarchy of production, leading to competition, crises, and wars ; on the other hand, the class character of society, owing to which one part of society inevitably finds itself in mortal enmity with the other part (class war). Capitalist society is like a badly constructed machine, in which one part is continually interfering with the movements of another (see § 13. " Fundamental Contradictions of the capitalist System "). That is why it was inevitable that this machine would break down sooner or later.

It is evident that the new society must be much more solidly constructed than capitalism. As soon as the fundamental contradictions of capitalism have destroyed the capitalist system, upon the ruins of that system there must arise a new society which will be free from the contradictions of the old. That is to say, the communist method of production must present the following characteristics : In the first place it must be an *organised* society ; it must be free from anarchy of production, from competition between individual entrepreneurs, from wars and crises. In the second place it must be a *classless* society, not a society in which the two halves are at eternal enmity one with the other ; it must not be a society in which one class exploits the other. Now a society in which there are no classes, and in which production is organised, can only be *a society of comrades, a communist society based upon labour.*

Let us examine this society more closely.

The basis of communist society must be the social ownership of the means of production and exchange. Machinery, locomotives, steamships, factory buildings, warehouses, grain elevators, mines, telegraphs and telephones, the land, sheep, horses, and cattle, must all be at the disposal of society. All these means of production must be under the control of society as a whole, and not as at present under the control of individual capitalists or capitalist combines. What do we mean by " society as a whole " ? We mean that ownership and control is not the privilege of a class but of all the persons who make up society. In these circumstances society will be transformed into a huge working organisation for cooperative production. There will then be neither disintegration of production nor anarchy of production. In such a social order, production will be organised. No longer will one enterprise compete with another ; the factories, workshops, mines, and other productive institutions will all be subdivisions, as it were, of one vast people's workshop, which will embrace the entire national economy of production. It is obvious that so comprehensive an organisation presupposes a general plan of production. If all the factories and workshops together with the whole of agricultural production are combined to form an immense cooperative enterprise, it is obvious that everything must be precisely calculated. We must know in advance how much labour to assign to the various branches of industry ; what products are required and how much of each it is necessary to produce ; how and where machines must be provided. These and similar details must be thought out beforehand, with approximate accuracy at least ; and the work must be guided in conformity with our calculations. This is how the organisation of communist production will be effected. Without a general plan, without a general directive system, and without careful calculation and book-keeping, there can be no organisation. But in the communist social order, there is such a plan.

Mere organisation does not, however, suffice. The essence of the matter lies in this, that the organisation shall be a cooperative organisation of *all* the members of society. The communist system, in addition to affecting organisation, is further distinguished by the fact that *it puts an end to exploitation,* that *it abolishes the division of society into classes.* We might conceive the organisation of production as being effected in the following manner : a small group of capitalists, a capitalist combine, controls everything ; production has been organised, so that capitalist no longer competes with capitalist ; conjointly they extract surplus value from the workers, who have been practically reduced to slavery. Here we have organisation, but we also have the exploitation of one class by another. Here there is a joint ownership of the means of production, but it is joint ownership by one class, an exploiting class. This is something very different from communism, although it is characterised by the organisation of production. Such an organisation of society would have removed only one of the fundamental contradictions, the anarchy of production. But it would have strengthened the other fundamental contradiction of capitalism, the division of society into two warring halves ; the class war would be intensified. Such a society would be organised along one line only ; on another line, that of class structure, it would still be rent asunder. Communist society does not merely organise production ; in addition, it frees people from oppression by others. It is organised throughout.

The cooperative character of communist production is likewise displayed in every detail of organisation. Under communism, for example, there will not be permanent managers of factories, nor will there be persons who do one and the same kind of work throughout their lives. Under capitalism, if a man is a bootmaker, he spends his whole life in making boots (the cobbler sticks to his last) ; if he is a pastrycook, he spends all his life baking cakes ; if he is the manager of a factory, he spends his days in issuing orders and in administrative work ; if he is a mere labourer, his whole life is spent in obeying orders. Nothing of this sort happens in communist society. Under communism people receive a many-sided culture, and find themselves at home in various branches of production : to-day I work in an administrative capacity, I reckon up how many felt boots or how many French rolls must be produced during the following month ; to-morrow I shall be working in a soap factory, next month perhaps in a steam laundry, and the month after in an electric power station. This will be possible when all the members of society have been suitably educated.

§ 20.

Distribution in the communist System. The communist method of production presupposes in addition that production is not for the market, but for use. Under communism, it is no longer the individual manufacturer or the individual peasant who produces ; the work of production is effected by the gigantic cooperative as a whole. In consequence of this change, we no longer have *commodities*, but only *products*. These products are not exchanged one for another ; they are neither bought nor sold. They are simply stored in the communal warehouses, and are subsequently delivered to those who need them. In such conditions, money will no longer be required. " How can that be ? " some of you will ask. " In that case one person will get too much and another too little. What sense is there in such a method of distribution ? " The answer is as follows. At first, doubtless, and perhaps for twenty or thirty years, it will be necessary to have various regulations. Maybe certain products will only be supplied to those persons who have a special entry in their work-book or on their work-card. Subsequently, when communist society has been consolidated and fully developed, no such regulations will be needed. There will be an ample quantity of all products, our present wounds will long since have been healed, and everyone will be able to get just as much as he needs. "But will not people find it to their interest to take more than they need ? " Certainly not. To-day, for example, no one thinks it worth while when he wants one seat in a tram, to take three tickets and keep two places

empty. It will be just the same in the case of all products.
A person will take from the communal storehouse precisely
as much as he needs, no more. No one will have any interest
in taking more than he wants in order to sell the surplus
to others, since all these others can satisfy their needs
whenever they please. Money will then have no value. Our
meaning is that at the outset, in the first days of communist society, products will probably be distributed in
accordance with the amount of work done by the appli-
cant ; at a later stage, however, they will simply be supplied
according to the needs of the comrades.

It has often been contended that in the future society everyone
will have the right to the full product of his labour. " What you
have made by your labour, that you will receive." This is false.
It would never be possible to realise it fully. Why not ? For this
reason, that if everyone were to receive the full product of his labour,
there would never be any possibility of developing, expanding, and
improving production. Part of the work done must always be devoted
to the development and improvement of production. If we had to
consume and to use up everything we have produced, then we could
never produce machines, for these cannot be eaten or worn. But
it is obvious that the bettering of life will go hand in hand with the
extension and improvement of machinery. It is plain that more
and more machines must continually be produced. Now this implies
that part of the labour which has been incorporated in the machines
will not be returned to the person who has done the work. It implies
that no one can ever receive the full product of his labour. But
nothing of the kind is necessary. With the aid of good machinery,
production will be so arranged that all needs will be satisfied.

To sum up, at the outset products will be distributed *in proportion
to the work done* (which does not mean that the worker will receive
" the full product of his labour ") ; subsequently, products will be
distributed *according to need*, for there will be an abundance of
everything.

§ 21.

Administration in the communist System. In a communist society there will be no classes. But if there will
be no classes, this implies that *in communist society there
will likewise be no State*. We have previously seen that the
State is a class organisation of the rulers. The State is always
directed by one class against the other. A bourgeois State
is directed against the proletariat, whereas a proletarian
State is directed against the bourgeoisie. In the communist

social order there are neither landlords, nor capitalists, nor wage workers ; there are simply people—comrades. If there are no classes, then there is no class war, and there are no class organisations. Consequently the State has ceased to exist. Since there is no class war, the State has become superfluous. There is no one to be held in restraint, and there is no one to impose restraint.

But how, they will ask us, can this vast organisation be set in motion without any administration ? Who is going to work out the plans for social production ? Who will distribute labour power ? Who is going to keep account of social income and expenditure ? In a word, who is going to supervise the whole affair ?

It is not difficult to answer these questions. The main direction will be entrusted to various kinds of book-keeping offices or statistical bureaux. There, from day to day, account will be kept of production and all its needs ; there also it will be decided whither workers must be sent, whence they must be taken, and how much work there is to be done. And inasmuch as, from childhood onwards, all will have been accustomed to social labour, and since all will understand that this work is necessary and that life goes easier when everything is done according to a prearranged plan and when the social order is like a well-oiled machine, all will work in accordance with the indications of these statistical bureaux. There will be no need for special ministers of State, for police and prisons, for laws and decrees—nothing of the sort. Just as in an orchestra all the performers watch the conductor's baton and act accordingly, so here all will consult the statistical reports and will direct their work accordingly.

The State, therefore, has ceased to exist. There are no groups and there is no class standing above all other classes. Moreover, in these statistical bureaux one person will work to-day, another to-morrow. The bureaucracy, the permanent officialdom, will disappear. The State will die out.

Manifestly this will only happen in the fully developed and strongly established communist system, after the complete and definitive victory of the proletariat ; nor will it follow immediately upon that victory. For a long time yet, the working class will have to fight against all its enemies, and in especial against the relics of the past, such as sloth, slackness, criminality, pride. All these will have to be stamped out. Two or three generations of persons will have to grow up under the new conditions before the need will pass for laws and punishments and for the use of repressive measures by the workers' State. Not until then will all the vestiges of the capitalist past disappear. Though in the intervening period the existence of the workers' State is indispensable, subsequently, in the fully developed communist system, when the vestiges of capitalism are extinct, the proletarian State authority will also pass away. The proletariat itself will become mingled with all the other strata of the population, for everyone will by degrees come to participate in the common labour. Within a few decades there will be quite a new world, with new people and new customs.

§ 22.

The Development of productive Forces in the communist System. (The Advantages of Communism.) As soon as victory has been achieved and as soon as all our wounds have been healed, the communist system will rapidly develop the forces of production. This more rapid development of the forces of production will be due to the following causes.

In the first place, there will have ensued the liberation of the vast quantity of human energy which is now absorbed in the class struggle. Just think how great is the waste of nervous energy, strength, and labour—upon the political struggle, upon strikes, revolts and their suppression, trials in the law-courts, police activities, the State authority, upon the daily effort of the two hostile classes. The class war now swallows up vast quantities of energy and material means. In the new system this energy will be liberated; people will no longer struggle one with another. The liberated energy will be devoted to the work of production.

Secondly, the energy and the material means which now are destroyed or wasted in competition, crises, and wars, will all be saved. If we consider how much is squandered upon wars alone, we shall realise that this amounts to an enormous quantity. How much, again, is lost to society through the struggle of sellers one with another, of buyers one with another, and of sellers with buyers. How much futile destruction results from commercial crises. How much needless outlay results from the disorganisation and confusion that prevail in production. All these energies, which now run to waste, will be saved in communist society.

Thirdly, the organisation of industry on a purposive plan will not merely save us from needless waste, in so far as large-scale production is always more economical. In addition, it will be possible to improve production from the technical side, for work will be conducted in very large factories and with the aid of perfected machinery. Under capitalism, there are definite limits to the introduction of new machinery. The capitalist only introduces new machinery when he cannot procure a sufficiency of cheap labour. If he can hire an abundance of cheap labour, the capitalist will never instal new machinery, since he can secure ample profit without this trouble. The capitalist finds machinery requisite only when it reduces his expenses for highly paid labour. Under capitalism, however, labour is usually cheap. The bad conditions that prevail among the working class become a hindrance to the improvement of manufacturing technique. This causal sequence is peculiarly obvious in agriculture. Here labour power has always been cheap, and for that reason, the introduction of machinery in agricultural work has been extremely slow. In communist society, our concern will not be for profit but for the workers. There every technical advance will be immediately adopted. The chains which capitalism imposed will no longer exist. Technical advances will continue to take place under communism, for all will now enjoy a good education, and those who under capitalism perished from want—mentally gifted workers, for instance—will be able to turn their capacities to full account.

In communist society parasitism will likewise disappear. There will be no place for the parasites who do nothing and who live at others' cost. That which in capitalist society is squandered by the capitalists in gluttony, drunkenness, and riotous living, will in communist society be devoted to the needs of production. The capitalists, their lackeys, and their hangers-on (priests, prostitutes, and the rest), will disappear, and all the members of society will be occupied in productive labour.

The communist method of production will signify an enormous development of productive forces. As a result, no worker in communist society will have to do as much work as of old. The working day will grow continually shorter, and people will be to an increasing extent freed from the chains imposed on them by nature. As soon as man is enabled to spend less time upon feeding and clothing himself, he will be able to devote more time to the work of mental development. Human culture will climb to heights never attained before. It will no longer be a class culture, but will become a genuinely human culture. Concurrently with the disappearance of man's tyranny over man, the tyranny of nature over man will likewise vanish. Men and women will for the first time be able to lead a life worthy of thinking beings instead of a life worthy of brute beasts.

The opponents of communism have always described it as a process of sharing things out equally. They declared that the communists wanted to confiscate everything and to divide everything up; to parcel out the land, to divide up the other means of production, and to share out also all the articles of consumption. Nothing could be more absurd than this notion. Above all, such a general division is impossible. We could share out land, horses and cattle, money, but could not share out railways, machinery, steamboats, and various other things of the sort. So much for that. Furthermore, such a division, as far as practicable, would not merely do no good to anyone, but would be a backward step for mankind. It would create a vast number of petty proprietors. But we have already seen that out of petty proprietorship and the competition among petty proprietors there issues large-scale proprietorship. Thus even if it were possible to realise such an equal division, the same old cycle would be reproduced.

Proletarian communism (or proletarian socialism) is a huge co-operative commonwealth. It is a sequence of the whole development of capitalist society and of the condition of the proletariat in that society. It must be carefully distinguished from the four following things :

1. *Lumpenproletarian socialism (anarchism)*. The anarchists reproach the communists on the ground that communism (so they contend) will maintain the State authority in the future society. As we have seen, the assertion is false. The essential difference consists in this, that the anarchists are far more concerned with dividing up than with the organisation of production ; and that they conceive

the organisation of production as taking the form, not of a huge cooperative commonwealth, but of a great number of " free," small, self-governing communes. It need hardly be said that such a social system would fail to liberate mankind from nature's yoke, for in it the forces of production would not be developed even to the degree to which they have been developed under capitalism. Anarchism would not increase production, but would disintegrate it. It is natural that, in practice, the anarchists should advocate the dividing up of articles of consumption and should oppose the organisation of large-scale production. They do not, for the most part, represent the interests and aspirations of the working class ; they represent those of what is termed the lümpenproletariat, the loafer-proletariat ; they represent the interests of those who live in bad conditions under capitalism, but who are quite incapable of independent creative work.

2. *Petty-bourgeois socialism.* This finds its main supporters, not in the proletariat, but in the decaying class of independent artisans, among the lower middle-class townsfolk, and in part among the intelligentsia (professional classes). It protests against large-scale capital, but it does so in the name of the " freedom " of petty enterprise. For the most part the petty-bourgeois socialists advocate bourgeois democracy and oppose the social revolution ; they hope to attain their ideals " peacefully "—through the development of cooperatives, a unified organisation of home workers, and so on. In Russia, most of the urban cooperatives formed by the social revolutionists exhibit this complexion. Under capitalism, cooperative enterprises are apt to degenerate into ordinary capitalistic organisations, and the cooperators can in this case hardly be distinguished from bourgeois.

3. *Agrarian peasant socialism.* This assumes various forms, and at times closely resembles peasant anarchism. Its most distinctive characteristic is the way in which it habitually fails to look upon socialism as a system of large-scale production, and the way in which it inclines towards dividing up and towards equalisation. Its main distinction from anarchism is that it demands the creation of a strong central authority which shall protect it, on the one hand from the landlords and on the other from the proletariat. In this form of socialism we have the " socialisation of the land " advocated by the social revolutionists, who desire to establish small-scale production in perpetuity, who dread the proletariat, and who oppose the formation of a great and united cooperative commonwealth. In addition, among certain strata of the peasantry, we find yet other varieties of socialism more or less akin to anarchism. Here the State authority is repudiated, but the advocates of these trends are distinguished by their pacifist views (various communistically inclined sectaries, such as the Duhobors, etc.). The agrarian types of socialism will not be eradicated until after the lapse of a good many years. They will disappear as soon as the masses of the peasantry come to realise the advantages of large-scale production. We shall return to this matter later in the book.

4. *Slaveholding and large-scale capitalistic socialism (so-called).* In this form we cannot discern so much as a trace of socialism. In the three varieties previously mentioned, we find at least some tincture of socialism, and we find in them a protest against oppression ; but in the fourth variety, the one we are now considering, the " socialism " is a mere word, fraudulently employed by those who want a new shuffle of the cards. This variety was introduced by bourgeois intellectuals and was taken over from them by the socialist advocates of class collaboration (and in part by Kautsky & Co.). Of such a character, for. example, was the communism of Plato, the philosopher of ancient Greece. The essential characteristic of his system was that the slaveholders' organisation would in " comradely " fashion and " jointly " exploit the mass of slaves—who were to have no legal rights. As far as the slave-owners were concerned there would be perfect equality and all things would be held in common. The case of the slaves was to be very different ; they were to become mere cattle. Obviously this has nothing whatever to do with socialism. A similar sort of " socialism " has been advocated by certain bourgeois professors under the name of " State socialism." The only difference from Plato's variety is that eontemporary proletarians have taken the place of the slaves, while the capitalist magnates sit in the seats of the mighty in place of the slave-owners. Here, likewise, there is no trace of socialism. We have State capitalism, based upon forced labour. To this matter we shall return.

Petty-bourgeois, agrarian, and lumpenproletarian socialism have one characteristic common to them all. Such varieties of non-proletarian socialism are outside the general course of evolution. The course of social evolution leads to the expansion of production. But in these non-proletarian varieties the whole trend is towards small-scale production. Inevitably, therefore, socialism of this kind is nothing more than a utopian dream. There is no likelihood of its actual realisation.

§ 23.

The Dictatorship of the Proletariat. For the realisation of the communist system the proletariat must have all authority and all power in its hands. The proletariat cannot overthrow the old world unless it has power in its hands, unless for a time it becomes the ruling class. Manifestly the bourgeoisie will not abandon its position without a fight. For the bourgeoisie, communism signifies the loss of its former power, the loss of its " freedom " to extort blood and sweat from the workers ; the loss of its right to rent, interest, and profit. Consequently the communist revolution of the proletariat, the communist transformation of society, is fiercely resisted by the exploiters. It follows that the principal task of the workers' government is to crush this opposition ruthlessly. Precisely because the opposition will inevitably be so embittered, it is necessary that the workers' authority, the proletarian rule, shall take the form of a dictatorship. Now "dictatorship" signifies very strict methods of government and a resolute crushing of enemies. It is obvious that in such a state of affairs there can be no talk of "freedom" for everyone. The dictatorship of the proletariat is incompatible with freedom for the bourgeoisie. This is the very reason why the dictatorship of the proletariat is needed : to deprive the bourgeoisie of freedom ; to bind it hand and foot ; to make it impossible for it to carry on a struggle against the revolutionary proletariat. The more vigorous the resistance of the bourgeoisie, the more desperate the mobilisation of its forces, the more threatening its attitude, the sterner and harsher must be the proletarian dictatorship. In extreme cases the workers' government must not hesitate to use the method of the terror. Only when the suppression of the exploiters is complete, when they have ceased to resist, when it is no longer in their power to injure the working class, will the proletarian dictatorship grow progressively milder. Meanwhile the bourgeoisie, little by little, will fuse with the proletariat ; the workers' State will gradually die out; society as a whole will be transformed into a communist society in which there will be no classes.

Under the dictatorship of the proletariat (a temporary institution) the means of production will from the nature of the case belong, not to society as a whole, but only to the proletariat, to its State organisation. For the time being, the working class, that is the majority of the population, monopolises the means of production. Consequently there does not yet exist communist production in all its completeness. There still exists the division of society into classes ; there is still a governing class (the proletariat) ; all the means of production are monopolised by this new governing class ; there is still a State authority (the proletarian authority) which crushes its enemies. But as the resistance of the sometime capitalists, landlords, bankers, generals, and bishops, is crushed, in like measure the system of proletarian dictatorship will without any revolution undergo transformation into communism.

The dictatorship of the proletariat is not only an instrument for the crushing of enemies; it is likewise a lever for effecting economic transformation. Private ownership of the means of production must be replaced by social ownership; the bourgeoisie must be deprived of the means of production and exchange, must be " expropriated." Who will and can do this? Obviously no isolated individual could do it, even if he should be of proletarian origin. If it were to be done by an isolated individual or even by isolated groups of individuals, at the best it would be nothing more than a dividing up, and at the worst it would be a mere act of robbery. We understand, therefore, why the expropriation of the bourgeoisie must be effected by the *organised* power of the proletariat. Now this organised power takes the form of the dictatorial workers' State.

Objections to the dictatorship of the proletariat arise from various quarters. First of all come the *anarchists*. They say that they are in revolt against all authority and against every kind of State, whereas the communist bolsheviks are the sustainers of the Soviet Government. Every kind of government, they continue, involves the abuse of power and the limitation of freedom. For this reason it is necessary to overthrow the bolsheviks, the Soviet Government, the dictatorship of the proletariat. No dictatorship is necessary, no State is necessary. Such are the arguments of the anarchists. Only in appearance is their criticism revolutionary. In actual fact the anarchists do not stand more to the left, but more to the right than the bolsheviks. Why, indeed, do we need the dictatorship? We need it for the *organised* destruction of the bourgeois regime; we need it that we may crush the enemies of the proletariat *by force*. Quite öpenly we say, by force. The dictatorship is the axe in the hands of the proletariat. Anyone who is opposed to the dictatorship of the proletariat is one who is afraid of decisive action, is afraid of hurting the bourgeoisie, is no revolutionist. When we have completely vanquished the bourgeoisie, the need for the dictatorship of the proletariat will no longer exist. But as long as the life-and-death struggle continues it is absolutely incumbent upon the working class to crush its enemies utterly. AN EPOCH OF PROLETARIAN DICTATORSHIP MUST INEVITABLY INTERVENE BETWEEN A CAPITALIST AND A COMMUNIST SOCIETY.

Next, as objectors to the dictatorship, come the *social democrats*, and in especial the mensheviks. These worthies have completely forgotten what they wrote about the matter in former days. In our old program, drawn up by ourselves and the mensheviks together, it is expressly stated: " An essential condition of the social revolution is the dictatorship of the proletariat, that is to say the conquest of political power by the proletariat, which will enable the workers to crush all resistance on the part of the exploiters." The mensheviks signed this statement. But when the time came for action, they raised a clamour against the crushing of the freedom of the bourgeoisie, against the suppression of bourgeois newspapers, against the bolshevist "reign of terror," and so on. Even Plehanoff, at one time, thoroughly approved of the most ruthless measures against the bourgeoisie, saying that we could deprive the bourgeois of their electoral rights, and so on. Nowadays the mensheviks have forgotten all this ; they have taken refuge in the camp of the bourgeoisie.

Finally, a number of *moral* considerations are brought into the argument against us. We are told that we form our judgments like the savage Hottentots. The Hottentot says : " When I steal my neighbour's wife, it is good ; when he steals my wife, it is bad." The bolsheviks, it is contended, resemble these savages, for they say : " When the bourgeoisie uses force to crush the proletariat, it is bad ; but when the proletariat uses force to crush the bourgeoisie, it is good." Those who argue thus, do not know what they are talking about. In the case of the Hottentots we are concerned with two equal individuals who are stealing one another's wives for identical reasons. But the proletariat and the bourgeoisie are not on equal terms. Proletarians comprise an enormous class, bourgeois form a comparatively small group. The proletariat is fighting for the liberation of all mankind ; but the bourgeoisie is fighting for the maintenance of oppression, wars, exploitation. The proletariat is fighting for communism, the bourgeoisie for the preservation of capitalism. If capitalism and communism were one and the same thing, then the bourgeoisie and the proletariat could be compared to the two Hottentots. The proletariat is fighting solely on behalf of the new social order. Whatever helps in the struggle is good ; whatever hinders, is bad.

§ 24.

The Conquest of political Power. The proletariat makes its dictatorship actual through the conquest of the State power. But what do we mean by the conquest of power ? Many persons imagine that it is quite an easy matter to wrest power from the bourgeoisie, as easy as to transfer a ball from one pocket to another. First, power is in the hands of the bourgeoisie ; then the proletariat will drive the bourgeoisie from power and will take the reins into its own hands. According to this view, the problem is not the creation of a new power, but the seizure of a power that already exists.

Such a notion is utterly false, and a very little reflection will show us where the error lies.

The State power is an organisation. The bourgeois State power is a bourgeois organisation, and in that organisation people are assigned their roles in a distinctive manner. At the head of the army are generals, members of the wealthy class; at the head of the administration are ministers, members of the wealthy class; and so on. When the proletariat is fighting for power, against whom and what is it fighting? In the first place, against this bourgeois organisation. Now when it is fighting this organisation, its task is to deliver blows that will destroy the organisation. But since the main strength of the government resides in the army, if we wish to gain the victory over the bourgeoisie, the first essential is to disorganise and destroy the bourgeois army. The German communists could not overthrow the regime of Scheidemann and Noske unless they could destroy the army of White Guards. If the opposing army remain intact, the victory of the revolution will be impossible; if the revolution be victorious, the army of the bourgeoisie will disintegrate and crumble. This, for example, is why the victory over tsarism signified no more than a partial destruction of the tsarist State and a partial decomposition of the army; but the victory of the November revolution denoted the final overthrow of the State organisation of the Provisional Government and the total dissolution of the Kerenskyite army.

Thus the revolution destroys the old power and creates a new one, a different power from that which existed before. Of course the new power takes over some of the constituent parts of the old, but it uses them in a different way.

It follows that the conquest of State power is not the conquest of the pre-existent organisation, but the creation of a new organisation, an organisation brought into being by the class which has been victorious in the struggle.

The practical importance of this question is enormous. The German bolsheviks, for example, have been reproached (as the Russian bolsheviks were formerly reproached) on the ground that they have led to disintegration in the army and have promoted indiscipline, have encouraged disobedience to officers. This used to be considered, and by many is still considered, a terrible charge. But there is nothing terrible about it. We must promote disintegration in an army which is ranged against the workers and is at the orders of the bourgeoisie, even though the latter consists of our fellow-countrymen. Failing this, the revolution will succumb. Consequently, there is nothing to be afraid of in working for the disintegration of such a bourgeois army ; a revolutionist who destroys the State apparatus of the bourgeoisie may consider that he is doing excellent service. Where bourgeois discipline remains intact, the bourgeoisie is invincible. Those who wish to overthrow the bourgeoisie must not shrink from hurting it.

§ 25.

The Communist Party and the Classes of capitalist Society. In order that the proletariat may gain the victory in any country, it is essential that it should be compact and well organised ; it is essential that it should have its own Communist Party which has clearly recognised the trend of capitalist development, which has understood the actual situation and the true interests of the working class, which has adequately interpreted that situation, which is competent to marshal the ranks and to conduct the battle. Nowhere and at no time has any party been able to enrol all the members of the class which it represents ; never has any class attained the requisite degree of consciousness. Generally speaking, those who organise themselves into a party are the most advanced members of a class ; those who best understand their class interests ; those who are most daring, most energetic, and most stubborn in the fight. For this reason, the number of adherents of the party is always considerably less than the number of those composing the class whose interests the party represents. Since, however, a party definitely represents the rightly interpreted interests of the class, parties usually play a leading role. The party leads the whole class, and the struggle between *classes* for power finds expression in the struggle between *political parties* for power. He who wishes to understand the nature of political parties must study the relationships of the various classes in capitalist society. Out of these relationships definite class interests arise. As we have already learned, the defence of class interests is the essential purpose of political parties.

Landowners. During the first period of capitalist development, agrarian economy was based upon the semi-slave labour of the peasants. The landowners leased lands to the peasants, receiving as rent payment either in money or in kind. One method of payment in kind was for the worker to spend half his time tilling the landowner's estate. The landowners as a class found it to their interest to prevent the peasants from going to the towns; they therefore resisted all innovation; they desired to maintain the old semi-slave conditions in the villages; they opposed the development of manufacturing industry. Such landowners possessed ancient patrimonial seigneurial domains; very few of them did any work on their own estates, and they lived for the most part like parasites on the backs of the peasants. As a result of this state of affairs, the parties representing the landowners have always been and still are the main props of reaction. These are the political parties that everywhere desire a return to the old order; they want to go back to the rule of the landlords, to restore the landlord-tsar (the monarch), to ensure the predominance of the " blue-blooded gentry," to effect the complete enslavement of the peasants and the workers. They form what are known as the conservative parties; it would be more accurate to term them the reactionary parties. Since from time immemorial the officers of the army and the navy have been drawn from the ranks of the landed gentry, it is perfectly natural that landowners' parties should always be on the best of terms with generals and admirals. This is what we find in every country throughout the world.

As an example may be mentioned the members of the Prussian junker caste (in Germany, the great landowners are known as " junkers ") who send some of their sons into the officers' corps. Similarly in Russia we have our landed gentry, the so-called back-woodsmen, " the aurochses," like some of the deputies to the duma —Markoff the Second, Krupensky, and others. The tsarist council of state was largely composed of members of this landlord class. Most of the wealthy landowners belonging to old families bear such titles as prince, count, etc.; they are the true descendants of ancestors who owned thousands of bondslaves. The landlords' parties in Russia were: the League of the Russian People; the Nationalist Party, led by Krupensky; the right Octobrists; etc.

The capitalist Bourgeoisie. The interest of this class is to secure the greatest possible profits out of the developing " national industry," that is to say out of surplus value extracted from the working class. Manifestly this interest does not fully coincide with that of the landowners. When capital makes its influence felt in village life, the old conditions are disturbed. The peasants are attracted into the towns; capital creates a vast proletariat, and it arouses new needs in the villages; the peasants, hitherto docile and quiet, grow " unruly." The landowners, the backwoodsmen, find these innovations unpleasing. On the other hand, the capitalist bourgeoisie regards them as full of promise. The more the workers are lured from the villages to the towns, the more wage labour, consequently, is available for the service of the capitalist, and the cheaper can the capitalist hire it. The more completely village life is ruined and the greater the extent to which the petty producers cease to produce various articles for themselves, the more essential do they find it to buy these products from the large-scale manufacturers. The more rapid, therefore, the disappearance of the old conditions in which the village produced everything for itself, the greater will be the expansion of the market for the sale of factory-produced commodities, and the higher will be the profits of the capitalist class.

For this reason the capitalist class rails at landlords of the old school. (There are, in addition, capitalist landlords; these run their estates with the help of wage labour and with the aid of machinery; their interests are closely akin to those of the bourgeoisie, and they usually adhere to the parties of the wealthier capitalists.) But of course the chief struggle of the capitalists is with the working class. When the working class is fighting mainly against the landlords and very little against the bourgeoisie, the latter eyes approvingly the struggle of the working class. This was the case in the year 1904, and in 1905 until October. But when the workers begin to realise their communist interests and to march against the bourgeoisie, then the bourgeoisie joins forces with the landlords against the workers. Everywhere, to-day, the parties of the capitalist bourgeoisie (the so-called liberal parties) are carrying on a fierce struggle against the revolutionary proletariat, and it is they who form the political general staff of the counter-revolution.

Among such parties in Russia, two may be mentioned. First of all we have the Party of Popular Freedom, also known as the Party of Constitutional Democrats; from the initials of its name (C. D.) its members are generally spoken of as the "Cadets." Secondly there are the Octobrists, who have now almost disappeared. Members of the industrial bourgeoisie, capitalist landlords, bankers, and the champions of all these (the major intelligentsia—university professors, successful lawyers and authors, factory managers, etc.) form the nuclei of these parties. In the year 1905 the Cadets were murmuring against the autocracy, but they were already afraid of the workers and the peasants; after the revolution of March, 1917, they became the leaders of all the forces that were marshalled against the party of the working class, against the communist bolsheviks. In the years 1918 and 1919 the Cadets took the lead in all the plots against the Soviet Government, and they participated in the administrations of General Denikin and Admiral Kolchak. In a word, they led the bloody reaction, and finally they even formed a coalition with the landowners' parties. For under the pressure of the working-class movement all groups of wealthy proprietors unite in a single camp of reactionaries, led by the most energetic section among them

The urban Petty Bourgeoisie. To this group belong the independent artisans, the small shopkeepers, the minor intelligentsia comprising the salariat, and the lesser officialdom. In reality they do not constitute a class, but a motley crowd. All these elements are exploited more or less by capital, and they are often overworked. Many of them are ruined in the course of capitalist development. The conditions of their work, however, are such that for the most part they fail to realise how hopeless is their situation under capitalism. Let us consider, for instance, the independent artisan. He is as industrious as an ant. Capital exploits him in various ways: the usurer exploits him; the shop for which he works, exploits him; and so on. The artisan feels himself to be a "master"; he works with his own tools, and in appearance he is "independent," although in reality he is completely entangled in the web of the capitalist spider. He lives in the perennial hope of bettering himself, thinking always, "I shall soon be able to extend my business, then I shall buy for myself"; he is careful not to mix with the workers, and in his manners he avoids imitating them, affecting the manners of the gentry, for he always hopes to become a "gentleman" himself. Consequently, although he is as poor as a church mouse, he usually feels more akin to the man who exploits him than he does to the workers. The petty-bourgeois

parties commonly assemble under the standard of the
" radicals " or the " republicans," but sometimes under
that of the " socialists " (refer to the small-type paragraphs
of § 22). It is extremely difficult to shake such people out
of this wrong attitude of mind, which is their misfortune
not their fault.

In Russia, more commonly than elsewhere, the petty-bourgeois
parties have been apt to wear a socialist mask. This was done by
the populist socialists, the social revolutionaries, and in part by the
mensheviks. It is necessary to point out that the social revolutionaries tended to rely mainly upon the middle peasants and the rich
peasants for support.

The Peasantry. In the rural districts, the peasantry
occupies a position closely akin to that occupied by the
petty bourgeoisie in the towns. It too, properly speaking,
does not constitute a single class, for under capitalism it
is continually splitting up into classes. In every village
and hamlet we find that some of the peasants go to look
for work in the towns, and thus in time become completely
transformed into proletarians ; others develop into wealthy
and usurious peasants. The " middle " peasants form an
unstable stratum. Many of them are ruined in course of
time ; they become " horseless men," and eventually seek
work as agricultural labourers or as factory hands ; others
are more successful, " get on in the world," gather wealth,
become " master peasants," hire agricultural labourers,
make use of machinery—in a word, they are transformed
into capitalist entrepreneurs. That is why we are entitled
to say that the peasantry does not properly speaking form
a single class. Among the peasants we must distinguish
at least three groups. First we have the rich peasants,
the master peasants, who constitute a rural bourgeoisie, for
they are exploiters of wage labour. Next come the middle
peasants, who work their own little farms and do not exploit
wage labour. Thirdly and lastly, we have the poor peasants
forming the rural semi-proletariat and proletariat.

It is easy to understand that the members of these
respective groups, owing to the difference in their positions,
will take different views of the class struggle between the
proletariat and the bourgeoisie. The rich peasants are as

a rule allied with the bourgeoisie, and very often with the great landlords as well. In Germany, for example, those who are termed " great peasants " are united in a single organisation with the priests and the landlords. We find the same thing in Switzerland and in Austria, and to some extent also in France. In Russia, during the year 1918, the rich peasants supported all the counter-revolutionary plots. Those belonging to the semi-proletarian and proletarian strata naturally back the workers in their struggle with the bourgeoisie and the rich peasants. As far as the middle peasants are concerned, the matter is much more complicated.

If the middle peasants would only realise that for the majority among them there is no way out under capitalism, that only a few of them can ever hope to become rich peasants, whereas most of them are fated to live in penury, then they would be ready to give unstinted support to the workers. But their misfortune lies in this, that the same thing happens to them as happens in the towns to the independent artisans and the members of the petty bourgeoisie. Every one of them, at the bottom of his heart, cherishes the hope of getting on, of growing rich. But, on the other hand, the middle peasant is oppressed by the capitalist, the money-lender, the landlord, and the rich peasant. The result is, as a rule, that the middle peasant see-saws between the proletariat and the bourgeoisie. He is unable wholeheartedly to adopt the working-class platform, but at the same time he is terribly afraid of the landowner.

This wobbling has been peculiarly plain in Russia. The middle peasants supported the workers against the landlords and the rich peasants. Then, growing afraid lest they should not be so well off in the " commune," they listened to the advice of the rich peasants and opposed the workers. Still later, when danger threatened from the side of the landowning class (Denikin, Kolchak), they were once more inclined to espouse the cause of the workers.

The same vacillation has been displayed in the party struggle. At one time the middle peasants would adhere to the party of the workers, the party of the communist bolsheviks ; at another time they would adhere to the party of the rich peasants, the party of the essers (social revolutionaries).

The working Class (*the Proletariat*). This class consists of those who " have nothing to lose but their chains." Not only are they exploited by the capitalists; but in addition, as we have already learned, the very course of capitalist development leads to their solidarisation into a homogeneous power, consisting of persons accustomed to work together and to fight together. For this reason, the working class is the most progressive class in capitalist society. For this reason, likewise, the party of the working class is the most progressive, the most revolutionary party that can possibly exist.

It is natural, moreover, that the aim of this party should be to bring about the communist revolution. To this end, the proletarian party must be absolutely uncompromising. Its function is not to chaffer with the bourgeoisie, but to hurl the bourgeoisie from power and to crush the resistance of the capitalists. This party must " reveal the absolute conflict of interests as between exploiters and exploited " (the words were used in our old program, which was signed by the mensheviks ; but, alas, the mensheviks have quite forgotten them, and are now hand in glove with the bourgeoisie).

What, however, should be the attitude of our party towards the petty bourgeoisie, towards the non-proletarian poorer strata of our large towns, and towards the middle peasants ?

This is clear from what has been said above. We must never weary in our proofs and explanations, in order to convince them that their hopes for a better life under capitalism are the outcome of fraud by others or are due to their own self-deception. We must patiently and clearly demonstrate to the middle peasants that they ought unhesitatingly to enter the proletarian camp, and despite all difficulties fight shoulder to shoulder with the workers ; it is our duty to show them that the only peasants to gain by the victory of the bourgeoisie will be the rich peasants, who will in that case become transformed into a new landlord class. In a word, we must bring all those who work, to make common cause with the proletariat ; must enable all those who work, to see things from the working-class point of view. Those who belong to the petty bourgeoisie and to the stratum of the middle peasants, are full of prejudices arising out of the conditions of their lives. It is our duty to reveal the true posture of affairs. We must show that the position of the artisan and of the working peasant under capitalism is quite hopeless, and that they had better give up trying to amuse themselves with fancy pictures. We must tell the middle peasant that as long as capitalism lasts there will always be a landlord riding on his back : either one of the gentry, the old type of landlord ; or else a rich peasant, the landlord of the new type. In no other way than through the victory and the strengthening of the proletariat is there any possibility of rebuilding life on new foundations. But, since the victory of the proletariat can only be secured through the organisation of the workers and through the existence of a strong, solid, and resolute party, we must draw into our ranks all those who labour, all those to whom the new life is dear, all those who have learned to think and to fight like proletarians.

How important the existence of a solid and militant communist party is, can be learned from the examples of Germany and Russia. In Germany, where the proletariat is highly developed, there was nevertheless prior to the war no such militant party of the working class as that of the communist bolsheviks in Russia. Only during the war did comrades Karl Liebknecht, Rosa Luxemburg, and others begin to found a distinctively communist party. This is why, during the years 1918 and 1919, notwithstanding a number of risings, the German workers proved unable to overthrow the bourgeoisie. In Russia, however, there existed our uncompromisingly communist party. Thanks to this the Russian proletariat was well led. Hence, despite all difficulties, the Russian proletariat was the first to secure a solid and speedy victory. In this respect our party may and does serve as an example to other communist parties. Its solidity and discipline are universally recognised. It is, in fact, the most militant party of the proletarian revolution, and as such it occupies the leading place.

Literature. MARX and ENGELS, The Communist Manifesto. LENIN, The State and Revolution. PLEHANOFF, The Centenary of the great French Revolution. BOGDANOFF, A short Course of economic Science BEBEL, Woman and Socialism (The State of the Future). BOGDA-NOFF, The red Star (utopian). KORSAK, The legalist Society and the Workers' Society (an essay in the collective work " Papers on realistic Philosophy ").

Concerning anarchism, the following works may be read : VOLSKY, The Theory and Practice of Anarchism. PREOBRAZHENSKY, Anarchism and Communism. BAZAROFF, Anarchist Communism and Marxism.

Concerning the classes of capitalist society, read : KAUTSKY, Class Interests.

Concerning the characteristics of the petty-bourgeois parties, read the following : MARX, The 18th Brumaire of Louis Napoleon Bonaparte. MARX, Revolution and Counter-Revolution in Germany. MARX, The Civil War in France.

CHAPTER FOUR

HOW THE DEVELOPMENT OF CAPITALISM LED TO THE COMMUNIST REVOLUTION

(IMPERIALISM, THE WAR, AND THE COLLAPSE OF CAPITALISM)

§ 26.

Financial Capital. We have previously seen that among the entrepreneurs there is a continuous and fierce struggle for buyers, and that the unfailing result of this struggle is the victory of the great entrepreneurs. Hence the lesser capitalists are ruined, so that capital and production as a whole accumulate in the hands of the great capitalists (the concentration and centralisation of capital). By the beginning of the eighties in the nineteenth century, the centralisation of capital was already far advanced. In place of the individual owners of enterprises there now appeared large numbers of joint-stock enterprises, cooperative concerns; but it must be carefully noted that these " cooperatives " were companies of capitalist shareholders. What was the significance of this development ? Why did joint-stock companies come into existence ? It is easy to answer the question. The time had arrived when every new undertaking required the command of a considerable quantity of capital. If an enterprise scantily furnished with capital was founded, its chance of life was poor ; on all sides it was surrounded by its more vigorous competitors, by enterprises which were manufacturing on a larger scale. If, therefore, a new enterprise was not to perish in its infancy, if the undertaking was to live and thrive, it had

to be built up on strong foundations. But strong foundations could only be provided by those who had plenty of
capital. The joint-stock company was the outcome of
this need. The essence of the matter is that a few great
capitalists make use of the capital of lesser capitalists, and
make use also of the savings that have accumulated in the
hands of non-capitalistic groups (employees, peasants,
civil servants, etc.). Matters are arranged in the following
way. Everyone contributes his portion ; everyone takes
a " share " or a number of " shares." In return for his
money he receives a " share certificate " which gives him
the right to receive a definite portion of the income. In
this way the accumulation of small sums promptly gives
rise to a large quantity of " joint-stock capital."

When joint-stock companies first came into existence,
certain bourgeois theorists, and in addition certain socialist
advocates of class collaboration, began to assure the world
that a new era was beginning. Capitalism, they declared,
was not destined to result in the dominion of a small group
of capitalists. Far from this ; out of his savings every
worker would be able to buy shares, and in this way
every worker would become a capitalist. Capital, they
said, was to an increasing extent being " democratised " ;
in course of time, the difference between the capitalists
and the workers would disappear without any revolution.

Of course this was utter nonsense. Things worked
out very differently. The great capitalists simply made
use of the lesser capitalists for their own purposes. The
centralisation of capital went on more rapidly than ever,
now that competition had taken the form of a struggle
between huge shareholding concerns.

It is easy to understand how the great capitalist shareholders
have been able to make the small shareholders their hodmen. The
small shareholder often lives in another town from that in which
the enterprise is centred, and cannot travel a hundred miles or more
to attend a shareholders' meeting. Even when some of the ordinary
shareholders turn up at the meeting, they are unorganised, and merely
jostle one another like blind puppies. But the big shareholders are
organised. They have a common plan ; they can do what they
please. Experience has shown that it suffices the great capitalist
to own one-third of all the shares, for this gives him absolute control
of the whole undertaking

But the development of the concentration and centralisation of capital was to advance still further. During the last few decades the place of individual enterprises and individual shareholding companies has largely been taken by great capitalist combines known as *syndicates, cartels,* and *trusts.* Why have these been formed ? What is their significance ?

Let us suppose that in a certain branch of production, textiles or engineering, for instance, the lesser capitalists have already disappeared. There remain only five or six huge firms, shareholding companies, producing nearly all the commodities in these particular branches of enterprise. They are carrying on a cut-throat competition ; they lower prices, and consequently make smaller profits. Let us now suppose that two of these concerns are larger and stronger than the others. Then these two will continue the struggle until their rivals have been ruined. Let us further suppose that the strength of the two remaining competitors is practically identical ; they work on a similar scale, they have the same sort of machinery, and they both employ about the same number of workers ; there is no notable difference between them as regards the net cost of production. What will happen then ? Neither can gain the victory ; both are being exhausted by the struggle ; neither of them is making any profit. The capitalist groups draw the same conclusion. Why, they ask themselves, should we go on cutting prices against one another ? Would it not be better for us to unite, to join forces in order to fleece the public ? If we combine, there will be no more competition ; we shall control the market, and we can force up prices to any figure we please.

Thus arises the combine, the league of capitalists, known as the syndicate or trust. The syndicate is distinguished from the trust in this way. When a *syndicate* is organised, the participating concerns agree that they will not sell their wares below a specified price ; or they agree to share out the orders ; or they agree to a territorial division of the market (you confine your sales to one district, and I will confine mine to another) ; and so on. In this arrangement, however, the management of the syndicate is not entitled to close down any of the undertakings ; these are all members of a league in which each retains a certain measure of independence. In the *trust*, on the other hand, there is so intimate a union that each individual undertaking completely loses its independence ; the management of the trust can close it down, reconstruct it, transfer it to another place, do whatever seems likely to be advantageous to the trust as a whole. The owner of the individual undertaking of course continues to receive his profits regularly, and these profits may even be larger than before ; but the entire management is vested in the solidly constructed capitalist combine, the trust.

Syndicates and trusts exercise an almost complete control over the market. They no longer fear competition, for they have crushed competition. Its place has been taken by capitalist *monopoly*, that is to say, by *the dominion of a single trust*.[1]

In this way the concentration and centralisation of capital gradually lead to the suppression of competition. Competition has devoured itself. The more frantic the development of capitalism, the quicker did centralisation proceed, because the ruin of the weaker capitalists was more speedily effected. In the end the centralisation of capital, arising out of competition, proved fatal to competition. " FREE COMPETITION " HAS BEEN REPLACED BY THE DOMINION OF CAPITALIST COMBINES, BY THE RULE OF SYNDICATES AND TRUSTS.

A few examples may be given, to show the enormous power wielded by trusts and syndicates. In the *United States* as long ago as 1900, that is to say in the very beginning of the twentieth century, the proportion of production in the hands of syndicates and trusts was as follows : Textiles, more than 50 per cent. ; glass, 54 per cent. ; paper, 60 per cent. ; metals (excluding iron and steel), 84 per cent. ; iron and steel, 84 per cent. ; chemicals, 81 per cent. ; etc. It need hardly be said that during the last two decades the power of the combines has enormously increased. In actual fact, the whole industrial production of the U.S. is to-day controlled by two trusts, the Standard Oil Trust and the Steel Trust ; all the other trusts are

[1] The word " monopoly " is derived from two Greek words, *monos* (alone, sole, single) and *polein* (to sell). In Russia, at one time, the use of the term " monopoly " was almost restricted to denoting the governmental monopoly in spirituous liquors. But there can exist a monopoly in any commodity ; and a monopoly may be held by a manufacturer or a group of manufacturers just as well as by the State.

dependents of these. In *Germany*, in the year 1913, 92·6 per cent. of the coal mined in the Rhenish-Westphalian region was in the hands of a single syndicate ; of all the steel produced within the German empire, nearly half was manufactured by the Steel Syndicate ; the Sugar Trust supplied 70 per cent. of the home demand and 80 per cent. of the export demand.

Even in *Russia* quite a number of branches of industry had already passed completely under the sway of the syndicates. " Produgol " produced 60 per cent. of the Donetz coal ; " Prodameta " [metal syndicate] controlled 88 to 93 per cent. of the production ; " Krovlya " supplied 60 per cent. of all the iron used for roofing ; " Prodwagon " was a syndicate of about 15 concerns building railway carriages ; the Copper Syndicate controlled 90 per cent. of the output of copper ; the Sugar Syndicate controlled the entire production of sugar ; and so on. According to the calculations of a Swiss expert, *at the beginning of the twentieth century half the capital of the world was already in the hands of trusts or syndicates.*

Syndicates and trusts do not only centralise homogeneous enterprises. With increasing frequency there arise trusts that simultaneously embrace several branches of production. How does this take place ?

The various branches of production are connected one with another principally by means of buying and selling. Let us consider the production of iron ore and of coal. Here we have to do with products which serve as raw material for iron foundries and engineering workshops ; in their turn these workshops turn out, let us suppose, machines ; the machines serve as means of production in a series of other branches ; and so on. Now let us imagine that we have an iron foundry. It buys iron ore and coal. Of course the interest of the smelting works is to buy the ore and the coal as cheaply as possible. But what if the ore and the coal are in the hands of another syndicate ? There then begins a struggle between the two syndicates, which ends either in the victory of one of them or else in a fusion of the two. In either event there arises a new syndicate, uniting both branches of production. It is obvious that such a union can be effected in the case, not merely of two, but of three or of ten branches of production. Such enterprises are termed " compound " (or " combined ") enterprises.

In this manner syndicates and trusts do more than organise individual branches of production ; they consolidate into a single organisation various kinds of production, uniting one branch with a second, a third, a fourth, etc. Formerly, in all branches, the entrepreneurs were independent of one another, and the whole work of production was dispersed in a hundred thousand petty factories. By the beginning of the twentieth century, production was already concentrated in the hands of huge trusts, each organising many branches of production.

Unions of individual branches of production came about in another way besides that of the formation of " combined " enterprises. The reader must now consider a phenomenon which is of even greater importance than " combined " enterprises. We refer to the dominion of the banks.

First of all it is necessary to say a few words about banks.

It has already been pointed out that when the concentration and centralisation of capital had advanced to a considerable degree, there arose a need for capital which could be employed for the immediate establishment of large-scale enterprises. This need was one of the causes of the development of joint-stock companies. The organisation of new enterprises required larger and ever larger quantities of capital.

Now let us consider what the capitalist does with the profit he receives. We know that he spends part of it upon his own immediate needs, in the way of food, clothing, and so on ; the remainder, he " saves." The question arises, How does he do this ? Is it possible for him at any moment to expand his business, to devote the " saved " part of his profits to this purpose? No, he cannot do so, for this reason. Money flows in continually, but only in driblets. The commodities he produces are sold from time to time, and from time to time money is received for them. Evidently, that he may use these receipts for the expansion of his enterprise, the accumulation of a considerable sum is requisite. He will therefore have to wait until he has secured as much money as he needs—let us suppose that it is for the purchase of new machinery. And until then, what is he to do ? Till then he cannot use the money. It lies idle. This does not happen to one or to two capitalists merely ; at one time or another it happens to all. *Free capital* is constantly available. We have, however, pointed out before that there is a demand for capital. On the one hand there are superfluous sums lying idle; on the other hand there is a need for these sums. The more rapid the centralisation of capital, the more vigorous is the demand for large sums of capital, but the greater likewise is the quantity of free capital. It is this state of affairs which gives the banks their importance. The capitalist, not wishing his money to lie idle, puts it in the bank, and the bank lends it to those who need it for the development of old enterprises or for the starting of new undertakings. Certain manufacturers deposit money in the bank, and the bank lends the money to other manufacturers. These latter, with the aid of the borrowed capital, extract surplus value. Part of their receipts is paid to the bank as interest. The bank then pays a portion of this last sum to its depositors, and keeps the rest as banking profits. Thus the machine grinds on. We can now understand why, during the latest phase of the capitalist regime, the role of the banks, their importance, and their activity, have expanded to a marvellous degree. The sums of capital sucked up by the banks are continually increasing. And to an increasing extent the banks invest capital in industry. Banking capital is ever " at work " in industry; it undergoes conversion into industrial capital. Industry grows dependent on the banks, which support it and nourish it with capital. Banking capital coalesces with industrial capital. Here we have the form of capital which is known as *financial capital*. To summarise, FINANCIAL CAPITAL IS BANKING CAPITAL WHICH HAS BEEN GRAFTED ON INDUSTRIAL CAPITAL.

Through the instrumentality of the banks, financial capital effects a yet more intimate union of all branches of industry than was effected by the direct combination of enterprises. Why is this ?

Let us suppose that we have before us a great bank. This great bank supplies with capital (or, as the phrase runs, " finances ") not merely one, but a large number of enterprises, or quite a number of syndicates. It is naturally to the bank's interest that these financial dependents should not clash one with another. The bank unites them all. Its persistent policy is to bring about an actual union of the undertakings into a whole which shall be under its own administration. The bank begins to hold the reins in quite a series of branches of industry. Its confidential agents are appointed directors of trusts, syndicates, and individual undertakings.

Thus in the end we arrive at the following picture. THE INDUSTRY OF THE WHOLE COUNTRY IS UNITED INTO SYNDICATES, TRUSTS, AND COMBINED ENTERPRISES. ALL THESE ARE UNITED BY BANKS. AT THE HEAD OF THE WHOLE ECONOMIC LIFE THERE IS A SMALL GROUP OF GREAT BANKERS WHO ADMINISTER INDUSTRY IN ITS ENTIRETY. THE GOVERNMENTAL AUTHORITY SIMPLY FULFILS THE WILL OF THESE BANKERS AND TRUST MAGNATES.

This is very well shown in the *United States*. Here the " democratic " administration of President Wilson is nothing more than a servant of the trusts. Congress merely carries out what has previously been decided at secret conclaves of trust magnates and bankers. The trusts spend vast sums in buying congressmen, in financing electoral campaigns, and the like. Myers, an American writer, reports that in the year 1904 the great life insurance companies spent the following sums in bribes : the Mutual, $364,254 ; the Equitable, $172,698 ; the New York, $204,019. The minister for finance, McAdoo, Wilson's son-in-law, is one of the leading bank and trust magnates. Senators, ministers of State, congressmen, are merely the henchmen of the great trusts, unless they themselves hold large interests in these bodies. The State authority, the governmental machinery of the " free republic," is nothing more than a workshop for the fleecing of the public.

We can therefore say that A CAPITALIST COUNTRY UNDER THE DOMINION OF FINANCIAL CAPITAL IS AS A WHOLE TRANSFORMED INTO AN IMMENSE COMBINED TRUST. AT THE HEAD OF THIS TRUST ARE THE BANKS. THE BOURGEOIS GOVERNMENT FORMS ITS EXECUTIVE COMMITTEE. The United States, Great Britain, France, Germany, etc., are nothing but State capitalist trusts, powerful organisations of trust magnates and bankers, exploiting and ruling hundreds of millions of wage slaves.

§ 27.

Imperialism. In individual countries the effect of the sway of financial capital is, in a certain measure, to put an end to the anarchy of capitalist production. The various producers, who have hitherto been fighting one another, now join forces in a State capitalist trust.

But what happens in this case to one of the fundamental contradictions of capitalism? We have said more than once that capitalism will inevitably break down because of its lack of organisation and because it is affected by the class struggle. Now if one of these two contradictions (see § 13) is invalid, may it not be that the prediction concerning the collapse of capitalism has no foundation?

The point we chiefly have to consider is this. In actual fact the anarchy of production and competition has not ceased. Or perhaps it would be better to say that it ceases in one place to break out worse than ever in another. Let us endeavour to explain the matter in detail.

Contemporary capitalism is world capitalism. All the countries are interconnected; they buy one from another. We cannot now find any country which is not under the heel of capitalism; we cannot find any country which produces for itself absolutely everything it needs.

There are numerous articles which can only be produced in certain places. Oranges do not grow in a cold country; whereas iron ore cannot be obtained from a country which has no deposits of it beneath the soil. Coffee, cocoa, and rubber are grown only in warm climates. Cotton is grown in the United States, India, Egypt, Turkestan, etc.; from these lands it is exported to all parts of the world. Coal is found in Britain, Germany, the United States, Austria, and Russia; but there is no coal in Italy, and Italy is entirely dependent upon supplies of British and German coal. Wheat is exported to all other countries from the United States, India, Russia, and Rumania.

On the other hand, certain countries are far advanced in their development, whilst others are backward. As a result of this, various products of urban industry in the more advanced lands are marketed in the backward countries. England, the United States, and Germany, in particular, send iron goods to all parts of the world. Germany is the chief exporter of chemical products.

Thus each country is dependent on the others; each sells to the others or buys from the others. How far this dependence can go, we may learn from the example of Britain. From three-fourths to four-fifths of the wheat needed by that country and half of the meat are imported, and in return for this the greater part of the goods produced in British factories has to be exported.

Let us now ask ourselves whether financial capital puts an end to competition in the world market. Does it create a world-wide organisation in virtue of the fact that it unites the capitalists in individual countries? Obviously this is not the case. The anarchy of production and of competition within each specific country ceases more or less completely because the individual entrepreneurs unite to form a State capitalist trust. All the fiercer grows the struggle between the various State capitalist trusts. This is what always happens when capital is centralised. When the small fry are ruined, then of course the number of competitors diminishes, for only the big fish are left. Among these latter, the struggle is now conducted upon a larger scale; instead of a fight between individual manufacturers, there ensues a fight between the trusts. Of course the number of the trusts is less than the number of the individual manufacturers. The struggle, therefore, has become fiercer and more destructive. When the capitalists in any particular country have defeated their lesser opponents and have organised themselves into a State capitalist trust, the number of competitors is still further reduced. For the competitors are now these titanic capitalist powers. Such competition involves expenditure and waste upon an unprecedented scale. The fight between the State capitalist trusts expresses itself during "peace" time in the rivalry of armaments. Ultimately it leads to a devastating war.

Thus, WHEREAS FINANCIAL CAPITAL PUTS AN END TO COMPETITION WITHIN THE INDIVIDUAL COUNTRIES, in due course and when the time is ripe, IT GIVES RISE TO A FIERCE AND EMBITTERED COMPETITION BETWEEN THE VARIOUS STATES.

How does this come about? Why, moreover, does competition between capitalist countries lead in the end to an annexationist policy and to war? Why cannot the competition be peaceful? When two manufacturers compete with one another, they do not attack one another with knives, but attempt to steal one another's custom by peaceful methods. Why, then, should competition in the world market assume so savage a form? Why should the competitors have recourse to arms? To these questions we must give a detailed answer.

First of all we must consider why it was necessary that the policy of the bourgeoisie should undergo a change concurrently with the transition from the old capitalism in which free competition prevailed, to the new capitalism in which financial capital holds sway.

Let us begin with the so-called tariff policy. In the international struggle, the bourgeois governmental authorities, each aiming at the protection of its own capitalists, have long since adopted the use of customs tariffs as a means of struggle. When, for example, the Russian textile manufacturers were afraid that their British or German competitors would introduce British or German textiles into Russia and would cut prices, the Russian government was accommodating enough to impose an import duty upon British and German textiles. Of course this hindered the import of foreign products into Russia. Manufacturers usually declare that tariffs are necessary for the encouragement of home industry. If, however, we study the tariff policies of the various countries, we can see that the real aim was very different. During the last few decades, the countries in which the capitalists have raised the greatest clamour for high import tariffs, the countries in which such tariffs have been imposed, are the greatest and strongest countries in the world. The United States has led in this movement. Could foreign competition possibly injure these countries ? " What are you making such a row about, John ? Who is hurting you ? You are the aggressor ! "

What is the real meaning of all this ? Let us suppose that in a certain country the textile industry has been monopolised by syndicates or trusts. What happens if an import duty is imposed ? The syndicated capitalists kill two birds with one stone. In the first place they free themselves from foreign competition. Secondly, to the buyers of their own land, they are able to raise prices by an amount nearly equal to that of the tariff. Suppose the import duty on textiles to be two shillings per yard. In that case the textile magnates need have no hesitation in adding two shillings, or at least 1s. 9d., per yard to the price of their goods. If the industry were not syndicated, the internal competition between the capitalists of the country we are considering would immediately lead to price cutting. But if there is a syndicate in control, it has no difficulty in raising prices, for the foreigner is kept out of the market by the customs barrier, and owing to the syndication of the industry there is no competition in the homeland. In so far as there are any imports, the State revenue benefits, while the syndicated manufacturers secure additional surplus value in consequence of the enhanced price. This can only take place where there is a syndicate or trust. But that is not the end of the affair. Thanks to these surplus profits, the syndicated manufacturers are able to introduce their goods into other countries and to sell them there below cost price simply in order to supplant all competitors in those countries. This is what they have actually done. It is a matter of common knowledge that the Russian Sugar Syndicate kept the price of sugar in Russia comparatively high, while selling sugar in England at a ridiculously low price in the hope of destroying competitors in that country. The saying became current that in England pigs were fed on Russian sugar. Thus the syndicated manufacturers, aided by the tariffs, are able at one and the same time to fleece their own countrymen and to bring foreign customers under their sway.

The consequences are of great importance. It is obvious that the surplus profits of the syndicate will increase proportionally with the increase in the number of sheep to be shorn, with the increase in the number of those who are penned within the tariff barriers. If the customs area be a small one, the opportunity for profit-making will also be small. If, on the other hand, the customs area be large and populous, the opportunities for profit-making will be correspondingly extensive. In that case the surplus profits will be very large, so that it will be possible to act boldly in the world market, and to act there with the hope of a substantial success. Now, the customs area usually coincides with the area administered by the State. How can this latter be enlarged ? By grabbing some foreign territory, by annexing it, by including it within one's own frontiers, within one's own governmental area. But this means war. It means that the dominion of syndicates is inevitably associated with wars of conquest. Every robber capitalist State endeavours to extend its frontiers ; the extension is demanded by the interests of the trust magnates, by the interests of financial capital. Now, he who talks of extending frontiers really talks of waging war.

In this manner, the tariff policy of the syndicate and trust magnates, in conjunction with their policy in the world market, leads to violent collisions. But here there are at work, tending towards war, additional causes.

We have seen that the development of production results in the continuous accumulation of surplus value. In every land of advanced capitalist development there is therefore continually expanding a mass of *superfluous capital* which returns less profit than in comparatively backward countries. The larger the accumulation of superfluous capital in any country, the more vigorous are the endeavours to export capital, to invest it abroad. This aim is preeminently favoured by tariff policy. In fact, import duties greatly hinder the import of goods. When, for instance, the Russian manufacturers imposed high duties upon German goods, it became difficult for the German manufacturers to introduce their products into Russia. (We are speaking, of course, of things that happened when the manufacturers were in power, before the days of the Soviet Government.)

But when they found it difficult to export their goods to Russia, another way was opened to the German capitalists. They began to introduce their *capital* into Russia. They built factories there ; they bought shares in Russian undertakings, or they started new enterprises, supplying these with capital. Did the duties offer any hindrance ? Nothing of the kind. Far from being a hindrance, they were a help ; they positively promoted the influx of capital. For this reason. When the German capitalist has a factory in Russia, and when he too becomes a member of the " Russian " syndicate, of course the Russian tariff helps him to earn surplus profit. The import duties are just as useful to him in fleecing the Russian public as they are to his Russian colleagues.

Capital moves from one country into another not only in order to found new enterprises in the latter or to support those which already exist. In many cases the introduction of capital takes the form of a *loan to the government* of the country into which the capital is introduced, a loan at a fixed rate of interest. This means that the borrowing government increases its *national debt*, becomes indebted to the lending government. In such cases the debtor government usually undertakes to float all loans (and especially war loans) among the industrials of the creditor State. Thus vast quantities of capital pass from one State to another, partly incorporated in buildings and manufacturing enterprises, and partly taking the form of State loans. Under the dominion of financial capital, the export of capital attains gigantic proportions.

We will give certain figures which can still teach us a great deal, although they are a trifle out of date. In the year 1902, *France* had in twenty-six foreign States investments to the approximate amount of thirty-five milliards of francs : about half of the sum was in the form of State loans. The lion's share had gone to *Russia* (ten milliards). Parenthetically we may remark that this is why the French bourgeoisie is so furious because we Russians have cancelled the tsarist debts and have refused to pay the French usurers. By the year 1905 the sum of foreign capital imported into Russia had already exceeded forty milliards. In the year 1911 the foreign investments of *Britain* amounted to about sixteen hundred million pounds sterling ; but if we include loans to the British colonies the sum invested overseas by the British amounted to three thousand million pounds sterling. *Germany*, prior to the war, had foreign investments amounting to something like thirty-five milliards of marks.—In a word, every capitalist government exports vast quantities of capital, in order, with the aid of this capital, to plunder foreign countries.

Moreover, the export of capital entails important consequences. The various powerful States begin to compete for the possession of those territorial areas or lesser States to which they wish to export capital. But here is another point to which we must draw attention. When capitalists export capital to a " foreign " land, the risk involved is not that of certain quantities of commodities, but that of immense sums of money running into millions and milliards. Evidently, therefore, there will arise a strong desire to take completely into their hands the lesser countries in which they have invested capital, and to send *armies* to protect this capital. In the exporting States there thus arises the aspiration to subject these territories to their own governmental authorities, to do so at all hazards, simply to conquer them, to annex them by force. There ensues on the part of various strong, plundering States a competitive invasion of the weak territories, and it is clear that in the long run the marauders must come into mutual collision. Such clashes have actually taken place. In consequence, the export of capital has led to *war*.

We have now some additional points to consider. With the growth of syndicates and the introduction of tariffs, the struggle for markets becomes greatly intensified. Already by the close of the nineteenth century there was no longer to be found any territory which remained quite free for the export of goods, or any region on which the capitalist had not yet set his foot. A great rise in the price of raw materials was beginning; metals, wool, timber, coal, and cotton were all growing dearer. During the years immediately preceding the war, there had been a fierce scramble for markets and *a struggle for new sources of raw materials*. The capitalists were nosing all over the world in quest of new coal mines, and new deposits of ore; they were hunting for new markets to which they could export the produce of their metal works, their weaving mills, and other factories; they wanted a new, a " fresh " public to plunder. In former days, often enough, the competitors in any country consisted of firms whose competition was " peaceful "; they remained on tolerably good terms. Under the sway of the banks and the trusts, a great change has taken place. Let us suppose that new deposits of copper have been discovered. They are immediately seized by a bank or a trust, which gets them wholly into its power, monopolises them. The capitalists of other countries are left to console themselves with the adage : " It's no use crying over spilt milk." The same considerations apply to the struggle for markets. Let us suppose that capital from afar finds its way to a remote colony. The sale of goods is thereupon organised on the grand scale. The business usually falls into the hands of one gigantic firm. Opening branches in the place, it exercises pressure upon the local authorities, endeavouring in this way, and by a thousand wiles and stratagems, to corner the market, to secure a *monopoly*, to exclude all competitors. It is obvious that monopolist capital and the magnates of trusts and syndicates must act after their kind. We are not living in the "good old times," but in an age of war between monopolist thieves and plunderers.

Inevitably, therefore, CONCURRENTLY WITH THE GROWTH OF FINANCIAL CAPITAL THERE MUST OCCUR A GREAT INTENSIFICATION OF THE STRUGGLE FOR MARKETS AND RAW MATERIALS, AND THIS CANNOT FAIL TO LEAD TO VIOLENT COLLISIONS.

During the last quarter of the nineteenth century the great robber States ruthlessly seized numerous regions belonging to lesser nations. Between 1876 and 1914 the so-called Great Powers annexed approximately ten million square miles of territory. In other words, they grabbed territory the total area of which is twice as large as that of Europe. The whole world had been partitioned among the big robbers ; all other countries have become their colonies, their tributaries, or their slaves.

Here are some examples. *Great Britain* since 1870 has annexed in Asia : Beluchistan, Burma, Wei-hai-wei, and the mainland adjacent to Hong-Kong ; she has enlarged the Straits Settlements ; she has acquired Cyprus, and British North Borneo. In Australasia and Oceania she has annexed a number of islands, has occupied the eastern part of New Guinea, has annexed a great part of the Solomon Islands, the island of Tonga, etc. Her new possessions in Africa are : Egypt, the northern Soudan, Uganda, Eastern Equatorial Africa, British Somaliland, Zanzibar and Pemba. She has swallowed up the two Boer republics, has occupied Rhodesia and British Central Africa, has annexed Nigeria, and so on, and so on.

France, since 1870, has acquired Annam ; conquered Tonkin ; annexed Laos, Tunis, Madagascar, large portions of Sahara, Soudan, and the Guinea coast ; has acquired areas on the Ivory Coast, in Dahomey, in Somaliland, etc. As a result, at the opening of the twentieth century the French colonies had an area which was nearly twenty times that of the mother country. (The British colonies at this date were more than one hundred times the size of the mother country.)

Germany began to participate in the game of grab somewhat later, towards 1884 ; but within a brief time she was able to secure a considerable share of the spoil.

Tsarist Russia has likewise pursued a robber policy on a large scale. Of late years this was principally directed towards Asia, and here a collision with Japan ensued, for Japan was trying to plunder Asia from the other side.

The *United States* annexed numerous islands in the Caribbean Sea, and subsequently practised an annexationist policy on the American continent   Her attitude towards Mexico has been extremely threatening.

In the year 1914 the homeland territories of the six Great Powers amounted in all to about six million square miles. The total area of their colonial possessions at the same date was approximately thirty million square miles.

It need hardly be said that in the first instance such robberies were effected at the expense of the lesser countries, of those that were unprotected and weak. They were the first to be ruined. Just as in the struggle between the manufacturers and the independent artisans the latter were the first to succumb, so here. The great State trusts, the great capitalists organised for robbery, began by smashing the lesser governments and seizing their possessions. In the world economy, the centralisation of capital advanced along the familiar lines ; the lesser States were ruined while the large robber States grew richer, larger, and more powerful.

As soon as they had annexed the whole world, they began to struggle more fiercely among themselves. It was inevitable that the brigands should now quarrel over the loot, should fight for a redistribution of the world. Giant robber States remained, and a life-and-death combat was to ensue among these survivors.

THE POLICY OF CONQUEST WHICH FINANCIAL CAPITAL PURSUES IN THE STRUGGLE FOR MARKETS, FOR THE SOURCES OF RAW MATERIAL, AND FOR PLACES IN WHICH CAPITAL CAN BE INVESTED, IS KNOWN AS IMPERIALISM. Imperialism is born of financial capital. Just as a tiger cannot live upon grass, so financial capital cannot exist without a policy of conquest, spoliation, violence, and war. The essential desire of every one of the financial capitalist State trusts is to dominate the world ; to establish a world empire, wherein the small group of capitalists belonging to the victorious nations shall hold undivided sway. The British imperialist, for example, dreams of a " Greater Britain " which shall rule the whole world—a world in which British trust magnates shall command the labour of Negroes and Russians, Germans and Chinese, Hindus and Armenians, slaves of all colours, black, white, yellow, and red. Britain is not far from the attainment of this ideal. But the more she grabs, the more she wants. The same thing happens with the imperialists of other nations. Russian imperialists

dream of a " Greater Russia "; German imperialists dream
of a " Greater Germany "; and so on. By these " great "
ones, there is of course practised a shameless spoliation of
all the rest.

In this manner, therefore, the reign of financial capital
must inevitably hurl all mankind into the bloody abyss
of a war for the benefit of bankers and trust magnates;
a war which is not fought for a people's own land but for
the plunder of other lands; a war that is waged in order
that the world may be subjugated by the financial capital
of the conquering country. Such was the nature of the first
great world war, during the years 1914 to 1918.

§ 28.

Militarism. The rule of financial capital, of the bank
barons and the trust magnates, finds expression in another
phenomenon of the utmost importance, namely, in the
unprecedented growth of expenditure on armaments—
upon army, navy, and air force. The reason for this is
obvious. In earlier days no brigand ever dreamed of world
dominion. Now, however, the thoughts of the imperialists
are seriously turned in this direction. Never before was
there a contest between such monstrously strong State
trusts. It is as an outcome of this new situation that the
States have armed to the teeth. The Great Powers, professional robbers, kept their eyes on one another, for each
dreaded lest his neighbour should attack him in the rear.
Every Great Power finds it necessary to maintain an army,
not only for colonial service, not only for the repression of
the workers, but in addition for the fight with fellow brigands.
If any of the Powers introduces some new system of armaments, the other Powers eagerly endeavour to outdo the
advance, for they fear to be left behind in the race. Thus
ensues a mad rivalry in armaments, each State trying to
outdo the rest. Gigantic enterprises are formed, the trusts
of the cannon kings—Putiloff, Krupp, Armstrong, Vickers,
etc. The armament trusts make enormous profits; they
are in league with the general staffs of the armies; they
endeavour to throw fuel on the flames, to promote opportunities for conflict, seeing that the size of their profits
depends upon war.

Such was the crazy picture presented by capitalist society just before the great war. The State trusts were bristling with bayonets; on land, at sea, and in the air, everything had been made ready for the world struggle; in the various national budgets, the military and naval estimates assumed an ever larger place. In Britain, for example, in 1875 the expenditure for war purposes comprised 38·6 per cent. of the annual estimates for all purposes, this being not much more than one-third; by 1907-8, the proportion had risen to 48·6 per cent., nearly half. In the U.S.A., the proportion of national expenditure upon war purposes for the year 1908 was 56·9 per cent., this being considerably more than half. It was the same in other lands. "Prussian militarism" flourished in all the great State trusts. The armament kings were filling their treasuries. The whole world was hastening at an accelerating pace towards the bloodiest of all wars, towards the world war of imperialism.

Of exceptional interest was the armament rivalry between the British and the German bourgeoisies. In the year 1912 England decided to lay down three superdreadnoughts for every two laid down by Germany. In 1913, according to the naval estimates, the German North Sea fleet was to contain 17 dreadnoughts as against 21 British dreadnoughts; in 1916 the number was to be 26 German and 36 British; and so on.

The expenditure upon army and navy increased as follows:

	Millions of Pounds Sterling.	
	1888.	1908.
Russia	21	47
France	30	41·5
Germany	18	40·5
Austria-Hungary	10	20
Italy	7·5	12
Britain	15	28
Japan	0·7	9
U.S.A.	10	20

In the course of 20 years the expenditure had been doubled; in the case of Japan it had been multiplied by 13. The armament dance became even more lively shortly before the war. *France* expended for war purposes £50,000,000 in 1910, and £74,000,000 in 1914. *Germany* spent £47,800,000 in 1906, and £94,300,000 in 1914; that is to say, the expenditure was doubled in eight years. Even more extraordinary was the *British* expenditure. In 1900 this amounted to £49,900,000; in 1910 it was already £69,400,000; in 1914, the figures were £80,400,000. In the year 1913 the naval expenditure of Britain alone amounted to a larger sum than the total of what all the Powers had spent upon their fleets in 1886. As regards tsarist *Russia*, in the year 1892 the country spent upon armaments £29,300,000 ; in 1902, £42,100,000 ; in 1906, £52,900,000. In the year 1914 the Russian war budget amounted to £97,500,000.

Expenditure upon war purposes swallowed an enormous proportion of the national revenue. In the case of Russia, for example, one-third of the budgeted sum was devoted to armaments : indeed, if we take loans into account, the proportion was even greater. Here are the figures. For every £100 spent in tsarist Russia, there were spent :

Upon army, navy, and interest on loans	40·14	
„ education	3·86	(13th part)
„ agriculture	4·06	(10th part)
„ administration, justice, diplomacy, railway service, industry and commerce, department of finance, etc.	51·94	

Total £100

The budgets of other States were of the same character. Look at " democratic " Britain, for instance. In the year 1904, for every £100 spent, there were spent :

Upon army and navy	53·8	⎫
„ interest upon National Debt and upon sinking fund	22·5	⎬ In all 76·3
„ civil service generally	23·7	⎭

Total £100

§ 29.

The imperialist War of 1914 to 1918. It was inevitable that the imperialist policy of the " Great Powers " should sooner or later bring them into collision. Indisputably, the game of grab played by *all* the " Great Powers " was the real cause of the war. Only an idiot can continue to believe that the war took place because the Serbs killed the Austrian crown prince or because the Germans invaded Belgium. At the outset, there was much dispute as to who was responsible for the catastrophe. The German capitalists maintained that Russia was the aggressor, whereas the Russians proclaimed everywhere that Germany began it. In Britain the word went round that the British had entered the struggle on behalf of " gallant little Belgium."

In France, everyone was writing, screaming, and singing to prove how gloriously France was behaving in defence of the heroic Belgian nation. Simultaneously in Austria and Germany it was being trumpeted that these two countries were repelling a Cossack invasion and were waging a purely defensive war.

From first to last, this was all nonsense; it was a fraud upon the workers. The fraud was necessary to enable the bourgeoisie to force their soldiers into battle. It was not the first time that the bourgeoisie had used such methods. We have previously seen that the trust magnates introduced high tariffs in order that, while plundering their fellow-countrymen, they could more readily conquer the foreign market. For them, therefore, the customs duties were a means of *attack*. But the bourgeoisie insisted that the duties were imposed in order to *protect* home industry. The same thing happened in the case of the war. The essence of the imperialist war which was to subject the world to the yoke of financial capital lay in this, that in it all were aggressors. To-day this is as clear as clear can be. The lackeys of tsardom declared that they were defending themselves. But when the November revolution opened the ministerial archives and when the secret treaties were published, documentary evidence was furnished that both the tsar and Kerensky, in concert with the British and the French, were carrying on the war for the sake of the spoils, that they wanted to seize Constantinople, to plunder Turkey and Persia, and to steal Galicia from Austria. These things are now as plain as that two and two make four.

The German imperialists were also in the end unmasked. Think of the Brest-Litovsk treaty; think of the plunderings in Poland, Lithuania, Ukraine, and Finland. The German revolution has likewise led to many disclosures. We have learned from documentary evidence that Germany was ready to attack for the sake of loot, and that she had designed to seize vast quantities of foreign territories and colonies.

What about the " noble " Allies? They, too, have been fully unmasked. No one can believe in their nobility after the Versailles treaty. They have stripped Germany bare; they have demanded a war indemnity of twelve and a half milliards; they have taken the whole German fleet and all

the German colonies; they have seized most of the loco-
motives and the milch cows as earnest for the indemnity.
They have ravaged Russia in the north and in the south.
They, too, have been fighting for plunder.

The communist bolsheviks said all this at the very outset
of the war. But at that time few believed them. To-day,
everyone outside a lunatic asylum can see that it is true.
Financial capital is a greedy and bloodthirsty robber, no
matter what the nationality of the capitalists may be. It
is all the same whether they are Russians, Germans, French-
men, Englishmen, Japanese, or Americans.

We see, then, that when we are talking of the imperialist
war it is absurd to say that one imperialist is guilty and that
another is blameless, to say that some imperialists were the
aggressors and that others were on the defensive. All such
assertions are made only in order to fool the workers. In
actual fact, the Powers had all begun with aggressions upon
the lesser peoples in whose lands they established their
colonies; they all entertained designs of world-wide plunder;
in every land alike the capitalists hoped to subject the whole
world to the financial capital of their own country.

Once it had started, the war could not fail to be a
world war. The reason is plain. Almost all the world
had been partitioned among the " Great Powers," and
the Powers were intimately connected by the ties of a
world-wide economic system. It is not surprising, therefore, that the war should involve all countries, should
affect both hemispheres.

Britain, France, Italy, Belgium, Russia, Germany,
Austria-Hungary, Serbia, Bulgaria, Rumania, Montenegro,
Japan, the United States, China, and a dozen petty States,
were drawn into the bloody vortex. The total population
of the world is somewhere near fifteen hundred millions.
The whole of this vast population suffered directly or indirectly from the miseries of the war, which was imposed upon
them by a small group of capitalist criminals. Never before
had the world seen such immense armies as were now
marshalled, never before had it known such monstrous
instruments of death and destruction. Nor had the world
ever witnessed such an irresistible mass of capital. Britain
and France forced into the service of their money-bags,

not only those who were British and French by birth, but in addition the thousands upon thousands of black-skinned and yellow-skinned colonial slaves. The civilised robbers did not hesitate to enroll cannibals among their soldiery, when cannibals were forthcoming. All this was done in the name of the most exalted ideals.

The war of 1914 had its prototypes in the colonial wars. Of this character were the following: the campaigns of the "civilised" Powers against China; the Spanish-American war; the Russo-Japanese war in the year 1904 (on account of Korea, Port Arthur, Manchuria, etc.); the Tripolitan campaign of Italy in 1912; the Boer war at the turn of the century, when "democratic" England brutally crushed the two South African republics. There were several occasions when a gigantic international conflagration threatened. The partition of Africa nearly led to war between Britain and France (the Fashoda incident). Germany and France were embroiled over Morocco. Tsarist Russia at one time almost went to war with Britain in connexion with the partition of Central Asia.

At the beginning of the world war, the conflict of interests between England and Germany concerning territorial predominance in Africa, Asia Minor, and the Balkans, came to the front. Events worked out in this way, that the allies of Britain were, first of all France, which hoped to wrest Alsace-Lorraine from Germany, and secondly Russia, in search of profiteering opportunities in the Balkans and Galicia. The robber imperialism of Germany secured its chief ally in Austria-Hungary. American imperialism entered the conflict comparatively late, after watching for a time how the European Powers were exhausting themselves by their struggles.

In addition to militarism, one of the most abominable methods employed in the rivalry between the imperialist Powers is *secret diplomacy*, which avails itself of secret treaties and plots, and which does not shrink from the use of the assassin's knife and the dynamiter's bomb. The real aims of the imperialist war were embodied in the secret treaties between Britain, France, and Russia, on the one hand, and between Germany, Austria-Hungary, Turkey, and Bulgaria, on the other. It is manifest that secret agents of the Entente were privy to the assassination of the Austrian crown prince, which occurred five weeks before the war. On the other hand, German diplomacy was by no means disconcerted by the murder. For example, Rohrbach, the German imperialist, wrote: "We may deem ourselves fortunate that the great anti-German conspiracy declared itself before the appointed time through the assassination of the archduke Franz Ferdinand. Two years later, the war would have been far more difficult." The German provocative agents would have been perfectly willing to murder the German crown prince in order to bring about the war; nor would British, French, or Russian secret agents have shrunk from the assassination of this same prince.

§ 30.

State Capitalism and the Classes. The conduct of the imperialist war was differentiated from that of all previous wars, not only by the dimensions of the conflict and by its devastating effects, but in addition by the fact that in every country actively engaged in the imperialist war the whole of economic life had to be subordinated to war purposes. In former conflicts the bourgeoisie could carry them on merely by providing funds. The world war, however, attained such huge proportions and affected such highly developed countries that money alone did not suffice. It became essential in this war that the steel foundries should devote themselves entirely to the making of heavy guns, whose calibre was continually being enlarged; that coal should be mined for war purposes alone; that metals, textiles, hides, everything, should be employed in war service. Naturally, therefore, the greatest hope of victory was for whichever of the State capitalist trusts could best harness production and transport to the chariot of war.

How was this to be achieved? Manifestly, the only way in which it could be achieved was by the complete centralisation of production. It would be necessary to arrange things in such a way that production would go on smoothly; that it would be well organised; that it would be entirely under the control of the fighters, that is to say of the general staff; that all the orders of those wearing epaulets and stars would be punctually carried out.

How could the bourgeoisie do this? The matter was quite simple. To that end it was necessary that the bourgeoisie should place private production, privately owned trusts and syndicates, at the disposal of the capitalist robber State. This is what they did for the duration of the war. Industry was " mobilised " and " militarised," that is to say it was placed under the orders of the State and of the military authorities. " But how ? " some of our readers will ask. " In that way the bourgeoisie would surely forfeit its income ? That would be nationalisation ! When everything has been handed over to the State, where will the bourgeoisie come in, and how will the capitalists reconcile themselves to such a condition of affairs ? " It is an actual fact that the bourgeoisie agreed to the arrangement. But there is nothing very remarkable in that, for the privately owned syndicates and trusts were not handed over to the workers' State, but to the imperialist State, the State which belonged to the bourgeoisie. Was there anything to alarm the bourgeoisie in such a prospect ? The capitalists simply transferred their possessions from one pocket to another ; the possessions remained as large as ever.

We must never forget the class character of the State. The State must not be conceived as constituting a " third power " standing above the classes ; from head to foot it is a class organisation. Under the dictatorship of the workers it is a working-class organisation. Under the dominion of the bourgeoisie it is just as definitely an *economic* organisation as is a trust or a syndicate.

We see, then, that when the bourgeoisie handed over the privately owned syndicates and trusts to the State, it handed them over to its own State, to the robber capitalist State and not to the proletarian State ; consequently it had nothing to lose by the change. Is it not precisely the same thing to a manufacturer, whom we may call Schulz or Smith, whether he receives his profits from the counting-house of a syndicate or from a State-bank ? Far from losing by the change, the bourgeoisie actually gained. There was a gain because, through the State centralisation of industry, the war machine was enabled to work to better effect, and there was a greater chance of winning the war of rapine.

It is not surprising, therefore, that in nearly all capitalist countries there took place during the war a development of *State capitalism* in the place of the capitalism of private syndicates or trusts. Germany, for example, gained many successes and was able for a lengthy period to resist attack from enemies of a greatly superior strength, simply because the German bourgeoisie was so successful in the organisation of its State capitalism.

The change to State capitalism was effected in various ways. In most cases a State monopoly of production and trade was instituted. This implied that production and trade were placed wholly in the hands of the bourgeois State. Sometimes the transformation was not effected all at once, but by instalments. This took place when the State merely bought some of the shares of the syndicate or trust.

An enterprise in which this had taken place was half private and half a State affair, but the bourgeois State held the leading strings. Furthermore, even when certain enterprises remained in private hands, they were often subjected to governmental control. Some enterprises were by special legislation forced to buy their raw materials from certain others, while the latter had to sell to the former in specified quantities and at fixed prices. The State prescribed working methods, specified what materials were to be used, and rationed these materials. Thus, in place of private capitalism, State capitalism came into being.

Under State capitalism, instead of the separate organisations of the bourgeoisie there now flourishes a united organisation, the State organisation. Down to the time of the war there existed in any capitalist country the State organisation of the bourgeoisie, and there also existed separately from the State large numbers of bourgeois organisations, such as syndicates, trusts, societies of entrepreneurs, landowners' organisations, political parties, journalists' unions, learned societies, artists' clubs, the church, societies for the clergy, Boy Scouts and cadet corps (White Guard organisations of youth), private detective bureaux, etc. Under State capitalism all these separate organisations fuse with the bourgeois State; they become, as it were, State departments, and they work in accordance with a general plan, subject to the " high command " ; in the mines and factories they do whatever is ordered by the general staff ; they write in the newspapers under the orders of the general staff ; they preach in the churches whatever will be useful to the robbers of the general staff ; their pictures, their books, and their poems, are produced under the orders of the general staff ; they invent machinery, weapons, poison gas, etc., to meet the needs of the general staff. In this manner the whole of life is militarised in order to secure for the bourgeoisie the continued receipt of its filthy lucre.

State capitalism signifies an enormous accession of strength to the great bourgeoisie. Just as under the working-class dictatorship, in the workers' State, the working class is more powerful in proportion as the soviet authority, the trade unions, the Communist Party, etc., work more harmoniously together, so under the dictatorship of the bourgeoisie the capitalist class is strong in proportion to the success with which all the bourgeois organisations pull together. State capitalism, centralising all these organisations, converting them all into the instruments of a single, united organisation, contributes immensely to the power of capital. Bourgeois dictatorship attains its climax in State capitalism.

State capitalism flourished during the war in all the large capitalist countries. In tsarist Russia, too, it began to make its way (in the form of war industry committees, monopolies, etc.). Subsequently, however, the Russian bourgeoisie, alarmed by the revolution of March, 1917, became afraid lest productive industry should pass into the hands of the proletariat together with the State authority. For this reason, after the March revolution, the bourgeoisie did not merely refrain from attempts to organise production, but positively sabotaged industry.

We see that State capitalism, far from putting an end to exploitation, actually increases the power of the bourgeoisie. Nevertheless the Scheidemannites in Germany, and social solidarians in other lands, have contended that this forced labour is socialism. As soon, they say, as everything is in the hands of the State, socialism will be realised. They fail to see that in such a system the State is not a proletarian State, since it is in the hands of those who are the malicious and deadly enemies of the proletariat.

State capitalism uniting and organising the bourgeoisie, increasing the power of capitalism, has, of course, greatly weakened the working class. Under State capitalism the workers became the white slaves of the capitalist State. They were deprived of the right to strike ; they were mobilised and militarised ; everyone who raised his voice against the war was hauled before the courts and sentenced as a traitor. In many countries the workers were deprived of all freedom of movement, being forbidden to transfer from one enterprise to another. " Free " wage workers were reduced to serfdom ; they were doomed to perish on the battlefields, not on behalf of their own cause but on behalf of that of their enemies. They were doomed to work themselves to death, not for their own sake or for that of their comrades or their children, but for the sake of their oppressors.

§ 31.

The Collapse of Capitalism, and the working Class. In this manner, at the outset, the war contributed to the centralisation and organisation of the capitalist economy. That which the syndicates, the banks, the trusts, and the combined undertakings, had not yet fully achieved, was speedily finished by State capitalism. It created a network out of all the organs regulating production and distribution. Thus it prepared the ground even more fully than before for the time when the proletariat would be able to take the now centralised large-scale production into its own hands.

It was inevitable that the war, whose burden pressed so heavily on the working class, should in due course lead to a rising of the proletarian masses. The leading characteristic of the war was that it was murderous to an unparalleled degree. The levying of troops advanced with giant strides. The proletariat was positively decimated on the battle-fields. The reports show that down to March, 1917, the number of dead, wounded, and missing, totalled 25 millions ; by January 1, 1918, the number of the killed had been approximately 8 millions. If we assume the average weight of a soldier to 150 lb., this means that between August 1, 1914, and January 1, 1918, the capitalists had brought to market twelve hundred million pounds of putrid human flesh. To estimate the real loss in human beings, we must add a few millions permanently invalided. Considering syphilis alone, this disease has been diffused by the war to an almost incredible extent, so that infection is now nearly universal. In consequence of the war people have become far less fit physically ; the most healthy, the most effective elements, those which formed the flower of the nations, have been destroyed. It need hardly be said that the brunt of the losses was borne by the workers and the peasants.

In the great centres of the warring States we can find whole communities of those who have been crippled and monstrously mutilated ; men whose faces have been shot away, wearing masks, sit in misery as living tokens to the delights of bourgeois civilisation.

The proletariat, however, was not simply massacred at the front. In addition, intolerable burdens were laid upon the shoulders of those who remained alive. The war necessitated a frenzied expenditure. At the very time when the factory owners were piling up immense profits which became distinctively known as " war profits," the workers were being subjected to heavy taxation for war purposes. The cost of the war continued to increase beyond measure.

In the autumn of 1919, at the peace conference, the French minister for finance declared that the war had cost the belligerents more than a trillion francs. The significance of such figures is far from easy to grasp. In former days the number of miles between one star and another was stated in similar terms. Now they are used to figure out the cost of these years of criminal slaughter. A trillion is a million millions. Such has been the upshot of the war devised by the capitalists. According to another estimate, the cost of the war was as follows :

					Millions of £.
Cost of the first year of war	..	..	..		9,100
,, second ,,	..	..	..		13,650
,, third ,,	..	..	..		20,470
,, first half of the fourth year (the last five months of 1917)			..	..	15,350
Total ..	..	..	..	..	£58,570 millions

Subsequently, the costs of the war increased even more, attaining figures astounding in their magnitude. Vast sums have to be raised in order to meet these costs. Naturally, therefore, the capitalist States have already begun to impose heavy burdens on the working class : either by direct taxation ; or by taxes on articles of consumption ; or, finally, in order to make the bourgeoisie too contribute, by a deliberate advance in the price of goods from patriotic motives. Prices have continued to rise. But the manufacturers, and especially those who have been manufacturing things wanted for the war, have pocketed unheard-of gains.

The *Russian* manufacturers were able to secure more than double the previous dividends, and in certain undertakings the profits were positively fabulous. Here are some of the figures : the naphtha firm of the Mirosyeff Brothers paid 40 per cent. ; Dansheffsky Ltd., 30 per cent. ; the Kalfa tobacco factory, 30 per cent. ; and so on. In *Germany*, during the years 1913 and 1914, the net profits in four branches of industry, namely chemical works, explosives, metal works, and motor car works, amounted to 133 millions ; during the years 1915 and 1916 the total profits in the same branches amounted to 259 millions, practically double. In the *United States* the profits of the Steel Trust during the first half of 1916 were three times as great as the profits during the first half of 1915. The total profits of the Trust in 1915 were 98 million dollars ; in the year 1917 they were 478 million dollars. Dividends of 200 per cent. were several times declared. Many more examples could be given. There was a similar huge increase in banking profits. During the war, the small fry among the manufacturers were ruined, whilst the big sharks were incredibly enriched. As for the proletariat, this fell under the yoke of taxes and rising prices.

The chief articles produced during the war were shrapnel, shells, high explosives, heavy guns, tanks, aeroplanes, poison gas, gunpowder, etc. An incredible quantity of these requisites was manufactured. In the United States, new towns grew up like mushrooms round the powder factories. The owners of the new powder factories, in their eagerness for profits, conducted work so carelessly that explosions were common. Of course the manufacturers of munitions made huge profits, so that their businesses flourished amazingly. But as far as the common people were concerned, matters grew continually worse. Things of real value, such as can be eaten, worn, etc., were produced in ever-diminishing quantities. With powder and shot people can shoot and can destroy, but powder and shot are of no use for food or clothing. The whole strength of the belligerents was, however, devoted to the production of powder and other instruments of death. The production of ordinary utilities was increasingly reduced. The workers were drafted into the armies, and productive industry was entirely turned to the purposes of war. There was continually a greater dearth of useful goods. Hence arose shortage of food and exorbitant prices. LACK OF BREAD, LACK OF COAL, LACK OF ALL USEFUL GOODS, AND MOREOVER A WORLD-WIDE LACK IN CONJUNCTION WITH WORLD-WIDE EXHAUSTION, SUCH WERE THE MAIN CONSEQUENCES OF THE CRIMINAL IMPERIALIST WAR.

Here are a few examples from different countries.
In *France* during the opening years of the war, agricultural production diminished as follows :

	Quintals.	
	1914.	1916.
Grain	42,272,600	15,300,500
Root crops	46,639,000	15,860,000
Plants used for industrial purposes	59,429,000	20,448,000

In *Britain* the reserves of iron ore fell off as follows :

In the end of 1912 the reserves were			..	241,000	tons
,,	,,	1913	,,	,,	,,	.. 138,000 ,,
,,	,,	1914	,,	,,	,,	.. 108,000 ,,
,,	,,	1915	,,	,,	,,	.. 113,000 ,,
,,	,,	1916	,,	,,	,,	.. 3,000 ,,
,,	,,	1917	,,	,,	,,	.. 600 ,,

In other words, the reserves of iron ore were practically exhausted by the end of 1917.

In *Germany* the production of cast iron was as follows :

1913	..	..	..	..	.. 19,300,000 tons
1916	..	..	..	..	.. 13,300,000 ,,
1917	..	..	..	..	.. 13,100,000 ,,
1918	..	..	..	..	.. 12,000,000 ,,

Owing to the lack of coal, the condition of industry throughout the world was desperate. In Central and Western Europe the main provider of coal was Britain. In Britain by the middle of 1918 the production of coal was reduced by 13 per cent. Already in 1917 the principal industries were practically without supplies of coal. Electrical works were receiving only one-sixth of the coal they needed, while textile undertakings were receiving only one-eleventh of the pre-war supply. At the time of the " peace " conference at Versailles nearly all the countries in the world were affected by a terrible coal crisis. Factories were closed down for lack of fuel and the railway services were reduced. An extensive disorganisation of industry and transport ensued.

The same thing happened in *Russia*. In 1917 the war had led to very bad conditions in the matter of coal supply. The industries of the Moscow district required 12,000,000 poods of coal per month [61 poods = 1 ton]. Kerensky's administration promised to supply 6,000,000 poods, half the normal amount. The actual supplies were as follows :

January, 1917..	..	..	..	1,800,000 poods
February ,, ..	..	..	..	1,300,000 poods
March ,, ..	..	..	..	800,000 poods

It is not surprising that Russian industry, far from displaying " a tremendous expansion," was almost arrested. Here, as throughout the world, the ruin of capitalism was beginning. In 1917, under the Kerensky regime, the closure of factories attained the following dimensions :

Month.				No. of Undertakings.	No. of Workers Employed.
March ..	..	..	..	74	6,646
April ..	..	..	..	55	2,816
May ..	..	..	..	108	8,701
June ..	..	..	..	125	38,455
July ..	..	..	..	206	47,754

Ruin was advancing with giant strides

If we wish to consider the rise in prices that resulted in part from scarcity and in part from the inflation of the currency, it suffices to turn to *Britain*, which of all the original belligerents was least affected by the war.

Here are the average prices of five of the chief articles of diet (tea, sugar, butter, bread, and meat):

	Tea and Sugar.	Bread, Meat and Butter.
Average prices 1901–1905	500	300
End of July, 1914	579	350
,, January, 1915	786	413
,, ,, 1916	946	465
,, ,, 1917	1310	561
,, ,, 1918	1221	681
,, May, 1918	1247	777

Thus in the course of the war, even in Britain, prices were more than doubled, and the increase in wages was very far from keeping pace with the increase in the cost of living. In other countries, conditions were very much worse. They were especially bad in Russia, where the war proved positively ruinous, and where the country was reduced to the position of a tattered beggar dependent upon the favour of the lords of capital.

In the *United States*, which was even less affected by the war than Britain, between 1913 and 1918 the prices of fifteen leading products increased by 160 per cent., while during the same period the rise in wages was only 80 per cent.

At length, even production for war purposes began to languish for lack of coal, steel, and other essentials. In every land, the United States alone excepted, poverty was rife; hunger, cold, and ruin, were advancing all over the globe. It need hardly be said that the chief sufferers from all these evils were the members of the working class, who thereupon attempted to protest. Upon them, now, war was declared, a war waged with the whole strength of the bourgeois robber States. In every land, in republican countries just as much as in monarchical, the working class was subjected to unexampled persecutions. The workers were not only deprived of the right to strike, but the slightest movement of protest was ruthlessly suppressed. In this way the dominion of capitalism led to *civil war between the classes*.

The resolution of the Third International concerning the White Terror gives a striking picture of the persecution of the workers during the war. It runs as follows : " At the very outset of the war, the ruling classes—who on the battlefields have slaughtered more than ten million men and have crippled and mutilated a vast number in addition—instituted in internal affairs a regime of bloody dictatorship (a bourgeois dictatorship). In Russia, the tsarist government shot and hanged the workers, organised anti-Jewish pogroms, and stifled every protest. The Austrian government savagely suppressed the risings of the peasants and the workers in Ukraine and Bohemia. The British bourgeoisie butchered some of the finest representatives of the Irish people. The German imperialists breathed threatenings and slaughter, and the insurgent bluejackets were the first victims of their brutal wrath. In France, the authorities shot down the Russian soldiers who refused to defend the financial interests of the French bankers. In the United States, the bourgeoisie lynched the internationalists, sentenced many of the best proletarians to twenty years' imprisonment and shot down workers on strike."

The capitalist system was breaking down. The anarchy of production had led to the war, and this had induced an enormous accentuation of the class conflict. Thus the war led to the revolution. Capitalism was beginning to disintegrate in two fundamental ways. (Refer to § 13.) The era of the collapse of capitalism had set in. Let us examine this collapse more closely.

Capitalist society was constructed upon one model throughout. A factory was organised just like a government office or like a division of the imperial army. At the top were the rich who commanded ; at the bottom were the poor, the workers and the salariat, who obeyed ; in between were the superintending engineers, the " non-commissioned officers " [the foremen], the higher grade employees, etc. It follows, therefore, that capitalist society can maintain itself in being so long only as the private soldier (drawn from the ranks of the workers) obeys the orders of the officer (drawn from the aristocracy, the landed gentry, or the wealthier bourgeoisie) ; so long only as in the government offices the subordinates obey the orders of their wealthy chiefs ; and so long only as in the factories the workers continue to obey the highly paid managers or the factory owners who live upon surplus value. But as soon as the working masses realise that they are nothing but pawns in the hands of their enemies, the ties are broken that bind the private soldier to the service of the officer and that bind the worker to the service of the factory owner. The workers cease to attend to the orders of the factory owner ; the private soldiers cease to attend to the orders of their officers ; the civil servants cease to attend to the orders of their chiefs. Then begins the period in which the *old* discipline is relaxed, that discipline which enabled the rich to rule the poor, which enabled the bourgeoisie to fleece the workers. This period will inevitably continue until the new class (the proletariat) has subjugated the bourgeoisie, has forced the bourgeoisie to serve the workers, has established a *new* discipline.

Such a condition of affairs, in which the old order has been destroyed and the new order has not yet been created, can be ended in no other way than by the complete victory of the proletariat in the civil war.

§ 32.

The Civil War. Civil war is an extremely intensified class war, and it occurs when the class war has led to revolution. The imperialist world war between the two groups of bourgeois States, the war waged for the repartition of the world, was carried on by the slaves of capital. It imposed such heavy burdens upon the workers that the class war was transformed into a civil war fought by the oppressed against their oppressors, the war which Marx had declared to be the only just war.

It was perfectly natural that capitalism should culminate in civil war, that the imperialist war between the bourgeois States should lead to a war between the classes. Our party foretold this development at the very outset of the war, in the year 1914, when no one dreamed of revolution. Nevertheless it was manifest that the intolerable burdens which the war imposed upon the working class must lead to an insurrection of the proletariat. It was, moreover, perfectly clear that the bourgeoisie could not possibly ensure a lasting peace, for the conflict of interests between the various groups of plunderers was too vital.

Our predictions have been entirely fulfilled. After the terrible years of war, brutality, and devastation, a civil war against the oppressors began. This civil war was opened by the Russian revolutions of March and November, 1917 ;

it was continued by the Finnish revolution, the Hungarian revolution, the Austrian revolution, and the German revolution ; revolutions in other countries have begun. The bourgeoisies cannot bring about a lasting peace. The Allies overcame Germany in November, 1918 ; the robbers' peace of Versailles was signed many months later ; but no one knows when the final settlement will be effected. It is plain to all that the peace of Versailles is not lasting. Quarrels have already broken out between the Jugo-Slavs and the Italians, between the Poles and the Czecho-Slovaks, between the Poles and the Lithuanians, between the Latvians and the Germans. In addition, all the bourgeois States have combined to attack the republic of the victorious Russian workers. Thus the imperialist war is ending in a civil war, of which the inevitable outcome will be the victory of the proletariat.

The civil war is not the result of any party's caprice ; its coming has been no chance matter. The civil war is a manifestation of the revolution, and the revolution was absolutely inevitable because the robber war of the imperialists had opened the eyes of the broad masses of the workers.

To think that the revolution can take place without civil war is equivalent to thinking that there can be a " peaceful " revolution. Anyone who believes this (as the mensheviks who utter laments concerning the hurtfulness of civil war believe it) is turning away from Marx to those antediluvian socialists who imagine that the factory owners can be talked over. We might just as well hope by petting a tiger to persuade the animal to live upon grass and to leave cattle alone ! Marx was an advocate of the civil war, that is to say of the fight of the armed proletariat against the bourgeoisie. Writing with reference to the Paris Commune (the rising of the Parisian workers in the year 1871), Marx declares that the communards had not been sufficiently resolute. He uses reproachful terms in the manifesto of the First International. [The Civil War in France.] We read : " Even the sergents-de-ville, instead of being disarmed and locked up, as ought to have been done, found the gates of Paris flung wide open, for their safe retreat to Versailles. The men of the ' party of order ' " [this was the name then given to the counter-revolutionaries] " were not only left unharmed ; they were allowed to rally and quietly to seize more than one stronghold in the very heart of Paris. . . . In its reluctance to continue the civil war opened by Thiers " [the French counterpart of Denikin] " . . . the Central Committee made a grave mistake. It was urgently necessary to attack Versailles, . . . to put an end, once for all, to the plots of Thiers and the Rurals. Instead of this, the ' party of order ' was again allowed to test its strength at the ballot-box, in the communal elections of March 26th." Here Marx clearly advocates the armed suppression of the counter-revolution; he advocates civil war. Engels, too, wrote as follows : " Would the Commune of Paris have held its ground for a single day unless it had put its trust in the authority of the armed people against the bourgeoisie ? Have we not, rather, the right to blame the Commune for having made so little use of its powers of compulsion ? " And this is how Engels defines the term revolution : " A revolution is an act in which one part of the population imposes its will upon the other part by means of rifles, bayonets, and artillery."

We see that the leaders of socialism took a very serious view of revolution. They understood that the proletariat cannot peacefully persuade the bourgeoisie; they understood that the workers must impose their will by means of victory in a civil war fought with " rifles, bayonets, and artillery."

Civil war ranges one against another, with arms in their hands, the two classes of capitalist society, the two classes whose interests are diametrically opposed. The fact that capitalist society is split up into two parts, that it essentially consists of at least two distinct societies—this fact is obscured at ordinary times. For what reason ? Because the slaves passively obey their masters. But in time of civil war this passive obedience comes to an end, and the oppressed portion of society rises against the oppressors. It is obvious that in such circumstances the classes cannot possibly " live harmoniously side by side." The army splits up into White Guards consisting of the aristocracy, the bourgeoisie, the richer members of the professional classes, and so on, and Red Guards consisting of workers and peasants. It is now impossible that there should be a parliament of any sort in which factory owners and workers sit together. How can they meet " peacefully " in parliament when they are shooting one another in the streets ? In time of civil war, class takes up arms against class. This is why the struggle can only end through a victory of one of the two classes. It cannot end in an agreement, or in any sort of compromise. Such a view has been fully confirmed by the experience of civil war in Russia and elsewhere (Germany and Hungary). There must speedily ensue a dictatorship, either of the proletariat or of the bourgeoisie. Government by the middle classes and their parties (the Social Revolutionary

Party, the Menshevik Party, etc.) is merely a bridge by which we pass to one side or the other. When the Soviet Government of Hungary was overthrown with the aid of the mensheviks, its place was taken for a brief space by a " coalition," but then an absolutist reactionary government was established. From time to time the Constitutional Social Revolutionary Party would come to the top in Ufa, Transvolgia, or Siberia, but within twenty-four hours it was always overthrown by Admiral Kolchak, who was supported by the great capitalists and the landlords. This meant the establishment of a landlord-capitalist dictatorship instead of a worker-peasant dictatorship.

A DECISIVE VICTORY OVER THE ENEMY AND THE REALISATION OF THE DICTATORSHIP OF THE PROLETARIAT—SUCH WILL BE THE INEVITABLE OUTCOME OF THE WORLD-WIDE CIVIL WAR.

§ 33.

The Forms of the Civil War and its Cost. The epoch of civil wars was ushered in by the Russian revolution, itself no more than the herald, the beginning, of a revolution that will be general and world-wide. The revolution began earlier in Russia than elsewhere because in Russia the decomposition of capitalism set in earlier. The Russian bourgeoisie and the Russian landowning class hoped for the conquest of Constantinople and Galicia. In conjunction with their allies they participated in the cooking of the hell's broth of 1914. Through their weakness and lack of organisation, they were the first to collapse, so that chaos and famine appeared in Russia earlier than elsewhere. For that reason it was especially easy for the Russian proletariat to deal with its class enemies. This is why the Russian workers were the first to gain a decisive victory, the first to establish their dictatorship.

We must not infer that the Russian communist revolution is the most thoroughgoing revolution in the world ; nor must we infer that the less developed capitalism is in any country, the more " revolutionary " will be that country and the nearer to communism. The logical consequence of such a view would be that the complete realisation of socialism would first occur in China, Persia, Turkey, and other countries where practically no proletariat has as yet come into existence. Were this the case, the teaching of Marx would be completely falsified.

Anyone who reasons thus, is confusing two things : on the one hand, the beginning of the revolution ; on the other hand, its character, its degree of thoroughness. The revolution began earlier in Russia owing to the immaturity and weakness of capitalist development in that country. But precisely because of that immaturity and weakness, precisely because Russia is a backward country where the proletariat is in a minority, where there is a large number of petty traders, and so on, it is difficult for us to organise an integral communist economy. In England the revolution will come later. But there the proletariat, after its victory, will organise communism more swiftly. In Britain the proletariat constitutes a very large majority of the population ; the workers are accustomed to collective labour ; production is highly centralised. That is why the revolution will come later in England, but why, when it comes, it will be more highly developed, more far-reaching than ours.

Many persons have supposed that the ferocious character of our civil war is due to the backwardness of our country, or to some peculiar " Asiatic " traits. The opponents of revolution in western Europe are in the habit of saying that " Asiatic socialism " flourishes in Russia, and that in " civilised " lands a revolutionary change will be effected without atrocities. Obviously this is all nonsense. Where capitalist development is far advanced, the resistance of the bourgeoisie will be more stubborn. The intelligentsia (the professional classes, the technicians, the managing engineers, the army officers, etc.) are more strongly solidarised with capital, and are for that reason far more hostile to communism. In such countries, therefore, the civil war will inevitably assume a more savage form than in Russia. The course of the German revolution has actually proved that the war assumes harsher forms in countries where capitalist development is farther advanced.

Those who complain of the bolshevist Terror forget that the bourgeoisie sticks at nothing for the protection of its money-bags. With reference to this matter, the resolution passed by the first congress of the Third International runs as follows :

" When the imperialist war was beginning to be transformed into civil war, and when for the governing class (the greatest criminals known to history) the danger was imminent that its merciless regime would collapse, its brutality grew greater than ever. . . .

" Russian generals, living embodiments of the tsarist system, organised the shooting down of the workers on a large scale, and continue to do this with the direct or indirect connivance of the traitors to socialism. When the Social Revolutionary Party and the Menshevik Party were in power, the prisons were filled with thousands of workers and peasants, and the generals had entire regiments shot for disobedience. Krasnoff and Denikin, with the kind cooperation of the allied governments, have slaughtered the workers by tens of thousands, hanging them, or shooting every tenth man. As a deterrent, they often leave whole rows of gibbeted corpses hanging for three days. In Ural and Transvolgia the bands of Czecho-Slovak White Guards have cut off prisoners' hands and feet, have drowned prisoners in the Volga, have buried them alive. In Siberia the generals have slaughtered communists by the thousand and have butchered innumerable workers and peasants.

" The German and Austrian bourgeois made an open display of their bestial tendencies in Ukraine, where they hanged on portable iron gallows the workers and peasants whom they had robbed, and hanged communists who were their own fellow-countrymen, our Austrian and German comrades. In Finland, one of the homes of bourgeois democracy, they helped the Finnish bourgeois to shoot from 13,000 to 14,000 proletarians and to torture more than 15,000 to death in the prisons. In Helsingfors, wishing to protect themselves from machine-gun fire, they drove women and children in front of their ranks. Thanks to their aid, the Finnish White Guards and their Swedish assistants were able to enjoy this orgy of blood when they had conquered the Finnish proletariat. In Tammerfors, they compelled women and children to dig their own graves before being slaughtered. In Viborg, they killed thousands of Russians, men, women, and children.

" Within their own frontiers the German bourgeois and the German social democrats, manifested an even greater degree of reactionary violence. Risings of the communist workers were drowned in blood ; Karl Liebknecht and Rosa Luxemburg were brutally murdered ; the Spartacist workers were massacred. The flag under which the bourgeoisie marches is the flag of the White Terror— the mass Terror and the individual Terror.

" We see the same picture in other lands. In democratic Switzerland everything is ready for the punishment of the workers should they dare to infringe capitalist law. In America it would seem that the prison, lynch law, and the electric chair, are the chosen symbols of democracy and freedom. In Hungary and Britain, in Czecho-Slovakia and Poland—everywhere it is the same. The bourgeois assassins do not shrink from the most atrocious actions. In the hope of strengthening their regime they encourage jingoism, and they organise abominable anti-Jewish pogroms, even worse than those which used to be organised by the tsarist police. . . . When the Polish reactionaries and the ' socialist ' rabble murdered the representatives of the Russian Red Cross, this was but an additional drop in the ocean of crimes and atrocities perpetrated by bourgeois cannibalism in its death agony."

As the civil war develops, it assumes new forms. When in any country the proletariat is oppressed beyond measure, it leads this war by a revolt against the State authority of the bourgeoisie. Now let us suppose that in one country or another the proletariat has been victorious and has taken the State authority into its own hands. What happens in this case ? The proletariat has the organised State power at its service, it has the proletarian army, it has the entire apparatus of power. Then the proletariat has to fight with the bourgeoisie of its own land, which organises plots and risings against the proletarian authority. Furthermore, the proletariat organised as the State has to fight with bourgeois States. Here the civil war assumes a new form, for the class war becomes war in the ordinary sense when the proletarian State is fighting against bourgeois States ; the workers are now not simply fighting against the bourgeoisie, but the workers' State is engaged in formal warfare against the imperialist States of capital. This war is carried on, not for the seizure of others' goods, but for the victory of communism, for the dictatorship of the working class.

This is what has actually occurred. After the Russian revolution of November, 1917, the Soviet Government was attacked upon all sides by the capitalists ; by the British, the Germans, and the French, by the Americans and the Japanese, and so on. The more the workers of other lands became infected by the example of the Russian revolution, the more firmly did international capitalism close its ranks against the revolution, the more vigorously did it attempt to establish a robber alliance of capitalists against the proletariat.

Upon the initiative of the trickster Wilson, the leader of American capitalism, an attempt to form such an alliance was made at the so-called peace conference of Versailles. The robber alliance was christened the League of Nations, this being intended to signify that it was a " league of peoples." In reality it is not a league of peoples, but a league of the capitalists of various countries and of their State authorities.

This league is in the nature of an attempt to form a world-wide trust of monstrous proportions which shall embrace the whole surface of the globe in a grasp of universal exploitation, and which, on the other hand, shall crush with the utmost ferocity the working-class movement of revolt and revolution. It is pure fable to say that the League of Nations has been founded to promote the cause of peace. In actual fact it has a twofold aim : the ruthless exploitation of the proletariat throughout the world, of all colonies and of the colonial slaves ; and the crushing of the incipient world revolution.

In the League of Nations, the U.S.A., which became inordinately rich during the war, plays the first fiddle. All the bourgeois States of Europe are now heavily indebted to America. The United States is very powerful for the additional reason that she has vast quantities of raw materials and fuel, and is a great wheat-producing country. She wishes to use these advantages in such a way as to make all her fellow robbers dependent on her. Infallibly she will become the leader of the League of Nations.

Very interesting is the way in which the United States veils its preeminently predatory policy behind a cloud of fine phrases. When, in pursuit of plunder, she entered the war, her watchwords were " the salvation of mankind," " the rescue of the enslaved peoples," and so on. It suited the United States that Europe should be disintegrated, should consist of dozens of petty lands, formally " independent " but substantially dependent upon America. This predatory interest was masked by an exalted phrase concerning " the right of the nations to self-determination." The capitalist gendarmerie, the White Guards, and the White Police, which, according to Wilson's plan, were to be ready everywhere to crush the revolution, would exist to ensure punishment for " breaches of the peace." In the year 1919 all the imperialists suddenly became pacifically minded, and raised a clamour to the effect that the bolsheviks were the real imperialists, the true enemies of peace. Plans for the stifling of the revolution masqueraded as zeal for peace and democracy.

The League of Nations has already shown itself to be an international policeman and executioner. Its executive officers overthrew the Soviet Republics in Hungary and Bavaria. They have continually endeavoured to crush the Russian proletariat ; in the north and in the south, in the west and in the east of Russia, the British, the American, the Japanese, the French, and other armies have made common cause with the Russian enemies of the working class. The League of Nations used black troops against the Russian and Hungarian workers (in Odessa and in Budapest). The depth of baseness to which the League of Nations can descend is shown by the fact that these " civilised " brigands entered into a Butchers' League in partnership with General Yudenich, who was chief of the so-called North-Western Administration. The League of Nations incites Finland, Poland, etc., to attack Soviet Russia ; with the aid of the consuls of the foreign Powers it organises conspiracies ; its agents blow up bridges, throw bombs at the communists, and so on. There is no atrocity of which the League of Nations is not capable.

The more vigorous the proletarian onslaught, the more firmly do the capitalists close their ranks. In the Communist Manifesto, penned in the year 1847, Marx and Engels wrote : " A spectre haunts Europe, the spectre of communism. All the powers of old Europe have united in a holy alliance to lay this spectre—the pope and the tsar, Metternich and Guizot, the French radicals and the German police." Many years have passed since then. The spectre of communism has begun to clothe itself in flesh and blood. In the campaign against it are arrayed, not only " old Europe," but the entire capitalist world. Nevertheless the League of Nations will be unable to fulfil its two aims, which are the organisation of the world economy into a single trust and the universal suppression of the revolution. There is not sufficient unity even among the Great Powers. The United States is hostile to Japan, and both these Powers are arming for the fight. It is hardly credible that there can be much friendly feeling between defeated Germany and the " disinterested " robber Entente. Here is certainly a rift in the lute. The lesser States are fighting one with another. Still more important is the occurrence of a number of colonial risings and wars—in India, Egypt, Ireland, etc. Enslaved countries are beginning to fight against their " civilised " European slave-drivers. To the civil war, the class war waged by the proletariat against the imperialist bourgeoisie, there are superadded colonial risings which help to undermine and destroy the dominion of world-wide imperialism. Thus the imperialist system is being broken up by two different groups of influences. On the one hand, we have the upward movement of the proletariat, the wars waged by the proletarian republics, and the revolts and the wars carried on by the nations enslaved to the imperialists. On the other hand, we have the oppositions and disharmonies among the great capitalist Powers. Instead of " lasting peace," there is complete chaos ; instead of universal repression of the proletariat, there is fierce civil war. In this civil war the strength of the proletariat waxes while the strength of the bourgeoisie wanes. The inevitable issue of the struggle will be the victory of the proletariat.

Certainly the victory of the proletarian dictatorship will not be achieved on easy terms. The civil war, like any other war, demands the sacrifice of persons and the sacrifice of material values. Every revolution involves such costs. A natural consequence is that in the opening phases of this civil war the devastation due to the imperialist war is in various places considerably increased. It is obvious that when the best workmen, instead of working or organising production, go to the front rifle in hand to defend themselves against the landlords and the military caste, the life of the factories must suffer. Plainly, the disorganisation that results from the civil war is harmful. Manifestly, the loss of comrades that ensues is a costly sacrifice. But this is inevitable in every revolution. During the bourgeois revolution in France, in the years 1789–1793, when the bourgeoisie was breaking the yoke of the landlords, the civil war brought much disorganisation in its train. When, however, the caste of landlords and aristocrats had been conquered, the development of France was rapid and extensive.

No one can fail to understand that in so gigantic a revolution as the universal revolution of the proletariat, which effects the overthrow of a system of oppression that required centuries to upbuild, the cost must be exceedingly great. We have seen that the civil war is now conducted upon a world-wide scale. In part it takes the form of a war waged by bourgeois States against proletarian States. The proletarian States which are defending themselves against the imperialist robbers, are waging the class war, which is in actual fact a holy war. But this war demands the sacrifice of blood. The wider the extent of the war, the larger will be the number of victims, and the more extensive will be the disorganisation.

But because revolution is costly, we must not for that reason set our faces against revolution. The capitalist system, the growth of centuries, culminated in the monstrous imperialist war, in which rivers of blood were shed. What civil war can compare in its destructive effects with the brutal disorganisation and devastation, with the loss of the accumulated wealth of mankind, that resulted from the imperialist war ? MANIFESTLY IT IS ESSENTIAL THAT HUMANITY SHALL MAKE AN END OF CAPITALISM ONCE

AND FOR ALL. WITH THIS GOAL IN VIEW, WE CAN ENDURE
THE PERIOD OF CIVIL WARS, AND CAN PAVE THE WAY FOR
COMMUNISM, WHICH WILL HEAL ALL OUR WOUNDS, AND
WILL QUICKLY LEAD TO THE FULL DEVELOPMENT OF THE
PRODUCTIVE FORCES OF HUMAN SOCIETY.

§ 34.

Chaos or Communism. The revolution as it develops
becomes a world revolution for the same reason that the
imperialist war became a world war. All important countries
are interconnected, they are all parts of the world economy,
nearly all of them were involved in the war, and were united
by the war in a common understanding. In all countries
alike, the war produced terrible devastation, led to famine,
and to the enslavement of the proletariat. Everywhere it
promoted the gradual decomposition and decay of capitalism,
and ultimately caused a revolt against the savage discipline
in the army, the factory, and the workshop. With the like
inevitability it led to the communist revolution of the
proletariat.

Once they had begun, the disintegration of capitalism
and the growth of the communist revolution could no longer
be stayed. The ruin of capitalism was imminent. Every
attempt to establish a truly human society upon the old
capitalist foundations is foredoomed to absolute failure.
The class consciousness of the proletarian masses is now so
fully developed, that they neither can nor will work for
capital. They refuse to slay one another in the interests
of capital, of colonial policy, etc. The army of William II
cannot possibly be reestablished in Germany to-day. And
just as it is impossible to reestablish an imperialist discipline
in the army, just as it has become impossible to compel
proletarian soldiers to subject themselves to the yoke of
junker generals, so is it impossible to reestablish the capitalist
discipline of labour, and to compel the workers to toil for a
master or the peasants to toil for a landlord. The new army
can only be created by the proletariat ; the new labour
discipline can only be created by the working class.

We are thus confronted by two alternatives, and two
only. There must either be complete disintegration, hell
broth, further brutalisation and disorder, *absolute chaos,*

or else communism. All attempts that have been made to reestablish capitalism in a country where for a time the masses have had power in their own hands, confirm this statement of alternatives. Neither the Finnish bourgeoisie nor the Hungarian bourgeoisie, neither Kolchak nor Denikin nor Skoropadsky, was in a position to restore economic life. They were unable to establish even their own bloody system upon a firm footing.

THE ONLY ISSUE FOR HUMANITY IS COMMUNISM. AND SINCE COMMUNISM CAN BE REALISED ONLY BY THE PROLETARIAT, THE PROLETARIAT IS TO-DAY THE TRUE SAVIOUR OF MANKIND FROM THE HORRORS OF CAPITALISM, FROM THE BARBARITIES OF EXPLOITATION, FROM COLONIAL POLICY, INCESSANT WARS, FAMINE, A LAPSE INTO SAVAGERY AND BRUTALISATION, FROM ALL THE ABOMINATIONS THAT ARE ENTAILED BY FINANCIAL CAPITAL AND IMPERIALISM. HEREIN LIES THE SPLENDID HISTORIC SIGNIFICANCE OF THE PROLETARIAT. THE WORKERS MAY SUFFER DEFEAT IN INDIVIDUAL BATTLES, AND EVEN IN INDIVIDUAL COUNTRIES. BUT THE VICTORY OF THE PROLETARIAT IS NO LESS CERTAIN THAN THE RUIN OF THE BOURGEOISIE IS INEVITABLE.

From the foregoing it is plain that all groups, classes, and parties which believe the reestablishment of capitalism to be possible, which imagine that the time is not yet ripe for the coming of socialism, are in fact, whether they wish it or not and whether they know it or not, playing the part of counter-revolutionaries and reactionaries. Of this character are all the parties that preach class collaboration. We shall return to the matter in the next chapter.

Literature. KAMENEFF, The economic System of Imperialism. LENIN, Imperialism as the latest Phase of Capitalism. BUHARIN, The World Economy and Imperialism. TSYPEROVICH, Syndicates and Trusts in Russia. ANTONOFF, Militarism. PAVLOVICH, What is Imperialism ? PAVLOVICH, The great Railways. PAVLOVICH, Militarism and Navalism. PAVLOVICH, The Results of the World War. HILFERDING, Financial Capital (a standard work of primary importance but difficult to read). KAUTSKY, The Road to Power. KERZHENTSEFF, British Imperialism. LOZOFFSKY, Iron and Coal, the Fight for Alsace-Lorraine. ZINOVIEFF, Austria and the World War. POKROFFSKY, France during the War. HERASKOFF, Britain during the War. LARIN, The victorious Land. LARIN, The Consequences of the War. ZINOVIEFF, The Triple Alliance and the Triple Entente. LOMOFF, The Break-up of Capitalism and the Organisation of Communism. OSINSKY, The Upbuilding of Socialism. LONDON, The Iron Heel.

CHAPTER FIVE

THE SECOND AND THE THIRD INTERNATIONAL

§ 35. Internationalism of the Workers' Movement essential to the Victory
of the communist Revolution. § 36. The Collapse of the Second
International and its Causes. § 37. The Watchwords "National
Defence" and "Pacifism." § 38. Jingo Socialists. § 39. The Centre.
§ 40. The Third International.

§ 35.

**Internationalism of the Workers' Movement essential
to the Victory of the communist Revolution.** The
communist revolution can be victorious only as a
world revolution. If a state of affairs arose in which one
country was ruled by the working class, while in other
countries the working class, not from fear but from conviction, remained submissive to capital, in the end the
great robber States would crush the workers' State of the
first country. During the years 1917–18–19 all the Powers
were trying to crush Soviet Russia ; in 1919 they crushed
Soviet Hungary. They were, however, unable to crush Soviet
Russia, for the internal conditions in their own countries
were critical, and the governments were all afraid of being
overthrown by their own workers, who demanded the withdrawal of the invading armies from Russia. The significance
of this is, in the first place, that the realisation of proletarian
dictatorship in one country is gravely imperilled unless
active assistance is given by the workers of other lands.
It signifies, in the second place, that, under such conditions,
when the workers have gained the victory in only one country,
the organisation of economic life in that country is a very
difficult matter. Such a country receives little or nothing
from abroad ; it is blockaded on all sides.

If, however, for the victory of communism, it is essential
that there should be a world revolution and that the workers
in various lands should render mutual aid one to another,

138

this implies that the international solidarity of the working class is an essential preliminary to victory. The conditions for the general struggle of the workers are like the conditions for the working-class struggle in each individual country. In any one country the workers cannot win strikes when these are isolated affairs ; they can only win strikes when the workers in separate factories combine for mutual support, when they found a joint organisation, and when they conduct a united campaign against all the factory owners. It is just the same for the workers living in the various bourgeois States. They can only gain the victory when they march shoulder to shoulder, when they do not quarrel among themselves, when the proletarians of all lands unite, feeling themselves to be a single class with interests common to them all. Complete mutual trust, a brotherly alliance, united revolutionary action against world capitalism—these alone can bring victory to the working class. THE WORKERS' COMMUNIST MOVE-MENT CAN CONQUER ONLY AS AN INTERNATIONAL COMMUNIST MOVEMENT.

The need for an international struggle on the part of the proletariat has long been recognised. In the forties of the last century, on the eve of the revolution of 1848, there already existed an international secret organisation known as the Communist Federation. Marx and Engels were its leaders. At the London conference of the organisation they were instructed to write a manifesto in its name. Such was the origin of the Manifesto of the Communist Party, in which the great champions of the proletariat gave the first exposition of communist teaching.

In 1864 there was constituted under Marx's leadership the International Working Men's Association, now commonly spoken of as the *First International*. In the First International there were associated a number of working-class leaders from various countries, but unity was lacking. Moreover, the organisation was not yet based upon the broad masses of the workers, but rather took the form of an international society of revolutionary propagandists. In 1871 the members of the International took part in the rising of the Parisian workers (the Commune of Paris). There ensued everywhere a persecution of the branches of the International. It collapsed in 1874, having been greatly weakened by internal dissensions, by the struggles between the adherents of Marx and those of the anarchist, Bakunin. After the break-up of the First International, the growth of socialist parties began in various countries. The more rapid the development of industry, the more rapid was the growth of these parties. The need for mutual support was felt so strongly, that in 1889 there was held an international socialist congress attended by delegates of the socialist parties of numerous countries. Thus the *Second International* came into being. The Second International remained in existence till 1914, when the war gave it its death blow. The causes of its failure will be discussed in the next section.

In the Communist Manifesto, Marx already sounded the war cry : " Proletarians of all lands, unite'! " Here are the concluding lines of the manifesto : " The communists disdain to conceal their views and aims. They openly declare that their ends can only be attained by the forcible overthrow of the existing social order. Let the ruling classes tremble at a communist revolution. The proletarians have nothing to lose but their chains. They have a world to win. Proletarians of all lands, unite ! "

It thus appears that the international solidarity of the proletariat is not a toy or a fine phrase, but a vital necessity, without which the working-class movement would be foredoomed to failure.

§ 36.

The Collapse of the Second International and its Causes.

When the great world war began in August, 1914, the socialist and social-democratic parties of the various belligerent lands (with the exception of Russia, Serbia, and at a later date Italy), instead of declaring war upon the war and instead of inciting the workers to revolt, rallied to the side of their respective governments, and gave their assistance to the campaign for plunder. On one and the same day, the socialist deputies in France and Germany voted the war credits in parliament, thus solidarising themselves with the robber governments. Instead of joining forces in a rising against the criminal bourgeoisie, the socialist parties took up separate stands, each under the banner of its " own " bourgeois government. The war began with the direct support of the socialist parties ; the leaders of these parties turned their coats and betrayed the cause of socialism. The Second International died an ignominious death.

It is interesting to note that, only a few days before the betrayal, the socialist press and the leaders of the socialist parties were holding forth against the war. Gustave Hervé, for example, the traitor to French socialism, wrote as follows in his newspaper " La Guerre Sociale " [The Class War, subsequently rechristened Victory] : " We are to fight in order to save the tsar's prestige ! . . . How delightful to die in so glorious a cause !" Three days before the outbreak of war, the French Socialist Party issued a manifesto against it, and the French syndicalists wrote in their journal, "Workers ! If you are not cowards, protest !" The German social democrats held numerous great meetings of protest. The memory of the resolution passed at the Basle international congress was still fresh, a resolution to the effect that in case of war all possible means must be employed " to incite the people to revolt and to hasten the collapse of capitalism." But within a day or two these same parties and these same leaders were insisting upon the need for " the defence of the fatherland " (this meaning the defence of the robber State of their " own " bourgeoisie). In Austria the " Arbeiter Zeitung " [Worker's Gazette] actually declared that the workers must rally to the defence of " German humanity " !

In order to understand the inglorious collapse of the Second International, we must study the development of the working-class movement prior to the war. Before this conflict, capitalism in Europe and the U.S.A. had largely owed its development to the frantic plunder of the colonies. The loathsome and sanguinary aspects of capitalism were here displayed with exceptional clearness. By brutal exploitation, by robbery, fraud, and force, values were extracted from the colonial nations, and were transmuted into profit for the sharks of European and American financial capital. The stronger the position of any State capitalist trust in the world market, the larger were the profits it could derive from the exploitation of the colonies. Out of these surplus profits the trust could afford to pay its wage slaves a trifle more than the ordinary wages of labour. Not of course to all the wage workers, but only to those who are usually spoken of as skilled workers. These strata of the working class are thereby won over to the side of capital. Their reasoning runs as follows : " If ' our ' industry finds a market in the African colonies, so much the better ; it will flourish all the more ; the boss will make larger profits, and we shall have a finger in the pie." Thus capital fetters its wage slaves to its own State, buying one section of them, who are attracted by a share in the colonial plunder.

The founders of scientific communism had already taken note of this phenomenon. Engels, for example, in a letter to Kautsky, wrote in the year 1882 : " You ask me what the British workers think about colonial policy. Very much the same as what they think about politics in general. Here there does not yet exist a labour party ; there are only conservatives and liberal radicals ; while the workers gladly participate in those advantages which accrue to the British in virtue of their monopoly on the world market and in the colonies." Upon this soil has flourished a peculiar form of servility, an attach- ment of the workers to the bourgeoisie of their own country, an abasement before them. Engels wrote in 1889 : " The most repulsive phenomenon here in England is the bourgeois respectability which soaks into the very marrow of the workers. . . . So deeply rooted is this inborn respect for ' betters ' and ' superiors ' that Mr. Bourgeois finds it an easy matter to catch the workers in his nets. I really believe that, at the bottom of his heart, John Burns is more flattered by his popularity with Cardinal Manning and other notables, with the bourgeoisie generally, than by his popularity with his own class."

The working masses were not accustomed to carry on a great fight upon the international scale. Indeed, they had no opportunity for anything of the sort. For the most part the activity of their organisations was confined within the limits of the State administered by their own bourgeoisie. " Their own " bourgeoisie managed to interest in colonial policy a section of the working class, and chiefly the stratum of skilled workers. The same bait was swallowed by the leaders of the working-class organisations, by the working- class bureaucracy, and by the parliamentary represen- tatives of the workers, these being all persons who had secured cosy corners, and were inclined to advocate " peace- ful," " quiet," and " law-abiding " methods. We have already pointed out that the bloodthirsty aspects of capitalism were especially displayed in the colonies. In Europe and the United States, industry was highly developed, and in these regions the struggle of the working class had assumed comparatively peaceful forms. Since 1871 there had been no great revolutions anywhere except in Russia, and in most countries there had been none since 1848. People were universally accustomed to the idea that the future development of capitalism would be peaceful, and even those who spoke of coming wars hardly believed their own words. A section of the workers, including the working- class leaders, was more and more inclined to accept the idea that the working class was interested in colonial policy and that the workers ought to join forces with their own bourgeoisie in order to promote, in this matter, " the common national welfare." Consequently, large numbers of the lower middle class flocked into the socialist parties. In Germany, for example, among the members of the social-democratic parliamentary group, there was quite a number of publicans and keepers of working-class restaurants. In 1892, out of 35 socialist M.P.'s, there were 4 following these occupations ; in 1905, there were 6 out of 81 ; in 1912, there were 12 out of 110.

It is not surprising that in critical moments their devotion to the imperialist robber State outweighed their devotion to international solidarity.

WE SEE, THEN, THAT THE CHIEF CAUSE OF THE BREAK-UP OF THE SECOND INTERNATIONAL WAS TO BE FOUND IN THE FACT THAT THE COLONIAL POLICY AND THE MONOPOLIST POSITION OF THE GREAT STATE CAPITALIST TRUSTS, HAD ATTACHED THE WORKERS—AND ESPECIALLY THE " UPPER STRATA " OF THE WORKING CLASS—TO THE IMPERIALIST BOURGEOIS STATE.

In the history of the working-class movement it has often happened that the workers have made common cause with their oppressors. For example, in the very early stages of development, the worker who sat at the same table with his master, looked upon his master's workshop almost as if it had been his own, and regarded his master not as an enemy but as a " giver of work." Only in course of time did the workers in various factories come to unite one with another against all the masters. When the great countries had themselves been converted into " State capitalist trusts," the workers continued to display towards these State capitalist trusts the same sort of devotion that in earlier days they had displayed towards individual masters.

Only the war has taught them that they must not take the side of their respective bourgeois States, but must join forces for the overthrow of these bourgeois States and for the realisation of the dictatorship of the proletariat.

§ 37.

The Watchwords " National Defence " and " Pacifism."

The leaders of the socialist parties and of the Second International justified their treason to the cause of the workers and to the common struggle of the working class by saying that it was essential to defend the fatherland.

We have seen that as far as the imperialist war was

concerned this was pure nonsense. In that war not one of the Great Powers was on the defensive; all were aggressors. The slogan "defence of the fatherland" (the defence of the bourgeois State) was humbug, and was shouted by the leaders in order to hide their treason.

Here it is necessary to consider the question in somewhat greater detail.

First of all, what is our fatherland? What is the real meaning of this word? Does it mean, people who all speak the same language; is it the same as "nation"? No, it is not, Let us consider, for example, tsarist Russia. When the Russian bourgeoisie clamoured for the defence of the fatherland, it was not thinking of the area in which people of one nationality were living, of the area, say, inhabited by the White Russians; it was referring to the peoples of various nationalities who are settled in Russia. What, in fact, did the bourgeoisie mean? Nothing else than the State authority of the Russian bourgeoisie and the landlords. This is what the capitalists wanted the Russian workers to defend. Really, of course, they were not thinking simply of defending it, but of extending its frontiers to include Constantinople and Cracow. When the German bourgeoisie sang the defence of the fatherland, what was the meaning in that case? Here the reference was to the authority of the German bourgeoisie, to an extension of the boundaries of the robber State ruled by William II.

We have, then, to enquire whether, under capitalism, the working class has any fatherland at all. Marx, in The Manifesto of the Communist Party, replied to this question by saying: "The workers have no country." What he said was true. Why? The answer is very simple. Because under capitalism the workers have no power; because under capitalism everything is in the hands of the bourgeoisie; because under capitalism the State is merely an instrument for the suppression and oppression of the working class. We have already seen that the task of the proletariat is to destroy the bourgeois State, not to defend it. Then only will the proletariat have a country, when it has seized the State authority and has become master of the country. Then, and only then, will it be the duty of the proletariat to defend its fatherland; for then it will be defending its own authority and its own cause; it will not be defending the authority of its enemies, and will not be defending the robber policy of its oppressors.

The bourgeoisie is well aware of all this. Here is evidence of the fact. When the proletariat had effected the conquest of power in Russia, the Russian bourgeoisie began to fight against Russia, forming an alliance with anyone who was willing—with the Germans, the Japanese, the British, the Americans, with all the world and his wife. Why? Because, having lost power in Russia, it had also lost the power of robbing and plundering, the power of bourgeois exploitation. The Russian capitalists were ready at any moment to destroy *proletarian* Russia, to destroy, that is, the Soviet Power. Let us take Hungary for another example. When the bourgeois had the power in their own hands, they issued appeals for the defence of the fatherland; but in order to destroy proletarian Hungary they were prompt to enter into an alliance with the Rumanians, the Czecho-Slovaks, the Austrians, and the Entente. We see, then, that the bourgeoisie knows perfectly well what it is about. Under the plea of the defence of the fatherland, it appeals to all citizens to defend its own bourgeois power, and it sentences for high treason all who refuse to assist. On the other hand, when it is a question of destroying the proletarian fatherland, it assembles all its forces and sticks at nothing.

The proletariat must take a leaf out of the bourgeois book; it must destroy the *bourgeois* fatherland and must do nothing for its defence or enlargement; but the proletariat must defend its *own* fatherland with all its might and to the last drop of its blood.

To these considerations the objector may reply as follows. Do you not know, he will say, that colonial policy and imperialism have helped the industrial development of the Great Powers, and that, thanks to this, crumbs from the masters' table fall to the working class? Surely this means that the worker should defend his master, should help his master against competitors?

It means nothing of the kind. Let us suppose that there are two manufacturers whom we will call Schultz and Petroff. They are rivals in the market. Schultz says to his men: " Friends, stand by me with all your strength. Do all the harm you can to the Petroff factory, to Petroff himself, to his workmen. Then my factory will flourish, for I shall have downed Petroff and my business will boom. I shall be able to give all you fellows a rise."

Petroff says just the same to his men. Now let us
suppose that Schultz has the best of it. It is quite
likely that in the flush of victory he will give his
workers a rise. But after a time he will cut down wages
to the old level. If now the workers in the Schultz factory
go on strike, and would like those who had formerly
worked in the Petroff factory to help them, the latter
would say : " Mighty fine ! You did us all the harm you
could, and now you come crawling to us for help ! Clear
out ! " It would be impossible to arrange for a general
strike. When the workers are disunited, the capitalist
is strong. Now that he has overthrown his competitor,
he is able to get the better of his disunited workers. For
a brief space the workers in Schultz's factory enjoyed higher
wages, but their gains were soon lost. Just the same thing
happens in the international struggle. The bourgeois State
is a masters' league. When one such league grows fat at
the expense of the others, it is able to bribe the workers.
The collapse of the Second International and the betrayal
of socialism by the leaders of the working-class movement
occurred because these leaders determined to " defend "
the crumbs that fell from the masters' table and hoped
for an increase in the amount of these crumbs. During the
war, when, owing to the aforesaid treason, the workers were
disunited, capital in all countries imposed terrible burdens
upon them. The workers came to realise their mis-
calculation ; they came to understand that their leaders
had sold them for the merest trifle. Thus began the rebirth
of socialism. We can readily understand that the first
protests came from the badly paid, unskilled workers. The
" aristocracy of labour " (the printers, for instance) and
the old leaders, continued to play a traitor's game.

Not content with using the slogan of the defence of the
(bourgeois) fatherland, the bourgeoisie has another means
with which to cheat and befool the working masses. We
refer to the so-called *pacifism*. This name is given to the
view that within the framework of capitalism—without
any revolution, without any revolt of the workers—a reign
of universal peace can be established. It would suffice,
we are told, to set up courts of arbitration between the
various Powers, to abolish secret diplomacy, to agree upon

disarmament (at first, perhaps, only to a limited extent). With this and a few similar measures, all would be well.

The basic error of pacifism is that the bourgeoisie simply will not carry out any of these fine things like disarmament. It is absolutely absurd to preach disarmament in an era of imperialism and civil war. The bourgeoisie will take care to be well armed ; and if the workers were to disarm or were to fail to arm themselves, they would be inviting destruction. We can thus realise how the pacifist watchwords cannot fail to lead the proletariat astray. PACIFISM TENDS TO PREVENT THE WORKERS FROM CONCENTRATING THEIR ATTENTION UPON THE ARMED STRUGGLE FOR COMMUNISM.

The best example of the fraudulent character of pacifism is furnished by the policy of Wilson, and by his fourteen points. Here, under a garnish of fine words, and in the name of the League of Nations, world-wide plunder and a civil war against the proletariat are promulgated. The following examples will show to what depths of baseness the pacifists can descend. Taft, sometime president of the U.S.A., was one of the founders of the American Peace Society, and at the same time a rabid imperialist. Ford, the famous American motorcar manufacturer, financed entire expeditions to Europe in order to trumpet his pacifist views ; but at the very same time he was netting millions of dollars from the work his factories were doing for the war. Fried, in his Handbook of the Peace Movement (*Handbuch der Friedensbewegung*, vol. ii, pp. 149–150) assures his readers that the joint expedition of the imperialists against China in 1900 proved the " brotherhood of the nations." He writes as follows : " The expedition to China furnished another proof of the ascendancy of the idea of peace in contemporary affairs. An *international association of armies* was displayed. . . . The armies marched, as a pacific force, under the command of a European generalissimo. We, the friends of peace, regard this world generalissimo " [he was writing about Count Waldersee, who was appointed generalissimo by William II] " as merely the forerunner of that world statesman who will be in a position to realise our ideal of peaceful methods." Here we see open and universal robbery designated " the brotherhood of the nations." In like manner, the robber League of Capitalists is dished up with the League of Nations' sauce.

§ 38.

Jingo Socialists. The false watchwords with which, day after day, the bourgeoisie deafened the masses, with which the newspapers were filled, and which clamoured from every hoarding, were also adopted as slogans by the traitors to socialism.

In nearly all countries, the old socialist parties were split up. Three trends were manifest. First of all, there were open and brazen-faced traitors, the jingo socialists. Secondly, there were secret and vacillating traitors, constituting the so-called centre. Thirdly, there were those who remained faithful to socialism. Out of the members of this third group, the communist parties were subsequently organised.

In nearly every country the leaders of the old socialist parties proved to be jingo socialists. Under the banner of socialism, they preached international hatred; under the lying watchword of the defence of the fatherland, they preached the support of the robber bourgeois States. Among the jingo socialists in Germany were Scheidemann, Noske, Ebert, David, Heine, and others; in England, Henderson; in the U.S.A., Russell, Gompers; in France, Renaudel, Albert-Thomas, Guesde, Jouhaux; in Russia, Plehanoff, Potresoff, the right essers (Breshko-Breshkoffskaya, Kerensky, Chernoff), and the right mensheviks (Liber, Rosanoff); in Austria, Renner, Seitz, Victor Adler; in Hungary, Garami, Buchinger, etc.

One and all they were for the " defence " of the bourgeois fatherland. Many of them openly declared themselves in favour of the robber policy of annexations and indemnities, and advocated the seizure of the colonial possessions of other nations. These were usually spoken of as the imperialist socialists. Throughout the war, they supported it, not only by voting the war credits, but by propaganda. In Russia, Plehanoff's manifesto was widely posted on the hoardings by Hvostoff, the tsarist minister of State. General Korniloff made Plehanoff a member of his administration. Kerensky (the social revolutionary) and Tseretelli (the menshevik), concealed the tsar's secret treaties from the people; in the July days, they bludgeoned the Petrograd proletariat; the social revolutionaries and the right mensheviks were members of Kolchak's administration; Rosanoff was one of Yudenich's spies. In a word, like all the bourgeoisie, they stood for the support of the robber bourgeois fatherland, and for the destruction of the proletarian soviet fatherland. The French jingo socialists, Guesde and Albert-Thomas, entered the robber government; they supported all the predatory plans of the Entente;

they stood for the suppression of the Russian revolution and for the sending of troops against the Russian workers. The German jingo socialists entered the ministry while William II was still on the throne (Scheidemann); they supported the emperor when he suppressed the Finnish revolution and when he ravaged Ukraine and Great Russia; members of the Social-Democratic Party (for instance, Winnig in Riga) conducted campaigns against the Russian and the Latvian workers; subsequently, the German jingo socialists murdered Karl Liebknecht and Rosa Luxemburg, and drowned in blood the risings of the communist workers of Berlin, Leipzig, Hamburg, Munich, etc. The Hungarian jingo socialists gave their support to the monarchical government as long as that was in power; afterwards they betrayed the Soviet Republic. IN A WORD, IN ALL COUNTRIES ALIKE, THE JINGO SOCIALISTS ASSUMED THE ROLE OF EXECUTIONERS AGAINST THE WORKING CLASS.

When Plehanoff was still a revolutionist, writing in the Russian newspaper " Iskra " (published in Switzerland) he declared that in the twentieth century, which was destined to witness the realisation of socialism, there would in all probability be a great split in the socialist ranks, and that a fierce struggle would ensue between the two factions. Just as, in the days of the French revolution (1789–1793), the extremist revolutionary party (nicknamed the Mountain) carried on a civil war against the moderates who were later organised as a counter-revolutionary party (spoken of as the Gironde) so— said Plehanoff—in the twentieth century, those who had at one time been brothers in opinion would probably be split into two warring sections, for some of them would have taken sides with the bourgeoisie.

Plehanoff's prophecy was fulfilled. But when he wrote he did not foresee that he himself would be among the traitors.

In this way the jingo socialists (sometimes spoken of as opportunists) are transformed into the open class enemies of the proletariat. During the great world revolution they fight in the ranks of the Whites against the Reds; they march shoulder to shoulder with the military caste, with the great bourgeoisie and with the landlords. It is perfectly clear that we must wage as relentless a war against them as against the bourgeoisie, whose agents they are.

The remnants of the Second International, which the members of these parties have endeavoured to revive, form merely a branch office of the League of Nations. The

SECOND INTERNATIONAL IS NOW ONE OF THE WEAPONS USED
BY THE BOURGEOISIE IN ITS FIGHT WITH THE PROLETARIAT.

§ 39.

The Centre. Another group of parties composed of those
who were once socialists constitutes the so-called " Centre."
Persons of this trend are said to form the " Centre " because
they waver between the communists on one side and the
jingo socialists on the other. Of this complexion are :
in Russia, the left mensheviks under the leadership of Martoff ;
in Germany, the " independents " (the Independent Social
Democratic Party), under the leadership of Kautsky and
Haase ; in France, the group led by Jean Longuet ; in
the U.S.A., the Socialist Party of America, under the
leadership of Hilquit ; in Great Britain, part of the
British Socialist Party, the Independent Labour Party ;
and so on.

At the outset of the war the centrists advocated the
defence of the fatherland (making common cause in this
matter with the traitors to socialism), and they opposed
the idea of revolution. Kautsky wrote that the " enemy
invasion " was the most terrible thing in the world, and
that the class struggle must be postponed until everything
was over. In Kautsky's opinion, as long as the war lasted,
there was nothing whatever for the International to do.
After the conclusion of " peace," Kautsky began to write
that everything was now in a state of such great confusion
that it was no use dreaming about socialism. The reasoning
amounts to this. While the war was on, we must drop
the class struggle, for it would be useless, and we must
wait until after the war ; when peace has come, there is
no use thinking about the class war, for the imperialist
war has entailed general exhaustion. It is plain that
Kautsky's theory is an avowal of absolute impotence, that
it is calculated to lead the proletariat utterly astray, and
that it is closely akin to rank treason. Worse still, when
we were in the very throes of revolution, Kautsky could
find nothing better to do than to raise the hunt against the
bolsheviks. Forgetting Marx's teaching, he persisted in
a campaign against the proletarian dictatorship, the Terror,
etc., ignoring the fact that in this way he was himself assisting

the White Terror of the bourgeoisie. His own hopes would appear to be now those of the ordinary pacifist; he wants courts of arbitration, and things of that sort. Thus he has come to resemble any bourgeois pacifist you care to name.

Although Kautsky's position is to the right of the Centre, we choose him as an example rather than another because his theory is typical of the centrist outlook.

The chief characteristic of centrist policy is the way in which it wobbles between the bourgeoisie and the proletariat. The Centre is unsteady on its legs; wants to reconcile irreconcilables; and at the critical moment betrays the proletariat. During the Russian November revolution, the Russian Centre (Martoff & Co.) vociferated against the use of force by the bolsheviks; it endeavoured to " reconcile " everybody, thus actually helping the White Guards, and reducing the energy of the proletariat in the hour of struggle. The mensheviks did not even exclude from their party those who had acted as spies and plotters for the military caste. In the crisis of the proletarian struggle, the Centre advocated a strike in the name of the Constituent Assembly against the dictatorship of the proletariat. During Kolchak's onslaught, some of these mensheviks, solidarising themselves with the bourgeois plotters, raised the slogan, " Stop the civil war " (the menshevik Pleskoff). In Germany the " independents " played a treacherous part at the time of the rising of the Berlin workers, for they practised their policy of " conciliation " while the fight was actually in progress, and thus contributed to the defeat. Among the independents there are many advocates of collaboration with the Scheidemannites. But the gravest charge against them is that they refrain from the advocacy of a mass rising against the bourgeoisie, and that they wish to drug the proletariat with pacifist hopes. In France and Britain, the Centre " condemns " the counter-revolution; it " protests " in words against the crushing of the revolution; but it displays utter incapacity for mass action.

At the present time the centrist group does quite as much harm as do the jingo socialists. The centrists, sometimes spoken of as the Kautskyites, are attempting, like the jingo socialists, to reanimate the corpse of the Second International and to " reconcile " it with the communists.   Unquestionably, a victory over the counter-revolution is impossible without a definite breach, and without a decisive struggle against them.

The attempts to revive the Second International took place under the benevolent patronage of the robber League of Nations.   For, in fact, the jingo socialists are faithful supporters of the decaying capitalist order, and are its very last props.   The imperialist war could never have continued to rage for five years but for the treachery of the socialist parties.   Directly the period of revolution began, the bourgeoisie looked to the socialist traitors for help in crushing the proletarian movement.   The sometime socialist parties were the chief obstacle in the way of the struggle of the working class for the overthrow of capitalism.   Throughout the war, every one of the traitor socialist parties echoed all that the bourgeoisie said.   After the peace of Versailles, when the League of Nations was founded, the remnants of the Second International (the Centre as well as the jingo socialists) began to reecho all the slogans uttered by the League of Nations.   The League accused the bolsheviks of terrorism, of violating democracy, of Red imperialism. The Second International repeated the accusations.   Instead of engaging in a decisive struggle against the imperialists, it voiced the imperialist war-cries.   Just as the various parties of socialist traitors had supported the respective bourgeois administrations, so did the Second International support the League of Nations.

§ 40.

The Third International.   The jingo socialists and the Centre adopted as their watchword during the war, the defence of the (bourgeois) fatherland, this meaning the defence of the State organisation of the enemies of the proletariat.   A logical sequel was the watchword of the " party truce," which signified universal submission to the bourgeois State.   The matter is perfectly clear.   When Plehanoff or Scheidemann considered it necessary to " defend " the tsarist or kaiserist fatherland, they had, of course, to insist that the workers must do absolutely nothing to interfere with the defence of the robber State.   Consequently, there must be no strikes, and still less must there be any talk of rising against the bourgeoisie. The socialist traitors reasoned as follows. First of all, they said, we must settle accounts with the " foreign " enemy, and then we shall see. For example, Plehanoff declared in his manifesto that there must be no strikes now that Russia was in danger. The workers of all the belligerent lands were enslaved by the bourgeoisie in like manner. But from the first days of the war there were groups of trusty socialists who realised that the " defence of the fatherland " and the " truce of parties " tied the proletariat hand and foot, and that to utter these slogans was treason to the workers. The bolsheviks saw this from the outset. As early as 1914 they declared that there must be no truce with the bourgeoisie, but unceasing struggle against the capitalists—revolution. The first duty of the proletariat in any country is to overthrow its own bourgeoisie—such was the opinion voiced by our party in the early days of the war. In Germany, too, there was formed a group of comrades led by Karl Liebknecht and Rosa Luxemburg. This group took the name of International, declaring that the international solidarity of the proletariat was the first of all duties. Soon Karl Liebknecht openly proclaimed the need for civil war, and incited the workers to armed insurrection against the bourgeoisie. Such was the origin of the party of the German bolsheviks—the Spartacist group. In the other countries, too, there was a split in the old parties. In Sweden there were bolsheviks, who formed what was known as the Left Socialist Party ; while in Norway the " lefts " gained entire control of the party. The Italian socialists took a firm stand throughout. In a word, there gradually came into existence the parties which stood for the revolution. An attempt to secure unified action was now made in Switzerland. In two conferences, at Zimmerwald and Kienthal respectively, were laid the foundations of the Third International. Soon, however, it became apparent that certain dubious elements from the Centre were adhering to the movement, and were in fact hindering it. Within the international union of Zimmerwald there was formed the so-called " Zimmerwald Left " under the leadership of Comrade Lenin. The Zimmerwald Left was in favour of decisive action. It fiercely criticised the Zimmerwald centre led by Kautsky.

After the November revolution and the establishment of the Soviet Power in Russia, that country came to occupy the most important place in the international movement. In order to distinguish itself from the party of the traitors to socialism, and in order to return to the fine old fighting name, our party now called itself the Communist Party. Under the impulsion of the Russian revolution, communist parties were formed in other lands. The Spartacus League changed its name to the Communist Party of Germany. A communist party was formed in Hungary, headed by Bela Kun, who had at one time been a prisoner of war in Russia. Parties were also formed in Austria, Czecho-Slovakia, Finland, etc., and subsequently in France. In the United States, the centre expelled the left wing from the party, and the lefts thereupon organised themselves into a fighting Communist Party. In Britain, negotiations for the formation of a united communist party were begun in the autumn of 1919. To sum up, after the split between the Centre and the Left, the formation and active development of real revolutionary workers' parties began everywhere. The development of these parties led to the formation of a new International, the *Communist International.* In March, 1919, at the Kremlin in Moscow, was held the first international communist congress, at which the Third, or Communist, International was formally constituted. The congress was attended by delegates from the German, Russian, Austrian, Hungarian, Swedish, Norwegian, and Finnish communists; communists from France, the U.S.A., Britain, etc., were also present.

The platform put forward by the German and Russian communists was adopted by the congress with complete unanimity, this showing that the proletariat had planted its feet solidly under the banner of the dictatorship of the proletariat, soviet power, and communism.

The Third International took the name of Communist International in conformity with that of the Communist Federation which had been headed by Karl Marx. In all its works the Third International shows that it is following in the footsteps of Marx, that it is on the revolutionary road towards the forcible overthrow of the capitalist system. It is not surprising that all who are live, trusty, and revolutionary minded members of the international proletariat are turning more and more eagerly towards the new International, and are joining forces to form the workers' vanguard.

The very name Communist International suffices to show that the organisation has absolutely nothing in common with the traitors to socialism.

Marx and Engels considered the name " social democrat " unsuitable for the party of the revolutionary proletariat. " Democrat " signifies one who advocates a particular form of rule. But, as we have previously seen, in the society of the future there will be no " State " of any kind. During the transitional period there will have to be a dictatorship of the workers. Those who have betrayed the working class look no farther than a bourgeois republic. We are out for communism.

In the preface to the 1888 edition of the Communist Manifesto, Engels wrote that the name socialist had in 1847, when the manifesto was penned, signified " men outside the working-class movement, and looking rather to the ' educated ' classes for support " ; but communism in 1847 was a working-class movement. We see the same thing to-day. The communists look for support to the rank and file of the workers ; the social democrats look for support to the aristocracy of the workers, to the professional classes, to the small shopkeepers, and to the petty bourgeoisie in general.

THE COMMUNIST INTERNATIONAL HAS THUS REALISED MARX'S DOCTRINES IN ACTUAL FACT, FOR IT HAS FREED THEM FROM THE ACCRETIONS WHICH HAD FORMED UPON THEM DURING THE " PEACEFUL " PERIOD OF CAPITALIST DEVELOPMENT. THAT WHICH THE GREAT TEACHER OF COMMUNISM WAS PREACHING SEVENTY YEARS AGO, IS BEING FULFILLED TO-DAY UNDER THE LEADERSHIP OF THE COMMUNIST INTERNATIONAL.

Literature. LENIN and ZINOVIEFF, Socialism and the War. LENIN and ZINOVIEFF, Up Stream. ZINOVIEFF, The War and the Crisis in Socialism. LENIN, The proletarian Revolution and the Renegade Kautsky. GORTER, Imperialism.

Zimmerwald Manifestos and Bulletins of the Zimmerwald Committee. The file of the " Communist International."

PART TWO

PRACTICAL

THE DICTATORSHIP OF THE PROLETARIAT AND THE UPBUILDING OF COMMUNISM

THE CONDITIONS OF COMMUNIST ACTIVITY IN RUSSIA

§ 41.

The international Situation of Russia. As we have previously noted, the necessity for the communist revolution arises above all from the circumstance that Russia has become intimately connected with the system of world economy. Our country is now merely a part of the world economy. If the question arises, in what way Russia can advance to the communist system in spite of the backward condition of the country, the answer will mainly be given by pointing to the international significance of the revolution. The proletarian revolution must to-day be a world revolution. On world lines only can it develop. Central and Western Europe will inevitably pass under the dictatorship of the proletariat, and in this way to communism. How, then, could Russia remain a capitalist country if Germany, France, and England were to pass under the proletarian dictatorship ? It is plain that Russia must become involved in the movement to socialism. Her backwardness, the comparatively undeveloped state of her industry, and so on, would all be overcome if Russia were to form part of an international, or even merely a European, soviet republic, and thus to be associated with more advanced lands. It is true that Europe will be terribly exhausted and weakened after the devastation of the war and after the revolution. But a vigorous and highly developed proletariat will be able in the course of a few years to

reestablish the industrial system on a firm footing, and
even backward Russia will be able to do the same. Russia
possesses great natural resources in the form of timber, coal,
mineral oil, iron, etc. ; she has vast corn lands ; with
proper organisation and under peace conditions, all could
be turned to proper account. For our part, we could help
our western comrades with Russian raw materials. Provided that the whole of Europe were to be under the authority
of the proletariat, there would be such a development of
production as would provide amply for all needs. Since,
however, the proletariat will inevitably rise to power everywhere, it is obvious that the mission of the Russian working
class is to do its utmost on behalf of the transformation
to communism. It is for this reason, as we have learned
in Part One, that our party has made the prompt establishment of communism its definite aim.

§ 42.

Large-scale Industry in Russia. Russian manufacturing
industry, however, though a small affair in comparison
with Russian agriculture, had been organised in accordance with the methods of large-scale capitalist production. In Part One we pointed out that in the most
important branches of capitalist production in Russia
there were enterprises employing ten thousand workers
and upwards. From 1907 onwards, the centralisation of
Russian industry made rapid progress, and production
passed under the control of a network of syndicates and
trusts. When the war began, the bourgeoisie started the
organisation of State capitalism. This confirms our view
that Russian industry can be organised and administered
as a unified whole, even though the process may offer difficulties. It is interesting to note that the right social
revolutionaries and the mensheviks, who are never weary of
proclaiming that socialism is absolutely impossible in
Russia, have always advocated the State regulation and
control of industry. But they only believed in the necessity
for this when all authority was in the hands of the bourgeoisie, when the " regulating " and " controlling " power
was to be that of the capitalist State. In other words,
the mensheviks and the essers, despite their protestations

of patriotism, were in favour of State capitalism on the Prussian model. But it is perfectly plain that we cannot believe State capitalism to be possible unless we also believe in the possibility of the socialist organisation of economic life. The only difference between the two systems lies in this, that in one case industry is organised by the bourgeois State, and that in the other case it is organised by the proletarian State. If industrial production in Russia were so backward that there could be no possibility of its being organised by the proletarian State, then there could be no possibility of organising it upon State capitalist foundations either. In a country where large-scale industry does not exist, and where production is carried on by quantities of small masters, it will be impossible to organise industry even upon State capitalist lines. We know perfectly well that the centralisation of industry only becomes possible when the centralisation of capital has advanced to a certain stage. Now Russian capitalism had already reached this stage of centralisation. Even the opponents of communism recognised this by the very fact that they considered it possible for the bourgeois State to " regulate industry." The backwardness of Russian economic life did not consist in the absence of great factories, for there were plenty ; it consisted in the fact that manufacturing industry taken as a whole was of small extent when compared with agriculture. The logical inference is that, despite all difficulties, the Russian proletariat must organise industry in a proletarian fashion, and must maintain its grip of industry until help comes from the west. As far as Russian agriculture is concerned, we must establish a number of focal points where comrades carry on cooperative production. When, however, Russian manufacturing industry is able to join forces with the productive industry of the west, then the joint organisation of production will speedily enable us to draw the petty producers and the peasants into a general and immense cooperative organisation. If, for instance, there existed one great European system of production organised by the working class, then vast quantities of the products of urban industry could be supplied to the rural districts. But town industry will have to furnish these products to the countryside in an organised manner. No longer, as of old, would a hundred thousand petty traders, middlemen, and speculators, cater for the needs of the rural districts.   These needs would be satisfied from State warehouses.   Manifestly, the peasants, too, would have in return to hand over their grain in an organised manner.   By degrees the country districts would become accustomed to social production.   A stage farther on, and rural life would be that of a great cooperative family.   A vigorous and well-organised industrial system would ultimately lead to a communal life in the villages as well.   With the aid of such a system, it would be possible to come to the help of the peasant, who would realise that life on the new plan was a great deal better.

But to reach this goal is difficult.   Many years must pass before the necessary changes can be effected and before life can run smoothly along the new lines.   Why it is difficult will be explained below.

§ 43.

The disastrous Legacy of the imperialist War.   Until the world revolution is victorious, Russia must act alone. Now the Russian working class received a disastrous heritage when it conquered power in the year 1917.   The whole country was disorganised and impoverished.

The war had sapped all the country's strength.   More than half the factories had been compelled to devote themselves to war work, and had squandered materials in the work of destruction.   In the year 1915, out of the eleven and a half milliards of the " national income," six milliards were spent upon the war.   At the very beginning of the revolution, the terrible consequences of the war became apparent.   The output of engineering works had fallen by 40 per cent., and that of textile works by 20 per cent. ; a great reduction was quickly apparent in the supply of coal, iron, and steel.   Between March 1st and August 1st (old style), 1917, 568 enterprises were closed down, and more than 100,000 proletarians were thrown out of work.   The national debt reached unprecedented figures.   Month by month, day by day, the condition of the country became more desperate.

It is plain that the proletariat, when it rose to power

in November, 1917, was faced by a task of unexampled difficulty, by the task of constructing a socialist economy in an utterly disorganised land. The disastrous heritage grew yet more disastrous at the close of the old imperialist war. The mere demobilisation of our army involved enormous expenditure. The transport system had already been shattered and disrupted by the war; demobilisation was the finishing stroke, and the railway system broke down almost completely. Thus transport came practically to an end as well as production.

This is absolutely no argument against the workers' revolution. Had the bourgeoisie remained in power, it would have continued to wage the great imperialist war, would have continued to pay vast sums as interest to the French and to the British, and would have thrown all the burden—this is the chief thing to remember—upon the shoulders of the workers and peasants. Our poverty and exhaustion would more than ever have incited the proletariat to undertake the rebuilding of the old world upon new foundations; with even more economy and with a yet more careful system of organisation would it have been necessary to utilise our old resources; and it would have been necessary to transfer as much of the cost as possible to the bourgeoisie, would have been necessary to protect the working class with whatever powers and by whatever means were at the disposal of the proletarian authority. But this necessary work was thrust upon the revolutionary proletariat under conditions of almost incredible difficulty. The workers had to clear up the mess which the imperialist lords had made.

§ 44.

The Civil War and the Struggle with international Imperialism. The bourgeoisie continued to do everything in its power to hinder the working class from organising production, and to prevent the upbuilding of a workers' society. Immediately after the victory of the proletariat, the bourgeoisie instituted a widespread policy of sabotage. All those who had been high officials, all the managing engineers, teachers, and bank clerks, all those who had been masters, did everything they could to hinder work.

Plot followed upon plot; one counter-revolutionary rising succeeded another. The Russian bourgeoisie entered into alliances with the Czecho-Slovaks, the Entente, the Germans, the Poles, etc.; an attempt was made to crush the Russian proletariat by never-ending fights. The proletariat had to create a huge army, one able to repel the onslaughts of the armies sent by the landlords and capitalists of all lands. The imperialists of the whole world hurled their forces against the Russian proletariat.

This war is for the proletariat a holy war, a war of deliverance, but none the less it involves terrible costs. The remnants of productive industry had to be devoted to the service of the Red Army; thousands of the best organisers among the workers were called to the front. Furthermore, almost at the very outset, the bourgeoisie was able to secure a strong grip of certain regions peculiarly important to the economic life of the country. The military leaders of the Don Cossacks succeeded in depriving the working class of the Donetz coal basin. The British seized the Baku oil-fields. The corn lands of Ukraine, Siberia, and part of Transvolgia, were in the hands of the counter-revolution. The working class, therefore, had not merely to stand to arms and to meet the onslaught of innumerable foes; it was compelled in addition to carry on its proletarian economy in default of some of the most important means of production —in default of fuel and raw materials.

These considerations show us what a martyr's road the workers had to tread. Their first task was to overthrow their enemies. Not until this had been done could they begin to upbuild the new life properly.

In its struggle with the working class, the bourgeoisie likewise availed itself of all the means that could effect the economic overthrow of the Russian proletariat. The capitalists encircled Russia on all sides; the land was rigidly blockaded for years; in their retreats the Whites burned and destroyed everything. For example, Admiral Kolchak burned ten million poods of grain, destroyed a good half of the Volga fleet, and so on. The resistance of the bourgeoisie, its frantic struggles, the aid given to it by world-wide imperialism—these constituted the second great obstacle in the path of the working class.

§ 45.

The petty-bourgeois Character of Russia, the Lack of extensive organisatory Experience on the Part of the Proletariat, etc. We have already seen that production in Russia was sufficiently centralised for the question to arise whether it could be nationalised under proletarian control, whether it could be transferred to the ownership of the workers' State, and whether its organisation on new foundations could be undertaken. But in comparison with the whole economic life of the country, manufacturing industry was still very weak. By far the greater part of the population of Russia is not urban but rural. At the census of 1897, the town population comprised 16,000,000 and the country population comprised 101,000,000 (this includes Siberia, etc., but excludes Finland). In 1913, according to Oganoffsky's estimate, the urban population of Russia was, in round figures, 30,000,000, and the rural population 140,000,000. At that date, therefore, the urban population was a little less than 18 per cent. of the whole. Moreover, of the town dwellers, by no means all belong to the proletariat. The urban population includes the commercial class, the manufacturers, the petty bourgeoisie, and the professional classes. In all, these strata number millions. It is true, of course, that in the country districts we find ex-workmen, semi-proletarians, and the poor peasants. These elements support the workers. But they are less class-conscious than the urban workers, and are not so well organised.

The enormous majority of the population of Russia consists of petty owners. Although they groan under the yoke of the capitalists and the landlords, they are so much accustomed to their system of separate, proprietary, individual economy, that it is very difficult to win them over to the idea of the common cause, to induce them to participate in the upbuilding of a cooperative commonwealth. Ingrained in the mind of every petty proprietor is the notion of grasping something that shall be entirely his own and shall have been taken away from another, the notion of working only for his own account. This is why there will be great difficulties in installing communism in Russia, even if the other difficulties be left out of account.

Our weakness is also reflected in the working class. Generally speaking, the Russian workers are revolutionary minded ; they have a fighting spirit. But we find among them backward elements, persons unaccustomed to organisation. Not all the workers are like those of Petrograd. Many of them are backward and ignorant ; such persons are quite unused to work in a team. There are a great many workers who are newcomers into the town. Most of these have the peasant mentality, and solidarise themselves with the peasantry.

These deficiencies of the working class disappear in proportion as the workers are compelled to struggle for their own cause. It is, however, obvious that the backwardness of a certain proportion is a hindrance to the realisation of our task. But, of course, it does not render realisation impossible.

Literature. Report of the eighth Party Congress, and especially the speeches of LENIN and BUHARIN on the program ; also LENIN'S speech, The Chief Task of our Times.—Concerning the economic position of Russia, consult the following : TSYPEROVICH, Syndicates and Trusts in Russia. MILYUTIN, The Economic Organisation of Soviet Russia. OSINSKY, The Upbuilding of Socialism (the first chapter of this work contains convincing evidence that the devastation caused by the war had rendered socialism inevitable).

CHAPTER SIX

THE SOVIET POWER

§ 46.

The Soviet Power as a Form of proletarian Dictatorship.
Our party was the first to formulate and the first to realise the demand for Soviet Power. The great revolution of November, 1917, was carried through under the watchword, "All power to the soviets!" Until our party took the phrase as its device, the slogan had never been heard of. Not that the notion simply sprang out of our heads! Far from this being the case, the idea was engendered at the very core of life. As early as the revolution of 1905–6, class organisations of the workers, known as soviets of workers' delegates, came into existence. In the revolution of 1917, these organisations appeared in far greater abundance ; almost everywhere there sprouted like mushrooms workers' soviets, soldiers' soviets, and subsequently peasants' soviets. It became clear that these soviets, which had originated as instruments for use in the struggle for power, must inevitably be transformed into the instruments for the wielding of power.

Prior to the Russian revolution of 1917, much had been said and written concerning the dictatorship of the proletariat, but no one clearly understood in what form this dictatorship would be realised. Now, in the Russian revolution, the form of the dictatorship has become manifest as the Soviet Power. THE SOVIET POWER IS THE REALISA-

TION OF THE DICTATORSHIP OF THE PROLETARIAT, ORGANISED
IN ITS SOVIETS AS THE RULING CLASS, AND, WITH THE
AID OF THE PEASANTS, CRUSHING THE RESISTANCE OF THE
BOURGEOISIE AND THE LANDLORDS.

At one time most people believed that the dictatorship
of the proletariat would be possible in the form of a so-called
democratic republic, which would have to be established
by the Constituent Assembly, and which would be administered by a parliament representing all classes of the
population. Even now, the opportunists and the social
solidarians continue to hold the same opinion, declaring
that only the Constituent Assembly and a democratic
republic can save the country from the disasters of
civil war. Actual experience tells a very different tale.
In Germany, for instance, such a republic was set up after
the revolution of November, 1918. Nevertheless, during
the close of 1918 and during 1919 there were sanguinary
struggles. Continually the working class was demanding
the establishment of a soviet regime. The demand for a
soviet regime has in fact become the international watchword
of the proletariat. In all countries the workers sound this
war-cry, in conjunction with the demand for the dictatorship
of the proletariat. Life has confirmed the accuracy of
our slogan, "All power to the soviets," not in Russia alone,
but in every country where there is a proletariat.

§ 47.

Proletarian Democracy and bourgeois Democracy. A
bourgeois democratic republic is based upon universal
suffrage and upon the so-called " will of the people," the
" will of the whole nation," the " united will of all classes."
The advocates of a bourgeois democratic republic, of a
Constituent Assembly, etc., tell us that we are doing violence
to the united will of the nation. Let us consider this matter
first.

In Part One we learned that contemporary society
consists of classes with conflicting interests. For example,
long working hours may be profitable to the bourgeoisie,
but they are disadvantageous to the working class. Peace
between the classes is as impossible as peace between wolves
and sheep. Wolves want to eat sheep, so sheep must defend

themselves against wolves. But if this be so (and unquestionably it is so), then we have to ask whether it is possible for wolves and sheep to have a common will. Every intelligent person knows that it is absurd to talk of anything of the kind. There simply cannot be a will common to sheep and wolves. We must have one thing or the other : either a wolves' will, that of those who enslave the cheated and oppressed sheep ; or else a sheep's will, that of those who wish to deliver the sheep from the wolves and to drive out the plunderers. There can be no middle course in this matter. Now, it is as clear as daylight that the same thing applies to the two main classes of human society. In contemporary society, class is arrayed against class, the bourgeoisie against the proletariat, the proletariat against the bourgeoisie. Between them there is war to the knife. How can they possibly have a common will, a bourgeois-proletarian will ? Obviously there is no more possibility of bourgeois-proletarian desires and aspirations than of wolf-sheep desires and aspirations. We can either have the will of the bourgeoisie, of the class which imposes its will in various ways upon the oppressed majority of the people ; or else we can have the will of the proletariat, of the class which imposes its will upon the bourgeoisie. It is particularly stupid to speak of a will common to all classes, of interests common to the whole nation, in an epoch of civil war, in a period of revolution, when the old world is crumbling to pieces. The proletariat wants to transform the world ; the bourgeoisie wants to strengthen the old slavery.

How can there be a " common " will for bourgeoisie and proletariat ? It is manifest that the very phrase about a will common to the whole nation is humbug if the words are intended to apply to all classes. No such common will has been realised or can be realised.

But this fraud is necessary to the bourgeoisie, necessary for the maintenance of capitalist rule. The capitalists are in the minority. They cannot venture to say openly that this small minority rules. This is why the bourgeoisie has to cheat, declaring that it rules in the name of " the whole people," " all classes," " the entire nation," and so on.

How is the fraud carried out in a " democratic republic " ? The chief reason why the proletariat is enslaved to-day is because it is *economically* enslaved. Even in a democratic republic, the factories and workshops belong to the capitalists, and the land belongs to the capitalists and the landlords. The worker has nothing but his labour power ; the poor peasant has nothing beyond a tiny scrap of land. They are eternally compelled to labour under terrible conditions, for they are under the heel of the master. On paper, they can do a great deal ; in actual fact, they can do nothing. They can do nothing because all the wealth, all the power of capital, is in the hands of their enemies. This is what is termed *bourgeois democracy.*

Bourgeois republics exist in the United States, in Switzerland, and in France. But all these countries are ruled by unscrupulous imperialists, by the trust kings and the bank barons, malignant enemies of the working class. The most democratic republic which existed in the year 1919 was the German Republic with its National Assembly. Yet this was the republic to which the murderers of Karl Liebknecht belonged.

The Soviet Power realises a new, a much more perfect type of democracy—*proletarian democracy.* The essence of this proletarian democracy consists in this, that it *is based upon the transference of the means of production into the hands of the workers.* thus depriving the bourgeoisie of all power. In proletarian democracy, those who formerly constituted the oppressed masses, and their organisations, have become the instruments of rule. In the capitalist system of society, and therefore in bourgeois democratic republics, there existed organisations of workers and peasants. They were, however, overwhelmed by the organisations of the rich. Under proletarian democracy, on the other hand, the rich have been deprived of their wealth. The mass organisations of the workers, the semi-proletarian peasants, etc. (soviets, trade unions, factory committees, etc.), have become the actual foundations of the proletarian State authority. In the constitution of the Soviet Republic we find at the outset the statement : " Russia declares itself to be a republic of workers', soldiers', and peasants' delegates. All power, both central and local, is vested in these soviets."

Soviet democracy does not merely not exclude the workers'

organisations from government, but it actually makes of them the instruments of government. But since the soviets and the other organisations of the working class and the peasantry number their members by the million, the Soviet Power entrusts with new functions innumerable masses of persons who were formerly oppressed and degraded. To an ever greater extent the masses of the people, the workers and the poor peasants, come to participate in the joint labours of the soviets, the trade unions, and the factory committees. This is going on everywhere. In the country towns and in the villages, people who never did anything of the kind before are now actively participating in the work of administration and in the upbuilding of a new life. In this way the Soviet Power secures the widest self-government for the various localities, and at the same time summons the broad masses of the people to participate in the work of government.

It is evident that our party must devote itself to promoting the world-wide development of this new proletarian democracy. We must do our utmost to secure that the widest strata of the proletarians and the poor peasants shall participate to the utmost of their power in the work of the soviets. In one of his pamphlets, published before the November revolution, Comrade Lenin wrote very truly that our task was to see that every cook should be taught to take her share in governmental administration. Of course this is by no means an easy job, and there are many hindrances to its realisation. First among such obstacles comes the low cultural level of the masses. The workers' vanguard is but a small body. In this vanguard, the metal workers, for instance, are conspicuous. But a large proportion of the workers are backward, and this is especially true of the country districts. They lack initiative, they lack creative faculty ; they stand aside and let others take the first steps. The task of our party consists in the systematic and gradual attraction of these backward strata to participate in the general work of administration. Of course the only way of bringing new strata to participate in the work is to raise their cultural level and their capacity for organisation. This, likewise, is the task of our party.

§ 48.

The class Character and the Transitoriness of the proletarian Dictatorship. The bourgeoisie has everywhere concealed its class rule behind the mask of " the cause of the whole people." How could the bourgeoisie, a comparatively small group of parasites, openly acknowledge that it imposes its class will upon all ? How could the bourgeoisie venture to declare that the State is but a league of robbers ? Of course it could do nothing of the kind. Even when the bourgeoisie hoists the bloodstained standard of a militarist dictatorship, it continues to talk of " the cause of the whole people." But the capitalist class is peculiarly adroit in the way in which it cheats the people in the so-called democratic republics. In these, the bourgeoisie rules, and is able to maintain its dictatorship through keeping up certain appearances. The workers are given the right of exercising the parliamentary vote every three or four years, but they are carefully excluded from all power in the administration. Yet because universal suffrage exists, the capitalist class loudly declares that the " whole people " rules.

The Soviet Power openly proclaims its class character. It makes no attempt to conceal that it is a class power, that the Soviet State is the dictatorship of the poor. The point is emphasised in its very name ; the Soviet Government is called the Workers' and Peasants' Government. The constitution, that is to say the fundamental laws of our Soviet Republic, the constitution adopted by the third All-Russian Soviet Congress, expressly declares : " The third All-Russian Soviet Congress of workers', soldiers', and peasants' delegates, declares that now, in the hour of the decisive struggle between the proletariat and the exploiters, there can be no place for the exploiters in any of the instruments of power." The Soviet Power, therefore, not only proclaims its class character, but does not hesitate to deprive of electoral rights and to exclude from the instruments of power the representatives of those classes which are hostile to the proletariat and to the peasantry. For what reason can and must the Soviet Power act thus openly ? Because the Soviet Power really is the power of the working masses, the power of the majority of the population. It has no occasion to conceal that it was born in working-class quarters. Far from it, for the more conspicuously the Soviet Power insists upon its origin and its meaning, the closer will be the ties between itself and the masses, and the more outstanding will be its success in the struggle against the exploiters.

Of course this state of affairs will not last for ever. The essence of the matter lies herein, that it is necessary to crush the resistance of the exploiters. But as soon as the exploiters have been repressed, bridled, and tamed, as soon as they have been trained to work and have become workers like everyone else, the pressure upon them will be relaxed and the dictatorship of the proletariat will gradually disappear.

This is expressly stipulated in our constitution (Part II, Chapter 5): "The fundamental task of the constitution of the Russian Socialist Federative Soviet Republic—a constitution adapted to the needs of the present period of transition—consists in the establishment of the dictatorship of the urban and rural workers and of the poor peasants in the form of a strong All-Russian Soviet Power, whose purpose it will be to effect the complete crushing of the bourgeoisie, to put an end to the exploitation of one human being by another, and to realise socialism, in which there will be neither division into classes nor any State authority."

From this we may deduce the tasks of our party. The party must systematically expose the bourgeois fraud, which is worked as follows. Certain rights are conceded to the worker, but he is left in material dependence upon a master. Consequently the task of our party is to crush the exploiters by all the means at the disposal of the proletariat. Furthermore, it will be incumbent upon our party, in proportion as it is able to crush the exploiters and their hangers-on, in proportion as it is able to refashion them, by degrees to mitigate and to revoke the measures which it was at first necessary to enforce. Let us suppose, for example, that the professional classes have drawn nearer to the working class, that they are no longer hostile to the workers, that in all they do they are wholly on the side of the Soviet Power, that they are on the best of terms with the proletariat. When this happens (and it is only a question of time), it will be incumbent upon us to give the professional classes full civil rights, and to accept them into our family. To-day, when the whole world is in arms against the Workers' Republic, it would be premature to speak of such an extension of rights. But we must never cease to make it perfectly clear that the extension of rights will ultimately be given, and will be given all the sooner, in proportion as there comes a speedier end to the attempts made by the exploiters to overthrow communism. In this manner the proletarian State will gradually die out, and will undergo transformation into a Stateless communist society, wherein the division into classes will have completely disappeared.

§ 49.

Rights of the Workers under bourgeois Democracy and under the Soviet Power. One of the chief frauds of bourgeois democracy consists in this, that it gives only the appearance of rights. On paper we read that the workers can elect to parliament in perfect freedom ; that they have the same rights as the masters (they are said to be " equal before the law ") ; that they have the right of combination and of public meeting ; that they can publish any newspapers and books they please ; and so on. These things are called the " essence of democracy " ; we are assured that democracy is for everyone, for the whole people, for all the citizens, so that conditions are quite different from those in the Soviet Republic.

First of all we must point out that no such bourgeois democracy really exists. It existed a hundred years ago, but Mr. Bourgeois has done away with it long since.

The United States will serve as the best example of this. Here, during the war, the following laws were promulgated : It was forbidden to speak slightingly of the president ; it was forbidden to say anything to the discredit of the Allies ; it was forbidden to declare that the entry of the U.S. and of the Entente into the war was the outcome of sordid, material motives ; it was forbidden to advocate a premature peace ; it was forbidden to utter any public condemnation of the policy of the U.S. government ; it was forbidden to say anything to the credit of Germany ; it was forbidden to advocate the overthrow of the existing order, the abolition of private property, the class war, etc. The penalty for breaking any of these laws ranged from 3 to 20 years' imprisonment. In the course of a single year, about 1500 workers were arrested for such offences.

The working-class organisation known as the I.W.W. (Industrial Workers of the World) was savagely attacked, and some of its leaders were lynched. As an example of the "right to strike," we may mention the strike at the Arizona copper mines in the year 1917, when many of the workers were shot, others flogged, and others tarred and feathered; when whole families were hunted from their homes and reduced to beggary. Again, during the strike at Rockefeller's coal mines, at Ludlow in the State of Colorado, Rockefeller's gunmen shot and burned several hundred workmen and workwomen. Although Congress is elected by universal suffrage, it merely carries out the orders of the trust kings, for nearly all the congressmen are in the pay of the trusts. The uncrowned kings are the real dictators of America. Among them we may name : Rockefeller, the head of the Standard Oil Trust, which controls, in addition to the oil wells, a vast number of banks ; Morgan, the railway king, also in control of numerous banks ; Schwab, the steel king ; Swift, the head of the meat trust ; Dupont, the powder king, who amassed incredible wealth during the war. Suffice it to say that Rockefeller's income is $10,000 per *hour* ! Who can withstand such strength ? This gang of Schwabs and Rockefellers holds everything in its hands in the name of " democracy."

Even if what is termed bourgeois democracy did really exist, in comparison with the Soviet Power it would not be worth a cracked farthing. Paper laws are of no use to the working class unless the possibility of their realisation exists. But such a possibility of realisation does not exist under the capitalist regime, cannot exist under the system in which the capitalists own all the wealth. Even if the workers enjoy on paper the right of meeting, they often find it quite impossible to exercise such a right. For instance, the innkeepers, incited by the big sharks of capital, or moved by their own hostility to the workers, will frequently refuse to let rooms for meetings—and the workers have nowhere else to go. Here is another example. The workers wish to publish a newspaper, and they have the legal right to do so. But to exercise this right they need money, paper, offices, a printing press, etc. All these things are in the hands of the capitalists. The capitalists won't relax their grip. Nothing doing ! Out of the workers' paltry wage it is impossible to accumulate adequate funds. The result is that the bourgeoisie has masses of newspapers and can cheat the workers to its heart's content day after day ; whereas the workers, notwithstanding their legal " rights," have practically no press of their own.

Such is the real character of the workers' " freedom " under bourgeois democracy. The freedom exists solely on paper. The workers have what is termed " formal " freedom. In substance, however, they have no freedom, because their formal freedom cannot be translated into the realm of fact. It is the same here as in all other departments of life. According to bourgeois theory, master and man are equals in capitalist society, since " free contract " exists : the employer offers work ; the worker is free to accept or refuse. Thus it is upon paper ! In actual fact, the master is rich and well fed ; the worker is poor and hungry. He must work or starve. Is this equality ? There can be no equality between rich and poor, whatever the written word declares. This is why, in the capitalist regime, " freedom " has a bourgeois complexion.

In the Soviet Republic, on the other hand, freedom really exists for the working class. It exists because it is a freedom which can be translated into the realm of fact. Let us quote from the constitution of the Russian Socialist Federative Soviet Republic (Part II, Chapter 5).

" 14. In order to secure for the workers actual freedom of expression of opinion, the Russian Socialist Federative Soviet Republic abolishes the dependence of the press upon capital, and puts into the hands of the working class and the poor peasantry all the technical and material means for the publication of newspapers, pamphlets, books, and all other products of the printing press, and provides for their free distribution throughout the country.

" 15. In order to secure for the workers the actual right of assembly, the Russian Socialist Federative Soviet Republic gives to all citizens of the Soviet Republic the unrestricted right to hold meetings and congresses, to march in processions, etc., and puts into the hands of the working class and the poor peasants all the buildings suitable for the purpose of holding public meetings, together with the provision of light, heating, etc.

" 16. In order to secure for the workers actual freedom of combination, the Russian Socialist Federative Soviet Republic, having overthrown the economic and political power of the possessing classes, and having removed all the hindrances which hitherto in bourgeois society have prevented the workers and peasants from effectively realising the freedom of organisation and activity, furnishes to the workers and poor peasants every kind of assistance, material and moral, requisite for their combination and organisation.

" 17. In order to secure for the workers effective access to knowledge, the Russian Socialist Federative Soviet Republic makes it its duty to provide the workers and poor peasants with a complete, many-sided, and gratuitous education."

Herein we see the enormous difference between the spurious freedoms of bourgeois democracy and the effective freedoms of proletarian democracy.

The Soviet Power and our party have already done much in this direction. The mansions of the nobles, the theatres, the printing presses, paper, etc.—all these now belong to the working-class organisations and to the workers' State. Our further task is to help by all possible means towards the full realisation of these rights by the backward strata of the proletariat and the peasantry. This will be achieved in two ways. First of all, we must continually advance along the road we have marked out, and must do everything in our power to broaden the material foundations of the workers' freedom. We must, therefore, do our utmost to design and build new houses, set up new printing presses, instal workers' palaces, etc. Secondly, the backward strata of the population must be made intimately acquainted with those possibilities of freedom which already exist, but which they have not hitherto been able to profit by, owing to ignorance, mental darkness, and lack of culture.

§ 50.

The Equality of the Workers, irrespective of Sex, Creed, and Race. Bourgeois democracy proclaims in words a whole series of freedoms, but from the oppressed these freedoms are safeguarded by five locks and seven seals. Among other things, bourgeois democracy has often declared that people are equal irrespective of sex, creed, race, and nationality. Proudly has the pledge been given that under the bourgeois democratic system all are equals : women and men ; whites, yellows, and blacks ; Europeans and Asiatics ; Buddhists, Christians, and Jews. In reality, the bourgeoisie has failed to carry out these pledges. During the imperialist epoch, there has been all over the world a terrible increase in racial and national oppression. (For details see the next chapter.) But even as concerns women, bourgeois democracy is far from having realised equality. Woman has remained a being without rights, a domestic animal, part of the furniture of the marital couch.

The working woman in capitalist society is peculiarly oppressed, peculiarly deprived of rights. In all matters she has even less than the beggarly rights which the bourgeoisie grants to the working man. The right to the parliamentary vote has been conceded in a few countries only. As regards the right of inheritance, woman everywhere receives the beggar's portion. In family life she is always subject to her husband, and everything that goes wrong is considered to be her fault. In a word, bourgeois democracy everywhere exhibits as regards women laws and customs which strongly remind us of the customs of savages, who exchange, buy, punish, or steal women just as if they were chattels, dolls, or beasts of burden. Our Russian proverb runs, " A hen is not a bird, and a woman is not a person " ; here we have the valuation of a slave society. This state of affairs is extremely disadvantageous to the proletariat. There are more women than men amongst the workers. It is obvious that the struggle of the proletariat must be greatly hindered by the lack of equality between the two halves of which it is composed. Without the aid of the women of the proletariat, it is idle to dream of a general victory, it is idle to dream of the " freeing of labour." For this reason, it is greatly to the interest of the working class that there should be complete fighting comradeship between the female and the male portions of the proletariat, and that this comradeship should be strengthened by equality. The Soviet Power is the first to have realised such equality in all departments of life : in marriage, in the family, in political affairs, etc. In all things, throughout Soviet Russia, women are the equals of men.

It is incumbent upon our party to effect the realisation of this equality in actual life. Before all, we must make it clear to the broad masses of the workers that the subjection of women is extremely harmful to them. Hitherto among the workers it has been customary to look upon women as inferiors ; as for the peasants, they smile when a " mere woman " begins to take an interest in social affairs. In the Soviet Republic the working woman has exactly the same rights as the working man ; she can elect to the soviets and be elected to them ; she can hold any commissar's office ; can do any kind of work in the army, in economic life, and in the State administration.

But in Russia, working women are far more backward than working men. Many people look down upon them. In this matter persevering efforts are needed : among men, that they may cease blocking women's road ; among women, that they may learn to make a full use of their rights, may cease to be timid or diffident.

We must not forget that " every cook has to be taught to take her share in governmental administration." We have learned above that the really important matter is not the right that is written on paper, but the possibility of realising a right in practice. How can a working woman effectively realise her rights when she has to devote so much time to housekeeping, must go to the market and wait her turn there, must do the family washing, must look after her children, must bear the heavy burden of all this domestic drudgery ?

The aim of the Soviet Republic and of our party must be, to deliver working women from such slavery, to free the working woman from these obsolete and antediluvian conditions. The organisation of house communes (not places in which people will wrangle, but places in which they will live like human beings) with central wash-houses ; the organisation of communal kitchens ; the organisation of communal nurseries, kindergartens, playgrounds, summer colonies for children, schools with communal dining rooms, etc.—such are the things which will enfranchise woman, and will make it possible for her to interest herself in all those matters which now interest the proletarian man.

In an era of devastation and famine, it is, of course, difficult to do all these things as they ought to be done. Nevertheless, our party must in this manner do its utmost to attract the working woman to play her part in the common task.

National equality, racial equality, etc., will be considered in the next chapter. Here we shall merely quote the paragraphs in the constitution which touch on this topic (Part II, Chapter 5).

" 20. In view of the solidarity of the workers of all lands, the Russian Socialist Federative Soviet Republic grants the political rights of Russian citizens to foreigners living in the territories of the Russian Republic, provided they live by their own labour and either belong to the working class or are peasants who do not employ others' labour ; it recognises the right of the local soviets to grant Russian citizenship to such foreigners without any tedious formalities.

" 21. The Russian Socialist Federative Soviet Republic grants the right of asylum to all foreigners suffering persecution on account of political or religious offences.

" 22. The Russian Socialist Federative Soviet Republic, recognising the equal rights of all citizens irrespective of their racial or national origin, declares the institution or maintenance of any privilege or preferential advantage upon the ground of such origin to be contrary to the fundamental law of the republic ; no less contrary to the fundamental law is any sort of oppression of national minorities or any limitation of their equal rights."

§ 51.

Parliamentarism and the Soviet System. In bourgeois democratic States, at the head of everything stands what is known as parliament. This is a representative institution, the electoral franchise varying in different countries. In some, only the rich have the vote ; in some, a part of the poor are admitted to the franchise ; in a third group, all the men of a certain age can vote ; in a fourth country, all the women as well.

But even where parliament is elected by universal suffrage, the majority of the seats are invariably occupied by representatives of the bourgeoisie. Why does this always happen ? The reason is obvious in view of what we have already learned. Let us suppose that the workers, who form the majority in the country, have the right to vote. But let us further suppose that all the wealth is in the hands of the capitalists, that they own all the newspapers and all the places where public meetings can be held, and that artists, printing presses, and millions of leaflets are at their service ; that from all the pulpits the clergy advocate their cause ; let us suppose, moreover, that the poor workers are engaged day after day in exhausting toil, that they have no meeting-places, that clever fellows circulate among them (agents of the bourgeoisie, lawyers, journalists, and other glib talkers) advocating what seem to be excellent watchwords, and thus confusing the workers' minds ; let us remember the enormous financial resources of the trust magnates, which enable them to corrupt the workers' representatives—however honest these may have been at the outset—by offering comfortable jobs, by flattery in the daily press, and so on. Then we can understand why it is that even in such parliaments the majority always consists of the secret or declared agents of the bourgeoisie, of financial capital, of the bank kings.

It is, therefore, extraordinarily difficult for the working masses to elect any of their own folk as representatives.

Once a representative finds his way to parliament, the matter is finished ; he can defy the electors ; for three or four years his seat is secure. He is independent of them. He sells himself right and left. He cannot be recalled by the electors ; the law makes no provision for anything of the kind.

Such is the state of affairs in a bourgeois democratic republic under parliamentarism. It is very different in the Soviet Republic. Here the parasites—the traders and the factory owners, the prelates and the landlords, the military officers and the rich peasants—have no right to the vote. They can neither elect nor be elected. On the other hand, the exercise of the franchise by the workers and the poor peasants is simple and easy. Moreover, every delegate to the soviet can be recalled by the electors, who can send another in his place. If the delegate fulfils his duties badly, if he turns his coat, etc., he can be recalled. This right of recall has nowhere been so extensively adopted as in the Soviet Republic.

In a bourgeois republic, parliament is a " talking shop " ; the members do nothing but discuss and make speeches. The real work is done by officials, ministers of State, etc. Parliament passes laws ; it " controls " the ministers by asking them various questions ; it votes what the administration decides. In parliament is concentrated what is termed the legislative authority. But the executive authority is in the hands of the cabinet. Parliament, therefore, does nothing ; parliament merely talks. In the soviet system, affairs are arranged quite differently. The highest and most important instrument of government is the Congress of Soviets. The constitution states : " The All-Russian Congress of Soviets is the supreme authority of the Russian Socialist Federative Soviet Republic." It must meet at least twice a year. Having reviewed the general situation, it makes suitable decisions, which become laws. The members of the congress are not professional talkers, but real workers, with something definite to do. In the intervals between the congresses the supreme authority is vested in the Central Executive Committee, elected by the congress. The Central Executive Committee exercises at one and the same time legislative and executive functions ; that is to say, it not only passes laws, but conducts public affairs. Its departments are known as the People's Commissariats, and its members work in these commissariats. Thus the Central Executive Committee is a real *working* committee.

Like the Central Executive Committee, the other soviet institutions are closely unified, and are based upon a whole series of organisations of the working masses. The soviet institutions are based on the Communist Party, the trade unions, the factory committees, and the cooperatives. These organisations comprise many millions of workers, who all combine to support the Soviet Power. Through the instrumentality of these organisations, the toiling masses take an active part in the State administration. The Communist Party and the trade unions appoint their most trusted members to fill all the posts and to carry out all the functions. In this way the best among the workers are delegated, not merely to talk, but actually to administer. In the so-called democratic republic, nothing of this kind happens. There the working-class elector drops his ballot paper into the box, and then his part in the affair ends. The bourgeoisie assures him that he has fulfilled his " duties as a citizen " ; he need trouble himself no longer about affairs of State.

These arrangements conceal one of the fundamental frauds of the bourgeois system of government. The fraud is of the same nature as those previously explained. On paper it seems as if the workers were " participating " in some way. In actual fact they are altogether outside the current of affairs. Everything is administered and all the work is done by a special caste of bourgeois officials, quite distinct from the masses, and constituting what is known as the bureaucracy. The administrative apparatus is out of reach of the masses ; the masses have no contact with it whatever.

Down to the sixteenth or seventeenth century the State officials were drawn only from the nobility. During the change to the capitalist system, a professional officialdom came into existence. Of late years, this professional officialdom has been mainly recruited from the ranks of the so-called intelligentsia or professional classes, but the higher posts have been filled by members of the wealthier bourgeoisie. Even the lesser officials, however, are trained in a spirit of devotion towards the robber State ; the more talented among them look forward to a rise in rank, to orders and titles, to an " official career." The result is that most of these gentlemen are full of profound disdain for the " common people." The dimensions and growth of this officialdom may be learned from the following figures, which are taken from Olsheffsky's book *Bureaucracy*. In *Austria*, in the year 1874, they numbered in round figures 27,000 ; in 1891, they numbered 36,000 ; in 1900, they numbered 169,000. In *France*, the number of officials in the year 1891 was 1,500,000, this being approximately 4 per cent. of the population. In *Britain*, in the same year, there were about 1,000,000 officials [civil servants], this being approximately 2·6 per cent. of the population. In the *United States*, in the year 1890, there were 750,000 officials. Olsheffsky, himself a bourgeois, tells us that the bureaucracy is characterised by the following traits : routinism, redtapism, overbearing manners, pettiness. In all capitalist countries, administrative work is actually in the hands of an officialdom of this character. We must repeat that the highest officials are mainly recruited from the wealthier bourgeoisie, and from the circles of the nobility and the great landowners. This is inevitable in capitalist society, where the bourgeoisie rules.

In the Soviet Republic, the masses do not merely elect (electing, not venal lawyers, but their own folk), but they participate in the work of administration, for the soviets and the other organisations of the working masses are actually engaged in administrative work.

As far as the soviets are concerned, the elections are of such a character as will retain close contact between these bodies and the masses. For the elections to the soviets are not territorial in the residential sense, but are based upon the places where people work (factories, workshops, etc.) ; they are based, as the phrase runs, upon " productive units." Those who are united in their working life elect from among their number, as their delegates, the persons in whom they have the greatest confidence.

Thus the Soviet Power realises an enormously higher form, a far more genuinely popular form, of democracy—proletarian democracy.

What, then, is the further task of our party? Our common course is clear. Our party has to realise proletarian democracy to a greater and ever greater extent; to bring about an increasingly close contact between delegates or elected persons (those deputed to perform various tasks) and the masses; to induce the workers to participate more and more effectively in the work of administration; finally, to ensure that millions of eyes shall watch the delegates and control their work. Everything possible must be done to see to it that all persons entrusted with authority shall be held responsible and shall frequently be called to account.

The carrying out of these tasks is a great undertaking. There are many obstacles to be overcome. The obstacles must be surmounted. We must achieve a full and inseparable union of three elements: the State apparatus; the active masses of the proletariat, the builders of communism; and the poor peasants.

§ 52.

The Army and the Soviet Power. Proletarian democracy, like every other State authority, has its armed forces—its army and its navy. In the bourgeois democratic State, the army is used to keep down the workers and to defend the capitalists' money-bags. The proletarian army, the Red Army of the Soviet Republic, is used for the class purposes of the proletariat and for the struggle against the bourgeoisie. Consequently, in respect of the conditions of service and in respect of political rights, there is a vast difference between a bourgeois army and a proletarian army. The bourgeoisie finds it expedient to pretend that its army is " above politics." In reality, it uses the army as a means for promoting its predatory and counter-revolutionary policy under the flag of the defence of " national interests." It does everything in its power to sow division between the army and the people. By a thousand subterfuges, it deprives soldiers of the possibility of utilising their political rights. Things are very different in the Soviet Republic. In the first place, the proletariat frankly declares that the Red Army is an instrument for use in the political class struggle against the bourgeoisie. In the second place, the Soviet Power uses all possible means to bring about an intimate union between the army and the people. The workers are solidarised in the soviets with the soldiers of the Red Army ; these soviets are known as " Soviets of Workers' and Soldiers' Delegates." The workers and the soldiers study in the same schools, and attend the same courses of lectures, they mingle at public meetings ; they rub shoulders in demonstrations. Again and again, the workers have entrusted the fighting flag to the soldiers of the Red Army ; and again and again the soldiers have entrusted the colours to the workers. In the Soviet State, which is nothing else than a great republic of workers, success can only be achieved in the fight against our enemies when there is an indestructible unity between the Red Army and the revolutionary working class.

The more intimate the solidarity of the working class with the army and of the army with the working class, the more durable will be our fighting revolutionary strength. Obviously, then, our party must sustain, develop, and strengthen this unity. Experience has shown that intimate association with proletarian organisations exercises a remarkable influence upon the army. We need only recall the resistance to Kolchak in the summer of 1919 and to Denikin in the autumn of the same year. These victories could not have been achieved had not the army been assisted by workers from the party, from the trade unions, etc., who flocked to the colours. For this reason the Red Army of the proletariat is in actual fact, and not merely in words, the first people's army, the first army created by the will of the workers, organised by the workers, solidarised with them, indissolubly united with them, and, by means of its representatives in the soviets, participating in the administration of the country. The Red Army is not something distinct from the people ; it consists of the working class and the poor peasants ; and it marches under the leadership of the working class. The army lives in the most intimate association with the workers at the rear. It is the absolute duty of our party to be indefatigable in its endeavours to consolidate this unity.

§ 53.

The leading Role of the Proletariat. In our revolution, which is a communist revolution, the principal role, the role of leader, has been assigned to the proletariat. The proletariat is the most united and the best organised class. The proletariat is the only class whose conditions of life in capitalist society have been such as to lead to the acquirement of sound communist views ; to it alone have these conditions disclosed the true goal and the right way of attaining it. Naturally, therefore, the proletariat has led the van in this revolution. The peasants (the middle peasants and even some of the poor peasants) were far from steadfast. They were only successful when they joined forces with the proletariat. Conversely, whenever the peasants took a different line from the proletarians, they were inevitably enslaved by Denikin, Kolchak, or some other representative of the landlords, the capitalists, or the military caste.

This leading role, this dominant mission of the proletariat, finds expression in the soviet constitution. Our laws grant the proletariat certain preferential political rights. For example, the electoral arrangements of the Congresses of Soviets are of such a nature, that, proportionally to their numbers, the urban workers have more delegates than the peasants.

Here are the relevant paragraphs of the constitution.

" The All-Russian Congress of Soviets consists of representatives of the Town Soviets, which are entitled to send one delegate for every 25,000 electors, and of representatives of the Provincial Soviets, which are entitled to send one delegate for every 125,000 inhabitants." (Part III, Chapter 5, Par. 25.)

" Congresses of Soviets consist of : (a) Regional Congresses, composed of representatives from the Town Soviets and from the County Congresses of Soviets, in the proportion of one delegate to 25,000 inhabitants, and from the Towns in the proportion of one delegate to 5,000 electors, with the proviso that there shall not be more than 500 delegates for the whole Region—or composed of the representatives to the Provincial Congresses of Soviets, elected on the same basis, when the Provincial Congress meets immediately before the Regional Congress of Soviets. (*b*) Provincial Congresses composed of representatives of the Town Soviets and of the Rural District Congresses of Soviets, in the proportion of one delegate to 10,000 inhabitants, and from the Towns in the proportion of one delegate to 2,000 electors, with the proviso that there shall not be more than 300 delegates for the whole Province—but when a County Congress of Soviets takes place immediately before the Provincial Congress of Soviets, the elections shall be held after the manner of those, not to the Rural District Congress of Soviets, but to the County Congress of Soviets." (Part III, Chapter 10, Par. 53.)

In the towns, it will be seen, the delegates are elected proportionally to the number of electors, but in the villages, proportionally to the number of inhabitants (these comprising, not only the workers in the strict sense of the term, but also the rich peasants, the clergy, the rural bourgeoisie, etc., as well as the children, who have no electoral rights). It follows from this that the preference given to the urban workers as against the peasants is less extensive than might appear at first sight. But the preferential treatment is indubitable.

These constitutionally specified privileges merely give expression to what actually exists, namely that the solidly organised urban proletariat leads the disorganised rural masses.

It is the first duty of the Communist Party to do everything it can to make plain that these privileges are temporary. In proportion as the backward strata of the country dwellers grow more enlightened, when experience has convinced them that the measures adopted by the workers are right and profitable, when they realise that they must not walk with the bourgeoisie but only with the proletariat, obviously the above-described temporary inequality will cease to exist.

The Communist Party must utilise the privileges of the proletariat in order to influence the rural districts, in order to solidarise the more advanced workers with the peasants. Thus only will the revolutionary enlightenment of the poorer peasants be successfully achieved. The privileged position of the workers has not been given them that they may be exclusive or may separate themselves from the dwellers in the rural districts, but in order that they may make a good use of it, in order that, by their greater influence in the soviets and the administration, they may bring the working class into closer contact with village life, that they may inaugurate and sustain a comradely union of the proletariat with the middle peasants and the poor peasants. Thus the workers will be able to free the peasants from the influence of the rich peasants, the clergy, the sometime landlords, etc.

§ 54.

Bureaucracy and the Soviet Power. The Soviet Power has been organised, as the power of a new class, the proletariat, upon the ruins of the old bourgeois power. Before the proletariat could organise its own power, it had to break the power of its adversaries. With the aid of the Soviet Power, the proletariat seized and destroyed the vestiges of the old State. It broke up the old police force, abolished the remnants of the secret service, abolished the gendarmerie and the tsarist bourgeois law courts with their public prosecutors and salaried defenders ; it swept away many of the old government departments, annihilated the bourgeois ministries of State with their armies of officials, etc. What was the aim of all this ? And what is now the general task of our party ? We have referred to the matter already in Part One of the present work. The task is this, to replace the old officialdom by the masses themselves, to bring it to pass that the whole working population shall put its hand to the job of administration (working in some occupations by turns for brief spells, and in other occupations by turns for long spells). But we have had serious difficulties to encounter. The chief obstacles have been the following.

First of all came the imperfect development, the lack of enlightenment, the timidity, of the backward strata of the urban population and still more of the rural population. The vanguard, which consists of the bold spirits, of those who are active in body and in mind, of those who are well informed, constitutes a comparatively thin stratum. The others are very slow to move. A great many are still afraid to put their hands to the plough ; a great many are still ignorant of their own rights, and have not yet realised that they are the masters of the country. This is not difficult to understand. The masses have been oppressed and enslaved for centuries ; it is impossible that from their half-savage condition they should in a moment rise to a level at which they can govern the country. Those who first come to the front are those who belong to the most highly developed stratum ; the workers of Petrograd, for instance. These we encounter everywhere. We find them as army commissars, as organisers of production, as executive committee delegates in the rural districts, as propagandists, as members of the highest soviet institutions, as teachers. By degrees even the backward masses are leavened ; they cast the old things aside ; they assimilate the new ; little by little they teach themselves. It is, however, obvious that the low level of general culture must be a great hindrance to progress.

Secondly we had the lack of experience in the work of administration. This is manifest even in the best of the comrades. The working class has for the first time taken power into its hands. It has never done any administrative work, and no one has ever taught it how to do anything of the kind. On the contrary, for decades during the tsarist regime, and also during the brief Guchkoff-Kerensky administration, everything that was possible was done to prevent the proletariat from getting any such experience. Both the bourgeois and the feudalist State were organisations for keeping the workers down, not organisations for educating them. Naturally, therefore, the workers, having risen to power, will, while learning by experience, make a great many mistakes. By these mistakes they learn, but inevitably they make them.

Thirdly we had trouble with bourgeois specialists of the old school. The proletariat was forced to retain many of them in its service. It made them submit, set them to work, got the better of their sabotage. In the end, it has turned them to successful account. But these bourgeois experts are apt to cling to their old customs. They look down upon the masses with contempt, and will not mix with them on equal terms ; they often cling to the old and evil office routine ; they dilly-dally ; and their bad example tends to corrupt our own people.

Fourthly we had the withdrawal of the best energies to the army. During the most critical periods of the civil war, when the army was in urgent need of the most trusty and valiant fighters, it was often necessary to despatch the very best of our own people to the front. In consequence of this, there remained at the rear only a comparatively small number of the most advanced among the workers.

All these circumstances make our work extremely difficult, and tend to a certain degree to promote the reintroduction of bureaucracy into the Soviet system. This is a grave danger for the proletariat. The workers did not destroy the old official-ridden State with the intention of allowing it to grow up again from new roots. Our party, therefore, must do its utmost to avert this danger. It can only be averted by attracting the masses to take part in the work. The fundamental matter, of course, is to raise the general cultural level of the workers and peasants, to make an end of illiteracy, to diffuse enlightenment. In addition, however, a whole series of other measures is essential. Among these, our party advocates the following.

It is absolutely indispensable that every member of a soviet should play some definite part in the work of State administration. It is incumbent upon every member of a soviet, not merely to pass opinions upon the matters that come up for discussion, but himself to take part in the common task, in his own person to fill some social office.

The next essential is that there should be a continuous rotation in these functions. This implies that every comrade must, after a definite time, change over from one occupation to another, so that by degrees he shall become experienced in all the important branches of administrative work. The comrade must not stick for years to one and the same job, for if he does this he will become a routinist official of the old type. As soon as he has learned the routine of one office, he must remove to another.

Finally, our party recommends, as far as concerns the general arrangement of the work, that by degrees the entire working population shall be induced to participate in the State administration. Here, in fact, is the true foundation of our political system. Certain steps in this direction have already been taken. For example, ten thousand proletarians participated in the house-to-house visitations of the Petrograd bourgeoisie. Again, nearly the whole of the working population of Petrograd took part in safeguarding the city. Yet again, to relieve the men for other duties, working women entered the militia service. In the soviets it is possible to train non-members as assistants. By looking on, at first, they can learn the work of the executive committee and the sub-committees. The same thing can be done in the factory committees and in the trade unions, where all the members can take office by turns. In a word, in one way or another (practical experience will teach us the best methods), we must follow in the footsteps of the Paris Commune, must simplify the work of administration, attract the masses to participate in it, completely put an end to bureaucracy. The more extensive this participation of the masses is, the sooner will the dictatorship of the proletariat die out. As soon as all the adult and hale members of the population, all without exception, have come to participate in administration, the last vestiges of bureaucracy will disappear. Concurrently with the disappearance of our bourgeois antagonists, we shall be able to celebrate the obsequies of the State. The government of men will be replaced by the administration of things—the administration of machinery, buildings, locomotives, and other apparatus. The communist order of society will be fully installed.

The dying out of the State will proceed far more rapidly when a complete victory has been gained over the imperialists. To-day, when a fierce civil war is still raging, all our organisations have to be on a war footing. The instruments of the Soviet Power have had to be constructed on militarist lines. Often enough there is no time to summon the soviets, and as a rule, therefore, the executive committees have to decide everything.

This state of affairs is due to the military situation of the Soviet Republic. What exists to-day in Russia is not simply the dictatorship of the proletariat; it is a militarist-proletarian dictatorship. The republic is an armed camp. Obviously, the above-described conditions will not pass away while the need persists for the militarisation of all our organisations.

Literature. LENIN, The State and Revolution. LENIN, Will the Bolsheviks retain the Authority of the State ? OSINSKY, A Democratic Republic or a Soviet Republic ? LENIN, Theses concerning bourgeois and proletarian Democracy adopted by the first Congress of the Communist International. LENIN, The proletarian Revolution and the Renegade Kautsky. STUCHKA, The Constitution of the R.S.F.S.R. in Question and Answer. BUHARIN, Parliamentarism or Soviet Republic ? KARPINSKY, What the Soviet Power is. KARPINSKY and LATSIS, What the Soviet Power is and how it is built up.

CHAPTER SEVEN

COMMUNISM AND THE PROBLEM OF NATIONALITY

§ 55.

The Oppression of subject Nationalities. One of the forms of the oppression of man by man is the oppression of subject nationalities. Among the barriers by which human beings are separated, we have, in addition to the barriers of class, those of national disunity, of national enmity and hatred.

National enmity and ill-feeling are among the means by which the proletariat is stupefied and by which its class consciousness is dulled. The bourgeoisie knows how to cultivate these sentiments skilfully in order to promote its own interests.

Let us consider how class-conscious proletarians should approach the problem of nationality, and how they can best solve it so as to further the speedy victory of communism.

A nation or a people is the name given to a group of persons who are united by the use of a common tongue and who inhabit a definite area. There are additional characteristics of nationality, but these two are the most important and the most fundamental.[1]

A few examples will help us to understand what is meant by the oppression of a subject nationality. The tsarist government persecuted the Jews, forbade them to live in

[1] Long ago, the Jews inhabited a definite territory and possessed a common speech ; to-day they have no territory, and many of them do not understand Hebrew. The gypsies have their own language, but they do not inhabit any definite territory. The non-nomadic Tunguses in Siberia have a territory, but they have forgotten their distinctive tongue.

certain parts of Russia, refused to admit them into the State service, restricted their entry into the schools, organised anti-Jewish pogroms, etc. The tsarist government, moreover, would not allow the Ukrainians to have their children taught the Ukrainian language in the schools. The issue of newspapers in the Ukrainian tongue was forbidden. None of the subject nationalities in Russia were even permitted to decide whether they wished to form part of the Russian State or not.

The German government closed the Polish schools. The Austrian government prohibited the use of the Czech language and forcibly imposed German upon the Czechs. The British bourgeoisie regards the indigens of Africa and Asia with contempt ; it subjugates the backward semi-savage peoples, plunders them, and shoots them down when they attempt to deliver themselves from the British yoke.

In a word, when in any State the people of one nation possess all rights and the people of another nation possess only a part of these rights ; when one nation, the weaker nation, has been forcibly united to a stronger nation ; when the stronger nation has against the will of the weaker nation imposed upon the latter a foreign tongue, foreign customs, etc. ; when the people of the weaker nation are not allowed to lead their own lives—then we have what is termed oppression of a subject nationality, we have national enslavement.

[§ 56.

The Unity of the Proletariat. First of all, however, we must propound and decide an extremely important and fundamental problem. Should the Russian worker and the Russian peasant look upon the Germans, the French, the British, the Jews, the Chinese, or the Tartars, as enemies, irrespective of the class to which these belong ? Are the Russian workers and peasants entitled to hate or to regard with suspicion those who belong to another nation, for the sole reason that these latter speak a different tongue, that their skins are black or yellow, that they have different customs and laws ? Obviously, this would be quite wrong. The German workers, the French workers, the Negro workers, are just as much proletarians as the Russians are. No matter what tongue the workers of other lands may speak, the essential feature of their condition lies in this, that they are all exploited by capital, that they are all comrades, that they all alike suffer from poverty, oppression, and injustice.

Is the Russian worker to love the Russian capitalist because his fellow-countryman abuses him in the familiar Russian terms, because his employer cuffs him with a Russian fist, or lashes him with a Russian whip ? Of course not. Nor is the German workman likely to love the German capitalist any better because the latter taunts him in the German language and after the German fashion. The workers of all lands are brothers of one class, and they are the enemies of the capitalists of all lands.

The same considerations apply in the case of the poor peasants of every nation. To the Russian peasant (the poor peasant or the middle peasant), the semi-proletarian peasant of Hungary, or the poor peasant of Sicily or Belgium, is nearer and dearer than can possibly be the rich peasant of his own land who exploits him, or the skinflint landlord who happens to be born on Russian soil and to speak the Russian tongue.

But the workers of the whole world must not merely recognise themselves to be brothers by class, to be brothers in oppression and slavery. It would do no good if they were to rest content with railing against their capitalist compatriots in their respective tongues ; if in each land the sufferers were to wipe one another's tears, and only within their own State were to carry on the struggle against the enemy. Brothers in oppression and slavery must be brothers in one world-wide league for the struggle with the capitalists. Forgetting all the national differences that tend to hinder union, they must unite in one great army to carry on a joint war against capitalism. Only by closing their ranks in such an international alliance, can they hope to conquer world capitalism. This is why, more than seventy years ago, the founders of communism, Marx and Engels, in their famous Communist Manifesto, fulminated the splendid slogan : " Proletarians of all lands, unite ! "

It is essential that the working class should overcome all national prejudices and national enmities. This is requisite, not only for the world-wide attack upon capital and for the complete overthrow of the capitalist system, but also for the organisation of a single world-wide economic system. Soviet Russia cannot exist without Donetz coal, Baku mineral oil, Turkestan cotton ; but it is just as true that Central and Western Europe cannot do without Russian wood, hemp, flax, and platinum, or without American wheat ; it is just as true that Italy finds British coal a vital necessity, and that Britain urgently needs Egyptian cotton, etc., etc. The bourgeoisie has found itself unable to organise a world economy, and the bourgeois system has been ship-wrecked upon this difficulty. The proletariat is alone competent to organise such a system with success. To this end, however, it must proclaim the watchword, " All the world and all the wealth that it contains belong to the whole world of labour." This watchword implies that the German workers must completely renounce their national wealth, the British theirs, and so on. If national prejudice and national greed oppose the internationalisation of industry and agriculture, away with them, wherever they may show themselves and under whatever colours they may sail !

§ 57.

The Causes of national Enmity. But it does not suffice that the communists should declare war on the oppression of nationalities and upon national prejudices, that they should advocate international unity in the struggle against capitalism, and that they should desire to found a world-wide economic alliance of the victorious proletariat. We must seek a far quicker way towards the overthrow of all jingoism and national egoism, of national stupidity and pride, of mutual mistrust among the workers of the various nations. This legacy from a brutal period of human life and from the brutal nationalist quarrel of the feudal and capitalist epochs, still hangs like a heavy burden round the neck of the world proletariat.

National enmities are of very ancient date. There was a time when the different tribes were not content with fighting one another for lands and forests, but when the men of one tribe would actually eat those of another. Remnants of this brutal mistrust and enmity between nation and nation, between race and race, continue to exist between the workers and peasants of all lands. These vestiges of intertribal enmity are gradually dying out, in proportion as world commerce develops, as economic contact ensues, as migrations and minglings bring people of various stocks into close association on the same territory ; but especially do they die out owing to the universality of the class struggle of the workers of all lands.   Yet these vestiges of intertribal enmity do not merely fail to become extinct, but actually glow with renewed life, when to the old causes of national ill-feeling there is superadded an antagonism of class interests or the appearance of such antagonism.

The bourgeoisie in each country exploits and oppresses the proletariat of its own land. But it does its utmost to convince its own proletariat that the latter's enemies are not to be found among bourgeois fellow-countrymen, but among the peoples of other lands. The German bourgeoisie cries to the German workers, " Down with the French ! Down with the English ! " The British bourgeoisie cries to the British workers, "Down with the Germans ! " The bourgeoisies of all countries, especially of late, join in the cry, " Down with the Jews ! " The aim of this is to switch off the class struggle of the workers against their capitalist oppressors, into a struggle between nationalities.

The bourgeoisie, however, in its desire to divert the workers' minds from the struggle for socialism, is not content with inflaming national hatred. It endeavours in addition to give the workers a material interest in the oppression of other peoples. During the recent war, when the bourgeois were chanting the German national anthem " Germany, Germany above all," the bourgeois economists of Germany tried to convince the German workers that the latter stood to gain a great deal from the victory, stood to gain from the oppression and plunder of the workers of the conquered lands. Before the war the bourgeoisie made a practice of bribing the leaders of the working class with the lure of the profits derivable from colonial plunder and from the oppression of backward and weakly nationalities. The workers of the more advanced European lands, acting on the instigation of the most highly paid members of the working class, acceded to the proposals of the capitalists, and allowed themselves to be talked over by the jingo socialists into accepting the belief that they too would have a fatherland if only they would acquiesce in the plunder of the colonies and of the partially dependent nations. The worker who, under capitalism, proclaims himself a patriot, is selling for a copper or two his real fatherland, which is socialism; and thereby he becomes one of the oppressors of the backward and weak nations.

§ 58.

The equal Rights of the Nations and the Right to Self-Determination; Federation. The Communist Party, declaring a relentless war upon all oppression of man by man, takes a decisive stand against that oppression of subject nationalities which is indispensable to the existence of the bourgeois system. Even more relentlessly do communists resist the slightest participation in this oppression on the part of the working class. It does not suffice, however, that the proletariat of a great and strong country should repudiate all attempts at the oppression of the other peoples which the bourgeoisie or the aristocracy of its own land has crushed. It is also essential that the proletarians of oppressed nations should not feel any mistrust of their comrades who belong to the lands of the oppressors. When the Czechs were oppressed by the German bourgeoisie of Austria, the Czech workers looked upon all Germans as their oppressors. Our tsarist government oppressed the Poles, and the population of Poland has continued to cherish mistrust of all Russians; not merely of the Russian tsar, the Russian landlord, and the Russian capitalist. If we are to eradicate the mistrust felt by the workers of oppressed nations for the workers of oppressor nations, we must not merely proclaim national equality, but must realise it in practice. This equality must find expression in the granting of equal rights in the matter of language, education, religion, etc. Nor is this all. The proletariat must be ready to grant complete national self-determination, must be ready, that is, to concede to the workers who form the majority in any nation the full right to decide the question whether that nation is to be completely integrated with the other, or is to be federated with it, or is to be entirely separated from it.

Is it possible, the reader will ask, that the communists can advocate the severance of the nations ? How then will come into existence that unified proletarian world-embracing State which the communists aspire to found ? There seems to be a contradiction here.

There is no contradiction, however. In order to secure as speedily as possible the full union of all the workers of the world, it is sometimes necessary to countenance the temporary separation of one nation from another.

Let us consider the circumstances in which such a course may be requisite. We will suppose that in Bavaria, which now forms part of Germany, a soviet republic has been declared, while at Berlin the bourgeois dictatorship of Noske and Scheidemann still prevails. Is it right for the Bavarian communists, in that case, to strive for the independence of Bavaria ? Certainly ! And not only the Bavarian communists, but also the communists of other parts of Germany, must welcome the separation of Soviet Bavaria, for this will not be a separation from the German proletariat, but will be a deliverance from the yoke of the German bourgeoisie.

Here is the obverse example. A soviet republic has been proclaimed throughout Germany, Bavaria alone excepted. The Bavarian bourgeoisie desires separation from Soviet Germany, but the Bavarian proletariat desires union. What should the communists do ? It is obvious that the communists of Germany should help the Bavarian workers, and should offer armed resistance to the separatist endeavours of the Bavarian bourgeoisie. This would not be the oppression of Bavaria, but the oppression of the Bavarian bourgeoisie.

Again, the soviet power has been proclaimed both in England and in Ireland, both in the land of the oppressors and in the land of the oppressed. Furthermore, the Irish workers will not trust the English workers, who belong to a country which has oppressed Ireland for centuries. From the economic point of view, the separation will be harmful. What course should the English communists pursue in these circumstances ? Whatever happens, they must not use force, as the English bourgeoisie has done, to maintain the union with Ireland. They must grant the Irish absolute freedom to separate.   Why must they do this?

First of all, because it is necessary to convince the Irish workers that the oppression of Ireland has been the work of the English bourgeoisie and not of the English proletariat. The English workers have to win the Irish workers' confidence.

Secondly, because the Irish workers will have to learn by experience that it is disadvantageous for them to form a small independent State.   They will have to learn by experience that production in Ireland cannot be properly organised unless Ireland is in close political and economic union with proletarian England and other proletarian lands.

Finally, take the case of a nation with a bourgeois government which wishes to separate from a nation with a proletarian regime, and let us suppose that, in the nation which desires to separate, the majority of the workers or a notable proportion of them are in favour of the separation. We may suppose that the workers of the separating country are distrustful, not only of the capitalists, but also of the workers belonging to the country whose bourgeoisie has oppressed them in the past.   Even in this case it would be better to allow the proletariat of the separating land to come to terms in its own way with its own bourgeoisie, for otherwise the latter would retain the power of saying : " It is not I who oppress you, but the people of such and such a country."   The working class will speedily realise that the bourgeoisie has desired independence that it may independently flay its own proletariat.   The workers will speedily realise, moreover, that the proletariat of the neighbouring Soviet State desires the union, not for the sake of exploiting or oppressing the workers of the smaller land, but that all the workers may join in a common struggle for deliverance from exploitation and oppression.

Although, therefore, communists are, as a general principle, opposed to the severance of one nation from another, especially when the lands in question have close economic ties, they can nevertheless countenance temporary separations.   They will act as a mother acts when she allows her child to burn its fingers once that it may dread the fire evermore.

§ 59.

Who expresses the " Will of the Nation " ? The Communist Party recognises that the nations have the right to self-determination even up to the point of secession ; but it considers that the working majority of the nation and not the bourgeoisie embodies the will of the nation. It would, therefore, be more accurate to say that when we speak of recognising the right of the nations to self-determination, we are referring to the right of the working majority in any nation. As far as the bourgeoisie is concerned, inasmuch as during the period of civil war and proletarian dictatorship we deprive it of civic freedoms, we deprive it also of the right to any voice in the question of national affairs.

What have we to say concerning the right of self-determination and the right of secession in the case of nations at a comparatively low or extremely low level of cultural development ? What is to happen to nations which not only have no proletariat, but have not even a bourgeoisie, or if they have it, have it only in an immature form ? Consider, for example, the Tunguses, the Kalmucks, or the Buryats, who inhabit Russian territory. What is to be done if these nations demand complete separation from the great civilised nations ? Still more, what is to be done if they wish to secede from nations which have realised socialism ? Surely to permit such secessions would be to strengthen barbarism at the expense of civilisation ?

We are of opinion that when socialism has been realised in the more advanced countries of the world, the backward and semi-savage peoples will be perfectly willing to join the general alliance of the peoples. The imperialist bourgeoisie which has seized its colonial possessions and has annexed them by force has good reason to fear the secession of the colonies. The proletariat, having no desire to plunder the colonies, can procure from them by the exchange of goods such raw materials as are required, and can leave to the natives of backward lands the right to arrange their own internal affairs as they please. The Communist Party, therefore, wishing to put an end for ever to all forms of national oppression and national inequality, voices the demand for the national right of self-determination.

The proletariat of all lands will avail itself of this right, first of all in order to destroy nationalism, and secondly in order to form a voluntary federative league.

When this federative league proves incompetent to establish a world-wide economic system, and when the great majority has been convinced of its inadequacy by actual experience, the time will have come for the creation of one world-wide socialist republic.

If we examine the manner in which the bourgeoisie propounded and solved the problem of nationality (or, as mostly happened, complicated the issue), we see that in the days of its youth the capitalist class dealt with questions of nationality in one fashion, and that in the days of its old age and decay it is dealing with them quite differently.

When the bourgeoisie was an oppressed class, when the aristocracy headed by a king or a tsar held the reins of power, when kings and tsars gave away whole peoples as their daughters' dowries, then the bourgeoisie was not merely accustomed to say fine things about the freedom of the nations, but actually attempted to realise such freedoms in practice—or at least the bourgeoisie of each nation did so as far as its own case was concerned. For example, when Italy was ruled by the Austrian crown, the Italian bourgeoisie headed the movement for national independence, endeavouring to secure the deliverance of Italy from the foreign yoke and its union to form a single state. When Germany was split up into a large number of petty princedoms and was crushed beneath the heel of Napoleon, the German bourgeoisie endeavoured to promote the union of Germany into a single great State, and it fought for the deliverance of the country from the French enslavers. When France, having overthrown the autocracy of Louis XVI, was attacked by the monarchical States of the rest of Europe, the revolutionary French bourgeoisie led the defence of the country and composed the national anthem known as the Marseillaise. In a word, the bourgeoisie of the oppressed nations always took the van in the struggle for deliverance ; it created a rich national literature ; it produced numerous men of genius— painters, prose writers, poets, and philosophers. This is what happened in earlier days, when the bourgeoisie was an oppressed class.

Why did the bourgeoisie of oppressed nations strive on behalf of national freedom ? If we are to listen to bourgeois poets, if we are to heed the works of bourgeois artists, the motive which animated the bourgeoisie was its hatred of all national oppression, its longing for the freeing and self-determination of every national stock, however small. In truth, when the bourgeoisie in any country fought for the deliverance of that country from a foreign yoke, it was fighting for the establishment of its own bourgeois State ; for the power of fleecing the people of its own land without any competition on the part of other exploiters ; for the right to the whole of the surplus value created by the town and country workers of their own land.

The history of all capitalist countries bears witness to this truth. When the bourgeoisie is oppressed in conjunction with the working people of its own nation, it clamours for the freedom of the nations in general, and insists upon the wrongfulness of any kind of national enslavement. But as soon as the capitalist class has secured power and has expelled the foreign conquerors—be these aristocrats or bourgeois—it does its utmost to subjugate any weak nationality whose subjugation may seem profitable. The revolutionary French bourgeoisie, as represented by Danton, Robespierre, and the other noted figures of the first epoch of the revolution, appealed to all the peoples of the world on behalf of deliverance from every form of tyranny ; the Marseillaise, written by Rouget de l'Isle, and sung by the armies of the revolution, is dear to the hearts of all oppressed peoples. But this same French bourgeoisie, having entered the second phase of its revolution under the regime of Napoleon, subjugated the peoples of Spain, Italy, Germany, and Austria, to the strains of the aforesaid Marseillaise, and continued to plunder them throughout the Napoleonic wars. When the German bourgeoisie was subject to oppression, such writers as Schiller with his *Wilhelm Tell* voiced the struggle of the peoples against foreign tyrants. But this same German bourgeoisie under the leadership of Bismarck and Moltke forcibly annexed the French provinces of Alsace-Lorraine, seized Schleswig from the Danes, tyrannised over the Poles of Posen, etc. The Italian bourgeoisie, having delivered itself from the yoke of the Austrian aristocracy, was perfectly ready to shoot down the conquered Bedouins of Tripoli, the Albanians and the Dalmatians on the shores of the Adriatic, and the Turks in Anatolia.

Why did these things happen, and why do they happen now ? Why has the bourgeoisie invariably voiced the demand for national freedom, and why has it never been able to realise such freedom in actual fact ?

The explanation is that every bourgeois State which has freed itself from the yoke of another nation inevitably strives to extend its own dominion. In any capitalist country you please to select, you will find that the bourgeoisie is not content with the exploitation of its own proletariat. The capitalists need raw materials from all the ends of the earth. They therefore strive to acquire colonies, whence, after subjugating the natives, they can without hindrance procure the raw materials they need for their factories. They require markets for the sale of their wares, and they endeavour to find such markets in backward lands, being quite unconcerned as to how this may affect the general population or the still immature bourgeoisies of such countries. They need territories to which they can export surplus capital, so that they may extract profits from these distant workers, and they enslave such territories, disposing of them as freely as they do of their own land. If during the conquest of colonies and during the economic enslavement of backward lands, another powerful bourgeoisie is encountered as a competitor, the dispute is settled by war, and this tends to take the form of such a world war as the one which has just been finished in Europe. The great war did not end the enslavement of the colonies and of the backward lands ; if any change has taken place for these, it has only been a change of masters. Furthermore, as the outcome of the war, Germany, Austria, and Bulgaria, which were free countries, have been enslaved. In this manner it has come to pass that the development of the bourgeois system, far from leading to a reduction in the number of the countries which are enslaved by other countries and by the bourgeoisies of these, has led to a positive increase in the number of enslaved lands. The bourgeois dominion has culminated in universal national oppression, for the whole world is now enslaved by the victorious group of capitalist States.

§ 60.

Antisemitism and the Proletariat. One of the worst forms of national enmity is antisemitism, that is to say, racial hostility towards the Jews, who belong to the Semitic stock (of which the Arabs form another great branch). The tsarist autocracy raised the hunt against the Jews in the hope of averting the workers' and peasants' revolution. " You are poor because the Jews fleece you," said the members of the Black Hundreds ; and they endeavoured to direct the discontent of the oppressed workers and peasants away from the landlords and the bourgeoisie, and to turn it against the whole Jewish nation. Among the Jews, as among other nationalities, there are different classes. It is only the bourgeois strata of the Jewish race which exploit the people, and these bourgeois strata plunder in common with the capitalists of other nationalities. In the outlying regions of tsarist Russia, where the Jews were allowed to reside, the Jewish workers and artisans lived in terrible poverty and degradation, so that their condition was even worse than that of the ordinary workers in other parts of Russia.

The Russian bourgeoisie raised the hunt against the Jews, not only in the hope of diverting the anger of the exploited workers, but also in the hope of freeing themselves from competitors in commerce and industry.

Of late years, anti-Jewish feeling has increased among

the bourgeois classes of nearly all countries. The bourgeoisie in other countries besides Russia can take example from Nicholas II in the attempt to inflame anti-Jewish feeling, not only in order to get rid of rival exploiters, but also in order to break the force of the revolutionary movement. Until recently, very little was heard of antisemitism in Germany, Great Britain, and the United States. To-day, even British ministers of State sometimes deliver antisemitic orations. This is an infallible sign that the bourgeois system in the west is on the eve of a collapse, and that the bourgeoisie is endeavouring to ward off the workers' revolution by throwing Rothschilds and Mendelssohns to the workers as sops. In Russia, antisemitism was in abeyance during the March revolution, but the movement regained strength as the civil war between the bourgeoisie and the proletariat grew fiercer; and the attacks on the Jews became more and more bitter in proportion as the attempts of the bourgeoisie to recapture power proved fruitless.

All these considerations combine to prove that antisemitism is one of the forms of resistance to socialism. It is disastrous that any worker or peasant should in this matter allow himself to be led astray by the enemies of his class.

Literature. LENIN, The Right of Self-Determination. STALIN, Marxism and the Problem of Nationality. ZALEFFSKY, The International and the Problem of Nationality. PETROFF, Truth and Falsehood about the Jews. KAUTSKY, The Jews. BEBEL, Antisemitism and the Proletariat. STEKLOFF, The last Word in Antisemitism.

CHAPTER EIGHT

THE PROGRAM OF THE COMMUNISTS IN RELATION TO ARMY ORGANISATION

§ 61.

Our old Army Program, and the Question of War in a socialist State. In § 12 we explained how the standing army of the bourgeois State is constructed and for what purposes it is used. The socialists of all countries, including the Russian social democrats, used to demand the abolition of standing armies. Instead of a standing army, the socialists wanted the general arming of the people (a citizen army) ; they demanded the abolition of the officers' caste, and the election of officers by the rank and file.

Let us consider what should be the communists' attitude towards these demands.

The first question that arises in this connexion is, on behalf of what form of social order the before-mentioned demands were made. Were they made for a bourgeois society, or for a socialist society, or for a society in the throes of the struggle between bourgeoisdom and socialism ?

The socialist parties adhering to the Second International had no clear ideas concerning the nature of the society in relation to which their program was drawn up. For the most part, indeed, their program related to a bourgeois society. What the socialists usually had in their minds as model was the Swiss Republic, where there is no standing army but a national militia.

It is obvious that the army program of the socialists was unrealisable in bourgeois society, above all during an epoch in which the class struggle was continually growing more acute. To abolish barracks signifies the abolition of the places where the workers and the peasants are trained to become the executioners of their own class brothers. It signifies the abolition of the only places in which it is possible to transform the workers into an army which will be ready to use its weapons against other nations at any moment which may suit the capitalists. To abolish the officers' caste signifies the abolition of the beast tamers who are alone competent to maintain an iron discipline, and who are alone able to subject the armed people to the will of the bourgeois class. The election of officers would enable the armed workers and peasants to choose officers from among themselves, officers who would not be bourgeois. For the bourgeoisie to agree to such proposals would mean that it was consenting to the formation of an army which was intended to subvert its own regime.

The whole history of capitalism in Europe has demonstrated and continues to demonstrate the impossibility of carrying out the old army program of the socialist party within the framework of bourgeois society, of carrying it out while society is divided into classes and in days when the class struggle is growing more acute. In proportion as the class struggle is intensified do we find that the bourgeois rulers are disinclined to arm the whole nation and are determined to put arms in the hands of their trusted White Guards only. The army program of the socialists, in so far as they hoped to realise it in the bourgeois regime, was, therefore, nothing but petty-bourgeois utopism.

Is it not possible, however, that the program was formulated with the definite aim of overthrowing the bourgeois regime ? This was not the case. The bourgeoisie wishes to defend itself against the working class, which hopes to seize power. It will therefore never entertain the idea of arming the workers. The bourgeoisie has introduced universal military service and has entrusted the worker-soldier with a rifle only for so long as it can hope that the soldiers drawn from the people will continue to obey the orders of their capitalist rulers. But directly the people thinks of fighting for its own hand, the people must be disarmed! All shrewd bourgeois politicians are well aware of this. Conversely, it would be quite unreasonable for the workers and peasants to think of arming the whole nation, when what they wish is to arm themselves that they may overthrow the bourgeoisie and seize power. It follows, therefore, that for the transitional period in which the proletariat is struggling for power, the old army program of the socialists is futile. Such a program is only applicable for the very brief period during which the pre-existing bourgeois standing army is being broken up. It is only applicable during the period when the officers' caste is being abolished and when the question of the election of officers by the rank and file arises. In the year 1917, the bolsheviks actually carried out this idea, which was part of their old pogram. By suppressing the officers' caste in what had been the tsarist army and in the Kerenskyite army, the bolsheviks deprived that army of its sting, so that it was no longer subject to the bourgeois-landlord class.

On the other hand, for a society in which socialism has been victorious, the old army program is fully applicable. When the proletariat has overthrown the bourgeoisie and has abolished class in quite a number of countries, it will be possible to carry out a general arming of the people. Then the working population alone will be armed, for in a socialist society all will be workers. It will be possible to do away with barrack life completely. It will also be possible to introduce the election of officers, a method which during the period of accentuated civil war is, except in rare and fortunate cases, unsuitable for the proletarian army.

A very natural question now arises. What need can there be for the general arming of the people in lands where a socialist regime prevails? In certain countries, let us suppose, the bourgeoisie has been conquered; those who were bourgeois have become workers; there can be no question of war between socialist States. But it is necessary to remember that socialism cannot gain the victory simultaneously in all the countries of the world. Some countries will, of course, lag behind the others in the matter of abolishing class and of realising socialism. In such circumstances, the countries in which the bourgeoisie has been overthrown and where all the bourgeois have become workers, may have to fight or to be prepared to fight against the bourgeoisies of those States in which the dictatorship of the proletariat has not yet been established ; or they may have to give armed assistance to the proletariat of those lands in which the dictatorship of the working class has been inaugurated but in which the struggle with the bourgeoisie has not yet been carried to a successful issue.

§ 62.

The Need for the Red Army ; its Class Composition. Most of the socialists who adhere to the Second International consider that socialism can be realised by securing a parliamentary majority. Since the socialists of this calibre were cradled in such ideas, since they were nurtured in the peaceful atmosphere of petty-bourgeois villadom, it was natural that they should give no heed to the possibility of or the need for organising a proletarian army in the period of the fight for socialism. Other socialists, though they recognised the inevitability of a forcible transformation effected by the armed workers, failed nevertheless to foresee that this armed struggle would be long drawn out, that Europe would have to pass through a phase, not only of socialist revolutions, but also of socialist wars. Consequently not one of the socialist programs voiced the need for the organisation of the Red Army, that is to say, of an army consisting of the armed workers and peasants. First in all the world,[1] the Russian working class was able to create such an army. We mean that, first in all the world, the Russian workers were able to get a firm grip of the State authority, and were able to defend what they had gained against the attacks of the Russian bourgeoisie and against the onslaughts of international capitalism. It is perfectly clear that without the Red Army the Russian workers and peasants would have found it impossible to maintain a single one of the achievements of their revolution. Without the Red Army they would have been crushed by the forces

---

[1] We are speaking in the text of an army in the full sense of the term. If we are asked where the first beginnings of such a Red Army are to be found, we can point to the army of the Paris Commune as the precursor of our Red Army—to the army which the workers of Paris created in the year 1871.

of reaction at home and abroad. A Red Army cannot be established upon the foundation of universal military service. While the struggle is still in progress, the proletariat, even though success is in sight, cannot venture to entrust rifles to members of the urban bourgeoisie or to the rich peasants. The proletarian army must be exclusively composed of persons belonging to the working class, of persons who do not exploit labour and who are directly interested in the victory of the workers' revolution. Only the industrial workers of the towns and the poor peasants from the villages should form the nucleus and the foundation of the Red Army, which will be converted into an army of all the working population by the adhesion of the middle peasants. As far as the members of the bourgeoisie and of the rich stratum of the peasantry are concerned, they must fulfil their military obligations to the proletarian State by militia duties at a distance from the fighting front. Of course this must not be considered to imply that a sufficiently powerful proletarian authority will refrain, in its turn, from compelling the exploiters to shoot at their White friends in the opposing trenches, just as the bourgeoisie, with the aid of its standing army, forced the proletarians to shoot their class brothers.

The standing army of the bourgeoisie, although it is established upon the basis of universal military service, and although in appearance it is an army of the whole people, is in reality a class army. But the proletariat need not hide the class character of its army, any more than it hides the class character of its dictatorship. The Red Army is one of the organs of the Soviet State, and is, generally speaking, constructed upon the same type as the other State organs of the proletarian dictatorship. Just as in the Soviet elections the soviet constitution gives no vote to persons whose whole economic and political position that constitution aims at undermining, so in the Red Army there is no place for those for whose destruction in the civil war the Red Army exists.

§ 63.

Universal military Training of the Workers. One of the primary aims of the system of military training for the workers which the Russian Soviet Republic has set out to realise, must be to reduce barrack life to a minimum. As far as possible, the workers and peasants must not be withdrawn from the work of production while they are being trained for military service. This will greatly diminish expenditure upon the army and will obviate the slackening down and disorganisation of production. Workers and peasants who are trained to arms in their spare time, fit themselves to be soldiers of the revolution without ceasing to be producers of value.

The second great need in connexion with the universal military training of the workers is to create in every town, and in every rural district, proletarian and peasant reserves able to take the field at a moment's notice on the approach of the enemy. The experience of the civil war in Russia has shown how important such reserves are for the success of the socialist campaign. It suffices to remember how the regiments of the workers' reserves successfully defended Petrograd from the White Guards ; or to think of the workers of the Ural region and the Donetz basin ; or of the workers and peasants in the town and province of Orenburg, in the town of Uralsk, etc.

§ 64.

Self-imposed Discipline versus Discipline imposed from above. Self-imposed discipline is impossible in an imperialist army. The very nature of such an army forbids the idea. An imperialist army consists of various social groups. The workers and peasants have been forcibly herded into the barracks of the bourgeois army. Should they begin to realise their own interests, far from consciously submitting to the discipline imposed by their epauletted superiors, they would consciously resist this discipline. For this reason, the discipline of bourgeois armies must be maintained by force; for this reason, flogging, tortures of every kind, and mass shootings, are not simply occasional incidents, but the very foundations of order, discipline, " military education."

On the other hand, in the Red Army, which is formed by the workers and the peasants and which defends their interests, coercive discipline must to an ever greater extent be replaced by the workers' voluntary acceptance of the discipline of the civil war. As the Red Army grows more clearly aware of its own nature, the Red soldiers come to realise that in the last resort they are commanded by the whole working class, through the instrumentality of the workers' State and its military staff. Thus the discipline of the Red Army is the submission of the minority (the soldiers) to the interests of the majority of the workers. Every reasonable order is backed, not by the commanding officer and his arbitrary will, not by the bourgeois minority and its predatory interests, but by the whole Workers' and Peasants' Republic. In the Red Army, therefore, propaganda and agitation, the political education of the rank and file, assume peculiar importance.

§ 65.

The political Commissars and the communist Groups.

In the Russian Soviet Republic, in which all workers can express their will through the soviets, the workers and peasants have for the last two years been electing communists to the various executive organs. The Communist Party—we put the matter in bourgeois phraseology—has become by the will of the masses the ruling party of the republic, for no other party was capable of conducting the victorious workers' and peasants' revolution to a successful issue. As a result of this, our party has become as it were a huge executive committee of the proletarian dictatorship. This is why the communists fill the leading role in the Red Army. The political commissars are the representatives of the class will of the proletariat in the army; they are mandated by the party and the military centres. Thereby are determined the mutual relationships of the commissar alike with the military staff and with the communist groups of the division to which he is assigned. The communist group is a section of the ruling party; the commissar is a plenipotentiary of the party as a whole. Thence derives his leading role, both in the army division, and in the communist groups of that division. Thence, likewise, his right to supervise the military staff. He is a political leader who acts as overseer to watch the technical experts performing their duties.

The task of the communist groups is to give to the soldiers of the Red Army clear ideas concerning the civil war, and concerning the need that they should subordinate their interests to the interests of all the workers. A further duty of the members of the communist groups in the army is, by personal example, to display their devotion to the revolution, and to arouse in their fellow-soldiers a desire to emulate this example. The members of the communist groups are further entitled to watch how their own commissar and other commissars perform their communist duties, and they can endeavour (by appealing to the supreme party organisations or to responsible commissars) to secure that necessary measures shall be carried into effect. Thus only can the Communist Party—without any infringement of general military discipline on the part of Red soldiers who are communists—secure complete control over all its members and prevent any misuse of power on their side.

Apart from the communist groups in the army and apart from the political commissars, the political education of the Red Army is supervised by a whole network of political sections in the divisions and in the armies at the various fronts, and it is also supervised by the propaganda sections of the Commissariat for War. In its various departments, the proletarian State of Russia has created a mighty instrument for the enlightenment and organisation of its army, and it endeavours to secure the maximum of result with the minimum of effort. Thanks to the existence of this apparatus, the work of agitation and enlightenment in our army is not carried on fortuitously, but has a systematised character. The newspaper, the spoken word at meetings, and scholastic instruction, are ensured for every soldier of the Red Army.

Unfortunately, however, the above-described organisations have not escaped the common lot of all the organisations of the Soviet Power. They have succumbed to bureaucracy ; they have tended towards a detachment from the masses, on the one hand, and from the party, on the other ; and in practice they have often shown themselves to be harbours of refuge for idlers and incapables who belong to the party war-office officialdom. A vigorous campaign against such abuses would seem to be of far more urgent importance to the Communist Party than the campaign against bureaucracy and slackness in the general soviet mechanism, for upon the success of the former campaign our speedy victory in the civil war must be said in a sense to depend.

§ 66.

Structure of the Red Army. In our system of universal military training, barrack life must be reduced to a minimum, so that ultimately the Red barracks may completely disappear. The structure of the Red Army must be gradually approximated to the structure of the productive units of the workers, whereby the artificial character of military unification will be overcome. We may express the matter more clearly by saying that the typical standing army of tsarist days, the standing army in the State of the bourgeoisie and the landed gentry, was composed of persons belonging to the most diverse classes. Those who were called up for service were forcibly dragged from their natural surroundings : the worker, from the factory ; the peasant, from the plough ; the clerk, from the desk ; the shopman, from the counter. The recruits were then artificially assembled in barracks, and distributed in the various army divisions. It was advantageous to the bourgeois State to break off all connexion between the proletarian recruit and his factory and between the peasant recruit and his village, so as to make of worker and peasant alike blind tools for the oppression of the labouring masses, and so that it might be easy to employ the workers and peasants of one province to shoot down those of another.

In the upbuilding of the Red Army, the Communist Party works in the opposite way. Although the conditions of the civil war have frequently compelled the party to make the best of the old methods of organisation, the essential aspiration is towards something utterly different. Our aim has been to ensure that the army subdivisions in the course of their construction (the company, the battalion, the regiment, the brigade, etc.) shall harmonise as far as may be with the factory, the workshop, the village, the hamlet, and so on. In other words, our aim is to remodel the artificial military unity—a unity which existed only for its own sake—into a natural, productive unity of the workers, and thus to reduce the artificiality of army life. The proletarian divisions built up in this manner are more compact ; they are disciplined by the very method of production ; and there is, therefore, the less need for a discipline imposed from above.

The formation of a sturdy, class-conscious proletarian nucleus is of primary importance to the Red Army. In such a country as Russia, in which peasants constitute the enormous majority of the population, the dictatorship of the proletariat necessarily means that the proletarian minority shall lead and organise the peasant majority (the middle peasantry) ; and that the peasant majority shall follow the lead of the organising proletariat, and shall have complete confidence in the political wisdom and constructive capacity of the urban workers. This statement is fully applicable to the Red Army, which is strong and disciplined precisely in proportion as its skeletal framework is proletarian and communist. To assemble this skeletal material, to distribute it properly, and to clothe the framework with a sufficient quantity of the disintegrated but far more abundant peasant material—this constitutes the fundamental organisatory task of the Communist Party in the upbuilding of the Red Army.

§ 67.

The Officers of the Red Army. The upbuilding of the Red Army was begun upon the ruins of the old tsarist army. The proletariat, when it gained the victory in the November revolution, had not a Red officers' corps of its own. There were only three ways in which the workers could make effective use of the experiences of the world war, could apply them to the civil war, could apply to the military training of its own army the technical military experiences that had been accumulated in the fallen regime. The first possibility was to create entirely new staffs out of the Reds, and to use members of the old officers' caste only as instructors. A second way would have been to hand over the command of the new army to the officers of the old army under the supervision of commissars. A third possible course was a combination of these two methods. Time pressed ; the civil war had begun ; the new army must be quickly created, and must be sent to the fight without delay. The proletarian authorities, therefore, had to adopt the third method. They began to organise schools for Red officers, who in general were only fitted for the lower grades. In addition, quite a number of the officers of the old army were invited to participate in the upbuilding of the Red Army and to share in its command.

The utilisation of the officers of the old army involved difficulties which were numerous and grave, and which have not yet been overcome. These officers could be divided into three groups, two small and one large. Some were more or less strongly sympathetic towards the Soviet Power. Others were definitely opposed to the new regime; they sided with the class enemies of the proletariat, and have continued to give these enemies active assistance. The third group, larger than both the others put together, consisted of the average officers who inclined to the winning side, and who were willing to serve the Soviet Government just as the wage worker serves the capitalist who buys labour power. Now the Communist Party had obviously to make all possible use of the services of the sympathetic minority. As regards the other minority, every means of repression had to be employed to render these reactionaries harmless. Finally, as far as the average officers were concerned, those whose political attitude in the civil war was neutral, the proletariat had to retain them in its service, and to ensure that they did their work conscientiously whether at the front or at the rear.

The utilisation of the old officers gave valuable results in the upbuilding of the Red Army. In this matter we were able to turn to useful account the technical experience in military affairs that had been acquired by the bourgeois and landlord regime. Their utilisation, however, entailed terrible dangers, for it occasionally involved widespread treachery on the part of the officers, and enormous sacrifices of the Red soldiers, who were betrayed and handed over in masses to the enemy.

The principal task of the Communist Party in this connexion is, in the first place, the effective training of our own commanders for the Red Army—the training of Red officers, of communists who shall be fitted for work on the general staff by a course of training at the Red Academy which has been established by the Soviet Power. Secondly we have to ensure a closer association between the communist commissars and all the other members of the party in the fighting forces, for the effective supervision and control of all the non-communist officers.

§ 68.

Should Army Officers be elected, or should they be appointed from above? The army of the capitalist State, based upon universal military service, is mainly composed of peasants and workers, under the command of officers drawn from the nobility and the bourgeoisie. When in our old program we demanded the election of officers, our aim was to ensure that the army command should be taken out of the hands of the exploiting classes. We were assuming that the army might be democratised while political power still remained in the hands of the bourgeoisie. Of course the idea was utterly unrealisable, for no bourgeoisie in the world could ever be expected to hand over without resistance the military apparatus of oppression. But in the struggle against militarism, in the campaign against the privileges of the officers' caste, our demand for the election of officers proved of enormous importance, and it was no less important owing to the way in which it contributed to the general disintegration of the imperialist armies.

The Red Army, on the other hand, is under proletarian control. The workers administer it through the central soviet organs, which they themselves elect. In all grades of army life, the proletariat is in control through the instrumentality of the communist commissars, who both at the front and at the rear are mainly drawn from among the workers. In these circumstances, the question of electing officers becomes a question of purely technical significance. The matter of real importance is that we should know what will make the army, in its present condition, the most efficient fighting force. From this point of view, will it be best to elect the officers, or to appoint them from above? When we take into consideration that our Red Army is mainly recruited from among the peasantry, when we recall the hardships to which it is exposed, its exhaustion by two wars, and the low level of class consciousness among the peasants who have joined the army— it will become obvious to us that the practice of electing officers cannot fail to exercise a disintegrating influence in our forces. Of course this does not exclude the possibility that in different circumstances the election of officers might do no harm; for instance, in volunteer units, firmly compacted out of men who all possess strong, revolutionary sentiments. Here, election would throw up practically the same officers as those who would have been appointed from above. As a general rule, however, the election of officers, although it may be regarded as an ideal method, would for practical reasons prove dangerous and harmful at the present juncture. But by the time the working masses who are now enrolled in the Red Army have risen to a level at which the election of officers will be useful and necessary, it is probable that there will be no further need for armies in the world.

§ 69.

The Red Army is provisional. The bourgeoisie looks upon the capitalist system as the " natural " ordering of human society ; it regards its own regime as everlasting, and it therefore constructs the instrument of its power—the army—solidly, builds it to last for years and years if not for ever. The proletariat regards its own Red Army in quite another light. The Red Army has been created by the workers for the struggle with the White Army of capital. The Red Army issued out of the civil war; it will disappear when a complete victory has been gained in that war, when class has been abolished, when the dictatorship of the proletariat has spontaneously lapsed. The bourgeois army is born of bourgeois society, and the bourgeoisie wishes this child to live for ever because it reflects the imperishability of the bourgeois regime. The Red Army, on the other hand, is the child of the working class, and the workers desire for their child a natural and glorious death. The day when the Red Army can be permanently disbanded will be the day on which will be signalised the final victory of the communist system.

The Communist Party must make it clear to the soldiers

of the Red Army that if that army should gain the victory over the White Guards of capital the victors would be the soldiers of the last army in the world. But the party must also make it perfectly clear to all who participate in the upbuilding of the Red Army, it must convince all the proletarian and peasant troops, that the workers have only become soldiers for a brief space and owing to a temporary need, that the field of *production* is the natural field for their activities, that work in the Red Army must on no account lead to the formation of any caste permanently withdrawn from industry and agriculture.

When the formation of the Red Army was first begun, the formation of the army which sprang from the proletarian Red Guards, the mensheviks and the social revolutionaries fiercely attacked the communists, declaring that the latter were false to the watchword of the general arming of the people, and accusing them of creating a standing army consisting of only one class. But the fact that civil war cannot last for ever, makes it obvious that the Red Army cannot be a standing army. The real reason why our army is a class army is because the class struggle has reached the last extremity of bitterness. No one but a petty-bourgeois utopist, no one who is not hopelessly stupid, can object to the existence of a class army while recognising the class war. It is characteristic that the bourgeoisie, in this epoch which has ensued upon the settlement of the world war, no longer thinks it necessary, or even possible, to conceal the class character of its army. Most instructive, in this connexion, has been the fate of the standing army in Germany, Britain, and France. The German National Assembly was elected by universal suffrage. Its main support was Noske's force of volunteer counter-revolutionary troops. At the stage of the embitterment of the class struggle and at the stage of the decay of bourgeois society which Germany has now reached, it is impossible that an army based on universal military service can be used for the maintenance of bourgeois institutions. Similarly in France and Britain, during the year 1919 the government was mainly dependent upon the support, not of the army which had been raised by universal service and had gained the victory in the great war, but upon a voluntary force of counter-revolutionary soldiers and police. Thus, not merely in Russia from the close of 1917, but likewise all over Europe from the close of 1918, a characteristic phenomenon was the abandonment of universal military service and the adoption of a system of class armies. In Russia, the traitors to socialism—the mensheviks and the social revolutionaries—were strongly opposed to the formation of the Red Army of the proletariat, at the very time when in Central Europe their friends Noske and Scheidemann were organising the White Army of the bourgeoisie. Thus the struggle against the creation of the class army of the proletariat (a struggle conducted in the name of universal military service and in the name of " democracy ") showed itself in practice to be a struggle to found the class army of the bourgeoisie.

Passing now to consider the question of a national militia, we find that the example of Switzerland, the example of the most democratic of all the bourgeois republics, has shown the part which such a militia plays in the hour when the class struggle is accentuated. The national militia, the " people's militia," of Switzerland under a bourgeois regime proves to be precisely the same weapon for keeping the proletariat down as any standing army in less democratic lands. The arming of the whole nation will inevitably lead to this result whenever and wherever it is effected under the political and economic regime of capitalism.

THE COMMUNIST PARTY DOES NOT ADVOCATE THE UNIVERSAL ARMING OF THE PEOPLE, BUT THE UNIVERSAL ARMING OF THE WORKERS. ONLY IN A SOCIETY CONSISTING OF NONE BUT WORKERS, ONLY IN A CLASSLESS SOCIETY, WILL IT BE POSSIBLE TO ARM THE WHOLE PEOPLE.

Literature. There is very little literature. Trotsky has published articles in " Pravda " and " Isvestia." A symposium, Revolutionary War has been edited by Podvoisky and Pavlovich. TROTSKY, The international Situation and the Red Army. TROTSKY, The Soviet Power and international Imperialism. ZINOVIEFF, Our Situation and the Creation of the Red Army. ZINOVIEFF, Speech concerning the Red Army. YAROSLAVSKY, The New Army.

CHAPTER NINE

PROLETARIAN JUSTICE

§ 70.

The Administration of Justice in bourgeois Society. Among the various institutions of bourgeois society which serve to oppress and deceive the working masses, must be mentioned bourgeois justice. This estimable institution is carried on under the guidance of laws passed in the interests of the exploiting class. Whatever the composition of the court, its decisions are restricted in accordance with the volumes of statutes in which are incorporated all the privileges of capital and all the lack of privileges of the toiling masses.

As far as the organisation of bourgeois justice is concerned, this is in perfect harmony with the characteristics of the bourgeois State. Where the bourgeois State is comparatively frank in its methods, where it is free from hypocrisy in its determination that the decisions of the courts shall be favourable to the ruling class, there the judges are appointed from above ; but even when they are elected, only the members of the privileged stratum are entitled to vote. When the masses have been sufficiently brought to heel by capital, so that they are duly submissive and regard the laws of the bourgeois State as their own laws, the workers are permitted to a certain extent to be their own judges, just as they are allowed to vote exploiters and their henchmen into parliament. Thus originated trial by jury, thanks to which legal decisions made in the interests of capital can masquerade as decisions made by the " whole people."

§ 71.

The Election of the Judiciary by the Workers. The program of the socialists adhering to the Second International contained a demand for the popular election of the judiciary. In the epoch of the proletarian dictatorship, this demand assumes a no less impracticable and reactionary complexion than the demand for universal suffrage or the demand for the general arming of the people. When the proletariat is in power, it cannot permit the enemies of its class to become judges. The workers could hardly accept the representatives of capital or of the landed interest as administrators of the new laws which are intended to overthrow the capitalist regime! In fine, in the long succession of civil and criminal affairs, the proceedings of the courts must be conducted in the spirit of the new socialist society which is in course of construction.

For these reasons the Soviet Power did not merely destroy all the old machinery of justice which, while serving capital, hypocritically proclaimed itself to be the voice of the people. It went farther, and constituted new courts, making no attempt to conceal their class character. In the old law-courts, the class minority of exploiters passed judgment upon the working majority. The law-courts of the proletarian dictatorship are places where the working majority passes judgment upon the exploiting minority. They are specially constructed for this purpose. The judges are elected by the workers alone. The judges are elected solely from among the workers. For the exploiters the only right that remains is the right of being judged.

§ 72.

Unified popular Law-courts. In bourgeois society the administration of justice is an exceedingly cumbrous affair. Bourgeois jurists proudly declare that, thanks to the gradation of lower courts, higher courts, courts of appeal, and so on, absolute justice is ensured, and the number of miscarriages of justice reduced to a minimum. In actual fact, in the past and to-day, the working of this graded series

of law-courts has been and is to the unfailing advantage
of the possessing classes. Well-to-do persons, being able
to command the services of highly paid lawyers, can carry
a case from court to court until they secure a favourable
decision ; whereas a plaintiff who is poor often finds it
necessary to abandon his suit on grounds of expense. The
right of appeal secures an " equitable " decision only in
this sense, that it secures a judgment in the interest of
exploiting groups.

The unified popular law-court of the proletarian State
reduces to a minimum the time which elapses from the
moment when the case is brought before the court to the
moment when it is finally decided. The law's delay is
greatly diminished, and if proceedings are still sluggish,
this is only because all soviet institutions are imperfect
during the first months and years of the proletarian dictatorship. But the general upshot is that the courts have
been made accessible to the poorest and most unenlightened
strata of the population ; and they will become still more
accessible as soon as the epoch of intensified civil war is
over, and as soon as all the mutual relationships of the
citizens of the republic have assumed a more stable
character. " Inter arma leges silent " [in war time, the
laws are in abeyance] the Romans used to say. But
during the time of civil war the laws are not in abeyance
as far as the workers are concerned. The popular law-
courts continue to do their work, but it is impossible as
yet for the whole population to realise the nature of the
new courts of justice and rightly to appreciate their
advantages.

During this era when the old society is being
destroyed and the new society is being upbuilded, the
popular courts have a gigantic task to perform. The process
of change has been so rapid that soviet legislation has not
been able to keep pace with it. The laws of the bourgeois-
landlord system have been annulled ; but the laws of the
proletarian State have as yet merely been outlined, and
will never be committed to paper in their entirety. The
workers do not intend to perpetuate their dominion, and
they therefore have no need for endless tomes of written
laws. When they have expressed their will in one of the

fundamental decrees, they can leave the interpretation and application of these decrees, as far as practical details are concerned, to the popular courts in which the judges are elected by the workers. The only important matter is that the decisions of these courts shall bear witness to the complete breach with the customs and the ideology of the bourgeois system; that the people's judges shall decide the cases which come before them in accordance with the dictates of proletarian ideology, and not in accordance with those of bourgeois ideology. Dealing with the unending series of disputes which arise during the break-up of the old relationships, and during the realisation of the rights of the proletariat, the people's judges can carry to its proper issue the transformation which began with the November revolution of the year 1917, and which must inevitably involve all the mutual relationships of the citizens of the Soviet Republic. On the other hand, in dealing with the vast number of cases which occur independently of the peculiar conditions of the revolutionary era—minor criminal cases of a petty-bourgeois character—the popular courts must give expression to the entirely new attitude towards such offences which has been adopted by the revolutionary proletariat, thus effecting a revolution in the whole character of penal measures.

§ 73.

Revolutionary Tribunals. These popular courts—to which the judges are elected, from which the judges can be recalled, and in which every worker must fulfil his judicial duty when his turn comes—are looked upon by the Communist Party as the normal law-courts of the proletarian State. But in the epoch of the extremest intensification of the civil war, it has been found necessary to supplement the popular courts by the appointment of revolutionary tribunals. The function of the revolutionary tribunals is to deal speedily and mercilessly with the enemies of the proletarian revolution. Such courts are among the weapons for the crushing of the exploiters, and from this point of view they are just as much the instruments of proletarian offence and defence as the Red Guard, the Red Army, and the Extraordinary Commissions. Consequently, the revolutionary tribunals are organised on less democratic lines than the popular courts. They are appointed by the soviets, and are not directly elected by the workers.

§ 74.

Proletarian penal Methods. In the sanguinary struggle with capitalism, the working class cannot refrain from inflicting the last extremity of punishment upon its declared enemies. While the civil war continues, the abolition of the death penalty is impossible. But a dispassionate comparison of proletarian justice with the justice of the bourgeois counter-revolution shows the marvellous leniency of the workers' courts in comparison with the executioners of bourgeois justice. The workers pass death sentences in extreme cases only. This was especially characteristic of the legal proceedings during the first months of the proletarian dictatorship. It suffices to recall that in Petrograd the notorious Purishkevich was condemned to only two weeks' imprisonment by the revolutionary tribunal. We find that the progressive classes, the inheritors of the future, have dealt very gently with their enemies, whereas the classes that are dying have displayed almost incredible ferocity.

When we come to consider the punishments inflicted by proletarian courts of justice for criminal offences which have no counter-revolutionary bearing, we find them to be radically different from those inflicted for similar offences by bourgeois courts. This is what we should expect. The great majority of crimes committed in bourgeois society are either direct infringements of property rights or are indirectly connected with property. It is natural that the bourgeois State should take vengeance upon criminals, and that the punishments inflicted by bourgeois society should be various expressions of the vengeful sentiments of the infuriated owner. Just as absurd have been and are the punishments inflicted for casual offences, or for offences which arise out of the fundamentally imperfect character of personal relationships in bourgeois society (offences connected with the family relationships of society; those resulting from romanticist inclinations; those due to alcoholism or to mental degeneration; those due to ignorance, or to a suppression of social instinct, etc.). The proletarian law-court has to deal with offences for which the ground has been prepared by bourgeois society, by the society whose vestiges are still operative. A large number of professional criminals, trained to become such in the old order, survive to give work for the proletarian courts. But these courts are entirely free from the spirit of revenge. They cannot take vengeance upon people simply because these happen to have lived in bourgeois society. This is why our courts manifest a revolutionary change in the character of their decisions. More and more frequently do we find that conditional sentences are imposed, punishments that do not involve any punishment, their chief aim being to prevent a repetition of the offence. Another method is that of social censure, a method that can only be effective in a classless society, one in which a social consciousness and a social sense of responsibility have greatly increased. Imprisonment without any occupation, enforced parasitism, the penal method so frequently employed under the tsarist regime, is replaced by the enforcement of social labour. The aim of the proletarian courts is to ensure that the damage done to society by the criminal shall be made good by him through the performance of an increased amount of social labour. Finally, when the court has to deal with a habitual criminal (one whose liberation after his sentence has been performed will entail danger to the lives of other citizens), isolation of the criminal from society is enforced, but in such a way as to give the offender full opportunities for moral regeneration.

Most of the measures above described, involving a complete transformation of the customary penal methods, have already been recommended by the best bourgeois criminologists. But in bourgeois society they remain a dream. Nothing but the victory of the proletariat can ensure their realisation.

§ 75.

Proletarian Justice in the Future. As far as the revolutionary tribunals are concerned, this form of proletarian justice has no significance for future days, any more than the Red Army will have any significance for the future after it has conquered the White Guards, or any more than the Extraordinary Commissions have any significance for the future. In a word, all the instruments created by the proletariat for the critical period of the civil war are transient. When the counter-revolution has been successfully crushed, these instruments will no longer be needed, and they will disappear.

On the other hand, proletarian justice in the form of the elective popular courts will unquestionably survive the end of the civil war, and will for a long period have to continue the use of measures to deal with the vestiges of bourgeois society in its manifold manifestations. The abolition of classes will not result in the immediate abolition of class ideology, which is more long-lived than are the social conditions which have produced it, more enduring than the class instincts and class customs which have brought it into being. Besides, the abolition of class may prove a lengthy process. The transformation of the bourgeoisie into working folk and that of the peasants into the workers of a socialist society will be a tardy affair. The change in peasant ideology is likely to be very slow, and will give plenty of work to the law-courts. Moreover, during the period which must precede the full development of communist distribution, the period during which the articles of consumption are still privately owned, there will be ample occasion for delinquencies and crimes. Finally, anti-social offences arising out of personal egoism, and all sorts of offences against the common weal, will long continue to provide work for the courts. It is true that these courts will gradually change in character. As the State dies out, they will tend to become simply organs for the expression of public opinion. They will assume the character of courts of arbitration. Their decisions will no longer be enforced by physical means and will have a purely moral significance.

Literature. Communist literature dealing with bourgeois and proletarian courts of justice is scanty. Among the older works, the following may be recommended.

MARX, Address to the Jury at the Cologne Communists' Trial. ENGELS, The Origin of the Family, of private Property, and of the State. LASSALLE, Collected Works, especially : Speeches for the Defence, The Idea of the working Class, The Program of the Workers. ENGELS, Anti-Dühring (the parts dealing with the State). KAUTSKY, The Nature of political Offences. VAN KON, The economic Factors of Crime. GERNET, The social Factors of Crime.

Recent works. STUCHKA, The Constitution of the R.S.F.S.R. in Question and Answer. STUCHKA, The People's Court. HOICHBART, What should a People's Court be ?

CHAPTER TEN

COMMUNISM AND EDUCATION

§ 76.

The School under the bourgeois Regime. In bourgeois society the school has three principal tasks to fulfil. First, it inspires the coming generation of workers with devotion and respect for the capitalist regime. Secondly, it creates from the young of the ruling classes " cultured " controllers of the working population. Thirdly, it assists capitalist production in the application of sciences to technique, thus increasing capitalist profits.

As regards the first of these tasks, just as in the bourgeois army the " right spirit " is inculcated by the officers, so in the schools under the capitalist regime the necessary influence is mainly exercised by the caste of " officers of popular enlightenment." The teachers in the public elementary schools receive a special course of training by which they are prepared for their role of beast tamers. Only persons who have thoroughly acquired the bourgeois outlook have the entry into the schools as teachers. The ministries of education in the capitalist regime are ever on the watch, and they ruthlessly purge the teaching profession of all dangerous (by which they mean socialist) elements. The German public elementary schools served prior to the revolution as supplements to the barracks of William II, and were shining examples of the way in which the landed gentry and the bourgeoisie can make use of the school for the manufacture of faithful and blind slaves of capital. In the elementary schools of the capitalist regime, instruction is given in accordance with a definite program perfectly adapted for the breaking-in of the pupils to the capitalist system. All the text-books are written in an appropriate spirit. The whole of bourgeois literature subserves the same end, for it is written by persons who look upon the bourgeois social order as natural, perdurable, and the best of all possible regimes. In this way the scholars are imperceptibly stuffed with bourgeois ideology; they are infected with enthusiasm for all bourgeois virtues; they are inspired with esteem for wealth, renown, titles and orders; they aspire to get on in the world, they long for personal comfort, and so on. The work of bourgeois educationists is completed by the servants of the church with their religious instruction. Thanks to the intimate associations between capital and the church, the law of God invariably proves to be the law of the possessing classes.[1]

In capitalist society the second leading aim of bourgeois education is secured by carefully withholding secondary education and higher education from the working masses. Instruction in the middle schools, and still more in the high schools, is extremely costly, so that it is quite beyond the financial resources of the workers. The course of instruction, in middle and higher education, lasts for ten years or more. For this reason it is inaccessible to the worker and the peasant who, in order to feed their families, are compelled to send their children at a very early age to factory work or field work, or else must make the youngsters work at home. In actual practice, the middle and higher schools are the preserves of bourgeois youth. In them, the younger members of the governing classes are trained to succeed their fathers in careers of exploitation, or to fill the official and technical posts of the

[1] In tsarist Russia the method by which the masses of the people were kept in subjection to the aristocratic State was not, on the whole, that of a bourgeois-priestly-tsarist enlightenment, but simply that of withholding enlightenment of any sort. In this connexion we may refer to the notorious " theory " of the celebrated obscurantist Pobedonostseff, who considered popular ignorance to be the main prop of the autocracy.

capitalist State. In these schools, likewise, instruction has a definitely class character. In the domains of mathematics, the technique of industry, and the natural sciences, this may be less striking ; but the class character of the teaching is conspicuous in the case of the social sciences, whereby the pupils' outlook on the world is in reality formed. Bourgeois political economy is inculcated with all the most perfected methods for the " annihilation of Marx." Sociology and history are likewise taught from a purely capitalist outlook. The history of jurisprudence concludes with the treatment of bourgeois jurisprudence as the natural right of " the man and the citizen " ; etc., etc. To sum up, the higher and middle schools teach the children of the capitalists all the data that are requisite for the maintenance of bourgeois society and the whole system of capitalist exploitation. If any of the children of the workers, happening to be exceptionally gifted, should find their way into the higher schools, in the great majority of instances the bourgeois scholastic apparatus will serve as a means of detaching them from their own class kin, and will inoculate them with bourgeois ideology, so that in the long run the genius of these scions of the working class will be turned to account for the oppression of the workers.

Turning, finally, to the third task of capitalist education, we find that the school fulfils it as follows. In a class society where capitalism is dominant, science is divorced from labour. Not only does it become the property of the possessing classes. More than this, it becomes the profession of a small and comparatively narrow circle of individuals. Scientific instruction and scientific research are divorced from the labour process. In order that it may avail itself of the data of science and may turn them to account in production, bourgeois society has to create a number of institutions serving for the application of scientific discoveries to manufacturing technique ; and it has to create a number of technical schools which will facilitate the maintenance of production at the level rendered possible by the advance of " pure " science—by which is meant science divorced from labour. Furthermore, the polytechnic schools of capitalist society do not merely serve to supply capitalist society with technical experts ; they supply in addition those who will act as managers, those who will function as " captains of industry." In addition, to provide the personnel which will supervise the circulation of commodities, there have been founded numerous commercial schools and academies.

In all these organizations, whatever is linked up with production will endure. But everything which is concerned merely with *capitalist* production, will die out. There will persist everything which promotes the advancement of science ; there will perish that which promotes the severance of science from labour. There will be preserved the methods of technical instruction—but instruction in technical methods altogether apart from the performance of physical labour will be abolished. There will be preserved and extended the utilisation of science to further production. On the other hand, any hindrances to such utilisation of science, in so far as capital tends to make use of science only to the degree in which at any given moment science tends to raise profits, will be swept out of the way.

§ 77.

The destructive Tasks of Communism. In the matter of education, as in all other matters, the Communist Party is not merely faced by constructive tasks, for in the opening phases of its activity it is likewise faced by destructive tasks. In the educational system bequeathed to it by capitalist society, it must hasten to destroy everything which has made of the school an instrument of capitalist class rule.

In capitalist society, the higher stages of school life were the exclusive property of the exploiting classes. Such schools, in their unending series of higher classical schools, higher modern schools, institutes, cadet corps, etc., have to be destroyed.

The teaching staff of the bourgeois schools served the purposes of bourgeois culture and of fraud. We must ruthlessly expel from the proletarian school all those teachers of the old schools who either cannot or will not become instruments for the communist enlightenment of the masses.

In the schools of the old regime, teachers were engaged who had been indoctrinated with the bourgeois spirit ; in these schools methods of instruction were practised which served the class interests of the bourgeoisie. In our new schools, we must make a clean sweep of all such things.

The old school was intimately associated with religion —by compulsory religious teaching, compulsory attendance at prayers, and compulsory church-going. The new school forcibly expels religion from within its walls, under whatever guise it seeks entry and in whatever diluted form reactionary groups of parents may desire to drag it back again.

The old university created a close corporation of professors, a teachers' guild, which prevented the introduction of fresh teaching strength into the university. The close corporation of bourgeois professors must be dissolved, and the professorial chairs must be thrown open to all competent instructors.

Under the tsar, Russian was the only permissible language in the State service and in the school; the non-Russian subjects of the tsar were not allowed to receive instruction in their native tongue. In the new schools, all trace of national oppression disappears from the realm of instruction, for those of every nationality are entitled to receive education in their respective tongues.

§ 78.

The School as an Instrument of communist Education and Enlightenment. The bourgeoisie comprises a very small minority of the population. This, however, does not prevent it from supplementing the other instruments of class oppression by the use of the school to educate and break in the millions of workers, to inoculate them with bourgeois ideology. In this way the majority of the population is constrained to accept the outlook and the morality of a numerically insignificant fraction.

In capitalist countries, the proletariat and the semi-proletariat comprise the majority of the population. In Russia, the urban workers, though a minority, have in political matters become the leaders and the organisers of the struggle on behalf of all the toilers. It is natural, therefore, that the urban proletariat, having seized power, should use it primarily to this end, that it may raise all the backward strata of the working population to the requisite level of communist consciousness. The bourgeoisie used the school for the enslavement of all who live by labour. The proletariat will use the school to enfranchise them, to sweep away the last traces of spiritual slavery from the consciousness of the workers. Thanks to the schools, the bourgeoisie was able to impose upon proletarian children a bourgeois mentality. The task of the new communist schools is to impose upon bourgeois and petty-bourgeois children a proletarian mentality. In the realm of the mind, in the psychological sphere, the communist school must effect the same revolutionary overthrow of bourgeois society, must effect the same expropriation, that the Soviet Power has effected in the economic sphere by the nationalisation of the means of production. The minds of men must be made ready for the new social relationships. If the masses find it difficult to construct a communist society, this is because in many departments of mental life they still have both feet firmly planted upon the soil of bourgeois society, because they have not yet freed themselves from bourgeois prejudices. In part, therefore, it is the task of the new school to adapt the mentality of adults to the changed social conditions. Still more, however, it is the task of the new school to train up a younger generation whose whole ideology shall be deeply rooted in the soil of the new communist society.

The attainment of this end must be promoted by all our educational reforms, some of which have already been inaugurated, whilst others still await realisation.

§ 79.

Preparation for School Life. In bourgeois society, the child is regarded as the property of its parents—if not wholly, at least to a major degree. When parents say, " My daughter," " My son," the words do not simply imply the existence of a parental relationship, they also give expression to the parents' view that they have a right to educate their own children. From the socialist outlook, no such right exists. The individual human being does not belong to himself, but to society, to the human race. The individual can only live and thrive owing to the existence of society. The child, therefore, belongs to the society in which it lives, and thanks to which it came into being—and this society is something wider than the " society " of its own parents. To society, likewise, belongs the primary and basic right of educating children.   From this point of view, the parents' claim to bring up their own children and thereby to impress upon the children's psychology their own limitations, must not merely be rejected, but must be absolutely laughed out of court.   Society may entrust the education of children to the parents ; but it may refuse to do anything of the kind ; and there is all the more reason why society should refuse to entrust education to the parents, seeing that the faculty of educating children is far more rarely encountered than the faculty of begetting them.   Of one hundred mothers, we shall perhaps find one or two who are competent educators.   The future belongs to social education.   Social education will make it possible for socialist society to train the coming generation most successfully, at lowest cost, and with the least expenditure of energy.

The social education of children, therefore, must be realised for other reasons besides those of pedagogy.   It has enormous economic advantages.   Hundreds of thousands, millions of mothers will thereby be freed for productive work and for self-culture.   They will be freed from the soul-destroying routine of housework, and from the endless round of petty duties which are involved in the education of children in their own homes.

That is why the Soviet Power is striving to create a number of institutions for the improvement of social educa-tion, which are intended by degrees to universalise it.   To this class of institutions belong the kindergartens, to which manual workers, clerks, etc., can send their children, thus entrusting them to experts who will prepare the children for school life.   To this category, too, belong the homes or residential kindergartens.   There are also children's colonies, where the children either live permanently, or for a considerable period, away from their parents.   There are in addition the creches, institutions for the reception of children under four years of age ; in these the little ones are cared for while their parents are at work.

The Communist Party, therefore, must, on the one hand, ensure, through the working of soviet institutions, that there shall be a more rapid development of the places where children are prepared for school life, and it must ensure that there shall be a steady improvement in the training given at such places. On the other hand, by intensified propaganda among parents, the party must overcome bourgeois and petty-bourgeois prejudices concerning the necessity and superiority of home education. Here theoretical propaganda must be reinforced by the example of the best conducted educational institutions of the Soviet Power. Only too often, the unsatisfactory condition of the homes, creches, kindergartens, etc., deters parents from entrusting their children to these. It must be the task of the Communist Party, and especially of the women's sections, to induce parents to strive for the improvement of social education, not by holding aloof from it, but by sending their children to the appropriate institutions, and by exercising the widest possible control over them through parents' organisations.

§ 80.

The unified Labour School. The preparatory institutions are for children up to the age of seven. After that age, education and instruction must be effected in the school— not in the home. Education must be compulsory, which marks a great advance upon tsarist times. It must be gratuitous, and this also marks a great advance, for even in the most progressive bourgeois lands only elementary education is gratuitous. Education is naturally open to all, for the educational and cultural privileges of special groups of the population have now been abolished. Universal, equal, and compulsory education is made available for all children from the ages of seven to seventeen.

The school must be unified. This means, first of all, that the segregation of the sexes in the school must be done away with, that boys and girls must be educated together, that there must be co-education. Unification further signifies the abolition of the classification of schools as elementary schools, middle schools, and high schools, having no connexion one with another, and working in accordance with programs which are quite independent of one another. It implies that there must no longer be a division of the elementary, middle, and high schools into general schools on the one hand and specialist or technical schools on the other, or into common schools and schools for special classes of the population. The unified school provides a single gradated system, through which every learner in the socialist republic can and must pass. Boys and girls will begin with the kindergarten, and will work their way together through all stages to the top. This will conclude general compulsory education and also such technical education as is compulsory for every pupil.

It will be obvious to our readers that the unified school is not merely the ideal of every advanced educationist, but is the only possible type of school in a socialist society, that is to say, in a classless society or in one that is striving to abolish class. Socialism alone can realise this ideal of the unified school, although certain bourgeois educationists have entertained aspirations towards it.

The school of the socialist republic must be a labour school. This means that instruction and education must be united with labour and must be based upon labour. The matter is important for many reasons. It is important, first of all because of its bearing upon successful instruction. A child learns more easily, more willingly, and more thoroughly that which it learns, not from books or from the words of the teacher, but from the personal experience of what it is doing with its own hands. We can more easily understand our natural surroundings when we get to work upon nature in our attempts to modify it. This unification of instruction with labour has already begun in the most progressive bourgeois schools. It is impossible, however, to carry it out thoroughly in the bourgeois system, in which parasitic elements are deliberately cultivated, and in which physical work is separated from mental work by an impassable gulf.

Labour is necessary, not only for the healthy physical development of the children, but also for the proper development of all their faculties. Experience shows that the time they spend at school in practical work, far from retarding their progress in all kinds of theoretical knowledge, contributes greatly to their advance in the theoretical field.

Finally, for communist society, the labour school is absolutely indispensable. Every citizen in such a society must be acquainted with the elements, at least, of all crafts. In communist society there will be no close corporations, no stereotyped guilds, no petrified specialist groups. The most brilliant man of science must also be skilled in manual labour. To the pupil who is about to leave the unified labour school, communist society says : " You may or may not become a professor ; but in any case you must produce values." A child's first activities take the form of play ; play should gradually pass into work by an imperceptible transition, so that the child learns from the very outset to look upon labour, not as a disagreeable necessity or as a punishment, but as a natural and spontaneous expression of faculty. Labour should be a need, like the desire for food and drink ; this need must be instilled and developed in the communist school.

In communist society, with its vigorous technical progress, there will inevitably be vast and rapid transferences of labour power from one department to another. For example, a discovery in the weaving or the spinning industry may reduce the need for weavers and spinners, and may increase the number of workers required for cotton growing. In such cases, a redistribution of energies and occupations will be essential, and it can only be carried out with success if every worker in communist society is a master of several crafts. Bourgeois society meets these difficulties by the expedient of the industrial reserve army, which means that there is always a greater or smaller residue of unemployed. In communist society there will be no army of unemployed. The reserve of workers requisite for any branch of production in which a deficiency of labour power makes itself apparent, will be constituted by the competence of workers in other branches of production to fill the vacant places. The unified labour school, and nothing else, can provide for the training of workers who will be able to perform the most diverse functions of communist society.

§ 81.

Specialist Education. Up to the age of seventeen, all the young people in the republic must attend the unified labour school, acquiring there the sum of theoretical and practical knowledge indispensable to every citizen of communist society. But instruction must not end there. Specialist knowledge is requisite in addition to general knowledge. The totality of the most indispensable sciences is so vast, that no individual can grasp it in its entirety. The unification of education in the unified labour school is by no means intended to exclude specialist training. Our aim merely is to defer specialist training till the last stage is reached. Already during the later stages of work in the unified labour school, in the case of pupils between the ages of fourteen and seventeen, inclination towards one occupation or another will invariably become manifest. It is not merely possible, but it is also necessary, to give an outlet to the natural desire for a more intimate acquaintance with certain of the sciences. But of course this must not be done to the detriment of the general educational program of the labour school.

Real specialist training should not, however, begin until after the age of seventeen. The age limit is selected for various reasons. Until seventeen, the pupils at the labour school are scholars rather than workers. The fundamental aim of the labour processes in the school is not that of creating values and of contributing to the State budget, but that of conveying instruction. After the age of seventeen, the pupil becomes a worker. He must perform his quota of labour, must play his due part in producing goods for the human community. He can receive specialist instruction only in so far as he has first fulfilled his fundamental duty towards society. For this reason, as is right, specialist instruction for young people after the age of seventeen can only be given out of working hours. With the advance of manufacturing technique we may expect the working day to become less than eight hours, and in this way there will be provided for every member of communist society plenty of time for specialist education. In certain cases, and where persons of unusual talent are concerned, it may prove desirable to make exceptions in the form of exemption from labour for a certain number of years, in order to provide opportunity for study or for research work. If complete exemption from labour should seem undesirable in the social interest, there may be a special reduction of the working hours for such individuals.

§ 82.

The University. At the present time it is still impossible to foresee precisely what character the higher schools for specialist training will assume under communism. . They will probably be of various types. There will be places where brief courses will be given. There will be polytechnics and laboratory schools, at which instruction will be furnished while at the same time experimental research is being carried on ; in these, all distinction between professors and students will have disappeared. But even to-day we can be perfectly sure that the universities in their present form, with their present professorial staffs, have ceased to be serviceable institutions. They carry a stage farther the same sort of instruction which was provided in the bourgeois middle schools of the old type. For the time being these universities may be reformed by leavening the professorial staffs through the addition of persons who may not perhaps attain the standard of the " learned specialists of bourgeois society," but who will be fully competent to effect the necessary revolution in the teaching of the social sciences, and will be able to expel bourgeois culture from its last refuge. Furthermore, the composition of the audiences will be changed, for most of the students will be workers, and of course in this way technical science will pass into the possession of the working class. But the attendance of the workers at the universities will necessarily involve their maintenance at the cost of the State throughout the period of instruction. All this is considered in the educational section of the party program. (See pp. 387–9.)

§ 83.

Soviet Schools and Party Schools. During the Kerensky regime the tsarist school apparatus was left practically intact. The Communist Party, having attained to power, made it its business to destroy this apparatus entirely. Upon the ruins of the old class school the communists have begun the construction of the unified labour school, as the embryo of the normal labour school of communist society. They are endeavouring to eradicate from the bourgeois university everything which used to promote the maintenance of the capitalist dominion. The knowledge that has been accumulated during the ages when the possessing classes were in power, is being made accessible to all the workers. Thus is being begun the construction of the normal type of university for communist society.

But among all the sciences known to bourgeois culture, there was not one which gave any information as to how the proletarian revolution was to be achieved. Among all the schools which the bourgeoisie has founded and which communist society has begun to reconstruct, there was not one to teach how the proletarian State is to be upbuilded. The transitional period between capitalism and communism has given birth to a special type of school, which is intended to be serviceable to the revolution now in progress and to assist in the construction of the soviet apparatus. Such were the aims of the party and soviet schools which have grown up under our own eyes, in order to give brief and occasional courses of instruction, and which are being transformed into permanent institutions for the training of those who work in the party and in the soviets. The transformation was inevitable. The upbuilding of a soviet State is an entirely new undertaking. There is no historical precedent for anything of the kind. The work of the soviet institutions develops and improves day by day ; it is essential to success that every worker in the soviets should be able to avail himself of all the experience of his predecessors. Self-education in administrative work, such as can be effected by the participation of all the workers in the soviets, would seem to be insufficient. This experience must be collected, systematised, elaborated, and made available to all the workers who are engaged in the upbuilding of the soviet system, so that each relay of workers which comes to participate in the administration can be saved from committing the faults of its predecessors ; so that the new arrivals can learn, not from their own mistakes, but from the mistakes which have been made by others, and for which the State has once already had to pay. Now the schools for soviet work must also serve this end, and we already have in the Soviet Republic a central school of soviet work in the All-Russian Central Executive Committee, which is a permanent school. Soon, doubtless, similar schools of soviet work will be established in the capitals of all the provinces.

Passing now to consider the party schools, we find that they have undergone a radical change in character during the period of actual transition to communism. At first they were the schools of a definite party, supported by the proletariat, and in this stage they had a purely political character. Now they have become places where instruction is given in the communist transformation of society, and they are therefore State schools. At the same time they are military academies for the purposes of the civil war. It has only been thanks to these schools that the proletariat has been able to form an idea of the objective significance of the transformation which it is undergoing half unwittingly, almost instinctively—for as yet it only realises the narrower concrete aims, and is incompetent to grasp the nature of the revolutionary process as a whole. The party schools are not only able to provide the proletariat with a scientific explanation of the nature and goal of the revolution, but they can also teach the workers how to achieve the aims of the revolution by the shortest route and with the least expenditure of effort.

§ 84.

Extra-scholastic Instruction. Under the tsarist regime the vast majority of the working population was deliberately kept in a permanent state of ignorance and illiteracy. An enormous percentage of illiterates was handed down by the autocracy to the Soviet Power, which has naturally been compelled to adopt heroic measures in order to deliver itself from the legacy. The departments of public instruction have opened schools for adults unable to read and write, and have taken a number of additional steps to put an end to illiteracy. But apart from the utilisation of the scholastic apparatus of the Commissariat for Education, the Communist Party must do its utmost to ensure that the masses shall avail themselves of the opportunities that offer for the instruction of illiterates. Here the soviets for popular culture, elected from among all the workers and peasants who are interested in educational matters, must play their part. A further means has been the mobilisation of all

who can read and write for the instruction of all the
illiterates. Such a mobilisation is beginning in various
parts of the republic, and it is the business of the party
to ensure that the movement shall everywhere be conducted
in accordance with a definite plan.

In addition to carrying on the struggle against illiteracy,
the Soviet Power must devote much energy and much
material means to the assistance of the self-cultural
endeavours of the population, and especially of adults.
Numerous libraries have been inaugurated to satisfy the
demands of the working population. Wherever possible,
people's houses and clubs have been established and people's
universities have been created. The cinema, which has
hitherto served as a means for demoralising the masses
and for enriching the owners, is gradually, though very
slowly, becoming one of the most potent instruments for
the enlightenment of the masses and for their education
in the spirit of socialism. Lecture courses of various kinds,
gratuitous and accessible to all, can now, thanks to the
shorter working day, become a general possession of the
workers. In the future, of great significance in the matter
of enlightenment will be the careful organisation of holiday
excursions, which will enable the workers to become
acquainted with their own land and with the foreign world.
There can be no doubt that in days to come such excursions
will have immense importance for the workers of all
countries.

§ 85.

New Workers on behalf of Enlightenment. The educational reforms of the Soviet Power have been more successful
than the reforms and innovations effected in any other
department. There is an additional reason for this besides
the fact that the Soviet State devotes to popular education
an enormously greater proportion of its revenues than is
devoted to this purpose by any bourgeois State. Over
and above, we have to remember that the way for the
realisation of the idea of the unified labour school had
already to a notable extent been prepared by the most
advanced educationists of bourgeois society. The leading
Russian educationists have been able under the soviet

regime to realise in practice, to a notable extent, that which from a purely pedagogical outlook they had already come to regard as socially necessary. Among the educational workers who have rallied from the side of the bourgeoisie and the landed interest to the side of the Soviet Power, we find quite a number of individuals who were and still are opposed to the proletarian revolution in general, but who are heartily in favour of the revolution that has been achieved by the proletariat in the educational field.

These favourable conditions, however, by no means suffice to overcome the difficulties of the proletarian State as far as concerns the provision of genuinely communist educational workers. The number of communists among the teachers, as among specialists in general, is but an insignificant minority. Most teachers are opposed to communism. The majority of them, however, are persons with an official type of mind, who are ready to serve any government and to work to any schedule, but who have a special fondness for a program which was familiar to 'their fathers and their grandfathers. As concerns this matter, therefore, the communists have a twofold task. In the first place, they must mobilise all the best elements of the teaching profession, and by intensified activity must create among them nuclei of communist endeavour. In the second place, the Communist Party has to create out of the younger generation an entirely new school of educationists, consisting of persons who have from the very first been trained in the spirit of communism, and above all in the spirit of the communist educational program.

§ 86.

The Treasures of Art and Science made available to the Workers. Under capitalism, talent is looked upon as the private property of its immediate possessor, and is regarded as a means of enrichment. In capitalist society, the product of talented activity is a commodity which can be sold for one price or another, and thus becomes the possession of the person with the longest purse. A work of genius, a thing with infinite social significance, and one whose essential nature is that of a collective creation, can be purchased by a Russian named Kolupayeff or by an American named

Morgan, and the buyer is then entitled to change it or to destroy it as fancy dictates. If Tretyakoff, the famous Moscow merchant, had one fine day made up his mind to burn down his picture gallery instead of presenting it to the town of Moscow, there was no law in capitalist society by which he could have been called to account. As a result of the private purchase and sale of works of art, rare books, manuscripts, etc., many of them are rendered inaccessible to the broad masses of the people, and these rarities become the exclusive possessions of members of the exploiting class. The Soviet Republic has declared all works of art, collections, etc., to be social property, and it removes every obstacle to their social utilisation. The same purpose is served by the decrees aiming at the withdrawal from private ownership of great libraries, so that these also have become social property.

The Communist Party must see to it that the State authority continues to advance along such lines. In view of the present lack of books and of the impossibility of speedily issuing large editions and reprints, it is necessary that there should be a further restriction of private ownership, and that books should be assembled in public libraries, in schools, etc.

Furthermore, in the interests of enlightenment, and in order to secure for the widest possible number of persons the opportunity of visiting the theatre, all the theatres have been nationalised, and thus in an indirect way there has been achieved the socialisation of dramatic, musical, and vocal art.

By degrees, therefore, all the works of science and art —which were created in the first instance by the exploitation of the toiling masses, were a burden upon their backs, were produced at their cost—have now been restored to the real owners.

§ 87.

The State Propaganda of Communism. Now that the capitalist system has been overthrown, and now that upon its ruins the new communist society is being built up, the propaganda of communist ideas cannot be left solely to the Communist Party and cannot be conducted with its modest means alone. Communist propaganda has become a necessity for the whole society now undergoing regeneration. It must accelerate the inevitable process of transformation. To the innovators, who often work without being fully aware of what they are doing, communist propaganda must reveal the significance of their energies and their labours. It is therefore necessary that not merely the proletarian school but in addition the whole mechanism of the proletarian State should contribute to the work of communist propaganda. This propaganda must be carried on in the army ; it must be carried on in and by all the instruments of the Soviet Power.

The most powerful method of State communist propaganda is the State publishing activity. The nationalisation of all the reserves of paper and of all the printing establishments, makes it possible for the proletarian State, despite the great scarcity of paper, to publish by the million any literature which is peculiarly important for the masses at a given moment. Everything issued from the State presses is made available to the generality of the people by publication at a very low price, and by degrees it is becoming possible to issue books, pamphlets, newspapers, and posters, gratuitously. The State propaganda of communism becomes in the long run a means for the eradication of the last traces of bourgeois propaganda dating from the old regime ; and it is a powerful instrument for the creation of a new ideology, of new modes of thought, of a new outlook on the world.

§ 88.

Popular Education under Tsarism and under the Soviet Power. State expenditure upon popular education in Russia is set forth in the following table.

Year.						Roubles.
1891 ..	..	..	..	..	..	22,810,260
1911 ..	..	..	..	..	..	27,883,000
1916 ..	..	..	..	..	..	195,624,000
1917 ..	..	..	..	..	..	339,831,687
1918 ..	..	..	..	..	..	2,914,082,124
1919 (half-year)	..	..	..	..	3,888,000,000

We see that the transference of power to the proletariat was immediately followed by nearly a tenfold increase in the expenditure upon popular education.

In the year 1917 there were on September 1st, 38,387 elementary schools (in 26 provinces).

In the school year 1917–18 there were 52,274 elementary schools, with 4,138,982 pupils.

In the school year 1918–19 there were approximately 62,238 elementary schools.

As regards middle schools, in the school year 1917–18 there were 1830, and in the school year 1918–19 there were 3783.

Preparatory schools and similar institutions were quite unknown under the tsarist regime. In this matter the Soviet Power had to make an entirely new start. Notwithstanding the unfavourable circumstances, by October 1st, 1919, in 31 provinces, the kindergartens, play schools, and homes numbered 2615, and cared for 155,443 children. At this date, about 2·5 per cent. of all the children from three to five years of age were attending such institutions. In the towns, the percentage of children cared for in this way is now 10·1, and the proportion continually rises.

Literature dealing with the question of the Labour School. Regulations concerning the unified Labour School of the R.S.F.S.R. (1918). POSNER, The unified Labour School (1918). The Labour School, Reports of the Department of popular Education of the Moscow Soviet. BLONSKY, The School of the working Class. BLONSKY, The Labour School. LEVITIN, The Labour School. LEVITIN, International Problems of socialist Pedagogy. KRUPSKAYA, Popular Culture and Democracy. DUNE, The School and Society. SHARELMAN, The Labour School. SHARELMAN, In the Laboratory of an elementary School Teacher. GANSBERG, Pedagogics. GANSBERG, Creative Work in the School.—" The weekly Journal of the People's Commissariat for Education."—Report of the first All-Russian Congress on Education (1919).

Non-communist Literature on Education: KERSCHENSTEINER, The Idea of the Labour School. KERSCHENSTEINER, The Labour School (1918). GURLITT, The Problems of the general unified School. FERRIÈRE, The New School. WETEKAMP, Independent Activity and creative Work. SCHULZ, Educational Reforms of the social Democrats. FEDOROFF-HARTVIG, The Labour School and Collectivism (1918). YANZHUL, The Labour Principle in European Schools (1918). SHATSKY, The active Life. MÜNCH, The School of the Future.

CHAPTER ELEVEN

COMMUNISM AND RELIGION

§ 89.

Why Religion and Communism are incompatible. " Religion is the opium of the people," said Karl Marx. It is the task of the Communist Party to make this truth comprehensible to the widest possible circles of the labouring masses. It is the task of the party to impress firmly upon the minds of the workers, even upon the most backward, that religion has been in the past and still is to-day one of the most powerful means at the disposal of the oppressors for the maintenance of inequality, exploitation, and slavish obedience on the part of the toilers.

Many weak-kneed communists reason as follows : " Religion does not prevent my being a communist. I believe both in God and in communism. My faith in God does not hinder me from fighting for the cause of the proletarian revolution."

This train of thought is radically false. Religion and communism are incompatible, both theoretically and practically.

Every communist must regard social phenomena (the relationships between human beings, revolutions, wars, etc.) as processes which occur in accordance with definite laws. The laws of social development have been fully established by scientific communism on the basis of the theory of historical materialism which we owe to our great teachers Karl Marx and Friedrich Engels. This theory explains that social development is not brought about by any kind of supernatural forces. Nay more. The same theory has demonstrated that the very idea of God and of supernatural powers arises at a definite stage in human history, and at another definite stage begins to disappear as a childish notion which finds no confirmation in practical life and in the struggle between man and nature. But it is profitable to the predatory class to maintain the ignorance of the people and to maintain the people's childish belief in miracle (the key to the riddle really lies in the exploiters' pockets), and this is why religious prejudices are so tenacious, and why they confuse the minds even of persons who are in other respects able.

The general happenings throughout nature are, moreover, nowise dependent upon supernatural causes. Man has been extremely successful in the struggle with nature. He influences nature in his own interests, and controls natural forces, achieving these conquests, not thanks to his faith in God and in divine assistance, but in spite of this faith. He achieves his conquests thanks to the fact that in practical life and in all serious matters he invariably conducts himself as an atheist. Scientific communism, in its judgments concerning natural phenomena, is guided by the data of the natural sciences, which are in irreconcilable conflict with all religious imaginings.

In practice, no less than in theory, communism is incompatible with religious faith. The tactic of the Communist Party prescribes for the members of the party definite lines of conduct. The moral code of every religion in like manner prescribes for the faithful some definite line of conduct. For example, the Christian code runs : " Whosoever shall smite thee on thy right cheek, turn to him the other also." In most cases there is an irreconcilable conflict between the principles of communist tactics and the commandments of religion. A communist who rejects the commandments of religion and acts in accordance with the directions of the party, ceases to be one of the faithful. On the other hand, one who, while calling himself a communist, continues to cling to his religious faith, one who in the name of religious commandments infringes the prescriptions of the party, ceases thereby to be a communist.

The struggle with religion has two sides, and every communist must distinguish clearly between them. On the one hand we have the struggle with the church, as a special organisation existing for religious propaganda, materially interested in the maintenance of popular ignorance and religious enslavement. On the other hand we have the struggle with the widely diffused and deeply ingrained prejudices of the majority of the working population.

§ 90.

Separation of the Church from the State. The Christian catechism teaches that the church is a society of the faithful who are united by a common creed, by the sacraments, etc. For the communist, the church is a society of persons who are united by definite sources of income at the cost of the faithful, at the cost of their ignorance and lack of true culture. It is a society united with the society of other exploiters such as the landlords and the capitalists, united with their State, assisting that State in the oppression of the workers, and reciprocally receiving from the State help in the business of oppression. The union between church and State is of great antiquity. The association between the church and the feudalist State of the landowners was exceedingly intimate. This becomes clear when we remember that the autocratic-aristocratic State was sustained by the landed interest. The church was itself a landlord on the grand scale, owning millions upon millions of acres. These two powers were inevitably compelled to join forces against the labouring masses, and their alliance served to strengthen their dominion over the workers. During the period in which the urban bourgeoisie was in conflict with the feudal nobility, the bourgeoisie fiercely attacked the church, because the church owned territories which the bourgeoisie wanted for itself. The church, as landowner, was in receipt of revenues extracted from the workers— revenues which the bourgeoisie coveted. In some countries (France for instance), the struggle was extremely embittered ; in other countries (England, Germany, and Russia), it was less fierce. But this conflict explains why the demand for the separation of church and State was made by the liberal bourgeoisie and the bourgeois democracy. The real basis of the demand was a desire for the transfer to the bourgeoisie of the revenues allotted by the State to the church. But the demand for the separation of the church from the State was nowhere fully realised by the bourgeoisie. The reason is that everywhere the struggle carried on by the working class against the capitalists was growing more intense, and it seemed inexpedient to the bourgeoisie to break up the alliance between State and church. The capitalists thought it would be more advantageous to come to terms with the church, to buy its prayers on behalf of the struggle with socialism, to utilise its influence over the uncultured masses in order to keep alive in their minds the sentiment of slavish submissiveness to the exploiting State. ("All power comes from God.")

The work which the bourgeoisie in its struggle with the church had left unfinished was carried to an end by the proletarian State. One of the first decrees of the Soviet Power in Russia was the decree concerning the separation of the church from the State. All its landed estates were taken away from the church and handed over to the working population. All the capital of the church became the property of the workers. The endowments which had been assigned to the church under the tsarist regime were confiscated, although these endowments had been cheerfully continued under the administration of the "socialist" Kerensky. Religion has become the private affair of every citizen. The Soviet Power rejects all thoughts of using the church in any way whatever as a means for strengthening the proletarian State.

§ 91.

Separation of the School from the Church. The association of religious propaganda with scholastic instruction is the second powerful weapon employed by the clergy for the strengthening of the ecclesiastical regime and for increasing the influence of the church over the masses. The future of the human race, its youth, is entrusted to the priests. Under the tsars, the maintenance of religious fanaticism, the maintenance of stupidity and ignorance, was regarded as a matter of great importance to the State. Religion was the leading subject of instruction in the schools. In the schools, moreover, the autocracy supported the church, and the church supported the autocracy. In addition to compulsory religious teaching in the schools and compulsory attendance at religious services, the church had other weapons. It began to take charge of the whole of popular education, and for this purpose Russia was covered with a network of church schools.

Thanks to the union of school and church, our young people were from their earliest years thralls to religious superstition, this making it practically impossible to convey to their minds any integral outlook upon the universe. To one and the same question (for instance concerning the origin of the world) religion and science give conflicting answers, so that the impressionable mind of the pupil becomes a battle ground between exact knowledge and the gross errors of obscurantists.

In many countries, young people are trained, not only in a spirit of submissiveness towards the dominant regime, but also in a spirit of submissiveness towards the overthrown autocratic-ecclesiastico-feudal order. This happens in France. Even from the outlook of the bourgeois State, propaganda of such a kind is reactionary.

The program of bourgeois liberalism used to contain a demand for the separation of the school from the church. The liberals fought for the replacement of religious instruction in the schools by instruction in bourgeois morality ; and they demanded the closing of schools organised by religious associations and by monasteries. Nowhere, however, was this struggle carried through to an end. In France, for instance, where for two decades all the bourgeois ministries had solemnly pledged themselves to dissolve the religious orders, to confiscate their property, and to forbid their educational activities, there has been one compromise after another with the Catholic clergy. An excellent example of such a compromise between State and church was the recent action of Clemenceau. This minister in his day had been fiercely opposed to the church. In the end, however, he forgot his hostility, and personally distributed orders of distinction among the Catholic clergy as a reward for their patriotic services. In the struggle for the exploitation of other lands (the war with Germany), and in the domestic struggle with the working class, the bourgeois State and the church have entered into an alliance, and give one another mutual support.

This reconciliation of the bourgeoisie with the church finds expression, not merely in the abandonment by the bourgeoisie of its old anti-religious watchwords and of its campaign against religion, but in something more significant. To an increasing extent, the bourgeoisie is now becoming a " believing class." The forerunners of the contemporary European bourgeoisie were atheists, were freethinkers, were fiercely antagonistic to priests and priestdom. Their successors have taken a step backwards. A generation ago, the bourgeois, though they were themselves still atheistically inclined, though they did not believe in religious fairy tales, and though they laughed covertly at religion, nevertheless considered that the fables must be treated with respect in public, since religion was a useful restraint for the common people. To-day, the scions of the bourgeoisie are not content with looking upon religion as providing useful fetters for the people, but they have themselves begun to wear the chains. Under our very eyes, after the November revolution, the liberal bourgeois and the members of the professional classes crowded into the churches and prayed fervently to that which in happier days they had regarded with contempt. Such is the fate of all dying classes, whose last resource it is to seek " consolation " in religion.

Among the bourgeoisies of Central and Western Europe, which still hold the reins of power, a similar movement in favour of religion is observable. But if the bourgeois class begins to believe in God and the heavenly life, this merely means it has realised that its life here below is drawing to a close!

The separation of the school from the church aroused and continues to arouse protest from the backward elements among the workers and peasants. Many of the older generation persist in demanding that religion should still be taught in the schools as an optional subject. The Communist Party fights resolutely against all such attempts to turn back. The teaching of ecclesiastical obscurantism in the schools, even though the instruction should be merely optional, would imply the giving of State aid to the maintenance of religious prejudices. In that case the church would be provided with a ready-made audience of children —of children who are assembled in school for purposes which are the very opposite of those contemplated by religion. The church would have at its disposal schoolrooms belonging to the State, and would thereby be enabled to diffuse religious poison among our young people almost as freely as it could before the separation of the school from the church.

The decree whereby the school is separated from the church must be rigidly enforced, and the proletarian State must not make the slightest concession to medievalism. What has already been done to throw off the yoke of religion is all too little, for it still remains within the power of ignorant parents to cripple the minds of their children by teaching them religious fables. Under the Soviet Power there is freedom of conscience for adults. But this freedom of conscience for parents is tantamount to a freedom for them to poison the minds of their children with the opium which when they were young was poured into their own minds by the church. The parents force upon the children their own dullness, their own ignorance ; they proclaim as truth all sorts of nonsense ; and they thus greatly increase the difficulties which the unified labour school has to encounter. One of the most important tasks of the proletarian State is to liberate children from the reactionary influence exercised by their parents. The really radical way of doing this is the social education of the children, carried to its logical conclusion. As far as the immediate future is concerned, we must not rest content with the expulsion of religious propaganda from the school. We must see to it that the school assumes the offensive against religious propaganda in the home, so that from the very outset the children's minds shall be rendered immune to all those religious fairy tales which many grown-ups continue to regard as truth.

§ 92.

Struggle with the religious Prejudices of the Masses. It has been comparatively easy for the proletarian authority to effect the separation of the church from the State and of the school from the church, and these changes have been almost painlessly achieved. It is enormously more difficult to fight the religious prejudices which are already deeply rooted in the consciousness of the masses, and which cling so stubbornly to life. The struggle will be a long one, demanding much steadfastness and great patience. Upon this matter we read in our program : " The Russian Communist Party is guided by the conviction that nothing but the realisation of purposiveness and full awareness in all the social and economic activities of the masses can lead to the complete disappearance of religious prejudices." What do these words signify ?

Religious propaganda, belief in God and in all kinds of supernatural powers, find their most grateful soil where the institutions of social life are such as to incline the consciousness of the masses towards supernatural explanations of the phenomena of nature and society. The environment created by capitalist methods of production has a strong tendency in this direction. In capitalist society, production, and the exchange of products, are not effected with full consciousness and in accordance with a preconceived plan ; they proceed as if they were the outcome of elemental forces. The market controls the producer. No one knows whether commodities are being produced in excess or in deficiency. The producer does not fully understand how the great and complicated mechanism of capitalist production works ; why crises occur and unemployment suddenly becomes rife ; why prices rise at one time and fall at another ; and so on. The ordinary worker, knowing nothing of the real causes of the social happenings amid which his life takes place, readily inclines to accept the " will of God " as a universal explanation.

In organised communist society, on the other hand, the realms of production and distribution will no longer contain any mysteries for the worker. Every worker will not merely perform his allotted portion of social work. He will in addition participate in the elaboration of the general plan of production, and will at least have clear ideas upon the matter. Throughout the entire mechanism of social production there will no longer be anything mysterious, incomprehensible, or unexpected, and there will therefore be no further place for mystical explanations or for superstition. Just as the joiner who has made a table knows perfectly well how the table came to exist and that he need not lift his eyes towards heaven in order to find its creator, so in communist society all the workers will clearly understand what they have produced with their collective energies and how they have produced it.

For this reason, the mere fact of the organisation and strengthening of the socialist system, will deal religion an irrecoverable blow. THE TRANSITION FROM SOCIALISM TO COMMUNISM, THE TRANSITION FROM THE SOCIETY WHICH MAKES AN END OF CAPITALISM TO THE SOCIETY WHICH IS COMPLETELY FREED FROM ALL TRACES OF CLASS DIVISION AND CLASS STRUGGLE, WILL BRING ABOUT THE NATURAL DEATH OF ALL RELIGION AND ALL SUPERSTITION.

But this must by no means be taken to imply that we

can sit down at our ease, satisfied with having prophesied the decay of religion at some future date.

It is essential at the present time to wage with the utmost vigour the war against religious prejudices, for the church has now definitely become a counter-revolutionary organisation, and endeavours to use its religious influence over the masses in order to marshal them for the political struggle against the dictatorship of the proletariat. The Orthodox faith which is defended by the priests aims at an alliance with the monarchy. This is why the Soviet Power finds it necessary to engage at this juncture in widespread anti-religious propaganda. Our aims can be secured by the delivery of special lectures, by the holding of debates, and by the publication of suitable literature ; also by the general diffusion of scientific knowledge, which slowly but surely undermines the authority of religion. An excellent weapon in the fight with the church was used recently in many parts of the republic when the shrines were opened to show the " incorruptible " relics. This served to prove to the wide masses of the people, and precisely to those in whom religious faith was strongest, the base trickery upon which religion in general, and the creed of the Russian Orthodox church in particular, are grounded.

But the campaign against the backwardness of the masses in this matter of religion, must be conducted with patience and considerateness, as well as with energy and perseverance. The credulous crowd is extremely sensitive to anything which hurts its feelings. To thrust atheism upon the masses, and in conjunction therewith to interfere forcibly with religious practices and to make mock of the objects of popular reverence, would not assist but would hinder the campaign against religion. If the church were to be persecuted, it would win sympathy among the masses, for persecution would remind them of the almost forgotten days when there was an association between religion and the defence of national freedom ; it would strengthen the antisemitic movement ; and in general it would mobilise all the vestiges of an ideology which is already beginning to die out.

We propose to append a few figures, showing how the tsarist regime paid over the people's money to the church ;

how the church was directly supported by the common
people, who drained their slender purses to this end ; and
how wealth accumulated in the hands of the servants of Christ.

Through the synods and in other ways the tsarist government
annually supplied the church with the average amount of 50,000,000
roubles (at a time when the rouble was worth one hundred times as
much as to-day). The synods had 70,000,000 roubles to their credit
in the banks. The churches and the monasteries owned vast areas
of land. In the year 1905 the churches owned 1,872,000 desyatinas,
and the monasteries owned 740,000 desyatinas. Six of the largest
monasteries owned 182,000 desyatinas. The Solovyetsky monastery
owned 66,000 desyatinas ; the Sarovskaya, 26,000 ; the Alexandro-
Nevskaya, 25,000 ; and so on. In 1903, the churches and monasteries of Petrograd owned 266 rent-producing properties in the form
of houses, shops, building sites, etc. In Moscow, they owned 1054
rent-paying houses, not to mention 32 hotels. In Kiev, the churches
owned 114 houses. Here are the stipends of the metropolitans and
the archbishops. The metropolitan of Petrograd received 300,000
roubles per annum ; the metropolitans of Moscow and of Kiev were
paid 100,000 roubles per annum each ; the stipend of the archbishop
of Novgorod was 310,000 roubles.

There were about 30,000 church schools, and these were attended
by 1,000,000 pupils. More than 20,000 teachers of religion were
"at work" in the elementary schools of the Ministry for Education.

Everyone knows that the autocracy supported the Orthodox
church as the dominant and only true church. Many millions of
roubles were raised by taxing Musulmans (Tartars and Bashkirs),
Catholics (Poles), and Jews. This money was used by the Orthodox
clergy to demonstrate that all other faiths were false. Under the
tsarist regime, religious persecution attained unprecedented proportions. In the population of Russia, for every hundred inhabitants
there were (besides the 70 Orthodox,) 9 Catholics, 11 Mohammedans,
5 Protestants, 4 Jews, and 1 of various creeds. As for the number of
the Orthodox clergy, the following were the figures for the year 1909 :

The 52,869 churches of Russia were served by

Archpriests	2,912
Priests	46,730
Deacons	14,670
Readers	43,518

In the 455 monasteries there were

Monks	9,987
Lay-brethren	9,582

In the 418 nunneries there were

Nuns	14,008
Lay-sisters	46,811

Total	188,218

The figures relate exclusively to the Orthodox church. A similar parasitic caste is found in every nation, though of course professing some other religion. These masses of people, instead of extracting vast sums of money from the population in order to promote popular ignorance, would have been able, had they been engaged in manual work, to produce immense quantities of values. The socialist State, when its economic apparatus has been perfected, will introduce labour service for the clergy as for all unproductive classes, so that they will have to become workers or peasants. Of the State revenues paid to the church under the tsarist regime, more than 12,000,000 roubles went every year to the urban and rural clergy. It is plain enough why the reverend fathers were opposed to the separation of the church from the State, since this implied the separation of a dozen million roubles from their pockets. This sum, however, was but a fraction of the clerical incomes, which for the most part were derived from professional fees, land rents, and interest upon the capital of the church. No one has been able to ascertain the precise amount of the revenues of the Russian church. Approximately the sum may be considered to have been 150,000,000 roubles —at a time (we repeat) when the rouble was worth one hundred of our present roubles. A considerable proportion of this income is still paid by the people to the clergy.

Literature. KILCHEFFSKY, Wealth and Revenues of the Clergy. LUKIN, Church and State. MELGUNOFF, Church and State in the Days of Transition. MININ, Religion and Communism. STEPANOFF, The Origin of God. STEPANOFF, The Clergy, its Income, its Prayers, and its Curses. KUNOFF, The Origin of Religion and of Faith in God. KAUTSKY, The Origin of biblical History. KAUTSKY, The classical World, Judaism, and Christianity. KAUTSKY, The Catholic Church and social Democracy. BEBEL, Christianity and Socialism. STAMLER and VANDERVELDE, Social Democracy and Religion. LAFARGUE, The Origin of religious Belief. DANILOFF, The black Army. KILVER, Social Democracy and Christianity. BUHARIN, Church and School in the Soviet Republic. BUROFF, What is the Meaning of the Law concerning Freedom of Conscience ? LAFARGUE, The Myth of the Immaculate Conception. NIKOLSKY, Jesus and the early Christian Communities. VIPPER, The Rise of Christianity. POKROFFSKY, The History of Russia (article by Nikolsky). BEDNY Reverend Fathers.

CHAPTER TWELVE

THE ORGANISATION OF INDUSTRY

§ 93.

The Expropriation of the Bourgeoisie and the proletarian Nationalisation of large-scale Industry. The very first task of the proletariat, and of the Soviet Power as instrument of the proletarian dictatorship, was to wrest the means of production from the bourgeoisie, or, as the phrase runs, to expropriate the bourgeoisie. It is self-evident that we were not concerned with the expropriation of small-scale industry or with the expropriation of artisan production, but with the seizure of the means of production that were in the hands of the great capitalists, with establishing large-scale industry upon a new foundation, and with organising it in accordance with new principles. How could the Soviet Power do these things ? In Part One we learned that the proletariat must not attempt to divide up the factories and workshops, and must not plunder them, but must undertake the social, the cooperative, organisation of production. Obviously, in the epoch of proletarian dictatorship there is only one way of doing this, namely by *proletarian nationalisation*, by which we mean the transfer of all the means of production, distribution, and exchange into the hands of the proletarian State, the greatest and most powerful of working-class organisations.

We must carefully avoid confusing the nationalisation

of production under the bourgeois regime with the nationalisation of production under the proletarian regime. Nationalisation means "transfer into the hands of the State." But one who speaks of the State without qualification, and without enquiring whether the State is a bourgeois State or a proletarian State, misses the whole point. When the bourgeoisie is the ruling class and when it nationalises its trusts and syndicates, this nationalisation nowise involves the expropriation of the bourgeoisie. All that happens is that the bourgeoisie takes its goods out of one pocket and puts them into the other. Everything is transferred into the possession of its own State, the masters' State. The bourgeoisie continues to exploit the working class as heretofore. The working class, as heretofore, works not for itself but for the enemies of its class. Such nationalisation is bourgeois nationalisation. The result of such nationalisation is to produce the social order we considered in Part One under the name of State capitalism. It is a very different matter when nationalisation is effected under the rule of the proletariat. Now the factories, the workshops, the means of transport, and so on, are transferred to the proletarian Power ; they do not pass under the control of the organisation of the masters, but under the control of the organisation of the workers. In this case, therefore, there is actually effected the expropriation of the bourgeoisie. The capitalists actually forfeit the foundations of their wealth, their dominion, their energy, and their power. The whole basis of exploitation is destroyed. The proletarian State cannot exploit the proletariat, for the simple reason that it is itself an organisation of the proletariat. A man cannot climb upon his own back. The proletariat cannot exploit its own self. Under State capitalism, the bourgeoisie loses nothing by the fact that the private entrepreneurs have ceased to work separately, and have joined hands to fleece the public. In proletarian nationalisation, obversely, the workers in the separate factories lose nothing by the fact that they are not independent masters in their own factories, by the fact that all the enterprises belong to the working class in its entirety, to the greatest of all workers' organisations, which is known as the Soviet State.

The expropriation of the bourgeoisie, which was begun

immediately after the November revolution, has now been practically completed. Within the confines of Soviet Russia, the entire transport system (railways and waterways) has been nationalised, and from 80 to 90 per cent. of large-scale production is in the hands of the proletarian State. According to the reports of the Department for Factory and Workshop Statistics of the Supreme Economic Council, by September, 1919, there had been nationalised, in 30 provinces, 3330 enterprises, at which 1,012,000 workers and 27,000 employees were occupied. These figures underrate the amount of nationalisation, for we learn from other data that more than 4000 enterprises have already been nationalised. The biggest of the 3330 enterprises mentioned in the report are functioning. This is plain from the following figures. By September, 1919, 1375 national enterprises were actually at work, and in 1258 of these, 782,000 workers and 26,000 employees were occupied. Out of the million workers, nearly 800,000 are actually at work, notwithstanding the terribly difficult conditions prevailing in industry. There were 691 enterprises closed down, at which 170,000 workers should have been occupied. Details are lacking concerning 1248 enterprises occupying 57,000 workers. These are comparatively small enterprises.

In the autumn of 1919, the nationalised undertakings actually at work, and combined into " chiefs " or into " centres," were as follows :

I. Mining and kindred industries (under the general management of the Mountain Soviet).

    1. Chief-coal (chief administration of coal production).
    2. Chief-mines.
    3. Chief-petroleum.
    4. Chief-peat.
    5. Chief-slate.
    6. Chief-salt.
    7. Chief-gold.

II. Metal industries (under the general management of the Department for Metals of the Supreme Economic Council).

    1. Gomza (portmanteau word for State machine shops).
    2. Chief-aviation.
    3. Centro-copper.
    4. Chief-nails.
    5. Motor-car manufacture.

6. Group of Malzov workshops.
7. Group of Kaluga and Ryazan workshops.
8. Locomotive works in Podolia.

III. Electro-technical industries (" Ogep," a portmanteau word like Gomza. " Ogep " means United State Electrical Enterprises).

IV. Textile industries (" Chief-textile ").

V. Chemical industries (under the general management of the Department for Chemical Industries of the Supreme Economic Council).

1. Raw chemicals.
2. Chief-aniline-dyes.
3. Centro-varnish.
4. Chief-drugs.
5. Chief-matches.
6. Chief-glass.
7. Chief-potash.
8. Centro-cement.
9. Centro-paints.
10. Centro-asbestos.
11. Chief-hides.
12. Chief-furs.
13. Centro-bristles.
14. Chief-bone.
15. Centro-fat.
16. Chief-paper.
17. Chief-rubber.
18. Chemical wood-working.
19. Chief-vegetable-oils.
20. Centro-spirits.
21. Chief-tobacco.
22. Chief-starch.
23. Chief-sugar.

VI. Preparation of food-stuffs (Department for the Preparation of Food-Stuffs of the Supreme Economic Council).

1. Chief-flour.
2. Chief-sweets.
3. Centro-tea.
4. Centro-milk.
5. Chief-tinned-goods.
6. Centro-cold-storage.

VII. Chief-timber-committee.

VIII. Printing industries (Printing Department of the Supreme Economic Council).

IX. Central auto-section (assembly and repair of motor cars).

X. Centro-garment-working (small tailoring shops, etc.).

XI. Utilisation of waste products (Centro-Util.).

XII. War Transport.

XIII, Building materials and the building industry (Committee of State Building)

XIV. Munitions of war (Department of Munitions of War—" Centro-Voyenzag " [portmanteau word]).

XV. Transport, lading, and storage department of the Supreme Economic Council (" Tramot " Department for the Transport of Material of the Supreme Economic Council).

The expropriation of the bourgeoisie, based upon principle, must be carried to its logical conclusion. This is the first task which is incumbent on our party. But we must be careful not to forget that petty proprietors are not to be expropriated. The " nationalisation " of small-scale industry is absolutely out of the question : first of all, because it is beyond our powers to organise the dispersed fragments of petty industry ; and secondly because the Communist Party does not and cannot wish to alienate the many millions of small masters. Their adhesion to socialism will be quite voluntary, and will not result from their forcible expropriation. This fact must be especially borne in mind in those regions where small-scale production is widely prevalent.

Subject to this reservation, the first task we have to face is the completion of nationalisation.

§ 94.

Our Goal, the Development of Productivity. The foundation of our whole policy must be the widest possible development of productivity. The disorganisation of production has been so extensive, the post-war scarcity of all products is so conspicuous, that everything else must be subordinated to this one task. More products ! More boots, scythes, barrels, textiles, salt, clothing, corn, etc.—these are our primary need. How can the desired end be secured ? Only by increasing the productive forces of the country, by increased productivity. There is no other way.

But here we encounter a formidable difficulty, arising out of the onslaught made upon us by the world-wide forces of the counter-revolution. We are blockaded and put upon our defence, so that we are simultaneously deprived of labour power and cut off from the material means of production. We have to wrest by force of arms petroleum and coal from the landlords and capitalists. Here is our first great task. We have to set the work of production upon a proper footing. Here is our second great task. We are hard put to it, indeed !

Before the working class had become master of the whole country, this was not our affair. But now the working class is in power. Everything is at its disposal. It is responsible for the destiny of the country. Upon its shoulders rests the whole burden of saving the Soviet Republic from the miseries of famine, cold, and disorder. Before the working class rose to power, its main task was to destroy the old order. Now its main task is to construct the new order. Formerly it was the business of the bourgeoisie to organise production ; now it is the business of the proletariat. Evidently, therefore, in the days of the most widespread disorganisation, all the thoughts of the proletariat, as far as this matter is concerned, must be concentrated upon the organisation of industry and the increase of production. To increase production means to increase the output of labour, to produce more goods, to work better in every possible way, and day by day to achieve better results. The time for fine phrases is past, and the time for hard work has come. No longer does it devolve upon us to fight for our rights in Moscow or in Petrograd ; the working class has secured its rights, and is defending them at the front. What we have to do now is to increase the number of nails, horse-shoes, ploughs, locks, machines, great coats. These things have become absolutely vital if we are to avoid dying of hunger amid the ruin resulting from the war, if we are to be clothed, if we are to regain our strength, if we are to advance by rapid strides along the road to the new life.

The problem of increased production comprises a number of problems. How can we increase the quantity of the material means of production (machinery, coal, and raw materials) ; and how can we increase the amount of labour power ? How can we best organise production (what is the best way of planning out economic life as a whole, how should one branch of production be linked up with another, how should production be administered, what is the best and most economical way of allotting the reserves of raw material, how can we best dispose of the available labour power ?) How can we secure better work, in so far as this depends upon the workers themselves ? (the question of a comradely labour discipline ; that of the struggle against slovenliness, slackness, idleness, etc.) Last of all comes the question of applying science to production, the question of the work of skilled experts.

All these questions are of immense importance. We have to solve them practically, to solve them in action. We have to solve them, not in a single factory or for a single factory, but for the whole of a huge country, where the working class and the semi-proletariat are numbered by millions. It is evident that in this matter we must stick to one point of view, must drive the nail home, must increase the productivity of the whole country which is building its economic life upon the new foundation of communist labour.

Our opponents—the social revolutionaries, the mensheviks, the bourgeois, etc.—declare that we are not Marxists at all, that our communism is only a consumers' communism, a communism of distribution. The bolsheviks, they say, shear the bourgeois, compel the bourgeois to give up their houses ; the bolsheviks divide up the articles of consumption ; but they do not organise production. The charge is utterly unfounded. The productive forces of society consist of two things : of the material means of production, on the one hand ; and of living persons, the workers, on the other. The working class is the basic force of production. If machinery, tools, etc., have been destroyed, this is unfortunate, but the loss is not vital, for experienced workers can, even though at the cost of much labour, reproduce everything that is lacking. Very different is the state of affairs when the living force of production is destroyed, when the workers migrate to the villages, when cold and hunger lead them to abandon the towns, when the working class crumbles to pieces. This must be prevented at all costs. The organised expropriation of the means of consumption is in such a case the best way to protect living labour power. Communism of the articles of consumption is thus no more than an indispensable preliminary to our real aim, the organisation of production. The bourgeoisie everywhere wishes to impose upon the proletariat all the costs of the war, all the poverty which arises out of it, all the cold, all the hunger. For the sake of its own future, the proletariat must force the bourgeoisie to shoulder the burdens of the post-war period. But of course our leading task is the organisation of production and the development of productivity.

§ 95.

The purposive Organisation of economic Life. The break-up of capitalism left as its legacy to the proletariat, not only a widespread lack of the means of production, but also widespread confusion. Russia was utterly disintegrated ; the connexion between the various regions of the country had been destroyed ; intercourse between one industrial district and another had become extraordinarily difficult. As a result of the revolution, the factory owners had dropped the reins of administration, and at first, in many places, the factories were simply masterless. There then ensued an unsystematic seizure of the enterprises by the workers, who could wait no longer. A local " nationalisation " of this kind had begun before the November revolution. Of course it was not really nationalisation, but only the unorganised seizure of enterprises by the workers who had been employed in them ; not until later did the seizure become transformed into nationalisation. Even after the November revolution, nationalisation was at first conducted at haphazard. Manifestly, the primary need was to nationalise the largest and best equipped enterprises ; but things did not always work out this way. The general tendency was to nationalise those enterprises which the owners had abandoned and which could not be left uncared for. In many cases, however, enterprises were nationalised because their owners were especially hostile to the workers. It was natural that in the days of the civil war there should be a great many such enterprises ; but it was equally natural that among these there were not a few which were in bad order and practically unworkable. Quite a number of them, in especial, were mushroom growths of the war period, inaugurated for " defensive " purposes ; having been hastily put together, they collapsed with equal speed during the revolution. All this inevitably led at first to increased disorganisation.

At the outset, the Soviet Power and its instruments had no accurate reports of what was going on. There was no list of undertakings ; there were no tabulated statements of the supplies of raw materials, fuel, and finished commodities ; there was no account of the productive possibilities, no definite idea concerning how much the undertakings that were being nationalised were competent to produce. The bourgeoisie was dying, but it was dying intestate. The proletariat became the " heir " to the wealth of the bourgeoisie—but it became the heir in virtue of a seizure of the property in an embittered civil struggle. Obviously, therefore, in these early days, there could be no talk of any general economic plan. The old organisation, the capitalist system, had collapsed ; the new organisation, the socialist system, had not yet come into being.

NEVERTHELESS, ONE OF THE FUNDAMENTAL TASKS OF THE SOVIET POWER WAS AND IS THAT OF UNITING ALL THE ECONOMIC ACTIVITIES OF THE COUNTRY IN ACCORDANCE WITH A GENERAL PLAN OF DIRECTION BY THE STATE. Thus only is it possible to retain productivity at such a level as will permit a subsequent farther development. We have learned in Part One that one of the great merits of the communist system is that it puts an end to the chaos, to the " anarchy," of the capitalist system. Herein lies the very essence of communism. It would of course be absurd to expect that within a brief space of time, when hunger and cold are rife, when there is a lack of fuel and raw materials, it will be possible rapidly to achieve permanent and satisfactory results. But while it is true that people do not live in the foundations of their house, and that they cannot live in the house at all till it has been erected upon its foundations, and until the scaffolding has been removed, nevertheless the foundation is absolutely indispensable. This comparison may be applied to the upbuilding of communist society. The foundations of communist society are laid by the organisation of industry, and first of all by a purposive unification of industry under State control.

To carry out this design in practice, it was necessary, first of all, to take stock. We had to know precisely what resources were available for the proletarian Power. We had to know what supplies there were, how many enterprises, etc. By degrees, ties arose between what had formerly been independent enterprises. Central instruments came into existence for the supply of raw materials, fuel, and accessories. A network of organs for the local and central administration of industry was created, and this was already in a position to elaborate a general plan and to apply the plan all over the country.

The administrative apparatus of industry, regarded from above, is constructed as follows. At the head of each factory there is the *workers' factory administration*. This usually consists of the workers in the enterprise, who are members of the appropriate trade unions, and of members of the technical staff who are appointed subject to the approval of the central committee of the workers' trade union; two-thirds of the members of the factory administration are ordinary workers, and one-third belong to the technical staff. In certain cases, where we have to do with a number of comparatively small undertakings, there are *district administrations* in close touch with the *local economic councils,* and these in their turn are in touch with the local soviets of workers' delegates. Larger undertakings are directly subordinated to the so-called "chiefs" and "centres." These "chiefs" and "centres" constitute unions of whole branches of production. For example, the Chief-textiles supervises the whole textile industry; Chief-nails supervises all the production of nails; Chief-coal supervises all the production of coal. (Refer back to the small-type list in § 93.) The organisations which, under State capitalism, had been State trusts presiding over specific branches of production, have in our system become "chiefs" and "centres." The composition of these chiefs and centres is decided by the presidium or executive committee of the Supreme Economic Council (see below) and by the central committee of the respective trade union. Should any dissension arise, the place of this trade union is taken by the All-Russian Central Soviet of Trade Unions, which decides the composition of such a "centre" in conjunction with the presidium of the Supreme Economic Council. The local economic councils are usually responsible for the organisation of minor enterprises.

The "chiefs" and the "centres," in their turn, are united into groups of kindred industries. For example, such unions of "chiefs" constitute respectively the "Gomza" (State machine shops), the Centro-copper, the Chief-gold, the Chief-nails, etc.

Here, for instance, is a list of the groups comprising the Department for Metals.

		No. of Enterprises.
1. The factories of Sormovo and Kolomna (Gomza)		17
2. Central coke, furnace and iron works	.. ..	3
3. Iron mines of Kaluga and Ryazan	.. ..	9
4. Malzov works	.. ..	6
5. Centro-copper	.. ..	10
6. Avtozav (motor-car works)	.. .. ..	3

and so on.[1]

In the textile industry, at the head of which is Centro-textile, we have in addition the so-called " Kusts " (especially in the cotton industry) ; these unite undertakings which produce half-manufactured products in various stages of manufacture, and also finished products.

Speaking generally, it may be said that all this organisation is still in a state of flux ; new forms are continually arising, and old forms are continually dying out. This is inevitable during a time of febrile constructive activity, and when the conditions are so unfavourable because we may own the Ural region to-day and lose it to the enemy to-morrow, because we may be excluded from Ukraine to-day and may be in control there to-morrow.

Not only, then, are the individual branches of production unified, but these branches of production are further integrated into larger unities. It need hardly be said that such combinations of branches are formed, first of all, between branches of a kindred character. For example, the production of nails, that of machinery, that of copper, and that of copper utensils, etc., are combined into a metal group. This group of " chiefs " constitutes the Department for Metals of the Supreme Economic Council. There are several such departments. Besides the Department for Metals, we have the Department for Chemical Industries, the Department for Foods, the Printing Department, etc. In the autumn of 1919, the structure of these various departments was still far from uniform. In the Department for Metals, the predominant influence was exercised by the Central Committee of the All-Russian Union of Metalworkers. The metalworkers belong to the workers' vanguard ; they are mentally alert ; they are splendid workers ; for these reasons they have excellent administrative capacity. In

[1] From the report made by the committee of the Department for Metals to the presidium or executive of the Supreme Economic Council. The report was drafted by Comrade Milyutin.

some of the other departments the conditions are less favourable. For example, it was not until the autumn of 1919 that the workers began to participate in the administration of the Department for Chemical Industries, for not until that date had there been constituted any corporative unity in this class of work.

All the departments are subordinated to the Supreme Economic Council (Vysovnarhoz [or S.E.C.]). This consists of representatives of the Soviet of Trade Unions, of the All-Russian Central Executive Committee of Soviets, and of the people's commissaries. Its affairs are managed by a presidium. Thus the S.E.C. coordinates all the economic activities of the country, and the primary duty of the council is to draw up and to carry out a unified scheme for the State administration of economic life.

The activities of the Gomza demonstrate the capacity of the workers, with the aid of the requisite types of organisation, to increase production. The Union of Metalworkers, it will be remembered, has the decisive influence here.

QUANTITIES PRODUCED.

	Spare Parts of loco-motives, carriages, and trucks.	Armoured Trains.		Railway carriages.	Tanks, etc., refitted.	Field railway carriages.	Points.
		Loco-motives.	Plat-forms.	New plat-forms.			
During 2 months, Nov. and Dec., 1918 ..	Poods. 24,240	2	4	477	—	148	—
During 6 months, Jan. to June, 1919 ..	94,419	10	19	1,181	1,040	522	7,543 [1]

[1] Data furnished by Comrade Larin.

The period of time to which the second line in the table relates was three times as long as the period to which the first line relates. It will be seen that the production was more than three times as great.

With the aid of a certain amount of organisation, which is already progressing satisfactorily, it has become possible to make a more purposive use of the apparatus for controlling the supply of raw material than has hitherto been made by the " chiefs," and also to secure a better centralisation of production by restricting it to the best equipped undertakings. The latter is a logical consequence of the general

plan. Plainly, it is more advantageous to utilise the best
equipped undertakings, to concentrate all our energies upon
the maintenance of these, rather than to trouble ourselves
fruitlessly by having recourse to inefficient and badly equipped
undertakings. In this matter, likewise, we have of course
to reckon with the general scarcity of fuel and raw materials.
Owing to the scarcity, we have often been compelled to
close down some of the largest works (in the textile industry,
for instance). Even to-day we owe to these causes the
still persistent partial disorganisation of production. The
main trouble here, however, is not the lack of organisation
properly speaking, but the lack of material things requisite
for production.

Nevertheless, the centralisation of production advances
with irresistible strides. The Gomza, for instance, has
closed a considerable number of second-rate enterprises,
and has concentrated production in sixteen of the best-
equipped works. The electro-technical industry, which was
quite disintegrated under capitalism, has now been unified.
The same thing has happened in various other branches of
production (tobacco, farinaceous foods, sugar, textiles, etc.).

The wise and thrifty utilisation of the extant supplies
of materials and energy is a matter of immense importance.
At first, as we have seen, there were no inventories. A
number of warehouses were destroyed, and the stores they
contained were pillaged, or they disappeared no one knew
whither, before there had been any discussion of the right
utilisation of these resources. But in this field, likewise,
order was gradually introduced, although with great difficulty. In the case of many articles, we now have definite
information as to the amounts available. [See table, p. 271.]

It is perfectly plain that a great deal still remains to be
done to perfect the regulation and organisation of economic
life. Confusion and disorder are still widely prevalent.
The apparatus does not yet dovetail properly ; but the
general framework has already been constructed. Our
task now consists in advancing the work along three lines :
first, we must perfect the unification of all the economic
activities of the country ; secondly, we must perfect our
general plan of economic administration, must centralise
production more completely, must organise it better, and

must continue to improve our administrative apparatus; lastly, we must learn to make a still better use of all the raw materials and stores in the country.

The following table gives a comparative statement relating to the supply of fuel and of raw material in the years 1918 and 1919 respectively. The data have been furnished by Comrade Milyutin.

Kind of Fuel or of Raw Material.	1918.	1919.
A. Fuel.		
1. Coal from the Moscow and Borovitch areas ..	30,000,000 poods	30,000,000 poods
2. Wood used or stored ..	4,000,000 cubic sazhenes	5,000,000 cubic sazhenes
3. Peat	58,000,000 poods	60,000,000 poods
4. Petroleum	93,000,000 poods	— [1]
B. Raw Materials used or stored		
1. Flax	No record	5,500,000 poods
2. Cotton	,,	6,500,000 poods [2]
3. Wool	,,	2,000,000 poods
4. Hemp	,,	2,000,000 poods
5. Metals	30,000,000 poods	40,000,000 poods [3]
6. Furs	?	?

[1] Baku occupied by the British.
[2] Including Turkestan cotton now on the way.
[3] Including metals from the Urals.

The table shows that order was being established in many departments. It likewise shows that our chief trouble has been the loss of the petroleum supplies.

§ 96.

The Development of economic Cooperation with other Lands. The question of our relationships to the foreign world is closely connected with the question of the organisation of large-scale industry. Soviet Russia is encircled by a blockade, and this does immense harm to the country. The figures in the following table show how important the interruption of economic intercourse with other lands has been in its influence upon Russian manufacturing industry and agriculture.

IMPORTS INTO RUSSIA.

Year.	Food-stuffs.		Raw materials and half-manufactured articles.		Live stock.		Manufactured articles.		Totals.	
	Thousands of roubles.	Percentage	Thousands of roubles.	Percentage	Thousands of roubles.	Percentage	Thousands of roubles.	Percentage	Thousands of roubles.	Percentage
1909	182,872	100·0	442,556	100·0	7,972	100·0	272,937	100·0	906,336	100·0
1910	191,462	104·7	554,386	125·3	10,791	135·4	327,807	120·1	1,084,446	119·7
1911	206,909	113.1	553,143	125·0	10,997	137·9	390,633	143·1	1,161,682	128·2
1912	209,647	114·6	555,516	125·5	11,979	150·3	394,630	144·6	1,171,772	129·3
1913	273,898	130·1	667,989	150·9	17,615	221·0	450,532	165·1	1,374,034	151·6

Our chief imports were manufactured articles, and between 1909 and 1913 the quantity of these imports increased by 65 per cent. The import of raw materials and half-manufactured goods increased in the same period by 60 per cent. Thus the importance of imports notably augmented. The most notable imports were industrial machinery apparatus of various kinds, hardware, agricultural machinery, chemical products, electrical accessories, and other means of production. But there was also a steady increase in the import of articles of consumption (textiles, leather goods, etc.).

All intercourse with Germany was broken off at the outset of the war. When Soviet Russia was blockaded, trade relations with the Entente likewise came to an end. According to pre-war estimates, our total imports of goods amounted to nearly one and a half milliards of roubles. This shows what a loss the blockade has inflicted upon us.

The policy of our party must therefore aim at the reopening of economic relationships with other States—in so far, of course, as this is compatible with our general aims. The best guarantee, in this connexion, would be a decisive victory over the counter-revolution.

A second task concerns the mutual economic relationships between Russia and those countries in which the proletariat gains the upper hand. We must aim, not merely at economic exchanges with such countries, but if possible we must collaborate with them in accordance with a common economic plan. Should the proletariat prove victorious in Germany, we should establish a joint organ which would direct the common economic policy of the two soviet republics. It would decide what quantity of products German proletarian industry should send to Soviet Russia; how many skilled workers should migrate from Germany (to the Russian locomotive factories, for instance); and, conversely, what quantity of raw materials should be sent from Russia to Germany. We are perfectly well aware that Europe will be able to recover far more rapidly from the present state of disorganisation in the event of a union being formed between the various countries. Naturally, we have no intention to unite with any capitalist land. On the other hand, we can and must enter into a close economic alliance with soviet republics, must collaborate with them in accordance with a common economic plan. THE ECONOMIC PROLETARIAN CENTRALISATION OF PRODUCTION UPON AN INTERNATIONAL SCALE—SUCH IS OUR GOAL.

§ 97.

The Organisation of small-scale Industry, Handicraft, and Home Industry. We have seen that one of the chief obstacles to the upbuilding of communism in Russia arises from the fact that in general our country, like all undeveloped and backward lands, is one of petty enterprise. Above all is this true of Russian agriculture. But the manufacturing industry of Russia likewise retains vestiges of the old type of relationships; we have large numbers of home workers, independent artisans, and small-scale producers. According to pre-war statistics, in 34 provinces there were in all about 1,700,000 petty enterprises carried on by home workers.

In the following statement, these home industries are numerically classified according to the nature of the products.

I. MINERALS   66,400
       (pottery and earthenware, tiles, millstones, whet-
         stones, copper ware, lime)

II. WOOD   467,900
       (mats ;   vats, tubs, barrels ;   furniture ;   bast
         shoes ;   sledges and country carts ;   baskets and
         basket ware ;   wheels, fellies ;   charcoal, pitch,
         and tar ;   spoons and other wooden utensils ;
         boats and rafts—in all, 18 industries)

III. METALS	130,500

(nails, hatchets, and other smithy work ; locks
and knives ; jewelry, watches and clocks ;
foundry work ; window frames and door
frames ; buckets and pipes)

IV. SPINNING, WEAVING, ETC.	65,200

(weaving ; fulling ; spinning ; lace making ;
kerchief making ; net making and rope making ;
carpet making ; cap making ; brush making ;
etc.—11 industries in all)

V. LEATHER GOODS	208,300

(boots and shoes ; sheepskin coats ; small leather
goods ; saddlery ; fur mits ; combs)

VI. MISCELLANEOUS	185,400

(these comprise : tailoring .. .. } 104,900
various industries 73,800
the making of ikons 3,600
the making of concer-
tinas .. .. } 3,100

According to some estimates, the number of independent home workers was reduced by one million during the war, and this despite the fact that, owing to the disorganisation of large-scale manufacture, many workers took to home industry. The reduction is to be explained by the migration and dispersal of home workers in search of regions where there was more to eat. In the provinces of Vologda, Novgorod, and similar regions, where the food conditions were particularly bad, the falling off ranged from 20 to 25 per cent. On the other hand, in the provinces of Kursk, Orel, Simbirsk, and Tambov, there was an increase of from 15 to 20 per cent.

The proletarian Power is faced by the question, How is this mass of petty producers to be incorporated into the general system of the socialist economy now in course of construction ?

In the first place, it is absolutely clear that forcible expropriation is here quite inadmissible. The petty producers must not be bludgeoned into the socialist realm. We must do everything in our power to make it easy for them to undergo the necessary change, and to understand that it is not merely necessary but advantageous. This can be achieved by surrounding the home worker with certain conditions. What are these conditions ? How can they be secured ?

First of all, WE MUST INCLUDE HOME INDUSTRY IN THE

GENERAL SCHEME FOR THE STATE PROVISION OF FUEL AND RAW MATERIALS. For if the home worker receives from the State organisation of the proletariat the fuel and the raw materials which are requisite for his productive occupation, then he will become dependent upon that proletarian organisation. In former days, under capitalism, the dealer or the factory owner often supplied the home worker with raw materials, and thereby the latter became dependent upon the former: Of course the dealer or the factory owner " looked after " the home worker in this way in order to exploit him. The home worker was really working, not for himself, but for a capitalist. Of a very different character is the dependence of the home worker upon the proletarian State. The proletarian State, the workers' State, neither wants to, nor will, nor can, exploit the home worker. The proletarian State only wants to help the home workers to organise themselves jointly with the other workers. The proletarian State will not extract profit from the home workers (it does not extract profit from anyone) ; its aim is to attract the home workers and their organisations into the general labour organisation of industry. The home worker who is dependent upon the dealer or the factory owner, works for the dealer or the factory owner. He becomes their beast of burden. The home worker who is dependent upon the proletarian State is a social worker. Thus the first requisite is to include the home worker in the general scheme for the supply of fuel and raw materials.

Secondly, it is essential that THE HOME WORKER SHOULD RECEIVE FINANCIAL AID FROM THE STATE. Formerly, under capitalism, the usurious dealer likewise helped out the home worker in money matters. But he " supported " the home worker much as the cord supports the man who has been hanged. The dealer enslaved the home worker in the most barbarous fashion, for the dealer, spiderlike, sucked a golden juice out of the home worker. The proletarian State can really help the home worker with money, supplying the money to enable the home worker to execute State orders, with no intention of extracting profits, with no usurious aim whatever.

Thirdly, it is self-evident that THE PROLETARIAN STATE MUST PLACE ITS ORDERS WITH THE HOME WORKER IN ACCORD-

ANCE WITH A CENTRALISED SYSTEM. Supplying the home worker with raw materials, with fuel, with accessories, and in case of need with implements, the proletarian State authority places its orders in accordance with a definite plan, and is enabled to include the home worker in the general scheme of social production.

Thus the home workers will by degrees be drawn within the general system of production now being organised upon socialist foundations. They will be drawn within that system, not only by being supplied with certain products of social production, but also because they themselves will be directly working for the proletarian State in accordance with a plan prescribed for them by the instruments of the proletarian State.

Fourthly, THE HELP GIVEN TO THE HOME WORKERS (in the manner just described) MUST BE CONDITIONAL UPON THEIR ORGANISING THEMSELVES LIKE OTHER WORKERS. The proletarian State must give the preference to those home workers who unite, who organise themselves into *artels* or cooperatives of production. More important still, it must give the preference among such organisations, to those which are undertaking large-scale cooperative production instead of petty production.

Every entrepreneur, however small the scale of his operations, and even the independent home worker, has at the bottom of his heart a desire to become a great entrepreneur, a desire to " get on in the world," a desire to have an " establishment " of his own, to engage " hands," and so on. Under capitalism, artels or cooperatives of production have tended, as they have grown stronger, to degenerate, in actual fact, into capitalist undertakings. It will be very different under the proletarian dictatorship. Here there is no scope for capitalism. Instead, we have the State authority of the workers, which organises all possible kinds of unions among the workers, and which holds in its hands all the financial resources of the community, and, still more important, all the means of production. Formerly it was absurd to believe that artels could bring us nearer to socialism ; inevitably, in the course of their development they became transformed into capitalist companies. But now, when we are able to draw them within the organisation of the workers' State, such bodies can be helpful in the upbuilding of socialism. They can be helpful, not because the home workers are themselves eager for communism (many of the home workers, like petty entrepreneurs in general, are prejudiced against communism), but because new roads are being opened, while the old roads have been completely closed.

By encouraging the home workers to form labour organisations, we encourage their painless transformation into workers of the great united, organised, "mechanised" system of social production.

Much has already been done in this direction. For the winter season of 1919–20, for example, State orders were extensively placed among home workers : 2,000,000 pairs of felt boots ; 2,200,000 pairs of woollen mits ; large quantities of knitted goods ; bast shoes ; sheepskin jackets ; etc. An improvement in production has already become noticeable. For the winter season 1918–19 the deliveries of felt boots down to March 1st, 1919 (!) were only 300,000 pairs ; for the winter season 1919–20 there have already been delivered 500,000 pairs by November, 1919.

The advances were given in accordance with a definite plan ; raw materials, petroleum, illuminants, and fuel were supplied.. In the years 1918–19, the work of organisation took the following form. Conferences were summoned consisting of the representatives of cooperative organisations, of the home workers' leagues (Centrosoyus, Centrosectia, Moska, Kustarsbyt, etc.), and representatives of the section for home industry of the Supreme Economic Council. These conferences drew up a general plan. Kustarsbyt (the central league of cooperatives for the production and distribution of goods manufactured by home workers and artels) is the largest organisation of home workers which has been drawn into the general organisational scheme. It embraces 29 leagues with 1306 cooperatives, representing in all 631,860 homeworking enterprises. They receive their supplies either from the central organisation or through the local economic councils.

Under the soviet regime, the number of associations is steadily increasing.

It need hardly be said that, since the links between the various parts of the economic soviet apparatus are now in course of construction, no final forms have yet been attained. Everything is still in a state of flux. But there is one matter upon which we have to keep our attention fixed—the regulation of the apparatus, the harmony of organisation, the purposiveness of all our activities.

§ 98.

The Organisation of Industry and of Trade Unions. In Russia, the apparatus which has proved preeminently suitable for the new tasks in the domain of organising and administering industry has consisted of the trade unions.

In capitalist society the function of the trade unions —constituted first upon a craft basis and subsequently upon an industrial (productive) basis—was primarily to serve as a means for the struggle against capitalism, as a means for the economic struggle. During the days of storm and stress, the trade unions joined forces with the party of the working class, with the bolsheviks, to lead the general onslaught upon capital. The party, the unions, and the soviets marched side by side against the capitalist social order. After the conquest of political power, the role of the trade unions naturally underwent a change. Hitherto, for example, they had engaged in strikes against the capitalists. Now the capitalists no longer existed as ruling class, as masters, as entrepreneurs. Hitherto, the principal aim of the trade unions had been to effect the destruction of the system which then prevailed in the factories. But after November,1917, the time had arrived for the establishment of the new order.

The organisation of production—this was the new task of the trade unions in the epoch of proletarian dictatorship. The unions were able to bring together immense numbers of the proletariat. They were the most powerful of all the proletarian organisations, and they were directly associated with the work of production. In Russia, moreover, at the time of the revolution, they were in entire agreement with the idea of the proletarian dictatorship. It is not surprising, therefore, that it proved necessary to hand over to these organisations the actual responsibility for the management of production, including the management of the most important of all the elements of production—the management of labour power.

What should be the relationship between the trade unions and the State Power of the proletariat ?

Let us recall what the bourgeoisie did in order to secure its greatest successes. It built up the system of State capitalism, associating all its other organisations more closely with the State Power, this applying in especial to its economic organisations (syndicates, trusts, and employers' associations). The proletariat, which has to carry to a successful issue its struggle against capital, must in like manner centralise its organisations. It has its soviets of workers' delegates, which constitute the instruments of State authority ; it has trade unions ; it has cooperatives. Manifestly, if their work is to be effective they must be mutually interconnected. The question now arises, with which organisation must the others be linked up. The answer is simple. We must select the greatest and most powerful of all. Such an organism is constituted by the State organisation of the working class, by the Soviet Power. It follows, therefore, that THE TRADE UNIONS AND THE COOPERATIVES MUST DEVELOP IN SUCH A WAY THAT THEY WILL BE TRANSFORMED INTO ECONOMIC DEPARTMENTS AND INSTRUMENTS OF THE STATE AUTHORITY ; THEY MUST BE " STATIFIED."

The social solidarians (those who continually overlook the significance of the class struggle), when considering the part that must be played by the trade unions in the epoch of the proletarian dictatorship, usually adopt the point of view of those who demand " independence " for the trade-union movement. The unions, these gentry assure us, are class organisations, and for this reason they must remain entirely independent of the State authority.

It is quite easy to detect the fallacy which underlies what here masquerades as a " class " outlook. The " State " cannot be thus contrasted with " class " organisations, for the State is itself a class organisation. When mensheviks and others protest against a union with the workers' State, they are in fact expressing their hostility towards the workers' State. They are taking sides with the bourgeoisie. We note that they likewise advocate independence of the bourgeois State.

They speak slightingly of unions " supported by State funds." But now [in Russia] the State treasury belongs to the workers. Apparently the mensheviks would prefer that the State revenues should still belong to the bourgeoisie ! Independence of the workers' State Power really means dependence upon the bourgeoisie.

The new tasks which were incumbent upon the trade unions made it essential that with all possible speed they should become huge industrial (productive) unions. It is obvious that if the members of the trade unions are to be responsible for the organisation of production, the workers must be organised upon the lines of productive industry,

and not upon craft lines. In other words, for the proper
fulfilment of the new function it was requisite that the
trade unions should be so organised that all the workers
and employees in any enterprise should be united in one
union, and that for each enterprise no other union should
be available. Previously, the unions were so constructed
that the workers were organised in accordance with their
petty crafts. When subsequently endeavours were made
to organise on the lines of industry (production), confusion
still prevailed. For example, the Metalworkers' Union
accepted as members, not only the workers who were really
engaged in the metallurgical industry, but any worker whose
craft had something to do with metals, although the industry
with which he was connected had nothing to do with metal-
lurgy. Of course we do not achieve real industrial (productive) organisation when each undertaking or each branch
of production is treated as a separate organism. To achieve
the industrial organisation of production, we must organise
in an appropriate manner, in accordance with whole branches
of production, and must organise in a single union all the
workers and employees engaged in any particular branch.

As an example of the fusion of a number of small craft unions
to form a great industrial union, we may take the organisation of
the Petrograd metalworkers.

Before Amalgamation.
(At the end of 1917 and beginning of 1918.)

After Amalgamation.

1. Metalworkers' Union.
2. Stokers' Union.
3. Smelters' Union.
4. Welders' and Shearers' Union.
5. Patternmakers' Union.
6. Gold and Silversmiths' Union.
7. Watch and Clockmakers' Union.
8. Electricians' Union.
9. Machinists' Union.
10. Sorters' Union.

1. The Union of Metalworkers,
together with its Sections
(a branch of the All-
Russian Union of Metal-
workers) comprises all
the workers and em-
ployees engaged in metal-
lurgical industry.

In this way, in place of large numbers of little unions
organised upon a craft basis, there have come into existence
the great centralised industrial (productive) unions. THE
TASK OF OUR PARTY IN THIS CONNEXION IS TO HASTEN
THE TRANSFORMATION, AND TO FAVOUR THE FORMATION OF
INDUSTRIAL (PRODUCTIVE) UNIONS, EACH OF WHICH SHALL

ENROL ALL THE WORKERS AND EMPLOYEES WITHOUT EX-
CEPTION ENGAGED IN A SPECIFIC BRANCH OF INDUSTRIAL
PRODUCTION.

According to the data made available by the statistical department of the All-Russian Central Soviet of Trade Unions, the
membership of the unions was as follows:

In the first half of 1917			..	..	..	335,938
,,	second	,,	1917	..	..	..	943,547
,,	first	,,	1918	..	..	..	1,649,278
,,	second	,,	1918	..	..	..	2,250,278
,,	first	,,	1919	..	..	..	2,825,018

In the first half of the year 1919, the membership of 31 All-Russian
unions, excluding the Railwayworkers' Union and the Water Transportworkers' Union, was 2,801,000—the rest of the workers were
organised in local unions. If we add the 722,000 railwayworkers
and the 200,000 water transportworkers, we find that the total membership of the trade unions was more than 3,700,000. They have
33 central executive committees. In addition, there are still quite
a number of trade unions which have not yet been centralised. The
statistical department estimates that the total number of organised
workers (including the provinces occupied by the enemy) is 4,000,000.
We must not forget that the workers belonging to the factories
which are not running are still reckoned as workers of these factories,
and remain members of their respective unions.

In accordance with the laws of the Soviet Republic,
and in accordance with established practice, the trade
unions (industrial or productive unions) participate in the
work of all the central and local organs of the administration
of industry. They participate in the work of the commissariats, of the economic councils, of the Supreme Economic
Council, of the chiefs and the centres, of the workers' factory
administration—in a word, everywhere the trade unions play
an important, nay a decisive role.

Nevertheless, this taking control of production on the
part of the trade unions is still far from complete. There
are many branches of economic life in which the workers
have not yet assumed, as they should assume, control.
Especially does this apply to the " chiefs " and " centres."
In these we frequently find that bourgeois specialists are
at work, persons who are not subject to any proper control,
and who would like to reconstruct economic organisation
in accordance with their own plans, hoping for a return

of the " good old times," for the speedy transformation of the centres into capitalist trusts. To counteract any such designs, it is essential that THE TRADE UNIONS SHOULD TAKE AN EVER-INCREASING SHARE IN THE ADMINISTRATION OF INDUSTRY, UNTIL THE DAY WHEN THE WHOLE OF ECONOMIC LIFE, FROM THE BOTTOM TO THE TOP, SHALL CONSTITUTE A UNITY WHICH IS EFFECTIVELY CONTROLLED BY THE INDUSTRIAL (PRODUCTIVE) UNIONS.

On the lower levels of industrial administration, we must refer in especial to the activity of the factory committees. These are really cells of the trade unions, subordinated in each case to the guidance of the respective union. Elected by the workers of a given factory or workshop, these factory or workshop committees control affairs within the enterprise so far as labour power is concerned. They are responsible for engaging and dismissing workers ; they care for the workers' families ; they supervise the pay, regulate the hours of work, are supreme in matters of discipline, etc. They are, moreover, admirable elementary schools of administrative work for the broad masses of the people.

In this way the trade (industrial or productive) unions effect the closest association between the central organs of State administration, economic life, and the broad masses of the workers.

The first, the most important, function of the industrial (productive) unions is to an ever-increasing degree to ensure that the masses shall participate in the control of economic life. Taking the factory committees as their foundation, and uniting practically all the workers, the industrial (productive) unions must induce more and ever more workers to interest themselves in the organisation of production. Direct practical experience of administrative work is here especially valuable (for example, on the factory committees, in the workers' factory administrations, in the economic councils, the " chiefs," etc.). Of great value, likewise, is a special work of enlightenment undertaken by the unions (courses of instruction, etc.).

This introduction of the masses to participation in constructive work is also the best way of counteracting the tendency to bureaucracy in the economic apparatus of the Soviet Power. In places where there are very few workers but a great number of " soviet employees," bureaucracy is apt to assume formidable proportions. Routinism, red tape, bad manners, slackness, sabotage—there is too much of all these in the economic organisations. We know only one way of getting rid of such abuses, and it is by lifting the lower grades of workers to a higher level. For thus only can be ensured a genuine, popular control of the activities of all our economic institutions.

§ 99.

The Utilisation of Labour Power. Of extreme importance to the future of Russia is the right utilisation of the available supplies of labour power. When means of production are nearly exhausted and raw materials are very scarce, everything depends upon the right application of labour power. We have, then, the following duties to perform. We must utilise all the available labour power; in other words, we must take care that all the elements capable of work have something to do, that they are all employed. We have to remember that in days of famine everyone who eats without doing useful work is a dead weight upon society. There are plenty of such persons. Nevertheless, there is a great deal of work which can be done without any complicated means : for example, the removal of town refuse ; the repair of streets, high roads, and railways ; street cleaning ; emergency fortification work ; the cleaning of barracks ; etc. There are various kinds of work connected with the provision of fuel and raw materials, the felling of trees, the transport of timber, the procuring of peat, etc. Here, of course, we encounter a great many difficulties. We may have men and axes, but may lack food for the men, so that our wood-cutting schemes come to nothing. It is obvious, however, that the only way out of our many difficulties is through the right utilisation of the labour power at our disposal.

Associated with this problem is that of carrying out general mobilisations for the performance of one kind of social work or another. When work of fortification was urgently required, an excellent use was made of the labour power of the masses which would otherwise have run to waste. This task must be systematically performed. The universal obligation to labour is part of the constitution of the Russian Socialist Federative Soviet Republic, but in practice we are a long way from its realisation. Our first duty, then, is to see to it that all the labour power of the Workers' Republic shall be adequately utilised. Our second duty concerns the distribution and redistribution of labour power. It is sufficiently obvious that the productivity of labour will depend upon how far we can effect a purposive distribution of labour power throughout the various districts and throughout the various branches of work.

This distribution of labour power, the supply of labour power to the places where it is required, will need an enormous amount of registration of labour power, if the assignments are to be made intelligently. Unless we know precisely what means we have to dispose of, we cannot dispose of them to advantage. Here is work which the Soviet Power cannot perform properly without the collaboration of the trade unions, and indeed the work must be done through the instrumentality of the trade unions.

§ 100.

Comradely Labour Discipline. The productivity of a country is not solely determined by the quantity of machinery, raw materials, and other material means of production it contains ; its productivity depends also upon labour power. In Russia at the present time, since the material means of production are so scanty, the condition of labour power, of living labour, assumes enormous importance.

The capitalist method of production kept the workers in subjection ; compelled them to work for their masters ; imposed upon them, in effect, the discipline of the lash.

The revolution undermined and overthrew this discipline of capitalist labour, completely abolished it, just as in the army it abolished the imperialist discipline, and made an end of the obedience of the soldiers to the tsarist officers. It is plain, however, that the task of socialist reconstruction will never be achieved without a new discipline. Here, likewise, comparison with the army holds good. We destroyed the old army. For a season, there was " anarchy," disorder, confusion. But we constructed a new army, on new foundations, and for new ends—an army which is in the hands of the proletariat, and fights against the land-lords and capitalists to whom the old army belonged.

The same thing is happening in the case of the " army of the toilers," in the case of the working class. The period of the destruction of the old discipline is over. There is now being inaugurated a new, a comradely labour discipline, not imposed and sustained by the masters, not imposed and sustained by the capitalist whip, but by the labour organisations themselves, by the factory committees, the workshop committees, and the trade unions. When we are organising production, we cannot leave out of account the organisation of labour in the factory.

A comradely labour discipline is one of the most important means for the organisation of social production and for the increase of productivity. Comradely discipline must be accompanied by the *complete spontaneity of the working class.* The workers must not wait for orders from above, must not lack initiative. Far from this, every improvement in production, every discovery of new methods of organising labour, must break trail for itself. Backward strata of the workers often fail to recognise how their work ought to be managed. But the means are to hand. The workers are organised in unions, and these unions control production ; every day the workers have before their eyes the factory and workshop committees and the workers' factory admin-istrations. Everything that is needed can be effected from below upwards through the instrumentality of the labour organisations, provided only that a little more zeal is dis-played, less timidity, a fuller realisation that the working class has now become the master of life.

Labour discipline must be based upon the feeling and *the consciousness that every worker is responsible to his class,* upon the consciousness that slackness and carelessness are treason to the common cause of the workers. The capi-talists no longer exist as a dominant caste. The workers no longer work for capitalists, usurers, and bankers ; they work for themselves. They are engaged upon their own affairs ; the edifice they are constructing belongs to the workers. Formerly, under the capitalist regime, it was not our business to trouble ourselves how their purses might best be filled. Now, another day has dawned. This sense of responsibility towards the whole working class must animate the mind of every worker.

Finally, labour discipline must be based upon *the strictest mutual control.* Since all the comrades know that a decline in the productivity of labour will involve the ruin of the whole working class, that if we fail to improve in this respect we shall inevitably perish, they must all supervise with a proprietary eye the common task of utilising the life-giving energies of nature. For labour is a struggle ; it is a struggle with nature. We have to win the victory over nature ; we must transform nature's crudities into clothing, fuel, and bread. And just as in the forefront of the struggle with the enemies of our class, with the capitalists, the landlords, and the military officers, we measure our successes, and keep a vigilant eye upon all who are afraid, all who are slack, all who are treacherous—so, here, we must control one another mutually. He betrays the workers' cause who fails now to help in getting the workers' cart out of the mire ; such a one is a blackleg.

It is plain that the work of creating a new labour discipline will be arduous, for it will involve *the re-education of the masses.* A slave psychology and slavish habits are still deeply ingrained. It is just as it was in the case of the army. When the tsar drove, the soldier moved on ; but when it was a case of defending his own cause, the soldier scratched his head and did nothing. Still, we were able to deal with this question of the army because the members of the workers' vanguard were well aware of what was at stake, and they did all that was necessary. Now we have to achieve similar results in the case of production. The re-education of the workers will be facilitated by the fact that the toiling masses themselves realise (and have been taught by daily experience) that their fate is in their own hands. They had a very good lesson when for a time, in various regions, the Soviet Power was overthrown by the counter-revolution. For instance, in the Urals, in Siberia, etc.

The communists, the workers' vanguard, gave a striking example of the new, comradely discipline when they instituted the so-called *Communist Saturdays*, when they worked voluntarily and gratuitously, increasing the productivity of labour far beyond the ordinary.

Comrade Lenin spoke of the Communist Saturdays as "the great initiative." The Moscow railwaymen were the first among the communists to organise Communist Saturdays, and from the very outset there was a notable increase in the productivity of their labour. On the Alexander Railway, 5 turners in 4 hours made 80 cylinders (213 % more than the ordinary production); 20 labourers, in 4 hours, assembled 600 poods of scrap iron and 70 carriage springs each weighing $3\frac{1}{2}$ poods (300 % more than the ordinary production). This was the beginning. Thereupon Petrograd adopted the Communist Saturdays, and organised them on the grand scale. Here are the figures:

					No. of Workers.	Cash Value of the five Days' Work.
1st Saturday	(August 16th)	..	..		5,175	
2nd ,	(August 23rd)	..	..		7,650	
3rd ,	(August 30th)	..	..		7,900	1,167,188 roubles
4th ,	(September 6th)	..	..		10,250	
5th ,	(September 13th)	..	..		10,500	

From Petrograd and Moscow, the Communist Saturdays made their way into the provinces, and non-members of the party began to work in the same way. The initiative of the Moscow railwaymen was so effective because they were the pioneers of a new discipline.

It need hardly be said that the establishment of the new labour discipline would be impracticable without the cooperation of the trade unions. Nay more, it is incumbent upon the trade unions to advance along this road, to try new methods and new paths. For here everything is experimental; we have no precedents.

Among the measures which have already been adopted, and which have in every possible way to be developed and perfected, our party lays stress upon the following:

1. *The introduction of account taking.* In Russia, we have been very backward in this respect. But without proper records no kind of organisation, investigation, or control can be achieved. Without records it is impossible to get to the root of the matter.

2. *The introduction of a normal working day and of a normal intensity of labour.* Here, too, we are as yet only in the first stage of development. The capitalists in their enterprises had fixed hours and a fixed standard of speed for the workers, with the aim of extracting surplus value. The hours and

speed were fixed by the masters' organisations. In Soviet Russia the hours of work and the intensity of labour are settled by the trade unions, that is to say by the workers' organisations, whose business it is to take further action in this field. The workers' organisations decide the possibilities of work, taking into account cold, hunger, the scarcity of materials, and the general disrepair of the machinery. As soon as hours and intensity have been prescribed, the worker does ill who fails to work up to the standard. We must establish a workers' code of honour, so that any worker who, without good reason, fails to contribute his quota to the common cause, shall be regarded as a contemptible loafer.

3. *The establishment of responsibility to comradely labour courts.* This implies, not merely that everyone will be under the supervision of his workmates, but that everyone will be positively called to account for bad work. In this matter, once more, it is not a master supervising his slaves, but the working class and its organisations enforcing the responsibility of individual members.

Many similar measures might be considered. They would one and all be directed towards the same end, which is to marshal the ranks of the army of the toilers, the army of the pioneers who are building the way to the new social order.

§ 101.

The Employment of bourgeois Experts. Contemporary large-scale production is inconceivable without managing engineers, technicians, learned specialists, investigators, and persons with peculiar practical experience. Among the ranks of the workers, very few come within these categories. Neither in the tsarist and feudalist regime nor in the bourgeois regime were the workers given any opportunity to learn. But we have to get on with the work, and there is only one way out of the difficulty. We must make use of those persons with specialised skill who served the bourgeoisie, not from fear, but from inclination. The party is well aware that this stratum of technicians and intellectuals, no less than the stratum of ex-managers and capitalist organisers, is saturated with bourgeois ideology. Nay more.

Many such persons are directly hostile to us, and would like to betray us to our class enemies. Nevertheless we have to take these bourgeois into our service. There is nothing else for us to do.

The experts and technicians have carried on a fierce struggle against the proletariat, in the first instance by sabotage. But the Soviet Power was able to put an end to sabotage. By degrees, many groups came over to our side, when they saw that the workers were creating as well as destroying, and that our party by no means intended to betray Russia to the German imperialists. Some of them are beginning to realise that the knell of capitalism has really sounded. A split in their ranks has begun. It devolves upon the proletariat to widen this breach to the utmost.

We should be wrong, of course, to expect fidelity from these " experts," to expect from them devotion to communism. It would be absurd to hope that such people, who are connected with the bourgeoisie by a thousand ties, will undergo a sudden transformation. But here the proletariat must act like a far-seeing employer. It needs the bourgeois experts, and it must compel them to work for it.

We must employ the following methods. Economic considerations dictate our giving every possible encouragement to those who work well ; we must not be stingy in the matter of their salaries. But towards any who prove to be counter-revolutionaries, who fight against the proletariat, who are traitors or saboteurs, we must be absolutely ruthless. The proletariat must prize those who serve it faithfully, and it knows how to prize them. But the workers cannot allow anyone to inflict an injury upon them unpunished, above all at such a time as this, when they have to suffer the pangs of hunger and a thousand additional evils.

We must, therefore, exercise strict control, more particularly when we are dealing with experts drawn from among the circles of the managers of great businesses and from among those who were capitalists on the grand scale. Such persons will frequently attempt to serve their own side in secret. We have to adopt the same measures in civil life that we have had to adopt at the front to deal with treachery on the part of ex-officers of the tsarist regime who have entered our service.

On the other hand, the party has to set its face against the unsound and childish view that we can entirely dispense with the services of experts. This would be preposterous. Such an idea can be entertained only by opinionated but ignorant persons who have never given any serious thought to the tasks which have now to be shouldered by the proletariat. The proletariat has to carry on contemporary production with the aid of the latest acquirements of science. Such, at least, must be its aim. It will, of course, create (it is already creating) its own Red managing engineers and technicians, just as it is producing its own Red commanding officers. But time presses. We have to use the materials that lie ready to hand, and need only be careful that when we are using them we take precautions against any ill-results, by an organised control of the work of all persons who are hostile to us in sentiment.

In this connexion, we have another question to consider, the question of remuneration. The aim of communism is to secure equal pay for all. Unfortunately, however, we cannot reach communism at one stride. We are only taking the first steps towards it. In this matter, likewise, we must be guided by utilitarian considerations.

If we were to give the experts the same pay that is received by a common labourer, it would not matter to them whether they were common labourers, engineers, or messenger boys. We should be stupid were we to attempt the enforcement of good work from such persons, who are accustomed to a different kind of life. It is better to give them more money if thereby we can secure better results. In this matter the proletariat must follow the example set by any intelligent employer. It must pay more in order to get better work from persons whose services happen to be indispensable at this juncture.

Manifestly, nevertheless, it remains our fundamental policy to work for a system of equal pay for all. The Soviet Power has already done a great deal in this direction. At one time the pay of the higher employees (managers, head bookkeepers, important engineers and organisers, scientific advisory experts, etc.), with the addition of various special fees, was many dozen times more than the pay of the ordinary labourer. Now the former are paid on the average only four times as much as the latter. Notwithstanding what was said above, we have already advanced a considerable distance towards the equalisation of rates of pay.

An equalisation is likewise being effected as regards the different grades of workers. According to the data furnished by Comrade Schmidt, in the year 1914 a daily wage of 50 kopecks was being paid to 4·43 per cent. of the workers, and in the same year there were a few workers (0·04 per cent.) who were earning more than 10 roubles a day. Thus the latter were in receipt of more than 20 times as much as the former. No doubt the lucky ones who earned such high wages in 1914 were very few in number ; but there were some. In the year 1916, the percentage of male workers whose daily earnings were only 50 kopecks was ½ per cent., whilst the percentage of those who earned more than 10 roubles was 1·15 per cent.

In accordance with the decree issued in the autumn of 1919, the minimum income was 1200 roubles and the maximum was 4800 roubles, the latter figure being the maximum for the "specialists" as well.

The detachment of many groups of technically skilled intellectuals from the bourgeoisie, and their espousal of the cause of the proletariat, will be accelerated in proportion as the Soviet Power becomes more perfectly stabilised. Inasmuch as the strengthening of the Soviet Power is inevitable, the adhesion of the intellectuals is likewise inevitable. It would, of course, be absurd of us to repulse them. Far from this, we must accept them into our service upon a basis of comradely collaboration, so that in intercourse with us they may have their angles rubbed off, so that through joining us in the common task they may become our own folk. They have a mass of foolish or mischievous prejudices, but under certain conditions they can and will cooperate with us. Already, through the instrumentality of the trade unions, they are gradually becoming associated with us in our work, are growing accustomed to the new state of affairs, and are even beginning to take kindly to us. Our main task, therefore, is to help in this development, and to go out to meet those elements which are themselves tending to draw near to us. In and through the industrial unions, because they and we are collaborating in the organisation of work, the two great divisions of those who labour, the mental workers and the manual workers, kept asunder by capitalism, will at length be reunited.

§ 102.

The Union of Production and Science. For the proper development of productivity, it is essential that science should be wedded to production. Under capitalism, large-scale production was already making extensive calls upon science. In the United States and in Germany, the great manufacturing institutions had special laboratories in which, by prolonged research, new methods and new apparatus were discovered. All this was done in the interest of profits upon privately owned capital. We, in our turn, must now organise in like manner for the sake of the whole of working society. The investigators of those days kept their discoveries secret. The valuable results of their researches went to fill the pockets and the strong boxes of the entrepreneurs. In contemporary Russia, no undertaking hides its discoveries from other undertakings; whatever is learned becomes the common property of all.

In this matter the Soviet Power has instituted a whole series of measures. It has established a number of scientific institutions of a technical and economic character, and has organised various laboratories and experimental stations. Scientific expeditions have been sent out, and among the fruitful results of these may be mentioned the discovery of petroleum wells and of deposits of schist. A means for manufacturing sugar out of sawdust has been discovered. In general, the scientific resources of the republic have been tabulated and have been turned to account.

We still lack many things, and some of these are things urgently necessary, beginning with fuel and ending with delicate scientific instruments. We must clearly realise the extreme importance of such work, and we must do our utmost to promote the union of science with technique and with the organisation of production. COMMUNISM SIGNIFIES INTELLIGENT, PURPOSIVE, AND, CONSEQUENTLY, SCIENTIFIC PRODUCTION. WE SHALL, THEREFORE, DO EVERYTHING IN OUR POWER TO SOLVE THE PROBLEM OF THE SCIENTIFIC ORGANISATION OF PRODUCTION.

Literature. OSINSKY, The Upbuilding of Socialism. MILYUTIN, Economic Development and the Dictatorship of the Proletariat. MILYUTIN, Articles in "Political Economy" for the year 1919. Reports of the eighth Party Congress (discussion of the party program). The Break-up of Capitalism and the Upbuilding of Communism. STEPANOFF, Workers' Control and Workers' Administration. Reports of the first and second All-Russian Economic Congresses. TSYPEROVICH, Syndicates and Trusts in Russia. TOMSKY, Articles on the trade-union movement in Russia appearing in "The Communist International." Reports of the trade-union congresses. Articles in "The Metalworkers' News." HOLZMANN, The Normalisation of Labour. LENIN, The great Initiative.

CHAPTER THIRTEEN

THE ORGANISATION OF AGRICULTURE

§ 103.

Agrarian Conditions in Russia prior to the Revolution. Even before the revolution, Russian agriculture was preeminently peasant agriculture. After the November revolution, after the expropriation of the landlords' estates, our agriculture became almost exclusively peasant agriculture, and almost exclusively small farming. In these circumstances, the Communist Party encountered wellnigh insuperable difficulties in the way of its campaign on behalf of large-scale collective farming. But the campaign is in progress, and even in this most difficult period, at the very outset, certain results have been achieved.

To understand the environment, to understand the conditions in which, as far as the rural districts are concerned, our party has to realise its program, we must study the data concerning Russian agriculture prior to the revolution and those concerning the changes which the revolution has brought about.

Prior to the revolution, landed property in European Russia was distributed as follows :

State lands	138,086,168	desyatinas
Peasant farms	138,767,587	,,
Land owned by private individuals and by institutions ..	118,332,788	,,

Nearly all the State lands consisted of forests, or were in other respects unsuitable for cultivation in their present condition. The land privately owned by individuals and institutions (apart from that held by the peasants) may be classified as follows:

Great estates	.. .. ..	101,735,343	desyatinas
Crown lands	.. .. ..	7,843,115	,,
Church lands	.. .. ..	1,871,858	,,
Monasteries and nunneries	..	733,777	,,
Municipal lands ..	.. ..	2,042,570	,,
Cossack territories	.. ..	3,459,240	,,
Various ..	.. .. ..	646,885	,,

As far as concerns the peasants' lands, according to the statistics of the year 1905 these comprised 12,277,355 farms, so that the average size of a peasant farm was 11·37 desyatinas. In the outlying provinces, where much of the land is unsuitable for cultivation, the peasant farms are considerably larger than this average, which means, of course, that land-hunger prevails among the peasantry of the central provinces of Russia. In actual fact, the average size of farms owned by the ex-serfs who comprise the majority of our peasant population is only 6·7 desyatinas. In some of the provinces, and in some of the counties, the farms are only half that size. By the year 1916, the number of peasant farms had risen to 15,492,202, although the share of the peasantry in the total cultivable land had increased very little. The land-hunger, therefore, had been greatly aggravated.

Since, however, most of the crown lands were unsuitable for cultivation, the only way in which the peasants could increase their holdings was at the expense of the land owned by "private individuals and by institutions."

Among these private individuals, those who had to be deprived of their estates were for the most part great landlords (owning 53,169,008 desyatinas), merchants, and rich peasants, and various cooperatives and companies of a moneymaking, bourgeois type. Individually owned estates exceeding 20 desyatinas comprised in all 82,841,413. The cooperatives owned 15,778,677 desyatinas. It was in these directions that the main onslaught of the peasant revolution moved. As far as concerns the land owned by institutions, the peasants were chiefly interested in the estates held by the church, the monasteries, and the nunneries, and also to some extent in the crown lands.

§ 104.

Agrarian Conditions in Russia subsequent to the Revolution. Before the revolution, privately owned land, and especially the land in the possession of the great landowners, was heavily embarrassed. Over 60,000,000 desyatinas were mortgaged, for a total sum of 3,497,894,600 roubles. In other words, the real owners of these estates were Russian and foreign banks. This explains why the various parties of the social solidarians, the social revolutionaries in especial, although they had clamoured for the assignment of all the privately owned lands to the peasants without compensation to the owners, were afraid to face the issue, or desired to postpone the confiscation when the day of realisation approached. It was only the party of communist bolsheviks, the party of those whose sole relationships with capitalism were the relationships of war to the knife, which (in contrast with the social solidarians) pushed to its logical conclusion the peasant revolution directed against the landlords. This revolution secured legislative expression in the Land Decree brought forward by the Communist Party and adopted by the second soviet congress.

By the terms of this decree and by those of the Fundamental Land Law adopted by the third congress, private ownership of the soil was formally abolished. All the land of the republic was placed at the disposal of any and every person who is a working occupier and cultivates the soil by his own labour. There are no restrictions on account of nationality. The land is allotted equally among the population, in quantities not exceeding that which can be properly tilled by the working occupier. Furthermore, in accordance with the prescriptions of the socialist land distribution, all the territories of the republic have been declared to be the property of the whole workers' and peasants' State, upon which devolves the supreme right of dealing with the land.

As the outcome of the land revolution, thus legally established, agrarian conditions in Russia have been completely transformed, and are still undergoing numerous changes.

Above all, throughout Great Russia, landed proprietorship, whether large-scale or small-scale, has been abolished. Thus, as regards land-ownership, the rich peasants have been placed upon the same footing as the medium-rich peasants.

On the other hand, the utilisation of the land by the poor and land-hungry peasants has been levelled up, and they have profited by a share in the cattle and farming implements of the rich peasants, and as a result of the division of the great estates.

As regards the equalisation of land-holdings throughout the various rural districts, counties, and provinces, the matter is still in progress, and is far from being completed.

At the present time it is impossible to give a conclusive picture of the results of the agrarian revolution. Speaking generally, we may say that almost all the land owned by private individuals, either in very large estates or in those of a considerable size, has passed into the hands of the peasants who work their own farms.

The private estates have been put under cultivation. The Soviet Power reserved for soviet agriculture approximately 2,000,000 desyatinas. The peasants are also cultivating part of the municipal territories. Furthermore, the peasants have received all the church lands, all the monastery and nunnery lands, and part of the crown lands. All in all, the peasants have secured about 40,000,000 desyatinas of land that was privately owned before the revolution.

In addition to the reserves of the Soviet Power, and in addition to the territories of the sugar refineries, there still remain at the disposal of the Soviet State nearly all the areas that used to be State land, and also the nationalised forests that used to belong to private landowners.

In this way the Russian Communist Party has carried on its fight for socialism despite the unfavourable conditions that prevail as far as the land question is concerned. By far the greater part of the land actually held by the State is unsuitable for cultivation. Most of the land fit for cultivation has been allotted to the lesser peasants, to those who work their own farms.

But however unfavourable the conditions for the socialisation of agriculture in Russia, and however stubborn the resistance made by the petty-bourgeois agricultural system, in rural Russia the future belongs exclusively to large-scale socialist agriculture.

§ 105.

Why does the Future belong to large-scale socialist Agriculture ? Large-scale capitalist methods have gained the victory over the methods of artisan production and peasant production, although it must be noted that in manufacturing industry this victory has been speedier and more complete than in agriculture. The communist economic system is yet more advantageous, yet more productive, than the capitalist economic system ; in like manner, communist farming on the large scale will prove more productive than peasant farming on the small scale. If a pound is heavier than an ounce, and a hundredweight is heavier than a pound, it is obvious that a hundredweight is a great deal heavier than an ounce.

We must, however, discuss the matter in detail, and make it perfectly plain.

The first requisite is that in socialist agriculture all the land of the republic should be utilised in such a way that in every district, farm, and field, that particular crop should be raised (rye, oats, hay, flax, hemp, beetroot, Jerusalem artichoke, etc.) which, having regard to the quality and the peculiarity of the soil, would grow most advantageously. Precisely which crop is the most suitable, is a matter for agricultural experts to determine. In our peasant system of agriculture the very opposite frequently happens. For instance, wheat is planted, and yields a very poor crop, in places where flax would thrive ; or rye is sown where wheat would do much better ; or something even more stupid may be done.

The general introduction of scientific methods in the utilisation of the land under cultivation, were the change simply to be one of a better choice of crops, would greatly increase the yield, even though in other respects everything should continue as before.

But the many-field system can only be introduced by

the adoption of medium-scale or large-scale agriculture in place of petty agriculture ; and of course the large-scale is more advantageous than the medium-scale. By the rotation of crops we are enabled to utilise the land far more thoroughly. To-day, our peasants, with the three-field system, leave at any given moment practically one-third of the land fallow.

For the peasants it is a practical impossibility to introduce a proper rotation of crops and the many-field system. It is impossible to the peasant who farms his land in isolation, for he has not enough land for a proper system. It is even more impossible when the communal land is cut up into strips.

In large-scale agriculture we avoid the waste of land which is inevitable, under petty culture, at the corners and edges of the fields. Our peasants waste hundreds of thousands of desyatinas in this way. According to my calculations the loss is equivalent to from 60,000,000 to 80,000,000 poods of grain.

Manuring is the principal means for maintaining the fertility of the soil. In large-scale agriculture, since a smaller number of horses will suffice for the work on any particular area of land, more horned cattle can be kept and there is therefore more manure from stall-fed beasts. In large-scale agriculture it is profitable to use artificial manures, or even artificially to make various kinds of manure, whereas these things are much less practicable in the case of petty agriculture.

Especially difficult, in small-scale agriculture, is it to arrange for ploughing at appropriate times, sufficiently deeply, and in a labour-saving manner. In this matter the isolated peasant is a mere dwarf when compared with his rival in socialist agriculture (and, indeed, as compared with his large-scale capitalist rival). The cheapest, quickest, and deepest ploughing is done with the aid of tractors. On the small strips of peasant culture, tractors have no place. Besides, it is less advantageous to work with a single tractor than with groups of eight or ten tractors in unison.

The same considerations apply to various other labour-saving machines. Steam threshers and steam harvesters can only be used in large-scale agriculture.

Finally, the full utilisation of all the farming implements is only possible in large-scale agriculture. For example for the full utilisation of

Implement.					Desyatinas of land.
a horse plough we require	..	..	..	..	27
a driller, a cutter, and a threshing machine (not steam-driven)	..	..	..	..	63
a steam thresher	..	..	..	..	225
a steam plough..	..	..	..	..	900

The use of steam ploughs and tractors will by itself suffice, though other conditions remain unaltered, to increase the productivity of the soil by fully one-third.

Even when we have to farm any area merely with the aid of horses, large-scale agriculture is more advantageous than petty agriculture, seeing that in the former each individual horse is utilised for a larger area. It has been calculated that in this respect large-scale agriculture requires only about one-third the number of horses.

Electricity can be used only in large-scale agriculture. And by the use of electricity on one large farm we can dispense with the need for a hundred small and badly constructed stables, for a hundred little kitchens, etc. We can conduct everything in one large and well-equipped building.

Dairy-farming can only be economically conducted on the large scale.

But the greatest saving of all is the economising of labour power, the possibility of reducing to one-half or one-third the countryman's hours of labour, not only without reducing the productivity of the land, but actually while increasing it threefold or fourfold.

Here is an example. According to the last census returns, those for the year 1916, there were in Russia 71,430,800 desyatinas of cultivable land. If we assume that this area is tilled once every year (every agriculturist knows that this is far too liberal an estimate), the peasants will have to use all the available labour power (that of 20,000,000 men) and all the available farm beasts. But to plough the same area with the aid of tractors (a tractor can plough from 8 to 10 desyatinas in one day, or considerably more if it works continuously), the labour of

1,000,000 workers would suffice. One man does the work of twenty.[1]

If in place of preparing 100 meals in separate kitchens, we prepare one dinner for the same number of persons in the kitchen of the village commune, 90 cooks out of the 100 will no longer be needed. Their services can be devoted to some other useful purpose, whereby the labour of yet others will be lightened.

Thus the task of the Communist Party is to do its utmost to establish a more perfect system of agriculture, a communist system, which will be competent to deliver our rural population from the barbaric waste of energy which occurs in the extant system of dwarf agriculture; to save Russia from the barbaric exhaustion of the soil which is now going on; from the barbaric and Asiatic methods of cattle keeping; from the barbaric methods of individual cookery.

How will the Communist Party achieve this great aim? There are various lines of advance. Let us consider the speediest first.

§ 106.

Soviet Agriculture. When the landlords' estates were seized by the peasants at the end of the year 1917, there were among these estates many on which model farms existed, where there was pedigree stock, and where up-to-date agricultural machinery was used. Some of these farms, which the soviets took under their care promptly, were saved from destruction, and they have become known as soviet farms. In addition, there passed into the system of soviet agriculture certain estates which could not be wholly distributed among the peasants because these already had as much land as they could work.

The soviet farms are the only ones in which large-scale socialist model farming, with all its advantages, can be carried on. Only by means of the soviet farms can we

---

[1] It is true that in addition to the men who are actually working the tractors we ought to take into account the workers who are employed in the workshops where the tractors are made, those who are employed in getting petroleum, etc., before we decide how many desyatinas of land one man can plough. This will somewhat reduce our estimate of the advantage of tractor ploughing, but the advantage will still remain exceedingly great.

demonstrate to the peasants the advantages of large-scale collective agriculture.

On the soviet farms we can introduce a proper rotation of crops, and can give practical proof of all the drawbacks of the three-field system.

Here, too, we can use all kinds of agricultural machinery, including the most complicated.

The soviet farms are the only places where pedigree stock can be preserved from destruction and can be bred. Only by the use of the soviet stud-farms shall we be able by degrees to improve the farm stock of the surrounding peasantry.

At the soviet farm it will be easy to have demonstration fields for the peasants, and also to improve the seed by selective methods. Already on these farms we have sorting machines for the selection of the best seeds, and the neighbouring peasant farmers have the use of the machines.

The soviet farms organise agricultural schools, arrange for lectures on agriculture, inaugurate agricultural exhibitions, etc.

They institute workshops for the repair of agricultural implements, primarily for their own immediate use, but secondarily for the assistance of the peasant farmers of the district.

The task of the Communist Party is to increase, wherever possible, the number of the soviet farms, and to enlarge them (as far as may be without interfering with the interests of peasant agriculture). By degrees we must assemble here the best breeding stock in the republic. Here we must organise the most perfect technical elaboration of agricultural produce. We must make an end of bureaucracy, must be careful to avoid the transformation of the soviet farms into something like monasteries, concerned only with the prosperity of their own employees and workers, and caring nothing for the Soviet State. The farms must gather together a staff of highly skilled workers ; they must not merely inaugurate workers' control, but must proceed in due course to the actual management of the estates by the workers. The peasants of the environing regions must be induced to interest themselves in the farms, must be led to examine the agricultural methods and plans of these, until they are gradually induced to regard the soviet farms as the direct concern of the entire working population.

In the autumn of 1919 there were 3536 soviet farms, the cultivable area of land upon these (without counting forest land) being 2,170,000 desyatinas.

§ 107.

Urban and suburban Agriculture (Market Gardening).[1] In view of the terrible food crisis which has been the inevitable outcome of the war and the revolution, a sound system of market gardening has become of extreme importance to the safety of the urban proletariat. This form of agriculture is beginning to flourish, and it will have a great future. The immediate task of municipal agriculture is to secure that every town shall have a sufficient area of cultivable land for the proper development of market gardening upon a large scale. Prior to the revolution, our towns owned about 2,000,000 desyatinas. The greater part of this area, occupied by buildings, pastures, parks, and vegetable gardens, still belongs to the towns. Part of the arable was assigned to the peasants, and has therefore been lost to the towns. But possession of such areas should be resumed by the towns. Further than this, all the environs of the towns should be expropriated, in so far as such a measure is requisite for a sound and generalised system of market gardening.

Already in the year 1919, in some of the towns, the agricultural sections of the soviets were successfully engaged in market gardening, and were securing supplies of vegetables sufficient for the population of these towns throughout an entire year. Further advance must be made along such lines. Every town must have at its disposal for market gardening an area large enough to supply the whole population of the town with kitchen-garden produce. Furthermore, it is essential that every town should have a large dairy-farm supplying at least enough milk for all the invalids and children in the town, and therefore having a sufficiency of land to provide fodder for the cattle. If the municipalities

---

[1] The familiar term "market gardening" is retained for the special form of agriculture described in this section, although the "kitchen-garden" products are no longer being produced for the capitalist market.—E. and C. P.

conduct their agriculture properly, they can supply the urban workers, not only with potatoes and cabbages, but also with meal (buckwheat, millet). In this way every town will be enabled to provide out of its own resources for the feeding of all the town's horses, which will make it easier to arrange for the nationalisation of the transport system. If we leave the two capital cities out of account, the experience already accumulated has shown that within the next year the practical realisation of such a scheme is possible for all the towns of the republic—provided they do not attempt to realise the utopian design of supplying their own inhabitants with corn.

Municipal soviet agriculture is of great importance for two additional reasons. The first of these is that it provides opportunity for the better utilisation of the enormous quantity of manure produced in every town in the form of street and household refuse, stable manure, and nightsoil. At present, the greater part of such manure is simply wasted. The second is that it provides for a better association of manufacturing industry with agriculture. Next year it will be possible for a definite proportion of the urban population to participate (without any interference with manufacturing industry) in agricultural production, by working in the large-scale market gardens adjoining the towns.

It is important that soviet agriculture and municipal market gardening should be something more than model enterprises. They must definitely help to relieve the food crisis. Experience has shown that in the most difficult season, just before the new crops are harvested in the rural districts and when the peasants have not begun or are only just beginning to thresh, the situation has been saved by the existence of the soviet farms. In the years 1918 and 1919, the first corn of the new harvest was provided by the soviet farms. In the future, the importance of the soviet farms in this respect will be greatly increased. By the utilisation of all the land on the soviet farms, the Soviet Republic will be enabled to provide about half of the corn needed to feed the urban workers and employees. This will tend to a notable extent to reduce the dependence of the townsfolk upon the peasants.

§ 108.

Communes and Artels. The soviet farms can increase
only at the expense of those areas which now lie fallow in
their environment, or at the expense of the crown lands
which are brought under cultivation by improved methods,
by reclamation and drainage. As regards Russian agriculture in general, this cannot become socialist agriculture
until peasant agriculture has entered the socialist road.
At the soviet farms, the peasants will be able to learn the
advantages of large-scale collective agriculture. But as far
as they themselves are concerned, they will only be able to
realise these advances through cooperative farming, through
uniting to form communes and artels. In capitalist society,
the change from the petty agriculture of the peasants to
large-scale agriculture was usually achieved by the destruction and proletarianisation of the smallholders. In socialist
society, large-scale collective farming will arise out of small-
scale farming chiefly through the union of a number of
small farms.

Among the peasants, the words " artel " and " commune "
mean almost the same thing. Many communes term
themselves artels, for the peasant is not fond of the word
" commune," and is afraid to use the name even when a
commune is perforce created in practice. Generally speaking,
the difference between the commune and the artel is that
the artel is only a productive union (a cooperative of production); whereas the commune is not only a productive
union but likewise a distributive union—a cooperative at
once for production, distribution, and consumption.

The number of communes and artels is rapidly increasing
in Soviet Russia. Here are the latest figures, those for the
autumn of 1919.

			Number.	Area of cultivable land.
Communes..	..	..	1901	150,000 desyatinas.
Artels	..	..	3698	
Associations for coopera-				480,000 ,,
tive farming	..	..	668	

The figures show that the tendency towards the formation of communes and artels has the character of a mass
movement and that it is progressive. But the figures also
show the weak side of these types of union. In the case

of the communes in especial, the average size of the area concerned is very small. What we are now considering is not a change from small-scale agriculture to large-scale agriculture, but a change to medium-scale agriculture or to something very little better. Hence the communes are unable to demonstrate either to their members or to the neighbouring population the real advantages of large-scale agriculture. Upon a farm of a few desyatinas, agricultural machinery cannot be utilised to the full extent of its powers; nor is it possible on such a farm to organise a proper rotation of the crops. Even so, the significance of these unions for the purposes of medium-scale agriculture is very great. They realise the advantages of the division of labour. Some of the women are released from housework, and are therefore able to help in the speedier finishing of the land work; on a given area, fewer horses are needed, the work is done in more timely fashion, and the ground is more thoroughly tilled; as a net result, better returns are secured than from the little plots of ordinary peasant agriculture.

The economy of labour power realised by the commune is further displayed by the fact that most of the communes engage in enterprises supplementary to land work. They build mills; undertake various small industries in the home; erect repairing shops; etc.

The communes can only advance along the road to socialism by a further process of union.

This can either be achieved by the fusion of two neighbouring communes; or else by the enlargement of particular communes through enrolling considerable numbers of new members from among the neighbouring peasants; or, finally, by the fusion of one or more communes with an adjacent soviet farm.

The chief task of the Communist Party as far as the rural districts is concerned is, at this juncture, to advance small-scale peasant agriculture to a higher stage, and as a first step to the stage of medium-scale communal agriculture. There is good reason to believe that the further development of the productivity of the land will mainly proceed along this route. It is within the power of the proletarian State to hasten the process, not only through the propaganda of word and deed (soviet farming), but also through the provision of all possible advantages to the communal farms now in course of creation—by furnishing them with financial support; by supplying them with seed, cattle, implements, and advice as to agricultural methods.

§ 109.

Cooperative Farming. The commune is an intimate union among peasants, not only for productive labour, but also for distributive purposes and for cooperative social life. The artel is a permanent union solely for productive purposes, for joint labour. Cooperative farming is an even less intimate association, looser than that of the artel, more casual so to speak. The inhabitants of any particular village who are unable, owing to internal dissensions, to unite for the formation of a commune, and who for the same reason are unable to form an artel, can at least engage in cooperative ploughing in a fashion which does not bind the cooperators to anything further. The net upshot of this is that everything remains as of old, with one important exception. The common land of the village is no longer divided up into strips, but is cooperatively farmed. Each small farm has its own vegetable garden; every peasant retains his own private property; but the machines and the horses work for a definite period on behalf of the whole village.

The regulations concerning the socialisation of the land which have been approved by the Central Executive Committee, provide likewise for this most primitive stage of collective agriculture. The advantages of such a form of union consist in the complete freedom of activity which is preserved for each peasant apart from the actual process of labour, so that every peasant can readily enter into such a union without risking the loss of his independence. But, in addition, cooperative farming entails quite a number of advantages: it puts an end to the division of the individual smallholder's land into long strips which are often widely separated one from another, and this reform renders the introduction of a many-field system possible; agricultural implements and machinery can be adequately utilised: there can be a more effective division of labour for the aid of households which lack workers, implements, cattle, etc.

Cooperative farming is the very first stage of collective agriculture; and we can therefore naturally expect that in so far as collective agriculture as yet exists, it will chiefly be in this form. The data relating to the 1919 season show that cooperative farming is already becoming established in quite a number of districts. Large areas have been divided into tithings and farmed cooperatively. In some cases part of the common land of the village has been cooperatively farmed in this way.

§ 110.

Agricultural Cooperation. Even before the revolution, cooperation for the full utilisation of the various agricultural products was widely diffused among the peasants. To this category belong the dairy-farming artels (cheese-making and butter-churning) which are widely distributed throughout the northern provinces and along the upper reaches of the Volga. Artels likewise exist for the early stages of linen manufacture, for the manufacture of raw sugar, for the drying of vegetables, for the compressing of hay. The Soviet Power supports all such undertakings. It is incumbent upon the Communist Party to assist the rural workers to form and extend cooperatives, and to encourage the peasants to improve working methods. At the same time, the party must do its utmost to resist the attempts of small-scale capital to entrench itself in such artels for a struggle against the Soviet Power and against large-scale socialist agriculture.

§ 111.

The State Utilisation of abandoned Areas; the Mobilisation of agricultural Experts; Lending Stations; Improvement of the Land; Land Settlements. The extreme disorganisation of agriculture resulting from the war has thrown large areas out of cultivation. The proletarian State cannot allow these regions to lie waste at the very time when a grave food crisis prevails in the towns and in the less fertile provinces. The Soviet State, therefore, undertakes the cultivation of all waste areas, no matter to whom they may belong. This measure is of especial importance in districts where the civil war has raged, for here in many cases the rich peasants have abandoned their farms and have withdrawn in the company of the retreating enemy. Of no less importance is the State garnering of crops abandoned by the owners, and of crops which the owners are unable to harvest unaided.

Russian agriculture can only be restored from its present disorganised condition by a number of resolute and revolutionary measures. One of these measures is the mobilisation of the labour power of all expert agriculturists, or, in a word, the institution of compulsory service for such persons. There have never been many skilled agriculturists in Russia. To-day, in view of the enormous task that lies before us in respect of the transformation of agricultural methods, and in view of the urgent need for increasing productivity in the rural districts, we cannot fail to be peculiarly aware of this lack. The mobilisation of expert agricultural knowledge is practically equivalent to the socialisation of such knowledge, and in truth it can be best and most purposively administered by the State.

The imperialist war made it impossible for Russia to import agricultural machinery. The native production of such machinery has never been equal to the demand. Many machines, and among them the best and the most complicated, have hitherto been imported from Germany, Sweden, and the United States of America. Furthermore, owing to the lack of metals, the scarcity of fuel, and many other causes, the native production of agricultural machinery has fallen to a minimum. All this has led to a serious dearth of farming implements. In view of the enormous demand for machinery and tools, and in view of the scanty supply of these requisites accessible to the proletarian State, it has become a matter of extreme importance that we should rightly distribute such implements as we have and should ensure their most advantageous utilisation. But as long as private ownership in agricultural implements exists, their proper utilisation remains impossible, seeing that for considerable periods the machines lie idle ; their owner is not using them at the very times when for lack of them his neighbours cannot plough their fields or cannot gather in the crops.

In order that we may render assistance to those strata

of the rural population which suffer most from lack of implements, and in order that we may guarantee that the implements shall be fully utilised, we must see to it that we do not supply machinery and tools for permanent use by private owners, but we must ensure that they shall be kept at *lending stations* where they will be available for all who need them. In other words, the machinery and tools intended for the use of the peasantry and allotted to particular regions (villages, rural districts, or circles), will not be sold to any individual peasant; they will be provided for the temporary use of all who need them, and a definite charge will be made to cover expenses. The depots where such arrangements are effected are known as lending stations. At these the machines and tools are stored, cleaned after use, and (in well-equipped stations) kept in repair. Lending stations already exist and function, although as yet there are very few of them. It behoves the Soviet Power to ensure that, as far as may be, all agricultural machinery, and without exception all the more complicated types of machine, intended for the rural districts, shall be supplied only to lending stations. There is no other way of securing that the machines shall be adequately used throughout their working life—to say nothing of the fact that in this way we shall help the poorer peasants whose means will not suffice for the buying of machines as private property. The machines confiscated from the rich peasants must also be kept at the lending stations. In the long run, a widely organised system for the provision of agricultural machinery through the instrumentality of the lending stations, will lead slowly but surely to the nationalisation of all the most important implements of agricultural production; and will consequently, in addition to giving immediate help to peasant industry, tend to promote its socialisation.

In the agricultural program of the proletarian Power, the improvement of the land must occupy an extremely important place. The Soviet Power has at the present time under its control millions of desyatinas which, although they are not cultivable as yet, might be made cultivable by a moderate amount of work in the way of cleansing, the grubbing-up of roots, drainage (either by open channels or by the laving of underground pipes), irrigation, etc. However strict the limits imposed upon the enlargement of the soviet farms, as far as concerns land already cultivated or immediately susceptible of cultivation, there is unlimited scope for the provision of areas which, by the above-mentioned methods of land improvement, our young socialist agriculture will be able to wrest from nature.

Land-improvement work is the most important of all the public work which the Soviet Power has to organise. It is, moreover, preeminently work in which we can make a good use of all the parasitic strata of society.

LAND SETTLEMENTS. The point has been omitted from our program, but it is necessary to consider it here, for the Soviet Power will be compelled sooner or later to give practical attention to the policy of land settlement.

Notwithstanding the redistribution of the landlords' estates, land-hunger is already manifest in a number of provinces. In outlying regions, on the other hand, there are huge areas of unoccupied land. Migration from the centre to the outskirts will be indispensable in the near future. It will be incumbent upon the proletarian State to ensure that the migrants to the newly settled districts shall not devote themselves to small-scale agriculture upon separate patches of land. We must see to it that everything is made ready for the newcomers, everything requisite for large-scale communist agriculture (communal farm buildings, communal land properly allotted for a many-field system, up-to-date agricultural machinery, and so on).

§ 112.

State Assistance to Peasant Agriculture. The soviet farms, the communes and the artels, in conjunction with all the above-described measures, will serve, by means of the organisation of large-scale collective agriculture, to enhance the productivity of agricultural labour and to increase the yield from the land. There is no other certain, speedy, and direct way of reaching the desired goal. But whatever successes we may achieve in this matter of organising soviet farms and communes, for a long time to come small-scale peasant farming will continue to exist; for a long time to come small-scale peasant farming will be the predominant form of Russian agriculture alike in respect of the area thus cultivated and in respect of the quantity of agricultural produce. The question therefore arises, How can we help this method of farming to increase the productivity of the land, even though it is still restricted by its petty-bourgeois limitations ?

Our program contains suggestions for a number of measures which the Soviet Power can apply to the help of small-scale peasant farming. They are the following.

First of all, help can be given in the apportionment of land. The chief evil of our rural life, one against which even the peasants are more and more inclined to kick, is the division of the cultivable land into long narrow strips. We continually find that the arables of one village will run right up to the kitchen gardens of the next village, and vice versa. Parts of the arable will be five or six miles from the dwellings, and are often left untilled. In order to put an end to this strip system, the peasants have, in elementary fashion, been endeavouring to do away with the obsolete method of apportioning the cultivable land, which conflicts for the most part with the new subdivisions made after the seizure of the landlords' estates. In so far as the struggle against the strip system is the forerunner of a more highly developed form of agriculture, and generally speaking in so far as the peasants need assistance in the apportionment of cultivable land, the Soviet Power must come to their aid with its surveyors and its agricultural experts.

For sowing, the Russian peasants commonly use unselected seed, just as it might have been sent to the mill. If they sowed selected seed, they would get much better crops, even though the conditions were unchanged in other respects. Still better harvests could be obtained by the use of better varieties of seed. These, however, the peasant can only secure from the State, which alone is in a position to purchase them from abroad, or to provide the farmers with what they need out of the small stock of improved seeds which has been saved from destruction on the soviet farms.

The live stock of our peasant farmers is largely degenerate. There is urgent need for an improvement in the breed. Such pedigree cattle as still remain in Russia are at the present time concentrated on the soviet estates and the soviet dairy-farms and stud-farms. The State will be able to give great assistance to the peasants in this matter of stock raising by the organisation of pairing stations on every soviet farm which has pedigree stock, and by the systematic distribution of thoroughbred males to pairing stations in every district.

Many of our peasants are still ignorant in respect of some of the most fundamental and important agricultural questions. It is evident, therefore, that the diffusion of a wider knowledge of these matters cannot fail to lead to improvements in the working of the land. In addition to giving lectures upon agricultural topics, which it is the duty of the soviet experts to deliver at various centres, brief courses of lectures must be given at the soviet farms. The farms will have model fields for demonstration purposes, will organise agricultural exhibitions, will distribute popular literature dealing with agricultural subjects, etc.

In addition to diffusing agricultural knowledge, the Soviet Power must directly provide expert assistance to the peasants. In view of the present scarcity of experts, the mobilisation of the entire personnel will achieve a useful result in this way, that the expert, whose services were in former days placed exclusively at the disposal of the great landlords, will now be made available to the peasants. Furthermore, the Soviet Power must take extensive measures to train agricultural experts from among the ranks of the peasants. Besides increasing the number of agricultural courses of lectures and the number of agricultural schools, the best method of achieving this end in the immediate future will be by the provision of special courses for the most gifted members of the communes and artels. In this way a vanguard of trained agriculturists can be recruited from the peasants' own ranks.

Of enormous importance to the peasants at this juncture is the provision of possibilities for the repair of agricultural implements. In view of the present iron famine, it is impossible for the small private workshops to undertake the necessary repairs. The State alone is in a position to organise the matter upon a sufficiently extensive scale, in part by enlarging the activities of the repairing shops on the soviet farms, and in part by covering the countryside with a network of shops especially instituted for the repair of agricultural implements.

Huge areas of peasant land now unfitted for cultivation are perfectly capable of being transformed into excellent arable. The necessary improvements are neglected to-day, partly because the work is beyond the means of any village community, and partly because the peasants are not acquainted with modern methods of land improvement. In this matter, therefore, the proletarian State can be of the utmost assistance to the peasants. Notwithstanding the civil war, in many districts excellent work is already being done along these lines.

During the decade 1901 to 1910, the yield per desyatina in various countries was as follows :

	Rye.	Wheat.	Barley.	Oats.	Potatoes.
Denmark	120	183	158	170	—
Holland	111	153	176	145	1079
England	—	149	127	118	908
Belgium	145	157	179	161	1042
Germany	109	130	127	122	900
Turkey	98	98	117	105	—
France	70	90	84	80	563
U.S.A.	67	64	93	74	421
Russia	50	45	51	50	410

Thus despite the fact that the Russian soil is much richer than that of western lands, our country is the last in the list as regards productivity. Per desyatina, Russia grows three and a half times less oats than Denmark and Belgium ; four times less wheat than Denmark, and three times less than Germany and England ; three times less rye than Belgium. Even in Turkey, the yield per desyatina is twice as great as the yield in Russia.

It is necessary to point out that the yield of our peasant farms is yet lower than that given in the above table, for the table records averages, and therefore includes the high productivity of the private landlords' estates, where the yield was from one-fifth greater to two and a half times greater than the yield of the peasant farms.

It follows, therefore, that without any increase of the land under cultivation our peasants could effect a twofold or a threefold increase in their harvests, simply by abandoning antiquated methods in favour of up-to-date ways of cultivating the soil.

§ 113.

The Union of manufacturing Industry with Agriculture.

The development of the towns which has been the outcome of the divorce of manufacturing industry from agriculture and of the predominant role assumed by manufacturing industry in the economic process of social life as a whole, has, in the later phases of capitalism, become a monstrous growth. The best energies of village life have systematically passed from the village to the town. Not merely has the urban population grown faster than the rural population, but town has positively grown at the expense of country. In many capitalist lands there has been an absolute decline in the rural population. Some of the towns, on the other hand, have swelled to fantastic proportions. The consequences have been disastrous both to town and country. Among the ill effects, may be mentioned : the depopulation of the villages and their relapse into primitive conditions ; the separation of rural life from urban culture ; a severance of the townsfolk from nature and from opportunities for health-giving agricultural work, with the resultant physical degeneration of the urban population ; the needless removal into the town of a number of branches of industry in which agricultural produce is elaborated ; extreme exhaustion of the soil, dependent upon the fact that the towns do not return to the land in the form of manure that which they extract from the land in the form of food ; and so on.

An approximation of town and country, a union between manufacturing industry and agriculture, a withdrawal of workers from factory occupations to agricultural—such, in this connexion, must be the immediate aims of communist reconstruction. A beginning has already been made in the assignment of tens of thousands of desyatinas of soviet land to various workshops, institutions, and enterprise which aim at the purposive and organised transfer of town workers to the soviet farms ; by the creation of market gardens for individual factories and workshops ; by Communist Saturdays in which urban workers visit neighbouring villages to help in agricultural labours ; by the mobilisation of soviet employees for work in the municipal market gardens ; and so on.

The Communist Party will continue to advance along

these lines, in the conviction that the future belongs to the
union of manufacturing industry with agriculture—a union
which will ultimately lead to the withdrawal from the towns
of the gross excess of urban population, and to the distribution
of this excess throughout the countryside.

§ 114.

**The Tactics of the Communist Party in relation to the
Peasants.** In our agrarian program we discuss what we
wish to realise in agriculture. Let us now consider how we
hope to realise our program ; to what strata of the population we look for support ; by what methods we think we
shall be able to win over the majority of the peasants to
our side, or at least to ensure their neutrality.

In the campaign against landlordism, the urban proletariat was supported by all the peasants, including the rich
peasants. This explains the rapid success of the November
revolution, for thereby was achieved the overthrow of the
bourgeois Provisional Government which had been endeavouring to postpone the liquidation of landlordism. But the
carrying into effect of the new agrarian law concerning the
so-called socialisation of the land, with its equal division
of the cultivable areas, transferred the rich peasants into the
counter-revolutionary camp. For the rich peasants lost part
of the purchased land which they had owned before the
revolution, and they lost the land which they had been able
to farm because they had rented it from the poor peasants.
They lost everything which they had secured when the
estates of the great landlords had been plundered. Finally,
it was made impossible for them to employ wage labour.
The rich peasants constitute the class which would have
become a landlord class if our revolution had never gone
beyond the limits of a bourgeois democratic revolution.
They constitute a class which is from its very nature mortally
hostile to all attempts in the direction of the socialistic
organisation of agriculture. The aim of the rich peasants
as a class is to bring about the development of our agricultural system in such a direction that it will come to resemble
that of Denmark or of the United States of America. But
for the proletarian authority and its socialistic policy,
Russian agriculture after the abolition of the old landlord

system would with remarkable celerity have developed into a system of bourgeois farming carried on by wage labour, with the aid of greatly improved methods of working the soil. In conjunction therewith there would have come into existence a huge class of semi-proletarian peasants. The rich peasant greeted the revolution inspired by the most rosy hopes and anticipations, but as a result of the revolution he found himself stripped of part of the land which he had owned before it occurred. As long as this class of rich peasants continues to exist, its members will inevitably prove to be irreconcilable enemies of the proletarian State and its agrarian policy. In its turn it can expect nothing from the Soviet Power but a pitiless struggle against its counter-revolutionary activities. The Soviet Power may eventually be compelled to undertake a deliberately planned expropriation of the rich peasants, mobilising them for social work, and above all for the task of improving peasant land and the land of the soviet farms.

The middle peasants form the great majority of the Russian peasants. These middle peasants secured their share of the landlords' estates with the aid of the urban proletariat, and only with its aid can they retain their grip upon this land in face of the counter-revolutionary movement on the part of the capitalists and the great landlords. Only in alliance with the proletariat, only under the leadership of the proletariat, only through the frank acceptance of this leadership, can the middle peasants save themselves from the onslaughts of world capitalism, from being plundered by the imperialists, from having to pay the vast debts incurred by the tsar and the Provisional Government. The system of petty agriculture is in any case doomed. It must inevitably be replaced by a more advantageous and more productive system, by the system of large-scale cooperative agriculture. Only through an alliance between the socialist proletariat and the middle peasants can this transformation be achieved without poverty, ruin, and incredible torment for the latter.

The petty-proprietor mentality of the middle peasants, however, inclines them to form an alliance with the rich peasants. An additional impulsion in this direction arises above all because the middle peasants are compelled to divide their superfluous grain with the town workers, or rather to hand over what they do not actually need for their own consumption without any prospect of receiving from the town workers in return the products of urban industry. It is therefore essential that the Communist Party should endeavour to detach the middle peasants from the rich peasants ; for the latter are in reality the agents of international capitalism, and are endeavouring to lead the peasantry as a whole into courses which will involve the loss of all that has been gained by the revolution. Furthermore, our party must make it perfectly clear to the middle peasants that only consideration for transient and temporary interests can induce them to make common cause with the rich peasants and with the bourgeoisie ; we must show them that their real, permanent, and far-reaching interests, as genuine workers, dictate an alliance with the urban proletariat. Finally, while striving to effect the socialist transformation of agriculture, we must be careful to avoid alienating the middle peasants by ill-considered and premature measures, and must make no attempt to coerce them into forming communes and artels. At the present juncture the principal task of communism in Russia is to bring it to pass that the workers upon their own initiative, and the peasants upon their own initiative, shall destroy the counter-revolution. When that has been achieved, there will no longer remain any insuperable obstacles in the way of the socialisation of agriculture. As regards the poor peasants, the proletarian and semi-proletarian strata of these have to a considerable extent, thanks to the revolution, been raised into the stratum of the middle peasants ; nevertheless, the stratum of the poor peasants still constitutes a main prop of the proletarian dictatorship. It was owing to the alliance with the poor peasants that the Soviet Power was enabled to deal some sturdy blows against the rich peasants, and to detach the middle peasants from the rich peasants. The communist mentality of the poor peasants rendered it possible to create instruments of the Soviet Power in the rural regions, thereby bringing about the first important and decisive military mobilisation of the peasantry.[1] Finally, up till

[1] When we are agitating to induce the peasants to participate actively in the civil war, we have to stress the reasons why they will find this parti.

now the poorer peasants have furnished most of the members of the communes and artels, and have actively assisted in the carrying out of the land decrees and of the other decrees of the Soviet Power.

The most important task of the Communist Party, as far as concerns the poor peasants, is to put an end to the disintegration that has affected this stratum since the dissolution of its committees. The best of all ways will be to unite the poor peasants upon the basis of production. Their influence in village life will be increased if they are enabled to participate in improved methods of agriculture. This can be achieved by enabling all the poor peasants to join forces in artels or in the communal cultivation of the land.

The reason why the rich peasant has so great an influence is because he is a successful farmer. But the farming of the rich peasant remains petty-bourgeois peasant agriculture. If the poor peasants combine to form communes they will be able to avail themselves of better agricultural methods than those ordinarily employed in peasant farming, and will thus from the economic outlook become as strong as the middle peasants, and even as strong as the rich peasants. The dictatorship of the poor peasants in rural life can be built up upon this economic foundation, upon the material superiority of the member of the commune over the small farmer. But it will not be a dictatorship of the poor peasants in the strict sense of the term ; it will not be the rule of "paupers and loafers" of which the rich peasants used to complain (not without reason) in the days of the committees of the poor peasants. It will be the rule of the vanguard of the rural workers, the rule of that minority which is two centuries ahead of the majority.

It is, however, extremely difficult to induce all the poor peasants to enter communes. Of late, considerable numbers of the middle peasants have joined communes, and they have been still more inclined to enter artels. In

cipation advantageous to themselves. What interests the peasant is not that we are fighting for socialism, but that we are fighting to make it impossible for the imperialists to exploit the petty proprietors in barbarous fashion, and to make it impossible for the imperialists to put the peasants' necks again under the yoke of landlord or merchant.

so far as the poor peasants will not abandon petty agriculture, we must induce them to form trade unions of poor peasants. These unions must carry on the struggle against the rich peasants, must continue the struggle which was not fought to a decisive issue by the committees of poor peasants. The poor peasants must unite for purposes of mutual aid ; they must enter into economic relationships with the State, in so far as they can undertake definite work for the State, receiving in return certain products on preferential terms, and various kinds of economic aid. Among the poor peasants of Russia there already exist large numbers of unions ; these are formed for various purposes, but they are for the most part purely local, and have a temporary and casual character. They must be fused to form larger unities. There is a great future for such unions among the poorer strata of the population in the provinces whose production of food-stuffs is very small—the districts, for instance, from which we get pitch and tar, the forest regions where timber is felled and stored, and so on.

Additional work for the Communist Party, as far as the poor peasants are concerned, is to bring them in closer contact with the urban proletariat, to rid them of their petty-bourgeois habits and of their futile hopes that they will be able to continue vigorous, independent, individualist farming. Wherever there is any considerable number of poor peasants, we must see to it that communist groups, or groups of sympathisers with communism, are formed. Every poor peasant should become a member of a commune. Every member of a commune should become a communist.

Literature. ENGELS, The Peasant Problem in France and Germany. LENIN, The agrarian Problem and the Critics of Marx. LENIN, The agrarian Problem in Russia at the Close of the Nineteenth Century.

Among popular pamphlets published since the revolution, the following may be mentioned : ZHEGUR, The Organisation of communist Agriculture. KY, Rural Communes. MESHCHERYAKOFF, Agricultural Communes. PREOBRAZHENSKY, Agricultural Communes. LARIN, The Urbanisation of Agriculture. MESHCHERYAKOFF, The Nationalisation of the Land. LENIN, Speech concerning the Condition of the middle Peasants, delivered at the eighth Congress of the Communist Party. SUMATOHIN, Let us live in a Commune ! LENIN, The Struggle for Bread.

CHAPTER FOURTEEN

THE ORGANISATION OF DISTRIBUTION

§ 115.

The Abolition of private Trade. To each method of production there corresponds a special method of distribution.
After the abolition of capitalist ownership in the means
of production, the Soviet Republic inevitably came into
conflict with the capitalist method of distribution, with
trade that is to say, and was compelled to undertake its
abolition by degrees. First of all, the great warehouses
were confiscated. This was likewise necessary on account
of the severe food crisis and on account of the general need
for goods. The articles which were being hoarded by speculators in anticipation of a rise in prices were distributed
among the working masses, and during the first weeks after
the November revolution this served to mitigate the crisis.

The nationalisation of the mercantile warehouses was
no more than a first step. The nationalisation of large-
scale trade soon followed. The measure was necessary
in the fight with speculation, and in order to take stock
of all the goods in the republic ; also and above all in
order that these goods might be distributed among the
working class. The Soviet Power introduced a system
of class rationing, not only for food-stuffs, but also for
manufactured articles in general and for all articles of
domestic use.

But perhaps the best way would have been for the
Soviet Power to have proceeded as follows : to confiscate
all the stores of goods which were in the hands of
private traders, and to distribute these goods in accordance
with the system of class rationing, without destroying

the apparatus of trade, which the Soviet State should rather have preserved, have utilised for its own purposes.

To some extent, indeed, we worked along these lines. But the goods were unfortunately confiscated too late, when the greater part of them had already been converted into money, which had been hidden by the owners. The whole apparatus of large-scale distribution was seized by the Soviet Power, and began to work on its behalf with the aid of the employees' trade unions. Only the heads of the businesses were discarded, for these had now become purely parasitic elements. Formerly it had been necessary to buy goods, to hunt them out, to make bargains. But now that the proletarian State had itself become the chief producer of goods in its nationalised workshops, it would have been absurd for the State to sell these goods to itself, and thus to maintain traders at its own expense. Furthermore, middlemen are superfluous as between the peasants and the State, and as between the State and the consumers—as soon as a State monopoly in grain has been established. Middlemen can offer no inducements which will encourage the peasants to hand the grain over to the State. The peasants have no occasion to seek buyers for the grain, for there are no buyers.

In so far, therefore, as the proletarian Power has taken over the production of a number of important articles, and in so far as it effects a notable proportion of production by the work of its own instruments, it needs its own apparatus of distribution. There is no place here for private trade.

But what is to happen in the case of petty private trade which serves for the distribution of the produce of small-scale independent home industry ? The Soviet Power has not yet taken possession of this branch of production. It has not yet succeeded in becoming the monopolist buyer of the produce of home industry. What is to happen in the case of the petty traders who are distributing such produce among the population (of course, at fancy prices)— articles which the agents of the Soviet Power are unable to provide at fixed prices ?

Indubitably this question is far more complicated than the problem of large-scale trade, for the fate of large-scale trade was settled by the mere fact of the general expropriation of capital. It would be absurd for the Soviet Power to prohibit petty trade when it is not itself in a position to replace the functions of this trade by the activity of its own organs of distribution. In certain cases, and above all in the regions from which the White Guards had recently been cleared out, local soviets and revolutionary committees prohibited private trade without providing their own apparatus for the supply of necessaries; or, even if such an apparatus existed, without ensuring that it should function regularly for the adequate supply of the population. As a result, private trade was driven under ground, and prices rose enormously.

Petty trade will cling tenaciously to life. Its extinction will be possible only in proportion as there passes through the hands of the State a larger and ever larger quantity of the products needed for the supply of the population. If to-day the Narkomprod [the People's Food Commissariat] exists side by side with the Suharevka [a Moscow market], this implies that the war between capitalism and socialism still continues in the domain of distribution. The struggle now rages round the positions occupied by petty trade. It will not cease until the State authority becomes the chief buyer of the products of petty industry; or until, as will ultimately happen, the State has itself become the manufacturer of all these products. Of course we are not here considering the cases in which petty traders sell products which are already supplied by the distributive organs of the State; we are not concerned with cases which are simply forms of the struggle against pilfering and against other defects of the soviet mechanism of distribution. In any case, petty trade will continue until, first, large-scale production has been adequately organised in the towns, and, secondly, there is proper provision for the supply of all such necessaries as are not yet produced by State monopoly.

Although the complete abolition of middlemen in the field of distribution is the aim of socialism, and although this aim will ultimately be realised, it is obvious that we cannot expect in the immediate future to achieve the entire destruction of the apparatus of retail trade.

§ 116.

The Apparatus of Distribution. Appropriate socialistic distributive organs must be created to deal with the great masses of products requisite for the supply of the population, in so far as these products now pass through or will shortly pass through the hands of the State. These distributive organs must have the following characteristics. They must be centralised. Centralisation will ensure the most equitable and accurate distribution. It will reduce the cost of maintenance of the apparatus, for under socialism this apparatus will require far less expenditure of labour power and of material means than were requisite for the apparatus of private trade. The socialist distributive apparatus must work swiftly. This is of the utmost importance. It is essential, not merely that the apparatus should demand the minimum expenditure of strength and means on the part of the State, but in addition that it should not involve the waste of a minute of any consumer's time. Otherwise, great loss would be involved for society as a whole through the unproductive expenditure of energy. Under a system of private trade and in the normal conditions of the capitalist economy, the consumer, provided he has money, can procure whatever he wants whenever he wants it. In these matters, the socialist apparatus of distribution must be at least as good as that of private trade. But in view of the high degree of centralisation, there is considerable risk that the socialist apparatus will degenerate into a cumbrous and dilatory machine in which a great many articles will rot before they reach the consumer. How is an efficient distributive apparatus to be constructed ?

Two possibilities were open to the Soviet Power. It could create an entirely new distributive apparatus ; or it could make use of all the organs of distribution created by capitalism, pressing these into the socialist service.

The Soviet Power adopted the latter course. While creating its own organs wherever necessary, especially in the opening period of the destruction of capitalist conditions, it concentrated its attention upon the cooperatives, aiming chiefly at the utilisation of the cooperative apparatus for the distribution of goods.

Cooperation in former Days. In capitalist society, the main function of the cooperatives is to free the consumer from the tyranny of the middleman, from the grip of the speculative trader; to secure trading profits for the union of consumers; and to provide consumers with goods of satisfactory quality. The cooperatives achieve these results with a considerable measure of success, but they do this only for their own members, only, that is to say, for a certain part of society.

The early cooperators fancied that capitalism would be peacefully renovated through the instrumentality of cooperation. What has really happened, however, amounts to this. With all its successes, cooperation has been able merely to overthrow retail trade with more or less success; but it has done nothing to break the power of wholesale trade, to which it is itself subordinate. We refer, of course, to distributive cooperation. As far as productive cooperation is concerned, this plays an insignificant part in the whole system of capitalist production, and exercises practically no influence upon the course and the development of capitalist industry. Speaking generally we may say that the titanic organisation of capital does not regard cooperation as a serious competitor. Capitalism felt fully capable of strangling cooperation like a kitten whenever it should think fit, and it was therefore content to leave the dreamers of the cooperative movement free to indulge their visions of the overthrow of capitalism, and to allow the cooperative book-keepers to plume themselves on the profits they had snatched from the petty traders. Cooperation adapted itself to capitalism, and came to play a definite part in the capitalist system of distribution. It was even advantageous to capitalism, for it reduced the cost of the capitalist apparatus of distribution, and thus set free a certain amount of trading capital for use in productive industry. On the other hand, cooperation, by reducing the number of petty middlemen and by bringing the consumer into closer contact with the large-scale capitalist producer, accelerated the exchange of commodities, guaranteed the prompt and conscientious payment of obligations, and in the last resort made the position of the industrial reserve army even worse than before—for the members of the industrial reserve have often been inclined to take refuge in the life of petty trade. Moreover, numerous investigations have shown that as far as cooperation among the peasants was concerned, its advantages were mostly confined to the vigorous and well-to-do peasants, whereas the poor peasants profited by it very little.

Considering the class to which their members respectively belong, the distributive cooperatives may be divided into workers' cooperatives, peasants' cooperatives, and the cooperatives of comparatively well-to-do town-dwellers— petty bourgeois and civil servants. The workers' cooperatives always form the extreme left wing among cooperative institutions in general; but as regards the class organisations of the proletariat they constitute the extreme right wing. In the peasant cooperatives, the well-to-do peasants have the decisive voice. In the third type of cooperative, the predominant place is occupied by the petty bourgeois intellectuals, of the same calibre as those whose mentality has dominated the whole cooperative movement—persons who believe that cooperation has a great mission for the destruction of capitalism by means of cooperative vouchers and loaves of cooperative bread.

The true nature of the cooperative movement was disclosed by the proletarian revolution in Russia. Except for some of the workers' cooperatives, this movement— especially as regards the intellectuals and the rich peasants among the cooperative leaders—assumed a definitely hostile attitude towards the socialist revolution. Indeed, the Siberian cooperatives, in the form of the organisation known as Purchase and Sale, and other distributive cooperatives, sided openly with the counter-revolution and advocated the crushing of the Soviet Republic with the assistance of world imperialism.

On October 1, 1917, there were 612 cooperative societies in Russia. Apparently, however, this figure is too low, for on January 1, 1918, according to estimates from various sources, there were 1000 such societies. In the Centrosoyus [the central cooperative league] there were 38,601 societies with a total membership of 13,694,196. Since, however, one and the same cooperative may belong to two or three different leagues, it is probable that the number of cooperatives and cooperators in Russia is smaller than this statement would suggest. As far as productive cooperation is concerned, in 1918 there existed in Russia 469 cooperative societies and leagues, small undertakings for the most part.

§ 118.

Contemporary Cooperation. In the capitalist regime, cooperation fulfils a definite role in the general system. In the soviet regime, the cooperative apparatus is destined either to die out gradually in conjunction with all the other apparatus of capitalist distribution, or else to enter the system of socialist distribution and to assume the role of a State distributive apparatus. The old leaders of the cooperatives—the mensheviks, the social revolutionaries, and the various " socialists " of the Kolchak type—would like to ensure for the cooperatives independence of the proletarian State, which means to ensure for them the freedom to die out. The Soviet Power, on the other hand, having an eye to the real interests of the great masses of the workers, and caring in particular for the interests of the cooperators themselves, pursues another path. Disregarding the opinions of the intellectuals who were leading the cooperatives, and refusing to discard the whole cooperative apparatus because of the counter-revolutionary activities of these leaders, the Soviet Power has continually endeavoured to fuse the cooperative distributive apparatus with the whole system of its own distributive organs. It has endeavoured to widen rather than to narrow the scale of cooperative activities. The practical aims of the Soviet Power and of the Communist Party, in this connexion, have been the following.

The normal cooperative of the bourgeois type is a voluntary union of citizens having a definite interest in the society. As a rule the society serves none but its own members ; and if it supplies products to the general population, it does so only in so far as this can be effected without harm to the members. We, on the other hand, consider it necessary that the entire population shall be organised in cooperatives, that every member of the community shall belong to a cooperative. Only then will distribution through the cooperatives signify distribution to the whole population.

In a distributive society of cooperators, the work is usually carried on under the administration of all the members of the society. In actual fact, as a rule, quite a small group of the members is responsible for the conduct of affairs, but this depends upon the members themselves. The constitution of the society puts the absolute control in the hands of the general assembly of the members. If all the citizens of the republic are enrolled in the cooperatives, they have full power to control these organisations from below upwards, thus controlling the entire apparatus of distribution in the proletarian State. Should the masses display sufficient independence, they could resolutely and successfully eradicate maladministration and bureaucracy from the work of distribution, and could thus ensure the requisite punctuality and accuracy throughout the State-cooperative organisation. When the consumers themselves participate in the work of distribution, the distributive organs will no longer hang in the air above the masses, but will become implements in the hands of the masses themselves. This will undoubtedly promote the development of a communistic consciousness, and will favour the growth of a comradely discipline among the workers. At the same time it will help the masses to understand the integral nature of the productive and distributive apparatus in socialist society. Further it is necessary, after enrolling the whole population in the cooperatives, that the leading part in these organisations shall be assigned to the proletarian stratum of the population. In the towns this will be secured through the more active participation of the urban workers in cooperative functions ; through securing the election of a communist and proletarian majority upon the administrative bodies ; and above all by seeing to it that the cooperatives which are transformed into urban consumers' communes shall be the workers' cooperatives and not the cooperatives founded by the petty bourgeois and the civil servants.

To the same end it is essential that there should be an intimate association between the cooperatives and the trade unions, that is to say between the respective organs of distribution and production. There is an immense future for such an association. In course of time the function of the State will be reduced to that of a central accountant's office, and then the living union of productive organisations with distributive organisations will be of overwhelming importance. Finally, it is essential that the communists should participate as a compact group in the construction of this system of cooperative distribution, and that they should secure the dominant role in the work.

In the rural districts it is important that the rich peasants should be excluded from the management of the cooperatives; that the comparatively well-to-do inhabitants of the countryside should not receive any privileges in the matter of distribution; and that the entire apparatus of the rural cooperatives should be controlled by the poor peasants and the class-conscious among the middle peasants.

§ 119.

Other Organs of Distribution. Since the November revolution there have come into existence various additional distributive organs created by the revolution. In the centre of these is the Narkomprod [the People's Food Commissariat] with all its subdepartments in the provinces and the counties. These organisations for the supply of food had and have their own distributive instruments in the form of a network of food depots and stores. At one time, in the rural districts, the committees of the poor peasants were distributing agents, thus forming a counterpoise to the cooperative distribution. Whereas the cooperatives distributed most of the products they received among the well-to-do peasants, the committees of the poor peasants distributed among the poor peasants the greater part and the best part of the goods they received from the State. An important role in distribution was played by the house committees in the large towns and by the house communes. The trade unions and the factory committees were likewise occupied in the work of distribution.

The task of the Soviet Power is to ensure that these multiple organs of distribution shall be replaced by a single distributive organ, or shall become parts of one integral distributive mechanism. In this connexion, for example, the house committees and the house communes play a useful part, for they enable consumers to secure the goods they need without standing about in queues for hours or days.

CHAPTER FIFTEEN

THE ORGANISATION OF BANKS AND MONETARY CIRCULATION

§ 120. The Nationalisation of the Banks and the Unified People's Bank. The Bank as a central Book-keeping Establishment. § 121. Money and the Dying-out of the monetary System.

§ 120.

The Nationalisation of the Banks and the Unified People's Bank. The Bank as a central Book-keeping Establishment. Few workers have a precise idea of what banks are, and what their function is in capitalist society. They conceive a bank to be a sort of huge treasure chest in which rich folk hoard money. The workers who have any savings and put them in a bank know that interest is paid upon these deposits, and they are aware that money deposited in a private bank sometimes vanishes: The savings are lost.

The first thing we have to understand is that a bank is not a money-box. At any given moment there is very little ready money in the bank. The essence of banking business is something quite different from the functioning as a fireproof safe for the money of people who have saved money. It is quite true that hundreds of millions of savings are paid into the bank, but these sums do not lie unused in the strong boxes. The money which flows into the banks is immediately put into circulation again. In the first place, it is lent to entrepreneurs who found factories, exploit workers, and pay part of their gains to the banks as interest on the loan—the bank, in its turn, paying part of its profits to its depositors. In the second place, the banks themselves found new undertakings with the funds they receive from depositors, or they finance extant undertakings. Finally the banks lend money to various States,[1] on which these

[1] For example, foreign banks lent more than 16,000,000 roubles to the tsarist Government and to Kerensky's government.

331

States pay interest. Thus, through the instrumentality of the governments, the banks plunder the populations of the debtor States.   Inasmuch as the banks belong to a small group of the wealthier capitalists, their work is seen in the last analysis to consist merely in the extraction of surplus value with the aid of their own capital and that of their depositors.

But the banks are not merely spiders sucking up the surplus labour of the workers and peasants.   They have an additional significance.   Let us suppose that I have some money and deposit it in the bank.   This means that I had certain commodities which I sold, transforming them into money.   The flow of new and ever new sums of money through all the banks, an increase in the total amount of capital in any society, signify that new and ever new masses of values are passing into circulation.   Money represents a product ; it is, so to speak, the certificate of a product. From the general circulation of money, we can approximately infer the general movement of products.   Inevitably, there-fore, the banks become, as it were, the book-keeping offices of capitalist society.

The foregoing considerations show us the function which the banks can perform in capitalist society, and what the proletariat must do with them as soon as it has seized power.

After the socialist revolution, or, rather, during the socialist revolution, the working class must seize all the banks, and, above all, the central State bank.   This is necessary, in the first place, simply in order that the workers may confiscate all the monetary deposits of the bourgeoisie, all the share certificates, and all the monetary obligations of the capitalists.   This act of confiscation will strike capitalist exploitation to the very heart.

We adopted this course after the November revolution, and our action was a crushing blow to the capitalist class of Russia.

What should the proletarian Power do with the confis-cated banks ?   It must turn to account everything that is of value in the capitalist banking system.   This means that the workers must preserve the banks as apparatus for keeping account of production, and as instruments for distributing financial resources.   Above all, there must be a thoroughgoing nationalisation of banking business. Not merely must all the banks taken from the bourgeoisie be converted into State institutions of the proletariat, but all future banking operations must be declared a State monopoly. The State alone can be allowed to found banks.

Furthermore, all the banks must be amalgamated. Superfluous banks must be abolished, and those which it is considered desirable to maintain must become branches of the unified bank of the Soviet Republic.

Instead of the manifold methods of account-keeping and instead of the various kinds of banking operations conducted by the bourgeois banks, in the unified people's bank there will be a single and simple method of keeping accounts. This will enable the proletarian State to draw up a complete picture showing where and how much the State has paid out, whence and how much it has received.

If, however, the revenue and expenditure of the State are recorded by the unified bank of the republic, what will happen to the bank when the State itself becomes, as it tends more and more to become, the sole administrator of a unified and gigantic apparatus organising the entire economic life of the country ?

It is obvious that the bank will then play the part that is played by the counting-house in any economic enterprise. The bank, as such, will gradually disappear. As our party program explains, the bank will become the central counting-house, "the central book-keeping establishment of communist society."

§ 121.

Money and the Dying-out of the monetary System. Communist society will know nothing of money. Every worker will produce goods for the general welfare. He will not receive any certificate to the effect that he has delivered the product to society ; he will receive no money, that is to say. In like manner, he will pay no money to society when he receives whatever he requires from the common store. A very different state of affairs prevails in socialist society, which is inevitable as an intermediate stage between capitalism and communism. Here money is needed, for it has a part to play in commodity economy.

If I, as a bootmaker, need a coat, I change my wares, the boots that I make, into money. Money is a commodity by means of which I can procure any other commodity I may please, and by means of which in the given case I can procure the particular thing I want, namely a coat. Every producer of commodities acts in the same way. In socialist society, this commodity economy will to some extent persist.

Let us suppose that the resistance of the bourgeoisie has been overcome, and that those who formerly constituted the ruling class have now become workers. But the peasants still remain. They do not work for the general account of society. Every peasant will endeavour to sell his surplus product to the State, to exchange it for the industrial products he needs for his own use. The peasant will remain a producer of commodities. That he may settle accounts with his neighbours and with the State, he will still need money ; just as the State will need money in order to settle accounts with all those members of society who have not yet become members of the general productive commune. Still more is it impossible to abolish money immediately, when private trade still continues to a considerable extent, and when the Soviet Power is not yet in a position to replace private trade entirely by socialist distribution. Finally, it would be disadvantageous to abolish money altogether so long as the issue of paper money is a substitute for taxation, so long as it helps the proletarian State to cope with the exceedingly difficult conditions now prevailing.

Socialism, however, is communism in course of construction ; it is incomplete communism. In proportion as the work of upbuilding communism is successfully effected, the need for money will disappear. In due time the State will probably be compelled to put an end to the expiring monetary circulation. This will be of especial importance in order to bring about the final disappearance of the laggards of the bourgeois classes who with hoarded money will continue to consume values created by the workers in a society which has proclaimed : " He who does not work, neither shall he eat."

Thus, from the very outset of the socialist revolution, money begins to lose its significance. All the nationalised undertakings, just like the single enterprise of a wealthy owner (for the owner of the unified enterprises is now the proletarian State), will have a common counting-house, and will have no need of money for reciprocal purchases and sales. By degrees a moneyless system of account-keeping will come to prevail. Thanks to this, money will no longer have anything to do with one great sphere of the national economy. As far as the peasants are concerned, in their case likewise money will cease by degrees to have any importance, and the direct exchange of commodities will come to the front once more. Even in private trade among the peasants, money will pass into the background, and the buyer will find himself able to procure corn only in exchange for products in kind, such as clothing, household utensils, furniture, etc. The gradual disappearance of money will likewise be promoted by the extensive issue of paper money by the State, in association with the great restriction in the exchange of commodities dependent upon the disorganisation of industry. The increasing depreciation of the currency is, essentially, an expression of the annulment of monetary values.

But the most forcible blow to the monetary system will be delivered by the introduction of budget-books and by the payment of the workers in kind. In the work-book will be entered how much the holder has done, and this will mean how much the State owes him. In accordance with the entries in his book, the worker will receive products from the consumers' stores. In such a system it will be impossible for those who do no work to procure goods for money. But the method can only be realised when the State has been able to concentrate into its own hands such a quantity of articles of consumption as is requisite for the supply of all the working members of socialist society. It will be impossible to carry it out until our disorganised industrial system has been reconstructed and expanded.

Speaking generally, the process of abolishing monetary circulation takes the following form to-day. First of all, money is expelled from the domain of product-exchange as far as the nationalised undertakings are concerned (factories, railways, soviet farms, etc.). Money likewise disappears from the domain of account-keeping between the State and the workers of the socialist State (that is, as far as concerns account-keeping between the Soviet Power on the one hand, and the employees and workers in soviet undertakings on the other). Furthermore, money becomes superfluous in so far as the direct exchange of goods is effected between the State and the small producers (the peasants and the home workers). Even within the realm of small-scale industry, the direct exchange of goods will tend to replace the use of money; but it may be that money will not completely disappear until small-scale industry itself disappears.

Literature. There is very little literature dealing with this subject. The following may be recommended: PYATAKOFF, The Proletariat and the Banks. SOKOLNIKOFF, The Nationalisation of the Banks.—Also the files of " Ekonomicheskaya Zhizn " [Economic Life], and " Narodnoe Hozyaistvo " [Political Economy].

CHAPTER SIXTEEN

FINANCE IN THE PROLETARIAN STATE

§ 122. The State as a parasitic Apparatus. § 123. The proletarian State as a productive Apparatus. § 124. The Budget of the proletarian State.

§ 122.

The State as a parasitic Apparatus. We have previously shown that the State is the organisation of force, that it is the expression of the dominion of one class over another class or over other classes. The bourgeois class, in the course of capitalist development, becomes to an increasing extent a class of idlers, who consume goods while doing nothing to help in the work of production. What view, then, are we to take of the bourgeois State, which serves to protect the ease and the income of these idlers from the exploited and incensed masses? The police and the gendarmerie, the standing army, the whole judicial apparatus, the entire machinery of administration—these comprise a huge mass of individuals not one of whom has ever produced a bushel of wheat, a yard of cloth, or so much as a pin or a needle. The whole organisation lives upon surplus value, which is produced by the workers and peasants. This surplus value is absorbed by the State in the form of direct and indirect taxation. For example, the tsarist government extracted in this way from the workers and peasants more than three milliards of roubles. (Translated into the terms of our present paper currency, this would represent three hundred milliards, which is thrice as much as all the money in Russia.) Only a small fraction of the State revenue was devoted to production, to such things as the building of roads and railways, bridges, ships, etc.

Turning to consider the proletarian State, we find that this likewise, so long as the civil war continues and so long as the resistance of the bourgeoisie has not been broken, must to a degree be an organ standing above production. The work of many of the instruments of the proletarian State is not work that effects the creation of new values. Indeed, many of the State instruments are maintained at the cost of the goods produced by the workers and peasants. To this category belong our military apparatus and the Red Army, the administrative system, all the means that are requisite for the struggle against the counter-revolution, and so on. But such features are not characteristic of the proletarian State; in these respects it is radically different from the exploiters' State. The essential characteristic of the proletarian State is its gradual transformation from an unproductive organisation to become an organisation for the administration of economic life.

§ 123.

The proletarian State as a productive Apparatus. Long before the end of the civil war, the proletarian State becomes mainly concerned with the production and distribution of goods. A mere enumeration of the central and local commissariats will make this perfectly plain. The most important of the soviet organisations is the Supreme Economic Council with its various subdepartments. This body is exclusively productive. The commissariats for agriculture, food, communications, and labour, are all likewise productive or distributive organisations, or organisations for the utilisation of labour power. In like manner the Commissariat for Popular Education, in proportion as its program for the institution of a unified labour school is realised, becomes an organisation for the preparation of skilled labour power. In the proletarian State, the Commissariat for Public Health is an instrument for the protection of the health of the workers; the Commissariat for Social Welfare is mainly concerned with the welfare of those who have been or will be workers (sanatoria, land settlements, etc.). Even the Commissariat for Administration finds its main activities engaged in supporting and leading the organs of local economic life, and in especial those of the municipalities. Taking it as a whole, the proletarian State mechanism becomes transformed into a huge organisation for the management of economic life, and for its advancement in every possible way. A study of the budget of the Soviet Republic will make this clear. Here are some characteristic items of expenditure.

Estimates for the half-year, January to June, 1919, in millions of roubles:

Supreme Economic Council	..	..	..	10,976
Commissariat for Food	..	..	..	..	8,153
,,	,, Communications	..	..	5,073
,,	,, Education	..	..	..	3,888
,,	,, Public Health	..	..	1,228
,,	,, Social Welfare	..	..	1,619
,,	,, Agriculture	..	..	..	533
,,	,, Army	..	..	..	12,150
,,	,, Navy	..	..	..	521
,,	,, Foreign Affairs	..	..	11
,,	,, National Affairs	..	..	17
,,	,, Justice ..	..	..	..	250
,,	,, Home Affairs	..	..	..	857
Extraordinary Commission	..	..	..	348

These figures show that the defence of the republic still requires vast sums of money. Putting on one side this item, which arises out of the peculiar conditions of the moment, we see that nine-tenths of the expenditure of the proletarian State is devoted to production, administration, the safeguarding of future functional capacity, the maintenance of labour power, etc. All this expenditure is purely economic.

Furthermore, in the Communist Saturdays the workers in the various productive organisations, the soldiers of the Red Army, and the war commissars, all combine to do their duty in the matter of productive labour—though at first, of course, the results are slender. Prior to the year 1919, there was no State in the world in which the civil servants were voluntarily engaged in such tasks as the repairing of locomotives and the lading of wood on behalf of the State.

§ 124.

The Budget of the proletarian State. We have seen that the expenditure of the proletarian State is increasingly devoted to productive purposes. The question now arises, from what sources its income will be derived.

The finances of the Russian Soviet Republic give some information upon this subject.

In the early days of its existence, the Soviet Power had certain extraordinary sources of revenue. It had the bank deposits which had been confiscated from the bourgeoisie; it had the cash resources of the late government; it had various sums which were secured by taxing the bourgeoisie, by the sale of goods confiscated from private traders and firms, etc. All these sources of income were small in relation to the necessary expenditure. As far as the local soviets were concerned, taxes levied upon the capitalists were for a considerable time their only source of revenue, but for the central government such taxes could not provide any notable means of support. Moreover, such a source of revenue was transient. The bourgeoisie was soon stripped bare; or else, and this is what usually happened, members of the bourgeois class vanished, after hiding their savings. A graduated income tax has not given and does not give satisfactory results. In so far as it is levied upon employees and workers, it is an absurdity, for the State is simply taking back in the form of a tax what it has paid in the form of salary or wages. In so far as it is levied upon the urban bourgeoisie, officially no bourgeois exist any longer. Legally the bourgeois cannot continue their former occupations. Such a tax, therefore, is extremely difficult to collect, and in actual experience this source of State revenue proved altogether inadequate. A graduated income tax might be far more lucrative when levied upon the rich peasants; but for its regular collection we should have to depend upon the work of local instruments of taxation, which would need to be organised by the local authorities, chiefly those of the rural districts. As far as the middle peasants are concerned, it is undesirable for political reasons to levy any tax upon them while the civil war continues, for such a measure would tend to alienate them from the proletariat. The attempt to raise an extraordinary revolutionary tax of ten milliards miscarried, for, after great efforts, less than two milliards were secured. The main source of revenue for the State has been the issue of paper money. This, in so far as the money is able to buy anything, is in reality a special form of taxation. Inasmuch as the issue of paper money accelerates the depreciation of the currency, it leads indirectly to the expropriation of the money capital of the bourgeoisie, for it reduces the purchasing capacity of this money capital to a fraction of that which it formerly possessed. It can readily be understood, that the issue of paper money cannot in the long run constitute a means of revenue for a State which aims at the ultimate abolition of money altogether. We are faced with this problem : What is the best foundation upon which the proletarian State can build up its revenues ?

Such a secure foundation is furnished by production. If the issue of paper money has hitherto proved to be a successful method of collecting State revenue, it is because this sort of tax can be collected without the taxpayer being aware that he is paying anything of the sort. No less inconspicuous is it when we secure revenue indirectly by means of State monopoly. This form of State revenue is, in reality, perfectly just. The cost of production of any articles which are produced by the State must include all the administrative charges requisite for the particular branch of production. The proletarian State apparatus actually realises such a form of administration. In practice this means that if the transport of passengers costs one milliard of roubles per annum, the State can fix the fares at such a figure that it will receive from this source the sum of twelve hundred million roubles. If the total cost of all manufactured articles is five milliards, they can be sold for six milliards, and so on. The excess is devoted to the maintenance of the State. Of course the revenues from monopoly are not to be conceived solely in the form of money, but also directly in the form of a definite quantity of goods.

If the proletarian State becomes transformed into an organ for the administration of the socialist economic system as a whole, the question of its upkeep, that is to say our old question of the budget, is greatly simplified. The affair is merely one of assigning a definite portion of goods to a definite item of economic expenditure.

But whereas the question of the State budget is now very simple, far less simple is the problem of how we are to determine precisely what portion of products can be consumed, that is to say, what portion can be expended in the economic system as a whole. It will be necessary to calculate with extreme forethought exactly what proportion of the total products can be consumed ungrudgingly, and exactly what proportion must be reserved as stores to use for the expansion of production, and so on.

We see, then, that in proportion as the State as a parasitic apparatus is destroyed, the problem of the State budget is merged into the general problem of the distribution of all products in a socialist society. The State budget will have become merely a small section of the integral budget of the cooperative commonwealth.

Literature. There is practically no literature dealing with this question. We may recommend POTYAEFF, The financial Policy of the Soviet Power.

CHAPTER SEVENTEEN

THE HOUSING PROBLEM

§ 125.

The Housing Problem in capitalist Society. The privileges of the bourgeois class are more conspicuous in the matter of housing than in any other domain. The bourgeois inhabit the best quarters of the towns. The well-to-do classes live in the best streets, in those which are cleanest, those where there are spacious gardens and plenty of trees. The working class, on the other hand, is in all lands stabled in the mean streets and in suburban quarters. It is not because most of the factories are usually situated in the outskirts of the town that the workers must dwell in the suburbs. Even if a factory is in the centre of a town, those who work there will none the less be herded somewhere in the outskirts. But those factory owners whose works are situated in the remote quarters of the town, themselves live in the centre.

Bourgeois families occupy entire dwellings, or flats with a great number of rooms. Their houses have more rooms than inhabitants. There are spacious gardens, bathrooms, and all the conveniences of life.

Working-class families are crowded into cellars, into single-roomed tenements, into tiny flats. Often enough they live in barrack dwellings, like prisoners who are herded in a gaol. Throughout the day the worker inhales factory smoke, filings, dust of every kind ; all night he breathes the air of a room in which as many as five or six children may be sleeping.

It is not surprising that statistics should show how quickly people die in working-class quarters—the folk

343

whose working hours are too long, whose dwellings are too narrow, and whose lives are too short. Here are some of the data. In Britain the average deathrate is 22 per thousand. In the bourgeois quarters, the deathrate is only 17 ; in the working-class quarters, it is 36 ; in some districts, where the poorest among the workers dwell, the deathrate is between 40 and 50. Turning to Belgium, we find that in the working-class quarters of Brussels 1 person in 29 dies every year, whereas in the best bourgeois quarters only 1 person in 53 dies each year. Thus the working-class deathrate is nearly twice as great as the bourgeois deathrate.

The mean duration of life in the case of the bourgeoisie, in the case of those who live in well-lighted, dry, and warm dwellings, is nearly half as long again as the mean duration of life of those who are crowded into the cellars and attics of the working-class quarters.

In Budapest, the mean duration of life of persons dying at an age exceeding 5 years, was as follows :

								Years.
Among those living	1 to	2	persons per room	..	47·16
,,	,,	,,	2 to	5	,,	,,	,,	.. 39·51
,,	,,	,,	5 to	10	,,	,,	,,	.. 37·10
more than			10		,,	,,	,,	.. 32·03

When we examine the figures relating to child mortality, the comparison between the working class and the bourgeoisie shows that the latter possess a still greater advantage in this respect. In those bourgeois dwellings where there is an average of only one person per room, the deathrate among infants (those under one year) is only one-fourth of the infantile deathrate in those working-class dwellings in which there are more than three persons per room. As regards children aged 1 to 5, the bourgeois deathrate is only half the working-class deathrate.

Not only do the workers in their gloomy and pestiferous habitations die on the average 15 years earlier than the bourgeois ; in addition they have to pay capitalist landlords for the privilege. Tribute goes to the house-owner for every corner, every cellar, and every garret, not to mention every real room or tenement. If you don't pay, here is the key of the street ! House rent always swallows a large proportion of the workers' wages, usually as much as 15 to 25 per cent. The cost of housing continually increases—for the workers—in capitalist lands. In Hamburg, for example, for every 100 marks [shillings] earned per month, there was paid in house rent :

Annual income ranging from		Percentages.		
		1868.	1881.	1900.
900 to 1200	Marks	19·8	24·1	24·7
1200 to 1800	,,	19·9	18·9	23·2
1800 to 2400	,,	20·3	19·5	21·6
6000 to 9000	,,	16·5	15·7	15·1
30,000 to 60,000	,,	6·7	8·1	6·0
more than 60,000	,,	3·7	3·9	3·0

Thus the smaller the income, the larger the percentage of that income which has to be devoted to house rent, and the more rapid likewise is the annual increase in the proportion that must be assigned to rent. In the case of the bourgeoisie, on the other hand, the percentage of income devoted to house rent is only one-sixth of that which must be paid by the workers, and this percentage, far from increasing, positively diminishes.

§ 126.

The Housing Problem in the proletarian State. The proletarian revolution effected an entire change in housing conditions. The Soviet Power nationalised the bourgeois dwellings ; in some cases it completely cancelled the arrears of rent in the working-class quarters, and in other cases reduced these arrears. But this is not all. Plans are being drawn up, and have in part already been put into operation, for the complete abolition of rent for the workers living in the nationalised dwellings. In the larger towns, there has begun a systematic transference of the workers from cellar dwellings, from ruinous houses, and from insanitary tenements, into the bourgeois villas and mansions of the central quarters of the towns. Furthermore, the workers are being systematically supplied with furniture and all necessary domestic utensils.

It is the business of the Communist Party to continue this policy, to perfect its housing economy, to institute a campaign against rough usage of the nationalised houses, to see that they are kept clean and in satisfactory repair, and to ensure that the drains, the water-pipes, the steam-heating apparatus, etc., are kept in good order.

But the Soviet Power, while pursuing on broad lines this policy of nationalising large-scale capitalist house property, sees no reason why the interests of the lesser house-owners should be infringed—the house-owners who are workers, employees, and other ordinary folk living in their own houses. Attempts to effect a general nationalisation of the small houses as well as of the large ones (such attempts were made in the provinces) had as their only result that the nationalised houses large and small had no one to care for them properly ; they fell into disrepair, and in many cases there was no one willing to live in them. On the other hand, feelings of animosity towards the Soviet Power were aroused among the owners of the small houses.

The Soviet Power, which was faced in the towns by a severe housing crisis resulting from the complete suspension of building activities, had to undertake the arduous task of justly apportioning the available housing accommodation. The housing departments of the soviets take charge of all the free dwellings in the towns, and allot them in accordance with a definite plan. The departments make schedules of all the available accommodation in the large houses, in the dwellings of families and individuals who have more rooms than they really need.

When the civil war is over and when the crisis in production has come to an end, there will be a great growth in the urban population. The proletariat which has taken refuge in the villages will return to the towns, and the excess of population in the rural districts will also make its way to the urban centres. The Soviet Power will have to deal with the question of building new houses, dwellings which will satisfy the needs of communist society. At the present moment it is difficult to say what type of buildings will be best : whether they should be large houses, fully equipped, with gardens, common dining halls, and the like ; or whether they should be small and well-designed separate dwellings for the workers. One thing is perfectly clear. The housing program must not conflict in any way with the proposed unification of industry and agriculture. It must favour the dispersal of the town over the countryside ; it must not increase the concentration of hundreds of thousands and millions of persons in limited areas—persons who by this concentration are deprived of the possibility of breathing fresh air, are cut off from nature, and are foredoomed to a premature death.

Literature. ENGELS, The Housing Question. FEDOROVICH, Working-class Dwellings. DEMENTYEFF, The Factory, its Merits and its Defects. SVETLOFFSKY, The Housing Question in Western Europe and in Russia. POKROFFSKAYA, The Improvement of working-class Dwellings in England.

CHAPTER EIGHTEEN

LABOUR PROTECTION AND SOCIAL WELFARE WORK

§ 127.

What is Labour Protection ? The working class fights to secure a communist system, because this system will deliver the workers from exploitation, and because communism will make it possible to develop productive forces to such an extent that it will no longer be necessary for people to devote the whole of their lives to the production of the necessaries of life. All the conquests, therefore, made by the working class on its way towards communism are in their essence directly or indirectly equivalent to labour protection ; they all promote an improvement in the position of the workers. Let us consider, for example, the political freedom of the working class in the Soviet Republic, and let us consider the position of the workers as ruling class. It is plain that this new political status implies a step forward in the path of labour protection. The same thing may be said of all the conquests of the working class, all without exception. But we must distinguish from labour protection in this general sense, certain more special senses of the term. In the latter case we are not thinking of the position of the working class in general, but of the position of the working class in the factory, in the workshop, in the mine ; in other words, we are thinking of the conditions which affect the workers in the actual labour process. Labour in factories and workshops, in the midst of machinery, and often in a

348

contaminated atmosphere, is very dangerous. The danger is increased by the undue length of the working day, whereby the workers are fatigued, whereby their energy is exhausted, so that their attention is apt to wander and the liability to accident is greatly increased. An unduly long working day entails, of itself, extreme exhaustion of the organism.

A few examples will suffice to show how the life of the workers is dependent upon their environment and upon the general conditions under which they work.

1. First of all comes the question of *accidents*. Here are some figures. At the Nevsky Shipbuilding Works in Petrograd, the records of accidents are as follows :

Year.	No. of accidents.	No. of workers.	No. of accidents per 1000 workers.
1914	4386	6186	709
1915	4689	7002	669
1916	2830	7602	371
1917	1269	6059	210

The decline in the number of accidents was mainly due to a series of special measures. But the figure of 210 accidents per 1000 workers is still far too high.

Sometimes accidents occur to 70 per cent. of the workers every year. According to the reports of a district surgeon, during harvest time in Ekaterinoslav province the country hospitals reminded him of field hospitals in war time. Of course such accidents are not peculiar Russia, but occur everywhere. In the British parliament, Ramsay MacDonald once pointed out that of 1200 miners killed at work, 1100 were killed owing to the neglect of the requisite precautionary measures by the capitalists.

The last example indicates that if we wish we can enormously reduce the number of accidents. But from the capitalist point of view the necessary measures would not " pay."

2. The second basic question is that of *injurious working environment and the occupational diseases and the mortality arising thereform.*

Let us consider, for instance, phosphorus manufacture.

Lazareff reported that in Russian phosphorus factories, where no precautionary measures were employed, five years sufficed to make of the worker a "living corpse." In chemical works, glass works, mines, etc., numerous so-called occupational diseases were rife. Like phenomena were observable in other branches of production. Varicose veins occurred in workers who had to stand too long; necrosis of the jaw in phosphorus workers; mercurial poisoning, arsenical poisoning, tuberculosis, etc.

Here are some figures. In England, during the years 1900–1902, among 1000 deaths of those following various occupations, the deaths from consumption were :

Clergy	55
Agriculturists and cattlemen	76
Barristers and solicitors	92
Civil servants	129
Glass workers	283
China and earthenware workers	285
Compositors	300
Brush makers	325
Knife grinders, etc.	533
Miners	579–816

According to the reports of Dr. Baranoff, the mortality from consumption in the proletariat was as follows :

Of 100 cigarette makers who died ..	63·4 died of consumption.
„ engravers who died	58·3 „ „
„ compositors who died	53·1 „ „
„ tailors who died	50·9 „ „
„ stonemasons who died	50·6 „ „
„ locksmiths, turners, bootmakers, bookbinders, tinplaters who died	46–47 „ „
„ cardboard makers, joiners who died	45–45·5 „ „

We learn from German statistics that the mortality from consumption among the Solingen metalpolishers was four times as great as that from any other illness.

3. In addition to causing manifest diseases, *bad working conditions give rise to a general deterioration of working-class physique.* This finds expression in the increasing number of men who are unfit for military service. Year by year

there is a larger number of weak-chested and undergrown persons ; and in the proletariat the proportion of such persons is far greater than among other strata of the population. In Switzerland, among those called up for militia service, the percentage of town workers who were unfit was 39·5, while the percentage of unfit rural workers was only 25. Similar conditions are observable in other lands. Among women, the deterioration of physique is frequently associated with a loss of the capacity for child-bearing.

Obviously, all these evils are closely linked with the conditions of production. The capitalist class has no interest in labour protection, and its policy towards labour power is merely a policy of plunder. The capitalists wish to squeeze the workers like lemons and throw away the skin. This is the policy likewise of " progressive " American capital. In the U.S.A., none but healthy workers are admitted into the factories ; their muscular development is carefully inspected and tested. Weakly workers are not even allowed to enter the country, for it is considered that these weaklings would constitute an inferior sort of working cattle. But in the States it is an exception for the workers to attain the age of forty-five. My Lord Capital sucks the life out of them in the most " progressive " manner possible.

The dictatorship of the proletariat is obviously the first means which has been found for putting this matter of labour protection upon a secure footing. The working class is directly interested in the preservation of labour power. It must display the utmost regard for this most precious and most important force of production. The communist system will have nothing to do with a foolish, criminal, and injurious waste of human strength ; it will work with the aid of a highly developed technique, whose first object will be the preservation of this strength. That is why labour protection is of such immense importance during the transition to the communist phase of human society.

LABOUR PROTECTION, THEN, SIGNIFIES THE SAFEGUARDING OF THE WORKERS FROM HARMFUL CONDITIONS OF PRODUCTION.

§ 128.

The chief Fields of Labour Protection. The most important requisite for the protection of the working class, and the most important safeguard against its physical deterioration, against illness, increased mortality, etc., is that there should be a *normal working day*. It is not surprising, therefore, that the working class has always put the struggle for the reduction of working hours in the forefront of the general struggle. The working day decides the expenditure of human energy which is converted into products. In capitalist society this energy is likewise converted into capitalist profit, and for this reason the capitalists are greatly interested in protracting the working day. But by overworking his strength, the worker reduces his capacity for further work; he wears himself out more speedily; his constitution is weakened; he falls ill more readily, and dies sooner. An abnormally long working day involves a predatory squandering of human energy. The establishment of a normal working day is the first step in labour protection.

The second step is *the protection of the specially weak elements of the working class*. This class does not consist solely of adult males. It contains also old men, young people, and women of various age. It is obvious that the power of resisting harmful conditions varies in different sections of the working class. What can be done easily and without any danger to health by a full-grown man may be extremely injurious to a woman, and absolutely dangerous to a half-grown child. Consider, for instance, the carrying of heavy weights. Women, moreover, require special protection at certain periods of life; during pregnancy, childbirth, and lactation. In these matters specific measures are essential. This is the field of women's protection and child protection.

Thirdly and lastly, a matter of great importance is *the technical and sanitary organisation of factories and workshops*. A great deal can be done, and still remains to be done, in the prevention of accidents, in the avoidance of noxious influences arising out of the work of production, in the general improvement of working conditions. Among bad conditions we think especially of dust, insufficient lighting, cold, draughts, dirt, etc.

The foregoing are the three main fields of labour protection.

§ 129.

What has been done in Russia as regards Labour Protection? The dictatorship of the proletariat has created conditions which make it possible to carry out in full the demands which have been put forward by all the socialist parties. In this matter, no legislature in the world can boast of legislation like that of the Soviet Republic. Our troubles (of which we have plenty, though they are diminishing) do not arise from bad laws, but from the fact that we have too little of many things, and that there is an absolute lack of certain essentials. The dearth, as we have seen, is due to the struggle carried on against us by world imperialism, and also to the imperialist war which the enemies of the working class have been waging among themselves.

Speaking generally, when we sum up what the Soviet Republic has done in the way of labour protection, and when we study the laws of the Soviet Republic, we derive the following picture.

(a) *The limitation of working hours.* In this matter the Soviet Power has carried various measures into effect.

1. We have at length realised the 8-hour day, confirming this by law (a step which the Coalition Government sedulously avoided); and there is a 6-hour working day for mental workers and for those working in offices.

2. Overtime is as a rule prohibited. It is permitted only to a limited extent in exceptional instances, and is paid at the rate of time-and-a-half.

3. In specially injurious trades the working hours are further reduced. Tobacco workers are employed for 7 hours a day; gas workers, for 6.

4. A normal 42-hour weekly rest has been established, and for this purpose the Saturday hours have everywhere been reduced to 6. Any workers who are unable to stop work on Sunday can rest on some other day of the week.

5. Once a year, every worker enjoys a holiday on full pay. The legally specified holiday is one month, but in the present difficult times (autumn, 1919) it has been reduced to a fortnight.

6. In especially injurious trades, and in the case of

adolescents who are going to land colonies, a supplementary holiday of a fortnight is given.

(b) *Protection of women's labour and child labour.*

1. As a rule, women must not work at night and must not work overtime. They may not be hired by the job.

2. Children under sixteen may not be engaged in industry. They are gradually being removed from the industrial field (in the first instance from all injurious trades); those who are withdrawn from industry are given material support and are sent to school.

3. Children under sixteen who still remain at work are employed for only 4 hours daily; young people from sixteen to eighteen have a working day of 6 hours.

4. Overtime, night work, and jobbing work, are prohibited in the case of all persons under the age of eighteen.

For the protection of motherhood, the following laws have been promulgated:

1. In pregnancy and childbirth all women, whether women actually engaged in industry or the wives of workers, receive an allowance throughout the period in which work is discontinued on account of pregnancy and childbirth. This allowance is equivalent to a full working wage.

2. Pregnant women engaged in physical work receive this allowance for eight weeks before delivery; mental workers and office employees receive it for six weeks before delivery.

3. After childbirth the allowance is continued respectively for eight weeks and six weeks.

4. Nursing mothers engaged in industry have half an hour's leave every three hours.

5. All mothers receive a supplementary allowance of 24 roubles a day for the feeding of the child for a period of nine months after birth. In addition they receive a lump sum of 720 roubles for the child's outfit.

In all these measures, which have already been carried into effect, there are certain divergences from the Code of Labour Laws. These divergences take the following form. In exceptional circumstances overtime is permitted, upon a number of days which is not to exceed 50 per annum in all. Children at ages from fourteen to sixteen may work in industry for hours not exceeding 4 per day. The month's holiday has been temporarily reduced to a fortnight. The duration of night work has been increased to 7 hours.

All these divergences have been necessitated by the extremely critical situation in which the Soviet Republic has been placed by the brutal attack of all the imperialist Powers.

(c) *Technical and sanitary organisation of the factories.* The following measures have been instituted:

1. A number of compulsory rules have been issued concerning technical measures for safety at work, concerning general sanitation, and concerning occupational hygiene. All these aim at a notable improvement of the working conditions in the factories and workshops.

2. In all injurious branches of production, arrangements have been made to provide special clothing which shall protect the worker from dust, gases, damp, etc.

3. All the workers are provided with overalls, which belong to the works, and are to be used by the worker during working hours only.

4. To supervise the actual carrying out of all labour protection measures, a system of Labour Inspection has been founded, elected by general conferences of the workers. In the case of individual trades characterised by peculiar working conditions, and in the case of trades (such as transport, the building trade, and agriculture) in which from the nature of the occupation the workers are peculiarly disintegrated, special committees for labour inspection are elected by the respective trade unions.

The figures relating to the personnel of the new inspectors show the extent to which the workers are themselves participating in this matter. Down to August 1, 1919, 53·5 per cent. of all the inspectors were manual workers. The real proportion was probably higher, for in the case of a good many of the inspectors the previous occupation was not stated. Among all the inspectors whose previous occupation is recorded, the proportion of those stated to have been manual workers is 62·5 per cent., and the proportion of those stated to have been employees is 15·5 per cent. Thus the manual workers and the employees together comprise 88 per cent. of all those whose occupation is stated !

The following table gives details down to August 1, 1919,

showing the distribution of inspectors according to previous occupation.

Occupation.	No. of individuals.	Percentage of total inspectors.	Percentage of those whose occupation is stated.
Workers	112	53·5	62·5
Masters, technicians, and draughts-			
men	21	10	11·5
Employees, salesmen and clerks ..	28	13·5	15·5
Surgeon's assistants	4	2	2
Pharmaceutical chemists	1	0·5	0·5
School teachers	5	2	2·5
Students	4	2	2
Doctors	5	2·5	2·5
Engineers	1	0·5	0·5
Lawyers	1	0·5	0·5
Occupation not stated	28	13	0
	210	100	100

In comparison with the previous half-year, the number of manual workers has increased (53·5 per cent. as against 47 per cent.; or 62·5 per cent. of all whose occupations were stated, as against 60 per cent.). The percentage of masters and technicians was practically unchanged (10 as against 11). There was a notable increase in the number of employees (13·5 per cent. as against 8 per cent.). Relatively, the number of the students declined from 6 per cent. to 2 per cent.; absolutely, the number of students was only one half in the second half-year of what it had been in the first half-year. The other figures were practically unchanged.

There thus originated in Russia a genuine *workers'* *inspection*, which merited the name in respect of its personnel no less than in respect of its aims.

Nevertheless, in the matter of labour protection much still remains to be done in the factories. In the enormous majority of cases the working conditions are still abominable, especially in the more backward forms of enterprise, where the workers are still uncultured and badly organised. In such dark corners everything is much as it was in the old days.

Often enough, indeed, it is impossible to undertake the necessary improvements at present, since these would need an entirely new installation and complete reorganisation. However, a great deal can be done even without these extensive changes, if only larger and yet larger sections of the masses become interested in the improvement of working conditions.

§ 130.

What is social Welfare Work? The capitalist system, as we have seen, aims at the extraction of profit from the working class. Wage workers, proletarians, were simply means of enrichment for the capitalist. When these living tools were worn out, when they had become unprofitable or superfluous, they were ruthlessly thrown away like a squeezed lemon or an egg-shell. The miseries of unemployment, illness, old age, mutilation, were nothing to the capitalist, who would jettison huge masses of persons without even trying to help them—or would help only the most devoted among their trusty servants, those from whom all the vital juices had already been sucked.

In the Soviet Republic the workers and the poor peasants are not the objects of exploitation. But it does not follow from this that there is not widespread poverty in the country. In Russia, perpetually harassed by its enemies, blockaded on all sides, cut off from its supplies of coal, petroleum, and raw materials, there is a terrible amount of poverty. It is no longer because the capitalist throws the workers out of the factories, but because the factories have to be closed for lack of fuel and raw material. Hence there is unemployment. It is not the unemployment of the old kind; it arises from very different causes, but it exists. As a legacy from the imperialist war we have invalids and cripples; we have the numerous victims of the counter-revolution; we have the aged, the sick, and the children—for all these helpless persons care is needed, and they are all a source of expense. The workers' government does not look upon the help which it gives them as a gift, an alms, or a benefaction. The workers' State makes their support its primary duty, above all in the case of those who are invalided from the army of labour or from the Red Army.

Our ultimate aim is to bring about the existence of a state of society in which all persons who for one reason or another have lost the capacity for work, all those who are unable to work, shall have assured support. We must ensure that old people shall enjoy a peaceful old age in which they will be provided with all the comforts of life; that children shall have everything suitable to their requirements; that invalids and cripples shall be able to live in the circumstances most appropriate to their condition; that those who are wearied and overworked shall be placed in curative surroundings, where they will receive all the care that used to be given to the wealthy bourgeois who were ailing; that no one shall any longer be perpetually harassed with anticipations of hard times.

To-day, of course, we are very far from having achieved anything like this. Thanks to the international robbers, our country is utterly impoverished. We lack the most ordinary requirements, such as drugs. The imperialists will not allow us to import them; they continue the blockade. But one thing at least cannot be denied. The Soviet Power spares nothing in the attempt to provide help and care for those who are unable to work.

§ 131.

The chief Provinces of social Welfare Work. There are two main departments of social welfare work. First of all there is the care for those persons who happen to be unemployed or who have lost their capacity for work while actually following their occupation (mental or manual). To this category belong cases of transient incapacity due to illness, accident, pregnancy, childbirth; and cases of permanent incapacity, due to a premature break-down in health, old age, chronic infirmity, etc. Secondly there is the care for persons who have sustained an accident or have lost the capacity for work while not actually engaged in work, while not employed in production. To this category belong those who were invalided during the imperialist war, men who were wounded while serving in the Red Army, the families of these Red soldiers, the victims of the counter-revolution, or of natural catastrophes and misfortunes (conflagrations, floods, epidemic disease, etc.). We also have to care for those who have been unfitted for work through conditions operative in the old order of society, the victims of the shameful social conditions that then prevailed. To this category belong professional beggars, the homeless and shelterless, mental defectives, etc.

Moreover, in case of death, help must be given to the family of the deceased.

The number of persons thus requiring care is enormous. Those of the first category, who are unemployed or who have lost the capacity for work but are in one way or another connected with the field of production, are the concern of the Commissariat for Labour which is actually under the control of the trade unions. Those of the second category are the concern of the Commissariat for Social Welfare.

§ 132.

Social Welfare Work in Russia. Considering its activities as a whole, the Soviet Power, in its welfare work, has achieved for the workers in the case of all kinds of incapacity for work, including unemployment, what has been achieved nowhere else in the world.

Here is a list of the measures which apply to persons of the first category :

1. All persons living by " wage labour " are exempt from any expenditure for social insurance.

2. Entrepreneurs are completely excluded from the work of organising social welfare and labour protection ; all the instruments of this work are based upon the representation of labour organisations.

3. Social welfare benefits apply to all cases of loss of capacity for work and to all cases of unemployment.

4. Social welfare benefits apply to members of a worker's family in case of any worker's death.

5. Allowances are given at the full rate of a worker's earnings in cases of illness, accident, quarantine, and other causes of temporary incapacity for work.

6. A life pension of 1800 roubles per month (in Moscow city) is payable to all who are permanently incapacitated for work, irrespective of the cause of the incapacity (whether old age, crippling, occupational disease, etc.), and regardless of the number of years of work.

7. An allowance for funeral expenses amounting to 1440 roubles is made in the case of every worker; and for every member of a worker's family a similar allowance is made, ranging from 400 to 800 roubles according to age.

8. In case of a worker's death, the family receives a life pension ranging up to 1200 roubles per month (in Moscow city), the amount varying in accordance with the size of the family.

9. For the better determination of questions concerning the amount of these allowances, special workers' committees are appointed in connexion with the departments for labour, and these committees will determine the pensions and allowances.

10. In all the provinces, medical boards shall be established under the chairmanship of workers, and these boards shall decide in each case the degree of incapacity.

11. In all the counties, special committees are to be appointed under the chairmanship of workers. These committees will supervise the treatment of sick workers and will exercise a general control.

12. To bring the system of welfare benefits into closer contact with all places where there are workers, centres are to be established for the receipt of applications for allowances and pensions and for the payment of the same. In large-scale enterprises, the allowances will be paid through the said enterprises.

13. There is no time limit for the payment of allowances. In case of illness, the allowance will be paid until health is restored; in case of permanent incapacity for work, the allowance will continue till death.

14. Social welfare benefit will be paid to all persons without exception who live by wage labour, and will be extended to home workers, independent artisans, and peasants.

15. For the second half of the year 1919 the Soviet Republic assigned a sum of five milliards of roubles for the social welfare benefits of workers and employees.

As far as concerns the second category of those who receive social welfare benefit, the most important benefit is that paid to the families of soldiers in the Red Army and to the Red soldiers themselves.

An invalided Red soldier who has completely lost the capacity for work (to the extent of more than 60 per cent.), receives a pension corresponding to the average wage of the locality where he lives. The pension decreases proportionally to a decrease in the degree of incapacity for work (in 15 to 30 per cent. incapacity, the ex-soldier's pension is one-third of the customary wage). The land of a Red soldier must be tilled and his farm must be properly supplied with seed. His family must receive a ration which is proportional to the number of the members of his family who are unable to work. The family of a Red soldier lives rent free and receives a supplementary food card. In the event of the death of a Red soldier, such members of his family as are unable to work and as are unprovided for by social welfare benefit will receive a pension amounting to 60 per cent. of the customary local wage for one person incapacitated for work, and a full wage for three or more persons incapacitated for work, etc., etc.

In the payment of allowances to the families of Red soldiers, there was expended during the first half of 1919 a sum of 1,200,000,000 roubles. The estimates for this expenditure for the second half of the same year were 3,500,000,000 roubles. According to the reports of Comrade Vinokuroff, in the autumn of 1919 the families of 4,500,000 Red soldiers were receiving allowances.

In addition, between July 4 and December 1, 1919, there was paid to the provinces a sum of more than two and a half milliards of roubles. There was assigned in aid of agriculture 200,000,000 roubles ; to housing, 150,000,000 roubles ; to pensions for Red soldiers, 100,000,000 roubles ; to allowances to those invalided from the war, 168,000,000 roubles.

One of the main defects of our social welfare work is the bad functioning of the apparatus. There is no proper record of the persons in receipt of benefit ; the assignment of funds to the various localities is faulty ; there is much waste of time in the subdepartments of the Commissariat for Social Welfare ; and so on. It is absolutely essential that our party should devote itself to the better organisation of these matters.

§ 133.

Other Measures for the Improvement of the Condition of the Working Class. In addition to the measures previously enumerated, several other measures prescribed in the Code of Labour Laws are of great importance to the condition of the working class. These measures are directly associated with the fact that the proletariat has become the ruling class, and they are therefore more comprehensive than the demands which used to be incorporated in the programs of the socialist parties. They may be summarised under three heads.

1. The participation of the labour organisations in the decision of questions relating to the engagement or discharge of workers. These matters are referred to the factory and workshop committees and to the workers' factory administrations.

2. The State regulation of wages. The most interesting matter in this connexion is that the rates of pay are elaborated by the trade unions and are submitted to the Commissariat for Labour, which itself is actually composed of representatives of the trade unions.

3. The compulsory search for work for the unemployed by special departments of the soviets and trade unions (the so-called departments for the distribution and registration of labour power).

All these measures are intimately connected with the dominant position of the labour organisations and of the trade unions in particular.

§ 134.

Further Tasks of the Party. The most important of all the duties of our party is to ensure the completest and most extensive realisation of the decrees and decisions of the Soviet Power. In many cases this practical realisation of a decree is lacking ; it exists on paper, but there is nothing corresponding to it in real life. The complete, precise, and accurate realisation of all decrees and decisions will be mainly secured by the correct functioning of an organisatory apparatus, wherein the centre is properly connected with the local organs, and wherein the local organs are properly connected with the centre whence the whole machine is run.

This in its turn is only possible in so far as the masses themselves can be induced to participate in the work. Hence it is necessary to adopt the following measures :

1. The work of organising and extending labour inspection must be actively taken in hand. New forces drawn from among the workers themselves must be continually flowing into this branch of activity. No one can know better than the actual workers, who are practically acquainted with labour conditions, wherein these conditions are faulty, and no one is more competent than they to recommend practical improvements.

2. Labour inspection must be extended to the fields of small-scale production and home industry. In such matters these branches of industry have always been ignored, although it is precisely here that the most abominable working conditions prevail. Inspection by the workers ought to be of great help in these fields.

3. Labour protection must be extended to all branches of work, including the building trade, land and water transport, domestic service, and agriculture. These branches of labour, in which the workers are disintegrated by the very conditions of their work, and in which the trade-union organisation of labour is therefore very difficult, must be included within the general system.

4. Industrial and agricultural labour must be absolutely prohibited during childhood, and there must be a further reduction of the working day in the case of young persons.

The eight-hour day, which is at present the standard for labour protection, is far from being regarded by our party as the limit in this matter of the reduction of working hours. In fact there is no precise limit. Everything depends upon the productivity of labour. At the present time, owing to the general decline in productive powers, and owing to the continued disorganisation, the working hours cannot as a general rule be less than eight. Often enough (this depends upon the military situation, etc.), the working day has to exceed the eight-hour standard. But at the first opportunity we must establish a six-hour day as the normal standard, applying to all workers the six-hour regulation which already applies to the employees —a very large number of persons.

On the other hand, in order to increase production, and in order to secure a continuous improvement in the quality of work, it has proved advantageous to introduce a system of payment which promotes emulation.

The general tasks of social welfare work will nowise be undertaken by the party in the spirit of the charitymonger or in a way which will encourage parasitism and idleness. It is the simple duty of the proletarian Power to give help where it is needed, just as it is the duty of the proletarian Power to facilitate for persons who have been demoralised by bad social conditions the return to a working life.

Literature. KAPLUN, Labour Protection and its Methods. MALYUTIN, On the Road to the bright Future of Communism. HELFER, The proletarian Revolution and the social Welfare of the Workers. PRESS, What is social Technique ? articles in " Vestnik Truda " [The Labour Herald] and in the publications of the Commissariat for Social Welfare. HOLZMANN, The Premium System in the metallurgical Industry.

CHAPTER NINETEEN

PUBLIC HYGIENE

§ 135. The Need for the special Protection of public Health. § 136. The Nationalisation of medical Institutions. § 137. The Labour Duty of medical Workers. § 138. Immediate Tasks in the Domain of public Hygiene.

§ 135.

The Need for the special Protection of public Health. Under capitalism the workers have always been compelled to live in unclean quarters of the towns, where epidemic disease is rife. It was only owing to the dread that they themselves would suffer from these epidemics, that the capitalists introduced certain measures to improve the sanitation of the areas in which their wage-slaves dwelt. As early as 1784 the British parliament manifested its liberal sentiments and began to concern itself about the workers. The reason for this activity was the report of a special parliamentary committee which had ascertained that a terrible epidemic of typhus had originated in the factories. Capitalism was only interested in the protection of public health in so far as this was necessary for its own safety.

As an ·outcome of the imperialist war, the condition of the great masses of the workers has changed considerably for the worse. The general circumstances, hunger, cold, etc., have given rise to devastating epidemics, causing widespread mortality, to successive outbreaks of cholera, typhus, and a new disease known as Spanish influenza. The last-named illness manifestly had a close connexion with the war. People's constitutions, exhausted and shattered, had no power to resist the germs of this disease. Everywhere the mortality was unprecedentedly high, so that the epidemic had a truly catastrophic character.

The war left another legacy, an extraordinary diffusion of venereal diseases, and notably of syphilis. Vast numbers of the soldiers became infected with this disease, and then, returning home, introduced it into their villages.

Never have venereal diseases been so widespread as they are to-day.

All these evils make it essential that we should be specially active on behalf of the protection of public health. Of course, in addition to the measures specifically classed under the head of hygiene, there are many other ways of carrying on the campaign against disease. For example, the solution of the housing problem is of immense importance. With the improvement of the workers' dwellings, numerous foci of epidemic illness will be destroyed. No less important is labour protection. Everyone will understand how much depends upon the food supply, upon the nutritive circumstances of the population.

But attention to these matters will not relieve us from the necessity of undertaking special hygienic measures, which must be applied on the grand scale.

To-day, when we are in a very bad position as regards the most elementary requisites for a healthy life, we must grasp at every available means of assistance in our struggle with the evil. Hence arises the urgent need for a special department of social work, the urgent need for measures for the protection of public health.

§ 136.

The Nationalisation of medical Institutions. Capitalist society had at its disposal a capitalistically organised system of medical work. Private hospitals and lunatic asylums, private health resorts, sanatoria, hydropathics, chemists' shops, electrotherapeutic, radiotherapeutic, and various other curative institutions, were organised on a profit-making basis. The major proportion of these comprised places for the cure of obesity, gout, and other aristocratic complaints. They were, that is to say, intended for the cure of diseases peculiar to the dominant classes of capitalist society. Workers could not visit the fashionable health resorts, nor were there any working-class invalids in the sanatoria.

The business of the retail chemists was in like manner pursued as a source of profit. Economically considered all these establishments were on precisely the same footing as any other profit-making enterprise.

It was therefore necessary to transform them from instruments for filling capitalists' purses into instruments for the service of the workers. The first step in this direction was the nationalisation of all such enterprises.

§ 137.

The Labour Duty of medical Workers. The great prevalence of epidemic diseases and the need for prompt measures to prevent their spread led to the consideration of the possibility of a purposive, organised, and extensive campaign in this direction. Since the number of available workers was comparatively small, the urgent need for their scheduling and mobilisation in this campaign against epidemics became immediately and spontaneously apparent.

Thanks to these measures, thanks to the full utilisation of practically all the available medical strength from the most distinguished professors down to the first-year students and the surgeons' assistants, it proved possible to get the better of the menacing epidemics—cholera and typhus.

Labour duty for medical workers has, however, a greater significance than that merely of " fireman's work." In association with the nationalisation of all curative enterprises, it is one of the germs of the organised social sanitation and social hygiene of the future.

§ 138.

Immediate Tasks in the Domain of public Hygiene. Our work is rendered extremely difficult owing to the terrible' dearth of many of the most ordinary essentials (proper food for use in the hospitals, drugs and instruments, etc.). In so far as the Communist Party is able to intervene actively in public health work, there are three main provinces for such activity.

The first essential is the resolute enforcement of broadly conceived sanitary measures. Attention must be given to the sanitary condition of all places of public resort. Many epidemics arise from the contamination of the water supply, from badly kept street gullies and storm-water pipes, middens and manure heaps, cesspools, closets, and so forth. The protection of earth, air, and water is the first requisite for public health. To the same category of measures belongs the organisation of communal kitchens and of the food supply generally upon a scientific and hygienic foundation. Owing to the scarcity of provisions, this task has hitherto been extremely difficult to fulfil; but it is already within our competence to ensure that the food shall be hygienically prepared in the communal kitchens, the children's kitchens, the hospitals, and all other public institutions. It is further necessary to organise measures to prevent the spread of epidemic diseases of a contagious character. This will be secured by the sanitary inspection of institutions, private houses, and schools; by the filtration of water, by the organisation of depots for the provision of boiled water, by disinfection, by the obligatory sterilisation of wearing apparel, etc.

The second essential is that there should be a carefully planned campaign against the so-called social diseases, that is to say against those diseases which affect masses of people and are brought about by social causes. Three diseases, above all, come within this category. First, tuberculosis, which is dependent upon bad working conditions. Secondly, venereal disease, whose present wide diffusion is mainly the outcome of the war. Thirdly, alcoholism: this partly arises from brutalisation, depression, and sordid surroundings; and it is partly due to parasitic degeneration. These diseases do not merely concern the adults who suffer from them; they exercise a disastrous influence upon the offspring. Humanity is gravely endangered by these influences, and above all because to-day their evil effects are exceptionally great owing to the prevalent condition of exhaustion.

Thirdly and lastly, it is of the utmost importance that the whole population should be able to secure gratuitous medical advice and treatment. Our main difficulty at present is due to the absolute lack of drugs. This dearth is not so much the result of the disorganisation of production in Russia as the result of the blockade. The " humane " Allies hope to crush us, not only by cutting us off from access to raw materials and fuel, not only by the " bony hand of hunger," but also by epidemic disease. This brings us back to our general struggle with world imperialism.

Literature. SEMASHKO, The Elements of Soviet Medical Science. LINDEMANN, The Struggle with Typhus.—Symposium : A Year's Work of the Commissariat for Public Hygiene.

PROGRAM

OF THE

COMMUNIST PARTY OF RUSSIA

PROGRAM OF THE COMMUNIST PARTY OF RUSSIA

ADOPTED AT THE EIGHTH PARTY CONGRESS, HELD MARCH 18 TO 23, 1919.

The November revolution [October 25th, old style ; November 7th, new style, 1917] in Russia, realised the dictatorship of the proletariat, which began to build the foundations of communist society, with the aid of the poor peasants or the semi-proletariat. The development of the revolution in Germany and Austria-Hungary, the growth of the revolutionary movement of the proletariat in all advanced lands, the spread of the soviet form of that movement (the form which aimed directly at realising the dictatorship of the proletariat)—these things combined to show that the era of the world-wide proletarian communist revolution had begun. §§ 1-5.

This revolution was the inevitable result of the development of capitalism, which had hitherto been dominant in the majority of civilised countries. If we ignore the misleading designation of the party as " social democratic," and use instead the word " communist," our old program accurately characterised in the following theses the nature of capitalism and of bourgeois society :

" As the chief characteristic of this society, we have commodity production upon the foundation of capitalist productive relationships, in accordance with which the most important and significant part of the means of the production and distribution of commodities is owned by a comparatively small class of persons, whereas the great majority of the population consists of proletarians and semi-proletarians compelled by their economic position to sell their labour power permanently or from time to time, compelled, that is to say, to become wage workers in the service of the capitalists, and to create by their labour the income of the higher classes of society. §§ 6-13.

§ 14. " The domain of capitalist productive relationships continually extends in proportion to the continued improvement of technique, which increases the economic importance of large-scale enterprises, and leads to the crushing out of petty independent producers, converting some of them into proletarians, restricting the role of the remainder in social and economic life, and in many places making them— more or less completely, more or less obviously, more or less miserably—the dependents of capital.

§ 15. " Moreover, this technical progress enables the entrepreneurs, to an increasing extent, to apply the labour of women and children to the process of producing and distributing commodities. In like measure, on the other hand, it leads to a comparative restriction of the demand on the part of the entrepreneurs for the living labour of the workers, so that the demand for labour power is necessarily inferior to the supply. Hence arise, first, an increase in the dependence of wage labour upon capital, and, secondly, a rise in the rate of exploitation.

§ 16. " This state of affairs in capitalist countries, and the continued intensification of their competition in the world market, give rise to more and more difficulty in disposing of the commodities which are produced in continually increasing quantities. Over-production, manifesting itself in more or less acute crises of production which are followed by more or less prolonged periods of stagnation, is the inevitable outcome of the development of productive strength in bourgeois society. Crises, and periods in which production is stagnant, lead, in their turn, to the more and more widespread ruin of the small producers, increase the dependence of wage labour upon capital, and give rise all the more speedily to a comparative or absolute worsening of the position of the working class.

§ 17. " In this manner, the improvement in technique, leading to an increase in the productivity of labour and to an increase in social wealth, entails in bourgeois society an increase in social inequality, a widening of the chasm between the haves and the have-nots, an increase in the insecurity of life, in unemployment, and in various kinds of deprivation for wider and wider circles among the labouring masses.

" In proportion as the contradictions peculiar to bourgeois

society grow and develop, so also does there increase the discontent of the toiling and exploited masses with the existing order of things, and so also do there increase the number and the solidarity of the proletarians and the intensity of their struggle with the exploiters. At the §18. same time the advance of technique, concentrating the means of production and distribution and socialising the labour process in capitalist undertakings, creates with greater and greater speed the material possibilities for the transformation of capitalist into communist productive relationships ; it creates, that is to say, the social revolution, which takes as its final aim all the activities of the international communist parties, regarded as conscious expressions of the class movement.

" Transforming private ownership of the means of §§ 19–22. production and distribution into social ownership, and leading to the purposive organisation of the social productive process for the safeguarding of the prosperity and the many-sided development of all the members of society, the social revolution of the proletariat puts an end to the division of society into classes, and thereby liberates the whole of oppressed mankind, thus abolishing all forms of exploitation of one section of society by another.

" A necessary condition for this social revolution is the §§ 23 & 2 dictatorship of the proletariat, this meaning the conquest by the proletariat of such a degree of political power as will enable it to crush the resistance of the exploiters. Determining to make the proletariat capable of fulfilling §25. its great historic mission, the international Communist Party organises the proletariat into an independent political party, opposed to all the bourgeois parties ; leads the workers in all the manifestations of the class struggle ; reveals to the exploited the irreconcilable conflict of interests between themselves and the exploiters ; and explains to the proletariat the historical significance and the necessary conditions of the imminent social revolution. At the same time, the party reveals to the other sections of the toiling and exploited masses the hopelessness of their condition in capitalist society, and shows them that the social revolution is indispensable in order that they may secure their own deliverance from the yoke of capital. The party of the working class, the Communist Party, summons to its ranks all strata of the toiling and exploited population in so far as they have accepted the proletarian outlook."

§ 26–28. The process of the concentration and centralisation of capital, destroying free competition, led in the beginning of the twentieth century to the creation of powerful, monopolist, capitalist combines—syndicates, cartels, and trusts—which acquired a decisive significance in economic life ; it led also to the amalgamation of banking capital with highly concentrated industrial capital, and to the vigorous export of capital into foreign lands. Trusts comprising whole groups of capitalist Powers began the economic partition of the world which had already been partitioned territorially among the richer countries. This epoch of financial capital, inevitably intensifying the struggle between the capitalist States, is the epoch of imperialism.

§ 29 & 30. Hence inevitably arise imperialist wars, wars for markets, for spheres for the investment of capital, for raw materials, and for labour power, that is to say, wars for world dominion and for power over small and weak nations. Such was the first great imperialist war of 1914 to 1918.

§ 31. The vast development of world capitalism ; the change from a system of free competition to a system in which monopolist capitalism was dominant ; the creation by the banks, and also by the capitalist combines, of an apparatus for the joint regulation of the process of the production and distribution of commodities ; the rise in the cost of living, the oppression of the workers by the employers' syndicates, the enslavement of the working class by the imperialist State, the colossal difficulties facing the proletariat in its economic and political struggle (phenomena inevitably associated with the growth of capitalist monopoly); the miseries, the poverty, and the ruin which issued from the imperialist war—all these things have inevitably contributed to the collapse of capitalism and to the transition to a higher type of social economy.

§ 32. The imperialist war could not end in a just peace or even in any sort of stable peace between the bourgeois governments. At the stage of development which capitalism has now reached this war must inevitably be transformed, and is being transformed under our very eyes, into a civil war between the exploited and toiling masses (led by the proletariat) and the bourgeoisie.

The vigorous onslaught made by the proletariat, and §§ 33 & 3 the victories secured by the workers in various lands, have intensified the resistance of the exploiters, and have led to the creation of new forms of international union among the capitalists (the League of Nations, etc.); these, organising upon a world scale, by the systematic exploitation of all the peoples of the globe, and concentrating their forces, aim at the direct crushing of the proletarian movement in all lands.

All this inevitably leads to the conjuncture of civil wars within the individual States, with revolutionary wars, waged in part by the proletarian States that are defending themselves against capitalist attack, and in part by the oppressed peoples that are endeavouring to throw off the yoke of the imperialist Powers.

In these circumstances the watchwords of pacifism, The latter international disarmament under capitalism, the founding part of § of courts of arbitration, etc., are something worse than reactionary utopism; they are a direct fraud upon the workers, aiming at the disarmament of the proletariat and at diverting it from the task of disarming the exploiters.

Nothing but the proletarian, the communist revolution can lead humanity out of the blind alley in which it has been placed by imperialism and imperialist wars. However great the difficulties in the way of the revolution, whatever temporary defeats it may sustain, however high the waves of the counter-revolution, the ultimate victory of the proletariat is assured.

To bring about the victory of the world-wide proletarian § 35. revolution it is essential that there should be absolute and mutual trust, the most intimate brotherly alliance, and the highest possible cohesion of the revolutionary activities of the working class in the more advanced lands.

These conditions cannot be realised without making it a matter of principle to break off relations with and to wage a pitiless struggle against that bourgeois perversion of socialism which is dominant in the leading official social democratic and socialist parties.

§§ 36 -38.   In this perversion there is displayed, on the one hand,
the trend of opportunism and jingo socialism, of that which
calls itself socialism but is in fact jingoism, the mask of
those who defend the predatory interests of their own
national bourgeoisie under colour of the false watchword
of the defence of the fatherland—a watchword applied
both generally, and specifically to the imperialist war of
1914 to 1918. This trend originated because the seizure
of colonies and the oppression of weak nations by the
advanced capitalist States has enabled the bourgeoisies
of these countries, out of the vast gains which have accrued
from such plunderings, to offer a privileged position to the
more highly skilled members of the proletariat, and thus
in effect to buy them in peace time by giving them an
advantageous petty-bourgeois status ; at the same time
the bourgeoisie takes into its service the leaders of this
stratum. The opportunists and the jingo socialists, having
become the servants of the bourgeoisie, are the direct class
enemies of the proletariat, especially to-day, when in alliance
with the capitalists they are endeavouring by force of arms
to crush the revolutionary movement of the proletariat in
their own and in other lands.

§ 39.   On the other hand, concurrently with the growth of
this bourgeois perversion of socialism, there appears the
centrist trend, which manifests itself in like manner in all
capitalist countries. The centre see-saws between the jingo
socialists and the communists, maintaining its union with
the former, and endeavouring to reconstruct the bankrupt
§ 40. Second International. As leader in the struggle of the
proletariat for emancipation, there is only the new, the
Third, the Communist International, to the ranks of
which belongs the Russian Communist Party. This International has in fact been created by the organisation of
communist parties out of the genuinely proletarian elements
among the socialist parties in various countries, and especially
Germany ; it was formally constituted in March, 1919, and
its first session was held in Moscow. The Communist
International, receiving more and more support from the
proletarian masses in all lands, has returned to Marxism
not merely in the name it has adopted, but also in its ideological and political tenets ; and in all its activities it realises

the revolutionary teaching of Marx, cleansed of bourgeois-opportunist perversions.

Concretely realising the tasks of the proletarian dicta- §§ 41-45 torship as applied to Russia, a land whose most notable peculiarity is the numerical predominance of the petty-bourgeois stratum of the population, the Russian Communist Party has defined these tasks in the following manner :

General Politics.

A bourgeois republic, however democratic, hallowed by §§ 46 & the watchwords of the will of the people, the will of the whole nation, the will of all classes, inevitably expresses— through the very fact that it is based upon the private ownership of the land and other means of production— the dictatorship of the bourgeoisie, of a machine for the exploitation and oppression of the immense majority of the workers by the capitalist clique. In contrast with this, proletarian or soviet democracy transforms the mass organisations of those who are oppressed by the capitalist class, of the proletarians and the semi-proletarians (the poor peasants), that is to say, of the immense majority of the population, into the permanent and unified foundation of the entire State apparatus, local and central, from the bottom to the top. Thereby the Soviet State realises, among other things, in an immeasurably wider form than ever before, local self-government, without any sort of authority imposed from above. It is the task of our party to work indefatigably on behalf of the complete inauguration of that higher type of democracy which needs for its right functioning the continuous uplifting of the level of culture, organisation, and initiative power of the masses.

In contrast with bourgeois democracy, which conceals § 48. the class character of the capitalist State, the Soviet Power openly recognises that every State will inevitably have a class character until the division of society into classes shall have completely disappeared, and therewith all State authority shall have vanished. The Soviet State, which by its very nature has led to the crushing of the resistance of the exploiters, and the Soviet Constitution, which is based upon the idea that all freedom is a fraud in so far as it conflicts with the deliverance of labour from the yoke of capital, does not shrink from depriving the exploiters of political rights. Our party, the party of the proletariat, while inexorably crushing the resistance of the exploiters, and while fighting in the field of ideas against the deep-rooted prejudices in accordance with which bourgeois rights and freedoms are regarded as inviolable, must at the same time make it perfectly clear that the forfeiture of political rights, and whatever limitations may be imposed upon freedom, are necessary only as temporary measures to cope with the attempts of the exploiters to regain their privileges. Concurrently with the disappearance of the objective possibility of the exploitation of man by man, there will likewise disappear the need for these temporary measures, and our party will aim at their restriction and ultimately at their complete abolition.

§ 49.   Bourgeois democracy is organised upon the basis of the formal diffusion of political rights and freedoms : for instance, the right of public meeting, the right of combination, the freedom of the press ; all citizens being regarded as equal in these respects. But in actual fact, as concerns administrative practice, and above all in view of their economic slavery, under bourgeois democracy the workers have always stood in the rear ranks, and have been unable to any notable extent to realise these rights and freedoms.

On the contrary, proletarian democracy, instead of formally proclaiming rights and freedoms, does in actual fact realise these rights and freedoms first of all and more than all for that very class of the population which was oppressed by capitalism, namely, for the proletariat and the peasantry. For this reason, the Soviet Power confiscates the possessions of the bourgeoisie, i.e. its printing presses, stores of paper, etc., in order to place them entirely at the disposal of the workers and their organisations.

The Russian Communist Party must induce wider and yet wider masses of the working population to avail themselves of democratic rights and freedoms, and it must enlarge the material possibilities in this direction.

§ 50.   Bourgeois democracy has repeatedly proclaimed the equality of individuals independently of sex, race, religion, and nationality ; but capitalism has nowhere been able to realise this equality of rights in practice, and in its imperialistic phase it has brought about an extreme intensification of racial and national oppression. Simply for the reason that the Soviet Power is the workers' Power, it has been able completely and in all spheres of life to effect for the first time in the world the entire abolition of the last traces of the inequality of women in the spheres of conjugal and family rights. At the present moment, it is the task of our party to labour in the field of ideas and in the field of education preeminently to this end, that it may effect the final destruction of all traces of former inequality and prejudice, especially among the backward strata of the proletariat and the peasantry.

Not content to proclaim a formal equality of rights for women, the party endeavours to free them from the material burdens of the old domestic economy by substituting for that economy communal housing, communal dining rooms, central wash houses, creches, etc.

§ 51.
The Soviet Power secures for the working masses, to an incomparably greater extent than was secured for them under bourgeois democracy and parliamentarism, the power of carrying on the election and recall of delegates; this is made easy and accessible for the benefit of the workers and the peasants. Thus the Soviet Power compensates the defects of the parliamentary system—especially the separation of the legislative and executive spheres characteristic of that system, the withdrawal of representative institutions from the masses, etc.

The Soviet State likewise approximates the State apparatus to the masses in this way, that the electoral units of the State, the fundamental cells out of which it is constructed, no longer consist of territorial constituencies, but are now productive units (factories and workshops).

Our party must concentrate its energies upon the task of bringing about a closer approximation between the instruments of power and the working masses, upon the basis of a clearer and fuller realisation by these masses of democracy in practice, especially by promoting the responsibility and accountability of the persons chiefly concerned.

§ 52.
Whereas bourgeois democracy, in spite of its professions

to the contrary, made of the army a tool of the well-to-do classes, detaching it from the working masses and setting it up against them, making it impossible or difficult for the soldier to exercise his political rights, the Soviet State brings the workers and the soldiers together in its organs, the soviets, in which they have equal rights and identical interests. It is the task of our party to safeguard and promote this union of the workers and the soldiers in the soviets, and to strengthen the indissoluble unity of the armed forces with the organisations of the proletariat and semi-proletariat.

§ 53.   The industrial urban proletariat, comprising that portion of the toiling masses which is most highly concentrated, most united, most enlightened, and most perfectly tempered for the struggle, must be the leader in all revolutions. From the first, the proletariat assumed this role in the soviets, and has continued to play the leading part throughout their development into organs of power. Our Soviet Constitution reflects this, by assigning certain preferential rights to the industrial proletariat, as compared with the comparatively disunited petty-bourgeois masses in the villages.

Recognising the temporary character of these privileges, which are historically dependent upon the difficulty of effecting the socialist organisation of the villages, the Russian Communist Party must do its utmost, unerringly and systematically, to make a good use of this situation of the industrial proletariat. As a counterpoise to the narrow trade and craft interests which capitalism promoted among the workers, our party must effect a closer union between the vanguard of the workers, on the one hand, and the comparatively backward and disintegrated masses of the rural proletariat and semi-proletariat, together with the middle peasants, on the other.

§ 54.   Only thanks to the soviet organisation of the State was it possible for the proletarian revolution at a single blow to overthrow and raze to the ground the old State apparatus of the bourgeoisie, with its officialdom and its judicial machinery. However, the comparatively low cultural level of the masses, the lack of the requisite experience of administrative work in those who have been summoned by the masses to fill responsible posts, the need for providing exceptional inducements to experts of the old school whose services are needed in difficult matters, in conjunction with the withdrawal of the most advanced stratum of the urban workers (who had to undertake war service), have led to a partial revival of bureaucracy within the soviet system.

Engaged in a decisive struggle with bureaucracy, the Russian Communist Party advocates the following measures for the complete eradication of this evil :

1. Every member of a soviet must undertake some definite work in the administrative service.

2. There must be a continuous rotation among those who engage in such duties, so that each member shall in turn gain experience in every branch of administration.

3. By degrees, the whole working population must be induced to take turns in the administrative service.

The complete and many-sided application of all these measures (which represent further steps along the road which the Paris Commune entered as a pioneer), in conjunction with a simplification of the function of administration when the workers shall have attained a higher cultural level, will lead to the disappearance of the State authority.

THE PROBLEM OF NATIONALITY.

Upon the question of nationality the Russian Communist Party adopts the following theses : §§ 55–57 & 60.

1. Of primary importance is the policy of uniting the proletarians and semi-proletarians of various nationalities in a joint revolutionary struggle for the overthrow of the landlords and the bourgeoisie.

2. In order to overcome the feelings of suspicion which §58. the working masses in any oppressed land entertain towards the proletariat of the oppressor State, it is essential to annul any and every privilege on the part of any national group, to secure complete national equality, and to recognise that colonies and oppressed nationalities have a full right to secede.

3. To secure these ends, the party recommends (as a transitional step towards complete union) a federative

union of all the States which are organised on a soviet basis.

§ 59.   4. With regard to the question, Who is entitled to express the will of a nation to secede, the Russian Communist Party adopts the historical class point of view, taking into account the stage of historical development which any particular nation happens to have reached—whether, for instance, it is passing from medievalism to bourgeois democracy, from bourgeois democracy to soviet or proletarian democracy, etc.

In each case, on the part of the proletariat of those nations which are or have been oppressor nations, it is necessary that there should be extreme discretion, and that the utmost consideration should be paid to the survival of national sentiments among the working masses of nations which have been oppressed or have been deprived of equal rights. Only by such a policy will it be possible to create conditions for the realisation of a durable and amicable union between the diverse national elements of the international proletariat. This has been proved by the experience of the union with the various national soviet republics adjacent to Soviet Russia.

Military Affairs.

§§ 61, 62, & 69.   As regards military affairs, the aims of the party are summed up in the following theses :

1. During the epoch when imperialism is breaking up and when the civil war rages, it is impossible to preserve the old army, and it is equally impossible to construct a new army upon a so-called non-class or whole-nation basis. The Red Army as the instrument of proletarian dictatorship must necessarily have a declared class character ; that is to say, it must be exclusively composed of the proletariat and of the kindred semi-proletarian strata of the peasantry. Only when class has completely disappeared, can such an army be transformed into a socialist militia comprising the whole people.

§ 63.   2. It is essential that all members of the proletariat and semi-proletariat should receive military training, and that suitable military instruction should be given in the schools.

3. The work of military training and instruction of §§ 64 & 65 the Red Army is effected upon a basis of class solidarity and socialist enlightenment. For this reason there must be political commissars, appointed from among trusty and self-denying communists, to cooperate with the military staff; and all the communist groups must be inspired with ideas of unity and self-imposed discipline.

4. To counteract the system of the old army, the follow- § 66. ing measures are requisite : the period of barrack life must be reduced to the utmost ; the barracks must be assimilated to the type of military and politico-military schools ; there must be the closest possible association between the military units and the factories, workshops, trade unions, and poor peasants' organisations.

5. The requisite solidarity and stability can only be § 67. supplied to the young revolutionary army by means of an officers' staff composed of class-conscious workers and peasants, appointed only as subalterns at the outset. Obviously, therefore, one of the most important tasks in the creation of the Red Army is to prepare for the duties of commanding officers those soldiers who are peculiarly capable and energetic and whose devotion to the cause of socialism is exceptionally ardent.

6. We must make the widest possible practical use of the operative and technical experience gained during the world war. In the fulfilment of this aim we must attract to the work of organising the army and to its effective leadership the military experts who were trained in the schools of the old army. But a necessary condition of the employment of such experts is that the political leader ship of the army and the effective control of the military staff shall be concentrated in the hands of the working class.

7. The demand for the election of officers, which had § 68. great importance as a matter of principle in relation to the bourgeois army whose commanders were especially trained as an apparatus for the class subjugation of the common soldiers (and, through the instrumentality of the common soldiers, the subjugation of the toiling masses), ceases to have any significance as a matter of principle in relation to the class army of the workers and peasants. A possible combination of election with appointment from above may

be expedient for the revolutionary class army simply on practical grounds. Whether this is so or not depends upon the cultural level of the military units, upon the degree of solidarity among the sections of the army, upon the efficiency of the commanding cadres, and upon similar considerations.

PROLETARIAN JUSTICE.

§ 70 & 71. Taking into its hands all the powers of the bourgeois State, and sweeping away the instruments of that State without leaving any vestiges, sweeping away the law-courts of the old order together with the bourgeois-democratic formula " election of the judges by the people," proletarian democracy issued the class watchword " election of judges from among the workers and by the workers alone." It applied this watchword throughout the administration of justice, and at the same time equalised the rights of the two sexes both in the matter of the election of judges and in the matter of compulsory jury service.

In order to enrol for the administration of justice the widest possible masses of the proletariat and the poor peasantry, it was arranged that there should participate in the courts judge-assessors [jurors], continually changed at brief intervals, and it was stipulated that jury lists should be drawn up, showing the membership of the mass organisations of the workers, the trade unions, etc.

72 & 73. Having created a unified popular law-court in place of the unending series of former courts in the social order which had been swept away (the system of higher and lower courts in various grades), the Soviet Power constructed its own judicial system, making it easily accessible to the population, and putting an end to all delays in the administration of justice.

Having annulled the laws of the overthrown administration, the Soviet Power left to the elected soviet courts the realisation of the will of the proletariat and the practical enforcement of its decrees. In cases which are not provided for by the decrees, or to which the decrees are not wholly applicable, the courts are to be guided by a socialist sense of equity.

§ 74. In the domain of penal justice, courts organised in this fashion have already effected a radical change in the character of punishment, realising in a large measure the conditional sentence, introducing social censure as a penal method, substituting compulsory labour while the offender remains at large for the deprivation of liberty, substituting educational establishments for prisons, and making it possible to realise as a practical measure the institution of comradely courts of law.

The Russian Communist Party, looking forward to the § 75. further development of justice along this road, must endeavour to secure that the whole working population shall participate by turns in the discharge of judicial duties, and that the penal system shall ultimately be transformed into a system of measures of an educative character.

EDUCATION.

In the domain of popular education the Russian Com- §§ 76 & 77 munist Party has accepted as its task the completion of the work begun by the November revolution of 1917, the transformation of the school so that from being an organ for maintaining the class dominion of the bourgeoisie, it shall become an organ for the complete abolition of the division of society into classes, an organ for the communist regeneration of society.

In the period of the dictatorship of the proletariat, § 78. that is to say, in the period when the conditions are being prepared which shall make it possible to achieve the complete realisation of communism, the school must be not merely a means for the conveyance of the principles of communism generally, but a means for the conveyance of the ideology and of the organisational and educational influence of the proletariat to the semi-proletarian and the non-proletarian strata of the working masses, to the end that there shall ultimately be educated a new generation capable of establishing communism. At the present time the first step along this road would appear to be the further development of the below-mentioned fundamental scholastic and cultural changes already introduced by the Soviet Power :

1. The introduction of gratuitous, compulsory, general §. 80 and technical instruction for all children of both sexes up

to the age of 17. (The technical education will supply an acquaintance with the theory and practice of the principal branches of production.)

§ 79.   2. The creation of a network of institutions preparatory to school life ; creches, kindergartens, children's homes, etc. ; for the improvement of social education and for the freeing of women.

§ 80.   3. The complete realisation of the principles of the unified labour school, with instruction in the native tongue, co-education, absolutely secular instruction (that is to say, education entirely free from any kind of religious influence), an instruction in which theory shall be closely linked with socially productive labour, an instruction which shall produce a many-sided development of the members of communist society.

4. The supply to all pupils, at the cost of the State, of food, clothing, foot gear, and scholastic requisites.

§ 85.   5. The creation of fresh relays of educational workers permeated with the ideas of communism.

§ 84.   6. The inducing of all the working population to participate actively in the spread of enlightenment (the development of soviets of public instruction, the mobilisation of all who can read and write, etc.).

84 & 83.   7. Many-sided State aid for the self-education of workers and peasants (the creation of a network of institutions for extra-scholastic instruction : libraries ; adult schools ; popular homes and universities ; courses ; lectures ; cinemas ; etc.).

§ 81.   8. The extensive development of professional training for pupils above the age of 17, in association with general polytechnic learning.

§ 82.   9. Easy access to the lecture halls of the universities for all who may desire it, and especially for workers ; the throwing open of the universities as a field for the teaching activities of all competent persons ; the removal of all artificial obstacles that may now prevent the access of fresh teaching strength into the professorial chairs ; attention to the material welfare of the pupils, so that it may become practically possible for proletarians and peasants to attend the universities.

§ 86.   10. In like manner it is essential to provide easy access for the workers to all art treasures, which have been created upon the basis of the exploitation of their labour, and which have hitherto been at the exclusive disposal of the exploiters.

11. The development of an extensive propaganda of communist ideas, and the utilisation to that end of all the apparatus and means of the State Power. § 87.

RELIGION.

With regard to religion, the Russian Communist Party is not content with having already decreed the separation of the church from the State and of the school from the church, that is, with having taken measures which bourgeois democracy includes in its programs but has nowhere carried out owing to the manifold associations that actually obtain between capital and religious propaganda. §§ 89-92.

The Russian Communist Party is guided by the conviction that nothing but the fulfilment of purposiveness and full awareness in all the social and economic activities of the masses can lead to the complete disappearance of religious prejudices. The party endeavours to secure the complete break-up of the union between the exploiting classes and the organisations for religious propaganda, thus cooperating in the actual deliverance of the working masses from religious prejudices, and organising the most extensive propaganda of scientific enlightenment and anti-religious conceptions. While doing this, we must carefully avoid anything that can wound the feelings of believers, for such a method can only lead to the strengthening of religious fanaticism.

ECONOMIC AFFAIRS.

The party must inexorably complete the expropriation of the bourgeoisie, which has already been begun, and which in the main and in essentials has been accomplished. As a result of this expropriation, the means of production and exchange pass into the ownership of the Soviet Republic, become, that is to say, the common property of all the workers. § 93.

It is an essential part of the economic policy of the Soviet Power to secure a universal increase in the productive forces of the country. In view of the widespread disorganisation, for the preservation of the country all other § 94.

considerations must be subordinated to one practical aim—a rapid increase, by all available means, in the quantity of goods urgently needed by the population. The success in the working of every soviet institution concerned with economic life, must be measured by the practical results that are secured in this matter of increased production.

In this connexion, the most important considerations are the following.

§ 95.　The break-up of the imperialist economy bequeathed as a legacy to the opening period of soviet reconstruction an utterly chaotic condition in respect both of the organisation and of the administration of production. Hence, one of our fundamental tasks, one of our most urgent needs, is to secure the greatest possible cohesion in all the economic activities of the country, which must be unified in accordance with a general governmental design. We must effect the maximum centralisation of production in the sense of uniting it into individual branches and groups of branches ; in the sense of concentrating it into the best possible productive units ; and in the sense of the speediest fulfilment of economic tasks. We must secure the maximum solidarisation of the whole economic apparatus, rationally and economically utilising all the material resources of the country.

§ 96.　To this end we must promote a close economic collaboration and a political alliance with other peoples, simultaneously striving to establish a unified economic plan in conjunction with those among them which have already established a soviet system.

§ 97.　With regard to small-scale production and home industry, we must make the widest possible use of it by giving government orders to the home workers. Home industry and small-scale production must be included within the general plan for the supply of raw materials and fuel ; and they must receive financial support on condition that the various home workers, home-workers' artels, productive cooperatives, and other petty undertakings may combine to form larger productive and industrial units. We must encourage such unions, while endeavouring by these and a series of other measures to counteract the endeavours of the home workers to become small independent manufacturers.

We must thus promote the painless transition of this obsolete form of production into the higher form of large-scale machinofacture.

§ 98. The organised apparatus of social production must primarily depend upon the trade unions. These unions must to an increasing extent free themselves from craft bonds. They must be transformed into huge productive unities, enrolling the majority of the workers, and in due time all the workers, in the respective branches of production.

Inasmuch as the trade unions are already (as specified in the laws of the Soviet Republic and as realised in practice) participants in all the local and central organs administering industry, they must proceed to the practical concentration into their own hands of the work of administration in the whole economic life of the country, making this their unified economic aim. Thus protecting the indissoluble union between the central State authority, the national economy, and the broad masses of the workers, the trade unions must in the fullest possible measure induce the workers to participate directly in the work of economic administration. The participation of the trade unions in the conduct of economic life, and the involvement by them of the broad masses of the people in this work, would appear at the same time to be our chief aid in the campaign against the bureaucratisation of the economic apparatus of the Soviet Power. This will also facilitate the establishment of an effective popular control over the results of production.

§ 99. For the purposive development of economic life, it is essential to utilise to the utmost all the labour power at the disposal of the State. Its correct assignment and reassignment as between the various territorial areas and as between the various branches of economic life is the main task of the economic policy of the Soviet Power. It can be fulfilled in no other way than by an intimate association between the Soviet Power and the trade unions. The general mobilisation by the Soviet Power of all members of the population who are physically and mentally fit for work (a mobilisation to be effected through the instrumentality of the trade unions), for the discharge of definite social duties, must be achieved far more widely and systematically than has hitherto been the case.

§ 100. Despite the disintegration of the capitalist organisations of labour, the productive energies of the country can be renovated and developed ; but the socialist method of production can be consolidated in no other way than through the establishment of a comradely discipline among the workers, through their achieving the utmost independence, through their acquiring a sense of responsibility, and through the strictest mutual control over productive work.

For the attainment of this end there is requisite persevering and systematic work for the education of the masses, which will now be facilitated by the fact that they are actually witnessing the overthrow of the capitalist, the landlord, and the trader, and by the fact that their own practical experience is convincing them that their wellbeing exclusively depends upon the disciplining of their own labour.

In this work of creating a new socialist discipline, the leading role is assigned to the trade unions. These latter, quitting the old rut, must for the realisation of the new aim put into practice various measures, such as the following : the introduction of account keeping ; the establishment of a normal working day and of a normal intensity of labour ; the inauguration of responsibility to comradely labour courts ; etc.

§ 101. This task of developing the forces of production requires for its performance the immediate, widespread, and many-sided utilisation of the experts (scientists and technicians) bequeathed to us as a legacy by capitalism. We must use them despite the fact that inevitably in most cases they have been nourished upon capitalist philosophy and have been trained in bourgeois habits. The party considers that the period of acute struggle with those belonging to this stratum—a struggle which originated in the sabotage they organised—has now come to an end, inasmuch as the strength of the sabotaging movement has been broken. The party, therefore, must pursue its policy in close alliance with the trade unions. On the one hand, it must avoid making any political concession to the members of the bourgeois stratum, and must ruthlessly suppress any leanings they may exhibit in the direction of the counter-revolution. On the other hand, it must no less ruthlessly wage war against the so-called radicalism (in fact, an ignorant form of self-conceit) of those who believe that the workers can overcome capitalism and the bourgeois system without learning from bourgeois experts, without making use of these experts, and without going to school with them for a considerable period.

While striving to secure equal remuneration for all labour, and while aiming at the establishment of complete communism, the Soviet Power cannot endeavour to effect the full realisation of this equality at the present moment, when hardly the first steps have been taken towards the transformation of capitalism into communism. Hence it will be necessary to maintain for a certain time the system of specially high remuneration for experts, so that they may work better than before and not worse. To this end, we must not shrink from the payment of premiums for exceptionally successful work and for work done in a managerial capacity.

In like manner we must place the bourgeois experts in an environment of comradely social labour. where they will rub shoulders with the rank and file of the workers and also with the most advanced among the class-conscious communists. In this way a mutual understanding will be secured, and the chasm bridged which existed under capitalism between mental workers and manual workers.

The Soviet Power has already adopted a whole series § 102. of measures aiming at the development of science and at its wedding to production. It has created a network of new institutes of applied science, laboratories, experimental stations, experimental works for the trial of new technical methods ; it has made improvements and inventions ; it has scheduled and organised the moral and material means at our disposal for scientific purposes ; etc. The Russian Communist Party supports all these measures ; it strives to further their development, and to assist in the creation of more favourable conditions for scientific study, and for the utilisation of science for the increase of the productive energy of the country.

AGRICULTURE.

§ 103–109.   The Soviet Power, having completely abolished **private** property in land, has already instituted a whole series of measures to promote the organisation of large-scale socialist agriculture. The most important of these measures are the following : (1) the founding of soviet farms, that is to say, of large-scale socialist economies ; (2) the support of artels or cooperatives for the communal cultivation of the land ; (3) the organisation of the State cultivation of all kinds of uncultivated land ; (4) the State mobilisation of all agricultural experts, so that energetic measures may be taken for the improvement of agricultural methods ; (5) the support of agricultural communes, as purely voluntary associations of agriculturists for the cooperative conduct of large-scale farming.

Regarding all these measures as integrally tending to favour the absolutely essential increase in the productivity of agricultural labour, the Russian Communist Party endeavours to make them as fully effective as possible, to diffuse them widely throughout the more backward regions of the country, and to encourage further advances of the same character.

§§ 110 & 111.   In especial the Russian Communist Party advocates :

1. Extensive State support for the agricultural cooperatives engaged in the elaboration of agricultural products.

2. The extensive introduction of methods for the improvement of the land.

3. The widespread and purposive supply of farming implements to the poor peasants and the middle peasants. This is to be effected by means of lending stations.

§ 112.   Having to reckon with the fact that small-scale peasant farming will continue to exist for many years to come, the Russian Communist Party endeavours to promote a series of measures tending to increase the productivity of peasant agriculture. Among such measures may be enumerated : (1) the regularisation of peasant tillage (the abolition of the strip system of culture, etc.) ; (2) the supply of better seed and of artificial manures to the peasants ; (3) the improvement of the breed of the peasants' live stock ;

(4) the general diffusion of expert agricultural knowledge ; (5) expert agricultural assistance to the peasants ; (6) repair of the peasants' agricultural implements at the soviet repairing shops ; (7) the foundation of lending stations, experimental stations, demonstration fields, etc. ; (8) the improvement of peasant lands.

The chasm between town and country is at all times § 113. one of the main causes of the backwardness of the rural districts, both as regards farming methods and as regards mental culture. But, in a profoundly critical epoch like the present, this cleavage involves for town and country alike the imminent danger of absolute ruin. The Russian Communist Party therefore regards the putting an end to this separation as one of the fundamental tasks of communist constructive policy. In addition to the general measures it advocates, it considers essential : the widespread and purposive attraction of industrial workers to communally conducted agricultural occupations ; the development of the activity of the Workers' Committee of Collaboration (a branch of State activity already instituted by the Soviet Power) ; and similar measures.

In all its work in the rural districts, the Russian § 114. Communist Party primarily relies for support upon the proletarian and semi-proletarian strata of these regions. It organises them, first of all, as an independent force, forming branches of the party in the villages, organisations of the poor peasants, a peculiar type of trade union for the rural proletarians and semi-proletarians, etc.—bringing these rural workers everywhere into close relations with the urban proletariat, and enfranchising them from the influence of the rural bourgeoisie and of the petty-proprietary interests.

As far as concerns the rich peasants—the rural bourgeoisie—the policy of the Russian Communist Party takes the form of a decisive struggle against their exploitative inclinations, and of measures to crush their resistance to the soviet policy.

In the case of the middle peasantry, the policy of the Russian Communist Party is, by degrees and of set purpose, to attract them to the work of socialist construction. The party aims at detaching them from the rich peasants, at bringing them over to the side of the working class by paying special attention to their needs. It attempts to overcome their backwardness in cultural matters by measures of an ideological character, carefully avoiding any coercive steps. On all occasions upon which their vital interests are touched, it endeavours to come to a practical agreement with them, making to them such concessions as will promote socialist reorganisation.

DISTRIBUTION.

115–119. In the sphere of distribution, the task of the Soviet Power at the present time is unerringly to continue the replacement of trade by a purposive distribution of goods, by a system of distribution organised by the State upon a national scale. The aim is to achieve the organisation of the whole population into an integral network of consumers' communes, which shall be able with the utmost speed, purposiveness, economy, and a minimal expenditure of labour, to distribute all the necessary goods, while strictly centralising the whole distributive apparatus.

Upon the foundation of consumers' communes and upon their unification there must be built up a genuine, all-embracing, and working cooperation, taking the form of an immense organisation of consumers, which shall become an apparatus for mass distribution more perfect than any known to the history of capitalism.

As a matter of principle, the Russian Communist Party holds that the proper course in connexion with this problem of distribution is, not to scrap the cooperative apparatus, but to develop it on communist lines. The party will pursue this policy systematically. It enjoins upon all the members of the party that they shall work in the cooperatives, and (with the assistance of the trade unions) shall administer them in the communist spirit ; that they shall promote independence and discipline throughout the working population united to form cooperatives ; that they shall endeavour to ensure that the entire population shall enter the cooperatives, and that these cooperatives shall merge into a single great cooperative comprising the whole Soviet Republic from top to bottom ; last of all, and above all, that the dominance of the proletariat over the other strata of the workers shall be continually maintained, and that everywhere there shall be put into practice various measures to facilitate and achieve the transition from petty-bourgeois cooperatives of the old capitalist type to consumers' communes led by the proletarians and the semi-proletarians.

Money and Banks.

Avoiding the mistakes made by the Commune of Paris, §§ 120–12 the Soviet Power in Russia first seized the State Bank, and then nationalised the private commercial banks, and formed a union of nationalised banks, and of their accumulated funds, merging them in the State Bank. In this way was created the framework of the People's Bank of the Soviet Republic. Thus, from being a centre for the economic dominion of financial capital and an instrument for the political rule of the exploiters, the bank became an instrument of the workers' power and a lever to promote economic transformation. In order to carry to its logical conclusion the work begun by the Soviet Power, the Russian Communist Party lays especial stress upon the following principles :

1. The monopolisation of all banking business in the hands of the Soviet State.

2. The radical transformation and simplification of banking operations, so that the whole banking system shall become an apparatus for the unified book-keeping of the Soviet Republic. In proportion as the organisation of a purposive social economy is achieved, this will lead to the disappearance of banks, and to their conversion into the central book-keeping establishment of communist society.

In the opening stage of the transition from capitalism to communism, and prior to the organisation of a fully developed system for the communist production and distribution of goods, the abolition of money is impossible. In these circumstances, the bourgeois elements of the population continue to use for speculation, profit-making, and the plundering of the workers, the monetary tokens that still remain in private ownership. Upon the basis of the nationalisation of banking, the Russian Communist Party endeavours to promote a series of measures favouring a moneyless system of account keeping, and paving the way for the abolition of money. These are : the compulsory deposit of money in the People's Bank; the introduction of budget-books; the replacement of money by written or printed tokens, by tickets giving the right to the receipt of goods but available for short periods only; etc.

FINANCE.

122-121.   During the epoch in which the socialisation of the means of production confiscated from the capitalists has begun, the State Power ceases to be a parasitic apparatus nourished upon the productive process. There now begins its transformation into an organisation directly fulfilling the function of administering the economic life of the country. To this extent the State budget will be a budget of the whole of the national economy. Under these conditions, the balancing of revenue and expenditure can only be effected by means of an accurate record of the production and distribution of goods systematically carried out by the State. As far as concerns the defraying of extraordinary State expenditure during the transitional period, the Russian Communist Party advocates that the system of levies upon the capitalists which was historically necessary and legitimate in the opening phase of the revolution, shall be replaced by a graduated income and property tax. But in so far as this tax ceases to be lucrative in view of the widely effected expropriation of the possessing classes, the State expenditure must be met by the direct conversion to this purpose of part of the income from various State monopolies.

THE HOUSING PROBLEM.

§§ 125 & 126.   The housing problem became extremely acute during the war period. To assist in its solution, the Soviet Power completely expropriated all the houses belonging to capitalist landlords and handed them over to the urban soviets. It effected mass settlements of workers from the suburbs in the bourgeois dwellings. It handed over the best of these dwellings to the workers' organisations, arranging for the upkeep of the houses at the cost of the State; it undertook to provide the workers' families with furniture, etc.

The Russian Communist Party, without doing anything contrary to the interests of non-capitalist house-owners, must use its utmost endeavours to discover and apply the best means for the improvement of the housing conditions of the working masses ; for putting an end to the overcrowding and the unsanitary condition of the older quarters of the cities ; for the destruction of dwellings unfit for habitation, the renovation of old houses, and the building of new houses suitable to the new conditions of working-class life ; in general for the rational rehousing of the workers.

Labour Protection and Social Welfare Work.

The establishment of the dictatorship of the proletariat §§ 127–129. made possible for the first time the full realisation of the minimum program of the socialist parties in the domain of labour protection. In its Code of Labour Laws, the Soviet Power has formally decreed : an eight-hour working day for all workers as the maximum working time—but for persons not exceeding eighteen years of age, and also in especially injurious branches of production, and also for miners, the working day must not exceed six hours ; a forty-two-hour period each week of uninterrupted rest for all workers ; overtime is as a rule prohibited ; the employment of the labour of children and of young persons under sixteen is prohibited ; night work, and work in injurious trades and also overtime, are prohibited in the case of all women and also in the case of young men under the age of eighteen ; for eight weeks before and eight weeks after childbirth women do no work, but continue to receive full pay, together with gratuitous medical attendance and medicine, and working women with children at the breast receive during working hours half-an-hour's leave every three hours ; the inspection of labour and sanitary inspection by soviets elected by the trade unions.

For all workers who do not exploit others' labour the §§ 130–132. legislation of the Soviet Power provides full social insurance against any kind of loss of capacity for labour, and also (for the first time in history) against unemployment at the sole expense of employers and the State, with complete independence on the part of the insured, together with the intimate participation of the trade unions.

More than this, in certain respects the Soviet Power § 133.

has gone beyond the minimum program, and in the before-mentioned Code of Labour Laws has arranged for the participation of the labour organisations in the decision of matters relating to the engagement and discharge of workers. For all workers who have worked continuously for not less than one year, a month's holiday on full pay is decreed. The Code provides for the State regulation of wages upon the basis of scales drawn up by the trade unions. The Code further arranges for the formation of special bodies or departments for the assignment and scheduling of labour power by the soviets and trade unions, making it compulsory to provide work for the unemployed.

§ 129. But the extreme disorganisation resulting from the war and the attack made by world imperialism, have compelled the Soviet Power to take certain steps backwards : to have recourse, in exceptional circumstances to overtime work, limiting this to fifty days in the year ; to permit the employment of young persons from fourteen to sixteen years of age, limiting their working day to four hours ; temporarily to arrange that the month's holiday shall be reduced to a fortnight ; to increase the duration of night work to seven hours.

§ 134. The Russian Communist Party must conduct extensive propaganda on behalf of the active participation of all workers in the energetic enforcement of the measures for labour protection. To this end the following measures are necessary :

1. The work of organising and extending labour inspection must be actively taken in hand. For this purpose, active workers, drawn from among the ranks of the manual workers, must be selected and trained, and this method of inspection must be extended to small-scale production and to home industry.

2. Labour protection must be extended to all branches of work, including the building trade, land and water transport, domestic service, and agriculture.

3. Industrial and agricultural labour must be absolutely prohibited during childhood, and there must be a further reduction of the working day in the case of young persons.

In addition, the Russian Communist Party must undertake the following tasks :

1. When there occurs a general increase in the productivity of labour there must be a maximum working day of six hours without any diminution in the rate of pay, and in addition to the six hours there shall be two hours' compulsory work without special pay, during which instruction shall be given in craftsmanship and the theory of production, practical instruction in the technique of State administrative work, and military training.

2. The introduction of a system of premiums which shall promote emulation, in order to increase the productivity of labour.

In the sphere of social welfare work, the Russian Communist Party endeavours to organise an extensive system of State aid, not only for the victims of the war and of misfortune arising from elemental causes, but also for the victims of abnormal social conditions ; it conducts a vigorous struggle against all forms of parasitism and idleness ; and it makes it its business to guide back to a working life all those whom circumstances have forced out of the ranks of the workers.

PUBLIC HYGIENE.

As the foundation of its activities in the domain of safeguarding public health, the Russian Communist Party proposes, first of all, the introduction of hygienic and sanitary measures aiming at the prevention of disease. The dictatorship of the proletariat has already made it possible to introduce quite a number of hygienic and curative measures which were impracticable within the framework of bourgeois society : for instance, the nationalisation of the business of the retail chemists, of large-scale curative institutions founded and run by private enterprise, of health resorts ; the establishment of labour duty for all medical workers ; etc. §§ **135-138.**

In conformity with this, the Russian Communist Party regards the following as its immediate tasks :

1. The vigorous pursuance of extensive sanitary measures undertaken in the interests of the workers, such as :

(*a*) improvement of the sanitary condition of all places of public resort ; the protection of earth, water, and air ;

(*b*) the organisation of communal kitchens and of the

food supply generally upon a scientific and hygienic foundation ;

(c) measures to prevent the spread of diseases of a contagious character ;

(d) sanitary legislation.

2. A campaign against social diseases (tuberculosis, venereal disease, alcoholism, etc.).

3. The gratuitous provision of medical advice and treatment for the whole population.

SELECTED READINGS

The literature relating to the authors of *The ABC of Communism* is generally limited. Western scholars have only recently begun to devote adequate attention to Bukharin and Preobrazhensky, but as yet there is no biography of either, and specialized studies are few. While commentaries by Soviet writers are voluminous, they are all colored by the Stalinist efforts to discredit the two men during the 1930's.

Useful general accounts dealing with the careers and thought of Bukharin and Preobrazhensky include Edward Hallet Carr, *A History of Soviet Russia* (New York: Macmillan Co., 1951–), of which seven volumes have been published thus far, carrying the account to 1926; Isaac Deutscher, *The Prophet Armed, The Prophet Unarmed,* and *The Prophet Outcast* (New York and London: Oxford University Press, 1954-63), a three-volume biography of Leon Trotsky containing a rich store of information and interpretation of the times during which he lived and the men surrounding him, including Bukharin and Preobrazhensky; Leonard Shapiro, *The Communist Party of the Soviet Union* (New York: Random House, Inc., 1960); and Robert V. Daniels, *The Conscience of the Revolution; Communist Opposition in Soviet Russia* (Cambridge: Harvard University Press, 1960).

More specialized studies of Bukharin and Preobrazhensky are Alexander Erlich, *The Soviet Industrialization Debate, 1924-1928* (Cambridge: Harvard University Press, 1960); Sidney Heitman, "Between Lenin and Stalin: Nikolai Bukharin," chapter 5 in Leopold Labedz (ed.), *Revisionism: Essays on the History of Marxist Ideas* (New York: Praeger, and London: Allen and Unwin, 1962) and "The Myth of Bukharin's Anarchism," in *The Rocky Mountain Social Science Journal* (Fort Collins, Colorado), I, no. 1 (April 1963), 38-53; and, for readers of German, Peter Knirsch, *Die Ökonomischen Anschauungen Nikolaj I. Bucharins* (Berlin: East European Institute of the Free University of Berlin, 1959).

Works by Bukharin available in English translation include *The Economic Theory of the Leisure Class* (New York: International Publishers, 1927); *Imperialism and World Economy* (New York: International Publishers, 1929); *Program of the Communists* (New York [?]: United Communist Party of America, 1918); *Historical Materialism; A System of Sociology* (New York: International Publishers, 1925); and *Building Up Socialism* (London, Communist Party of Great Britain, 1926). Also useful for an understanding of Bukharin's views on revolution is the 1928 "Program of the Communist International," largely written by Bukharin and published in numerous English editions. Those wishing to study Bukharin's thought in greater depth should consult Sidney Heitman, *Nikolai I. Bukharin; A Bibliography with Annotations, Including the Locations of His Works in Major American and European Libraries* (Stanford: The Hoover Institution, 1966) and the same author's forthcoming biography of Bukharin, to be published by the Stanford University Press.

Only one of Preobrazhensky's writings has been translated into English—his *The New Economics* (trans., Brian Pearce; New York: Oxford University Press, 1965), written in 1924-25, after he had broken with Bukharin. Otherwise, his published works, which dealt mainly with technical economic issues, have not been translated from Russian, and there are no special studies or guides to his works other than those indicated above.

For additional perspective on the ideas expressed in *The ABC of Communism,* the best critical studies by Western writers include Henry B. Mayo, *Introduction to Marxist Theory* (New York: Oxford University Press, 1960); Robert N. Carew Hunt, *The Theory and Practice of Communism; An Introduction* (5th ed.; New York: Macmillan Co., 1962); Alfred G. Meyer, *Communism* (New York, Random House, 1962); and Robert V. Daniels, *The Nature of Communism* (New York: Random House, Inc., 1962). For an up-to-date critical guide to other works in English on the history, ideology, and functioning of Russian and international communism, see the "Bibliographical Note" at the end of the last named book by Daniels, pp. 376-88.

GLOSSARY

[The translators have not attempted to supply an exhaustive glossary. Most of the terms used in the *A B C* are defined in the text or are used in senses which will be found in any dictionary. It has, however, been thought expedient to define all words employed in an unusual or restricted signification. Russian terms with no adequate English equivalent are also explained. A few historical references are included.]

artel. A union of working producers, either agricultural or industrial. A cooperative of production.

Cadets. The Constitutional Democrats (a political party). See p. 87.

centres. Unions of whole branches of production under the Soviet Power. For example, Centro-copper, Centro-milk, etc.

chiefs. An alternative term to the last. For example, Chief-coal, Chief-textile, etc.

commissar. A minister of State in the Soviet Republic.

commissariat. A ministry of State in the Soviet Republic.

Constituent Assembly. Properly speaking, this denotes a parliament specifically elected to draw up a constitution. In the *A B C* the reference is sometimes to the Constituent Assembly which met in January, 1918, and was forcibly dissolved by the bolsheviks ; at other times the term is used in a more general sense to denote any parliament elected democratically upon a territorial franchise. The context will show which is meant.

desyatina (also written **desiatine**). The usual Russian unit of measurement for farming land = approximately 2¾ acres. See **hectare.**

Duhobors. A Russian sect. The Duhobors are pacifists and conscientious objectors to military service.

employee. In the *A B C* this word is not used in the current English sense to denote *any* person employed by another. **Employee** is here contrasted with **worker,** which see. The employee earns a "salary," the worker earns a "wage." The former is (or regards himself as) a "brain-worker," and is therefore of a "superior class" to the "manual workers." Employees dress differently from workers and incline to have a bourgeois rather than a proletarian ideology. In so far as they are really proletarian in status, they comprise the "black-coated proletariat." Also known collectively as the **salariat,** which see. Also termed the **minor intelligentsia.** See **intelligentsia.**

Essers. The Social Revolutionaries (a political party). From the initials S. (ess) R. (er).

Gomza. The State machine shops of the Soviet Republic.

Hectare. A French superficial measure, = approximately 2½ acres See **desyatina.**

intelligentsia. A collective term used in Russia for those engaged in the "liberal professions"—lawyers, doctors, university professors, etc. Practically equivalent to the "professional classes" of this country. Strictly speaking these form the **major intelligentsia**. The other subclass comprises the **minor intelligentsia**. This is an alternative term for **salariat**. See **employee**.

kopeck. The hundredth part of a **rouble,** which see.

kulak. See **peasant**.

Kustarsbyt. See p. 277. The central league in which are organised the **kustarniks,** i.e., those engaged in home industry.

Kust. See p. 268.

octobrists. A political party which originated in connexion with the constitutional manifesto of Nicholas II on October 17, 1905.

old style. Dates recorded by the old Russian calendar, which was thirteen days behind that used in western countries. Thus January 1, 1917 (O.S.), was January 14, 1917, in this country, and so on. The Soviet Republic. has adopted the western calendar.

peasant and **peasantry.** The Russian peasants consist of three grades.

1. **Rich peasants.** These have large farms, on which wage labour is required. They are "master peasants," and therefore belong to the exploiting class. They are also known as **kulaks,** which conveys the idea that they are hard-fisted and usurious persons. (The village money-lenders and the avaricious liquor-sellers in the villages under the old regime were also known as **kulaks.**) The rich peasants correspond roughly to the "farmers" of the English countryside. But they are not "**tenant** farmers."

2. **Middle peasants.** These have small farms, which they work themselves without employing wage labour. They correspond to the smallholders of England and the crofters of Scotland.

3. **Poor peasants.** Landless rural workers, i.e. agricultural labourers forming the rural proletariat and **semi-proletariat,** which see.

pood. Russian unit of weight. 36 lbs. Approximately ⅓ of a cwt.

Purishkevich. A noted anti-semite, who had been a member of the duma in tsarist days. At a sitting of the "four dumas" in the summer of 1917, Purishkevich demanded the immediate suppression of the soviets and the proclamation of martial law.

revolution of 1917. Russian writers refer to the whole movement from the dethronement of the tsar in March to the establishment of the Soviet Power in November as "the revolution of 1917." When they wish to refer distinctively to one phase or the other, they speak of the "March revolution" and the "November revolution" respectively. Often, using the old calendar (see **old style**), they refer to the "February revolution" and the "October revolution," which is somewhat perplexing to non-Russian readers.

rouble. Russian standard coin. Before the war, the rouble was equivalent to 2s. 2d. in English money. Approximately ten roubles to the £1 sterling. The rouble is now enormously depreciated.

R.S.F.S.R. Initial letters of Russian Socialist Federative Soviet Republic.

salariat. The collectivity of employees or salary earners. See **employee**.

sazhene. Russian measure = 7 feet.

S.E.C. The Supreme Economic Council.

semi-proletarian. 1. A peasant who spends part of every year as a wage worker in a town. 2. A peasant who owns no land, a rural proletarian or agricultural labourer (a " poor peasant ").—The former is the strict meaning of the term, but it is used rather loosely. See **peasant.**

soviet. The Russian word for " council." In 1905 soviets or councils of workers' delegates were first set up. In their primary forms these bodies closely corresponded to the factory committees, shop-stewards' committees, workers' committees, etc., of Britain. Since the revolution of November, 1917, the word has had a political significance super-added to the primary meaning of " council of workers', soldiers', and peasants' delegates." This political significance is now familiar.

worker. This term is used in various senses. The context will show in which of the following meanings it is employed :

1. Most often it denotes all who are proletarian by status, members of the urban proletariat (as distinguished from the peasants), but not necessarily class-conscious members. See **peasant.**

2. In some cases it denotes the manual operatives in manufacturing industry, as contrasted with those who in England are sometimes termed the " black-coated proletariat." See **employee** and **salariat.**

3. In a great many instances it is used more comprehensively to denote all who live by labour, whether mainly mental or mainly manual, in contrast with those who live (or would fain live) by exploitation. Here the contrast is between " workers " and " bourgeois."

INDEX

Of related interest

Nikolai Bukharin

HISTORICAL MATERIALISM
A System of Sociology
New Introduction by Alfred G. Meyer

In *Historical Materialism* Bukharin achieves the rare feat of presenting revolutionary Marxism as a coherent and impressive
sociological system. His work was designed for, and widely used
by, higher Party circles, just as his earlier *ABC of Communism*
proved a popular primer for the less ideologically sophisticated
rank-and-file.

Leon Trotsky

THE NEW COURSE
and THE STRUGGLE FOR THE NEW COURSE
With a New Introduction by Max Shachtman

Written in 1923, *The New Course* was Trotsky's first blow in his
bitter and ill-fated struggle with Stalin. He sets forth the issues—
international revolution vs. "national-socialism," workers'
democracy vs. bureaucratic dictatorship. This book is indispensable to a clear understanding of the historic controversy that
led to Trotsky's brutal assassination in Mexico.

Write for information on available editions and current prices.

THE UNIVERSITY OF MICHIGAN PRESS
Ann Arbor, Michigan 48106